Elliot R. Wolfson

Library of Contemporary Jewish Philosophers

Editor-in-Chief

Hava Tirosh-Samuelson, *Arizona State University*

Editor

Aaron W. Hughes, *University of Rochester*

VOLUME 11

The titles published in this series are listed at brill.com/lcjp

Elliot R. Wolfson

Poetic Thinking

Edited by

Hava Tirosh-Samuelson and Aaron W. Hughes

BRILL

LEIDEN • BOSTON
2015

Cover illustration: Sönke Tollkühn. © Jewish Museum Berlin.

The series *Library of Contemporary Jewish Philosophers* was generously supported by the Baron Foundation.

Library of Congress Cataloging-in-Publication Data

Wolfson, Elliot R., author.
  Elliot R. Wolfson : poetic thinking / edited by Hava Tirosh-Samuelson and Aaron W. Hughes.
    pages cm. — (Library of contemporary Jewish philosophers, ISSN 2213-6010 ; volume 11)
  Includes bibliographical references.
  ISBN 978-90-04-29103-4 (hardback : alk. paper) — ISBN 978-90-04-29105-8 (e-book) —
  ISBN 978-90-04-29104-1 (pbk. : alk. paper) 1. Jewish philosophy—20th century. I. Tirosh-Samuelson, Hava, 1950- editor. II. Hughes, Aaron W., 1968- editor. III. Title. IV. Title: Poetic thinking.

  B5800.W645 2015
  181'.06—dc23

2014049626

This publication has been typeset in the multilingual "Brill" typeface. With over 5,100 characters covering Latin, IPA, Greek, and Cyrillic, this typeface is especially suitable for use in the humanities. For more information, please see www.brill.com/brill-typeface.

ISSN 2213-6010
ISBN 978-90-04-29104-1 (paperback)
ISBN 978-90-04-29105-8 (e-book)

This paperback is also published in hardback under ISBN 978-90-04-29103-4.

CONTENTS

THE CONTRIBUTORS

HAVA TIROSH-SAMUELSON (Ph.D, Hebrew University of Jerusalem, 1978) is Irving and Miriam Lowe Professor of Modern Judaism, the Director of Jewish Studies, and Professor of History at Arizona State University in Tempe, Arizona. Her research focuses on Jewish intellectual history, Judaism and ecology, science and religion, and feminist theory. In addition to numerous articles and book chapters in academic journals and edited volumes, she is the author of the award-winning *Between Worlds: The Life and Work of Rabbi David ben Judah Messer Leon* (SUNY Press, 1991) and the author of *Happiness in Premodern Judaism: Virtue, Knowledge, and Well-Being in Premodern Judaism* (Hebrew Union College Press, 2003). She is also the editor of *Judaism and Ecology: Created World and Revealed Word* (Harvard University Press, 2002); *Women and Gender in Jewish Philosophy* (Indiana University Press, 2004); *Judaism and the Phenomenon of Life: The Legacy of Hans Jonas* (Brill, 2008); *Building Better Humans? Refocusing the Debate on Transhumanism* (Peter Lang, 2011); *Hollywood's Chosen People: The Jewish Experience in American Cinema* (Wayne State University Press, 2012); and *Jewish Philosophy for the Twenty-First Century* (Brill, 2014). Professor Tirosh-Samuelson is the recipient of several large grants that have funded interdisciplinary research on religion, science, and technology.

AARON W. HUGHES (Ph.D., Indiana University Bloomington, 2000) holds the Philip S. Bernstein Chair in Jewish Studies at the University of Rochester. Hughes was educated at the University of Alberta, the Hebrew University of Jerusalem, and Oxford University. He has taught at Miami University of Ohio, McMaster University, the Hebrew University of Jerusalem, the University of Calgary, and the University at Buffalo. He is the author of over fifty articles and ten books, and the editor of seven books. His book titles include *Abrahamic Religions: On the Uses and Abuses of History* (Oxford, 2012); *Muslim Identities* (Columbia, 2013); *The Study of Judaism: Identity, Authenticity, Scholarship* (SUNY, 2013); and *Rethinking Jewish Philosophy: Beyond Particularism and Universalism* (Oxford, 2014). He is also the Editor-in-Chief of *Method and Theory in the Study of Religion*.

EDITORS' INTRODUCTION TO THE SERIES

It is customary to begin studies devoted to the topic of Jewish philosophy defining what exactly this term, concept, or even discipline is. We tend not to speak of Jewish mathematics, Jewish physics, or Jewish sociology, so why refer to something as "Jewish philosophy"? Indeed, this is the great paradox of Jewish philosophy. On the one hand it presumably names something that has to do with thinking, on the other it implies some sort of national, ethnic, or religious identity of those who engage in such activity. Is not philosophy just philosophy, regardless of who philosophizes? Why the need to append various racial, national, or religious adjectives to it?[1]

Jewish philosophy is indeed rooted in a paradox since it refers to philosophical activity carried out by those who call themselves Jews. As philosophy, this activity makes claims of universal validity, but as an activity by a well-defined group of people it is inherently particularistic. The question "What is Jewish philosophy?" therefore is inescapable, although over the centuries Jewish philosophers have given very different answers to it. For some, Jewish philosophy represents the relentless quest for truth. Although this truth itself may not be particularized, for such individuals, the use of the adjective "Jewish"—as a way to get at this truth—most decidedly is.[2] The Bible, the Mishnah, the Talmud, and related Jewish texts and genres are seen to provide particular insights into the more universal claims provided by the universal and totalizing gaze of philosophy. The problem is that these texts are not philosophical *on the surface*; they must, on the contrary, be interpreted to bring their philosophical insights to light. Within this context exegesis risks becoming eisegesis. Yet others eschew the term "philosophy" and instead envisage themselves as working in a decidedly

---

[1] Alexander Altmann once remarked:
It would be futile to attempt a presentation of Judaism as a philosophical system, or to speak of Jewish philosophy in the same sense as one speaks of American, English, French, or German philosophy. Judaism is a religion, and the truths it teaches are religious truths. They spring from the source of religious experience, not from pure reason.
See Alexander Altmann, "Judaism and World Philosophy," in *The Jews: Their History, Culture, and Religion*, ed. Louis Finkelstein (Philadelphia: Jewish Publication Society of America, 1949), vol. 2, 954.

[2] In this regard, see Norbert M. Samuelson, *Jewish Faith and Modern Science: On the Death and Rebirth of Jewish Philosophy* (New York: Rowman and Littlefield, 2008), e.g., 10–12.

Jewish key in order to articulate or clarify particular issues that have direct bearing on Jewish life and existence.[3] Between these two perspectives or orientations, there exist several other related approaches to the topic of Jewish philosophy, which can and have included ethics,[4] gender studies,[5] multiculturalism,[6] and postmodernism.[7]

Despite their differences in theory and method, what these approaches have in common is that they all represent the complex intersection of Judaism, variously defined, and a set of non-Jewish grids or lenses used to interpret this rich tradition. Framed somewhat differently, Jewish philosophy—whatever it is, however it is defined, or whether definition is even possible—represents the collision of particularistic demands and universal concerns. The *universal*, or that which is, in theory, open and accessible to all regardless of race, color, creed, or gender confronts the *particular*, or that which represents the sole concern of a specific group that, by nature or definition, is insular and specific-minded.

Because it is concerned with a particular people, the Jews, and how to frame their traditions in a universal and universalizing light that is believed to conform to the dictates of reason, Jewish philosophy can never be about pure thinking, if indeed there ever can be such a phenomenon. Rather Jewish philosophy—from antiquity to the present—always seems to have had and, for the most part continues to have, rather specific and perhaps

---

[3] See, e.g., Strauss's claim about Maimonides' *Guide of the Perplexed*, perhaps one of the most important and successful works of something called Jewish philosophy ever written. He claims that one "begins to understand the *Guide* once one sees that it is not a philosophic book—a book written by a philosopher for philosophers—but a Jewish book: a book written by a Jew for Jews." See Leo Strauss, "How to Begin to Study *The Guide of the Perplexed*," in *The Guide of the Perplexed*, trans. Shlomo Pines, 2 vols. (Chicago: University of Chicago Press, 1963), vol. 1, xiv.

Modern iterations of this may be found, for example, in J. David Bleich, *Bioethical Dilemmas: A Jewish Perspective*, 2 vols. (vol. 1, New York: Ktav, 1998; vol. 2, New York: Targum Press, 2006).

[4] See, e.g., David Novak, *Natural Law in Judaism* (Cambridge: Cambridge University Press, 1998); Elliot Dorff, *Love Your Neighbor and Yourself: A Jewish Approach to Modern Personal Ethics* (New York: Jewish Publication Society of America, 2006).

[5] E.g., the collection of essays in *Women and Gender in Jewish Philosophy*, ed. Hava Tirosh-Samuelson (Bloomington, IN: Indiana University Press, 2004).

[6] E.g., Jonathan Sacks, *The Dignity of Difference: How to Avoid a Clash of Civilizations* (London: Continuum, 2003); Jonathan Sacks, *To Heal a Fractured World: The Ethics of Responsibility* (New York: Schocken, 2007).

[7] E.g., Elliot R. Wolfson, *Language, Eros, Being: Kabbalistic Hermeneutics and Poetic Imagination* (New York: Fordham University Press, 2004); Elliot R. Wolfson, *Open Secret: Postmessianic Messianism and the Mystical Revision of Menahem Mendel Schneerson* (New York: Columbia University Press, 2009); Elliot R. Wolfson, *A Dream Interpreted within a Dream: Oneiropoiesis and the Prism of Imagination* (New York: Zone Books, 2011).

even practical concerns in mind. This *usually* translates into the notion that Judaism—at least the Judaism that Jewish philosophy seeks to articulate— is comprehensible to non-Jews and, framed in our contemporary context, that Judaism has a seat at the table, as it were, when it comes to pressing concerns in the realms of ethics and bioethics.

Jewish philosophy, as should already be apparent, is not a disinterested subject matter. It is, on the contrary, heavily invested in matters of Jewish peoplehood and in articulating its aims and objectives. Because of this interest in concrete issues (e.g., ethics, bioethics, medical ethics, feminism) Jewish philosophy—especially contemporary Jewish philosophy—is often constructive as opposed to being simply reflective. Because of this, it would seem to resemble what is customarily called "theology" more than it does philosophy. If philosophy represents the critical and systematic approach to ascertain the truth of a proposition based on rational argumentation, theology is the systematic and rational study of religion and the articulation of the nature of religious truths. The difference between theology and philosophy resides in their object of study. If the latter has "truth," however we may define this term, as its primary object of focus, the former is concerned with ascertaining religious dogma and belief. They would seem to be, in other words, mutually exclusive endeavors.

What we are accustomed to call "Jewish philosophy," then, is a paradox since it does not—indeed, cannot—engage in truth independent of religious claims. As such, it is unwilling to undo the major claims of Judaism (e.g., covenant, chosenness, revelation), even if it may occasionally redefine such claims.[8] So although medieval Jewish thinkers may well gravitate toward the systematic thought of Aristotle and his Arab interpreters and although modern Jewish thinkers may be attracted to the thought of Kant and Heidegger, the ideas of such non-Jewish thinkers are always applied to Jewish ideas and values. Indeed, if they were not, those who engaged in such activities would largely cease to be Jewish philosophers and would instead become just philosophers who just happened to be Jewish (e.g., Henri Bergson, Edmund Husserl, and Karl Popper).

Whether in its medieval or modern guise, Jewish philosophy has a tendency to be less philosophical simply for the sake of rational analysis and more constructive. Many of the volumes that appear in the Library of

---

[8] A good example of what we have in mind here is the thought of Maimonides. Although he might well redefine the notion of prophecy, he never abnegates the concept. On Maimonides on prophecy, see Howard Kreisel, *Prophecy: The History of an Idea in Medieval Jewish Philosophy* (Dordrecht: Kluwer, 2001), 148–56.

Contemporary Jewish Philosophers will bear this out. The truths of Judaism are upheld, albeit in often new and original ways. Although Jewish philosophy may well use non-Jewish ideas to articulate its claims, it never produces a vision that ends in the wholesale abandonment of Judaism.[9] Even though critics of Jewish philosophy may well argue that philosophy introduces "foreign" wisdom into the heart of Judaism, those we call Jewish philosophers do not perceive themselves to be tainting Judaism, but perfecting it or teasing out its originary meaning.[10]

The result is that Jewish philosophy is an attempt to produce a particular type of Judaism—one that is in tune with certain principles of rationalism. This rationalism, from the vantage point of the nineteenth century and up to the present, is believed to show Judaism in its best light, as the synthesis or nexus between a Greek-inflected universalism and the particularism of the Jewish tradition.

What is the status of philosophy among Jews in the modern period? Since their emancipation in the nineteenth century, Jews have gradually integrated into Western society and culture, including the academy. Ever since the academic study of Judaism began in the 1820s in Germany, Jewish philosophy has grown to become a distinctive academic discourse practiced by philosophers who now often hold positions in non-Jewish institutions of higher learning. The professionalization of Jewish philosophy has not been unproblematic, and Jewish philosophy has had to (and still has to) justify its legitimacy and validity. And even when Jewish philosophy is taught in Jewish institutions (for example, rabbinic seminaries or universities in Israel), it has to defend itself against those Jews who regard philosophy as alien to Judaism, or minimally, as secondary in importance to the inherently Jewish disciplines such as jurisprudence or exegesis. Jewish philosophy, in other words, must still confront the charge that it is not authentically Jewish.

The institutional setting for the practice of Jewish philosophy has shaped Jewish philosophy as an academic discourse. But regardless of the setting, Jewish philosophy as an academic discourse is quite distinct from Jewish

---

[9] This despite the claims of Yitzhak Baer who believed that philosophy had a negative influence on medieval Spanish Jews that made them more likely to convert to Christianity. See Israel Jacob Yuval, "Yitzhak Baer and the Search for Authentic Judaism," in *The Jewish Past Revisited: Reflections on Modern Jewish Historians*, ed. David N. Myers and David B. Ruderman (New Haven, CT: Yale University Press, 1998), 77–87.

[10] Indeed, Jewish philosophers in the medieval period did not even see themselves as introducing foreign ideas into Judaism. Instead they saw philosophical activity as a reclamation of their birthright since the Jews originally developed philosophy before the Greeks and others stole it from them.

philosophy as constructive theology, even though the two may often be produced by the same person.

Despite the lack of unanimity about the scope and methodology of Jewish philosophy, the Library of Contemporary Jewish Philosophers insists that Jewish philosophy has thrived in the past half century in ways that will probably seem surprising to most readers. When asked who are the Jewish philosophers of the twentieth century, most would certainly mention the obvious: Franz Rosenzweig (d. 1929), Martin Buber (d. 1965), and Emmanuel Levinas (d. 1995). Some would also be able to name Abraham Joshua Heschel (d. 1972), Mordecai Kaplan (d. 1983), Joseph Soloveitchik (d. 1993), and Hans Jonas (d. 1993). There is no doubt that these thinkers have either reshaped the discourse of Western thought for Jews and non-Jews or have inspired profound rethinking of modern Judaism. However, it is misleading to identify contemporary Jewish philosophy solely with these names, all of whom are now deceased.

In recent years it has been customary for Jews to think that Jewish philosophy has lost its creative edge or that Jewish philosophy is somehow profoundly irrelevant to Jewish life. Several reasons have given rise to this perception, not the least of which is, ironically enough, the very success of Jewish Studies as an academic discipline. Especially after 1967, Jewish Studies has blossomed in secular universities especially in the North American Diaspora, and Jewish philosophers have expressed their ideas in academic venues that have remained largely inaccessible to the public at large. Moreover, the fact that Jewish philosophers have used technical language and a certain way of argumentation has made their thought increasingly incomprehensible and therefore irrelevant to the public at large. At the same time that the Jewish public has had little interest in professional philosophy, the practitioners of philosophy (especially in the Anglo American departments of philosophy) have denied the philosophical merits of Jewish philosophy as too religious or too particularistic and excluded it entirely. The result is that Jewish philosophy is now largely generated by scholars who teach in departments/programs of Jewish Studies, in departments of Religious Studies, or in Jewish denominational seminaries.[11]

The purpose of the Library of Contemporary Jewish Philosophers is not only to dispel misperceptions about Jewish philosophy but also to help nudge the practice of Jewish philosophy out of the ethereal heights

---

[11] See the comments in Aaron W. Hughes and Elliot R. Wolfson, "Introduction: Charting an Alternative Course for the Study of Jewish Philosophy," in *New Directions in Jewish Philosophy*, ed. Aaron W. Hughes and Elliot R. Wolfson (Bloomington, IN: Indiana University Press, 2010), 1–16.

of academe to the more practical concerns of living Jewish communities. To the public at large this project documents the diversity, creativity, and richness of Jewish philosophical and intellectual activity during the second half of the twentieth century, and early twenty-first century, showing how Jewish thinkers have engaged new topics, themes, and methodologies and raised new philosophical questions. Indeed, Jewish philosophers have been intimately engaged in trying to understand and interpret the momentous changes of the twentieth century for Jews. These have included the Holocaust, the renewal of Jewish political sovereignty, secularism, postmodernism, feminism, and environmentalism. As a result, the Library of Contemporary Jewish Philosophers intentionally defines the scope of Jewish philosophy very broadly so as to engage and include theology, political theory, literary theory, intellectual history, ethics, and feminist theory, among other discourses. We believe that the overly stringent definition of "philosophy" has impoverished the practice of Jewish philosophy, obscuring the creativity and breadth of contemporary Jewish reflections. An accurate and forward looking view of Jewish philosophy must be inclusive.

To practitioners of Jewish philosophy this project claims that Jewish philosophical activity cannot and should not remain limited to professional academic pursuits. Rather, Jewish philosophy must be engaged in life as lived in the present by both Jews and non-Jews. Jews are no longer a people apart, instead they are part of the world and they live in this world through conversation with other civilizations and cultures. Jewish philosophy speaks to Jews and to non-Jews, encouraging them to reflect on problems and take a stand on a myriad of issues of grave importance. Jewish philosophy, in other words, is not only alive and well today, it is also of the utmost relevance to Jews and non-Jews.

The Library of Contemporary Jewish Philosophers is simultaneously a *documentary* and an *educational* project. As a documentary project, it intends to shape the legacy of outstanding thinkers for posterity, identifying their major philosophical ideas and making available their seminal essays, many of which are not easily accessible. A crucial aspect of this is the interview with the philosophers that functions, in many ways, as an oral history. The interview provides very personal comments by each philosopher as he or she reflects about a range of issues that have engaged them over the years. In this regard the Library of Contemporary Jewish Philosophers simultaneously records Jewish philosophical activity and demonstrates its creativity both as a constructive discourse as well as an academic field.

As an educational project, the Library of Contemporary Jewish Philosophers is intended to stimulate discussion, reflection, and debate about the meaning of Jewish existence at the dawn of the twenty-first century. The individual volumes and the entire set are intended to be used in a variety of educational settings: college-level courses, programs for adult Jewish learning, rabbinic training, and interreligious dialogues. By engaging or confronting the ideas of these philosophers, we hope that Jews and non-Jews alike will be encouraged to ponder the past, present, and future of Jewish philosophy, reflect on the challenges to and complexities of Jewish existence, and articulate Jewish philosophical responses to these challenges. We hope that, taken as individual volumes and as a collection, the Library of Contemporary Jewish Philosophers will inspire readers to ask philosophical, theological, ethical, and scientific questions that will enrich Jewish intellectual life for the remainder of the twenty-first century.

All of the volumes in the Library of Contemporary Jewish Philosophers have the same structure: an intellectual profile of the thinker, several seminal essays by the featured philosopher, an interview with him or her, and a select bibliography of 120 items, listing books, articles, book chapters, book reviews, and public addresses. As editors of the series we hope that the structure will encourage the reader to engage the volume through reflection, discussion, debate, and dialogue. As the love of wisdom, philosophy is inherently Jewish. Philosophy invites questions, cherishes debate and controversy, and ponders the meaning of life, especially Jewish life. We hope that the Library of Contemporary Jewish Philosophers will stimulate thinking and debate because it is our hope that the more Jews philosophize, the more they will make Judaism deeper, durable, and long-lasting. Finally, we invite readers to engage the thinkers featured in these volumes, to challenge and dispute them, so that Judaism will become ever stronger for future generations.

ELLIOT R. WOLFSON: AN INTELLECTUAL PORTRAIT

Aaron W. Hughes

on wings of moonlight
filled with vision unseen
i remain
Elliot R. Wolfson, "on wings of moonlight"[1]

It is fitting to open this essay with a poem because, as the subtitle of this volume should make clear, poetic locution resides at the heart of Wolfson's thinking. Poetry, for Wolfson, is not simply an aesthetic embellishment, but that which generates and unfolds philosophical meaning, thereby making understanding—and not just communication—possible. There is no "Truth" waiting to be objectively discovered and subsequently articulated behind language, only words that, when properly attuned to, reveal a dialectical process of covering and uncovering, of veiling and unveiling. To get beyond language would require a language of beyond, something that is tantamount to a cognitive impossibility. Instead Wolfson abides in the splendor and fullness of poetic thinking, therein trying to articulate the linguistic veil that many refuse to notice, yet behind which none can trespass. Philosophical activity, for Wolfson, is not about the clarification of terms, but about actualizing a form of *poesis*. But, if it is poetic, it is also necessarily lonely. The philosopher—as artist, as critic, as thinker—must negotiate between center and margins, trying to find a place that is often uncertain and certainly not traditional in the religious sense of the term.

Elliot R. Wolfson is one of the most original and creative thinkers operating within the idiom of the term that habitually, if problematically, is referred to as "Jewish philosophy." Although over the years he has contributed greatly to our scholarly understanding of kabbalah, or Jewish mysticism, it would be a mistake to define him solely by the contributions that he has made to this academic subfield. Since his youth, Wolfson has been a student of philosophy and he has frequently used Jewish mysticism as the source with which to engage in philosophical thinking. In his earlier work,

---

[1] Elliot R. Wolfson, "on wings of moonlight," quoted in Barbara E. Galli, *On Wings of Moonlight: Elliot R. Wolfson's Poetry in the Path of Rosenzweig and Celan* (Montreal and Kingston: McGill Queens University Press, 2007), 106.

for instance, kabbalistic texts have served as the muse for his examination of universal philosophical topics such as the function and processes of the imagination, the paradox of temporality, and the ontology of poetic language. Wolfson self-consciously works at the intersection of disciplines and what drives his creativity is his uncanny ability to put texts spanning diverse temporal, cultural, and religious periods in philosophical counterpoint. He reads, for example, premodern mystical texts in light of nineteenth- and twentieth-century French and German philosophers and vice versa, and the result is a living conversation that spans the ages as it simultaneously connects diverse linguistic expressions and interpretive modalities that Wolfson refuses to reduce to their simple historical contexts. Recent years have seen him work with an even broader array of texts that include religious works produced in Hinduism, Buddhism, and Islam, in addition to his ever-deeper engagement with the texts of Judaism, both philosophical and nonphilosophical. Yet, framing his interest in all of these texts is his engagement with philosophical hermeneutics.

Unlike many of the philosophers showcased in the Library of Contemporary Jewish Philosophers, Wolfson is not particularly interested in issues confronting contemporary Jews. Nor is he particularly interested in articulating a set of responses, Jewish or otherwise, to such issues. Rather, we must envisage Wolfson as a philosopher who is interested in topics that, although they may have social relevance if and when translated, are purely the domain of contemporary philosophy (more specifically, phenomenology and hermeneutics). This is important to note because Wolfson's goal is not to find a Jewish "essence" or mis/read texts in ways that contribute to contemporary problem-solving; rather, he shows us how to be close and sensitive readers who must be true to the integrity of the texts that we read. What, then, makes him a "Jewish philosopher"? The answer is simple: he comes at these universal problems through the particular texts of Judaism. "My upholding of the universal," he writes, "is certainly not meant to efface the particular; indeed, the universal I envision is one continuously shaped by the particular . . . and thus I resist (à la Hegel) both the universalization of the particular and the particularization of the universal."[2] In so doing, Wolfson affords us yet another paradigm of what it means to engage in the project of philosophy from a Jewish perspective. He is an extremely well-read scholar who uses a broad range of philosophic and religious traditions/

---

[2] Elliot R. Wolfson, *Giving Beyond the Gift: Apophasis and Overcoming Theomania* (New York: Fordham University Press, 2014), xiii–xiv.

categories to explicate philosophical questions out of the texts of the Jewish tradition. In so doing, he avoids the Christocentric assumptions of many working today within the context of the Continental philosophical tradition (e.g., Jean-Luc Marion).

Imagination forms the bedrock of all Wolfson's work. It functions as his point of departure and place of return, permitting him to read together texts that, on the surface, seem to have nothing to say to one another, and it is the faculty that offers him the creative wherewithal to carry such readings out boldly and fully. While the imagination is an artistic, mystical, and philosophical faculty, Wolfson articulates its transcendence and phenomenologically reveals its labyrinthine contours that can only be imagined from within its own imaginative structures. The imagination, in his own imaginative reading, becomes "the site wherein beings are brought to openness in the unconcealment of being as the letting-presence of the absence that prevails in the presencing of what is not yet present, the future that anticipates the past recollecting the future."[3] I have quoted this not to scare off the reader new to Wolfson's thought, but to show how language, imagination, and temporality are fundamentally connected and reveal themselves in his work though a prose style that reflects the creativity of language and the complexity of being. To unlock one is to understand the other, and, of course, vice versa. Once again, it is worth underscoring that, for Wolfson, philosophy is a poetic activity; one does not or cannot use language to arrive at a transcendent meaning, because meaning is in the very language, in the play of its words, conjuring up the symbolic imagery that permits us to encounter an imageless reality. Wolfson's prose, then, is intentionally difficult because that which he seeks to point toward, to un-conceal, is ultimately the very fragility of language, the way it haunts and tears the fabric of reality to open up a silent clearing that permits language to be heard in the first place. This is why his prose has a poetic dimension to it. It is also why his poetry and his artwork must be seen as two other sets of pathmarks (*Wegmarken* in the Heideggerian sense of the term) that chart the way.

Another feature that helps us understand Wolfson's thought and use of language comes by way of Buddhist philosophy, something that he has studied since a young man. In particular, he is drawn to the concept of *madhyamaka* developed by the Mahayana tradition, and that is often translated as the "middle path," though it should not be confused with the

---

[3] Elliot R. Wolfson, *Language, Eros, Being: Kabbalistic Hermeneutics and Poetic Imagination* (New York: Fordham University Press, 2005), 23.

"golden mean" of the Western philosophical tradition. *Madhyamaka* denies that things possess an inherent nature and that, instead, binary oppositions break down because each needs the other ultimately to define itself. The reciprocity between opposing terms means that we must dialectically overcome traditional dyadic structures and, thus, call into question the bivalent logic of linear reason. Silence or un-language, for example, needs language; truth un-truth; and so on. Framed formulaically: A is A; A is not-A, A is both A and not-A, and A is neither A nor not-A. This can lead Wolfson, for example, to posit "that the exteriority of the interior...is gauged by the interiority of the exterior"[4] or that "true liberation...would consist of being liberated from the need to be liberated."[5] By such locutions, Wolfson contends that concepts such as interiority or liberation are only graspable from their opposites, and vice versa, and that the only way to understand this semantically is through a chiasmic style of writing in which two terms or concepts that are related to one other are inverted.

Wolfson has spent a lifetime dedicated to mastering both Jewish texts and philosophical literature out of the conviction that the particularity of the former can serve indexically as a marker of the latter's universality. This is what motivated his work on Jewish mysticism in the first place, and this is why it is so rich, so textured, and, I dare say, misunderstood. He brings to the study of kabbalah a set of questions and concerns that are certainly nontraditional and that, as a result, lead to unexpected results that transcend simple or simplistic ethnico-historical understandings. His indebtedness to Maurice Merleau-Ponty, Edmond Jabès, Emmanuel Levinas, Jacques Derrida, Hélène Cixous, Luce Irigaray, Edmund Husserl, and, above all, Martin Heidegger are clear—all have become his conversation partners over the years as he has sought to uncover and inhabit the symbolic lifeworld of kabbalah. Although familiar, indebted, and responsible to the canons of both philological and historical scholarship, Wolfson is beholden to neither. This is what gives his work on kabbalah its philosophical depth. The formless form, the body of unembodiment, the intimate connections of anthropomorphism and theomorphism, and his deft attention to gender signification all increasingly became concepts not confined to kabbalistic texts, but philosophy more generally. But it is not an imposition of the latter on the former. Wolfson's work respects the integrity of original texts as he

---

[4] Wolfson, *Giving Beyond the Gift*, xiv.
[5] Elliot R. Wolfson, *Open Secret: Postmessianic Messianism and the Mystical Revision of Menaḥem Mendel Schneerson* (New York: Columbia University Press, 2009), 300.

undertakes the task of translating their insights into registers supplied by other intellectual and religious traditions.

This translation is what makes Wolfson's work so urgent and so exciting as he envisages the philosophical through the lens of Judaism and as he simultaneously envisages Judaism through the lens of the philosophical. This bifocality, in the lineage of Levinas, Derrida, and other Continental philosophers, finds Wolfson searching for a place that is defined by its very uncanniness, that is, its no-place-ness. It is this a-place/no-place, in the language of Derrida, whose "architecture" is "neither Greek nor Judaic," a space prior to the disentanglement of Jew and Greek. This has led Wolfson, both in his writing and in his teaching, to advocate for a Jewish philosophical thinking that belongs neither to the Jew nor to the Greek, a mode of thinking that resists reduction to either one of these demarcations.[6] It is a difficult, if not impossible task: to arrive at a place that is no-place and, perhaps, we should chart its course by the journey in and through language more than the actual telos.

Wolfson's lasting contribution must be to this type of philosophical thinking. Not simply to Jewish studies, not simply to the study of Jewish mysticism, but to showing how the texts of one religious tradition, to wit, Judaism, illumine more universal philosophical themes. These themes have included, in recent years, secrecy, messianism, apophasis, transcendence, and immanence. That he engages with these universal themes through the particulars of Judaism should not mean, as so many want it to, that his thinking is of relevance solely to Jewish studies. This is the lot of many in this field of Jewish studies—how to move to that universal that wants to relegate us to the confines of the particular, and how to get beyond the particular that is, perhaps necessarily, afraid of the mesmerizing lights of the universal's attraction.

Wolfson's work on Jewish mysticism, then, cannot be separated from his engagement with philosophy. As will become clear in the interview near the end of this volume, he also strongly resists the urge to have his work pigeon-holed within an ethnico-religious frame of reference. Indeed, his life work has been an attempt to dismantle the types of ontological essentialisms that plague so much of contemporaneous academic discussions. Resisting the label "Jewish philosopher" or "Jewish scholar," Wolfson sees himself as

---

[6] Wolfson articulates this complexity in, for example, his *Giving Beyond the Gift*, 158–68; and in Elliot R. Wolfson, "Skepticism and the Philosopher's Keeping Faith," in *Jewish Philosophy for the Twenty-First Century: Personal Reflections*, ed. Hava Tirosh-Samuelson and Aaron W. Hughes (Leiden: Brill, 2014), 481–515.

illumining larger philosophical problems using the particular language of Judaism as he simultaneously problematizes traditional Jewish concepts using the universal categories of philosophy. It is a delicate balance, to be sure, and he manages it with considerable aplomb that is undoubtedly made easier on account of his poetic sensitivity to language and the fragility of meaning that travels in its wake. Poet, painter, scholar—Wolfson uses all of these idioms, intertwinedly, to get at, to point the way toward, to reveal, that which cannot be spoken or that which dares not reveal its name.

Language and being for Wolfson open us onto a vista of ontological poetry in whose paths we make sense of ourselves, both individually and collectively. Poetic language, framed somewhat different, is what discloses ontology just as it is ontology that makes poetry possible. Maneuvering between poetry as thinking and thinking as poetry, we confront an amorphous space, the space in-between, the semantic locus upon which the chiasmus can but point fleetingly. It is this in-between-ness that becomes the foundation, source, and goal of Wolfson's thinking. Following the later Heidegger, about whom I shall discuss in greater detail below, Wolfson shows us the pathmarks that illumine our way ahead as it obfuscates our past and present, that demarcate our temporal coordinates as they betray our hermeneutic reversibility. It is to return to the imaginative faculty—as Wolfson so frequently does in his scholarly work, in his poetry, and in his painting—the place that reveals the ontological horizon, the locus where being is both projected and understood. Philosophy, poetry, and art become three variations on the same theme that fugue-like visit and revisit one another constantly. Wolfson, thus, uses language to limn the very limits of language.

If, in the words of Levinas, nomadism is intrinsic to poetic being in the world, Elliot Wolfson is a true nomad, someone who has chosen to eschew the sedentary nature of our traditional intellectual structures in the quest for meaning that unveils the place of transcendence as it simultaneously veils the transcendence of place. But it is a locus of alienation from Judaism because it steadfastly refuses to buy into or endorse the traditional narratives, predicated as they are upon outmoded concepts such as chosenness, election, or messianic fulfillment. In our palaces of amnesia, built out of stainless steel and colored in a drab grey, Wolfson asks us to be bold and risk the uncertainty, to embrace the ambiguity, that true thinking demands. This is a thinking that hears the muted call of Jewgreek and Greekjew, before their mutual unraveling. Wolfson encourages us to dismantle, yet not deconstruct (and I think there is a crucial difference between the two) these inflexible structures, the ephemeral abodes of human habitation. At a time when the humanities risk hiding behind the sociopolitical tribalism of identity politics or the shallowness of a certain kind of historical positivism, Wolfson—qua nomadic thinker—calls for iconoclasm, and the search for those ciphers that grant us access to the imaginal world, and he also shows us how the existence of that imaginal world lets us recognize phenomena as ciphers in the first place.

Wolfson is a scholar of Judaism, but only if we force ourselves to understand how the two words in that phrase—"scholar" and "Judaism"—pirouette in his thinking. Judaism serves, for him, as it should and as it must, as an indexical marker of and for the scholar's necessary if impossible desire for universality. Framed somewhat differently, for Wolfson the commensurability of the universal, which is after all philosophy's quest, only makes sense in light of Judaism's incommensurability and, of course, vice versa. The particular and the universal undermine one another in their mutual indeterminacy even when they are introduced to one another—as they have been from Halevi to Rosenzweig and beyond—wearing mutually overdetermined masks. This is what drives Wolfson's subtle readings of texts that, at first blush, ought to have nothing to say to one another. As nomadic thinker, Wolfson, artfully avoids the presumed existence of metaphysical absolutes or ontological essences, those communal abodes that invite us to dwell in comfort and that enable us to hear the mesmerizing cadences of sociability that often betray nothing more than a political or ideological patois.

The arc of Wolfson's thinking, the timeswerve that guides his hermeneutic discernment, is the avoidance of historical positivism that confines the past to its immediate and contemporaneous contexts. His attunement to philology combined with his unwillingness to be shackled by a simplistic chronological thinking has meant that Wolfson has forged a different foundation for himself and for those of us who have struggled with these issues, and no doubt others who will struggle with them in the future.

Biography and Career

Elliot R. Wolfson was born in Newark, New Jersey, in 1956, and grew up in Brooklyn, New York, in a neighborhood made up largely of East European refugees, Syrian Jews, and Italian Catholics. His father, a traditional rabbi, ensured that the young Wolfson had a yeshiva education, which meant studying many of the classical rabbinic texts associated with Orthodox

Judaism. It was an education, as he reveals in the interview, that also had its share of immersion in the world of Chabad, or ultra-Orthodoxy, which turned out to be his first personal and living encounter with Jewish mysticism.

Now, however, Wolfson is alienated from Judaism. It is, to be sure, an intimate estrangement. Wolfson understands "the" Jewish tradition in ways that few do, but he stands at its margins, which by his own locution means that he is at its very epicenter. Within this context, I think it is safe to say about Wolfson, as he himself has said about two of the major intellectual influences on his life, Jacques Derrida and his former teacher, Edith Wyschogrod, that he is "prepared to thrust aside the authority of tradition, and, as a consequence, [he has] accepted the fate of social dislocation and political estrangement, occupying a place that is no place, nomadically adrift without any discernible lifeline to be reanchored in a specific community."[7]

Wolfson is certainly not a newcomer to philosophy. He has spent much of his academic life in the pursuit of philosophical study and, as we have already seen, his understanding of kabbalistic and other mystical materials must be understood within the context of his larger interests in philosophy, especially that associated with the Continental tradition. In addition to his immersion in philosophy, Wolfson was interested from a young age in the study of religion, particularly Hinduism and Buddhism. Although he would not pursue these other religious traditions in his subsequent graduate study, they, along with Islam, continue to occupy his attention: he reads the texts associated with their traditions profusely, and they frequently appear in his work to illumine and be illumined by a particular text from Judaism. In this respect, it is certainly safe to say that Wolfson is a scholar of the comparative study of religion, in addition to his many other impressive talents.

As both an undergraduate and graduate student, Wolfson was interested in pursuing a career in philosophy, especially that associated with the subfields of phenomenology, hermeneutics, and existentialism. Within this context, one of his first, and most important teachers, was the late Edith Wyschogrod (1930–2009), with whom he studied at Queens College at the City University of New York, from which he received both a Bachelor of Arts and a Masters of Arts in 1979. Wyschogrod was, among other things, one of the first scholars to introduce the work of Emmanuel Levinas to an American audience. One can see the influence that she had on the young

---

[7] Wolfson, *Giving Beyond the Gift*, xviii.

Wolfson just by examining some of the major themes that she tackled in her *Emmanuel Levinas: The Problem of Ethical Metaphysics*: justice, alterity, the gift, and ontology in ways that connected post-Heideggerian Continental philosophy with the Jewish tradition.[8] In this and many of her other works, she was quick to respond to critics of the postmodernist project who contended that it was blind to ethical questions and simply nihilistic. Wyschogrod would leave an indelible mark on Wolfson and it was her, more than anyone, who appreciated, even in the earliest stages of his work after he had decided to pursue graduate study in Jewish mysticism, that he was using the kabbalistic material as a textual repository with which to think philosophically.

From Queens College, Wolfson went on to do further graduate study, not in philosophy but, as just noted, in Jewish mysticism, at Brandeis University, receiving a second M.A. (1983) and a Ph.D. (1986). At Brandeis he worked with, among others, the late Alexander Altmann, the doyen of Jewish Thought in America at that time. For his dissertation, Wolfson prepared a critical edition of *Sefer ha-Rimmon* (The Book of the Pomegranate) by Moses de León, the author of, among other works, the *Zohar*.[9] Wolfson recalls the following anecdote about how he came to this text in particular:

> Many years before [Altmann] wanted to edit the *Rimmon* himself. When he approached Scholem with his idea, the latter asked him not to undertake such a project for it was his intention to edit that text. Scholem suggested (ironically, perhaps) that instead Altmann edit de León's *Or Zaru'a*. Professor Altmann consented and, as we know, Scholem never did get around to editing the *Rimmon*. Professor Altmann thus encouraged me to help fulfill a personal desire of his by editing this voluminous work of de León.[10]

The text was also particularly suited to the young Wolfson because of the intersection of philosophy and mysticism found within. Wolfson has always taken to heart the statement by the thirteenth-century kabbalist Moses of Burgos that kabbalists stand on the heads of the philosophers. It is one of the reasons that Wolfson moves back and forth between philosophy and mysticism in his own work, showing how mystical elements emerge from philosophical texts and how philosophical insights appear in mystical sources. Indeed, Wolfson would eventually go on to show, more than

---

8 Edith Wyschogrod, *Emmanuel Levinas: The Problem of Ethical Metaphysics* (The Hague: Nijhoff, 1974; 2nd ed., New York: Fordham University Press, 2000).

9 The critical edition appeared as Elliot R. Wolfson, *The Book of the Pomegranate: Moses de Leon's Sefer Ha-Rimmon* (Atlanta: Scholars Press, 1988).

10 Wolfson, *The Book of the Pomegranate*, x.

anyone, how the line separating the so-called mystics and the so-called philosophers in medieval Judaism was as problematic as it was artificial. Within this context, *Sefer ha-Rimmon* belongs to the genre *ta'amei ha-mitzvot* (the reasons of the commandments) that was especially popular in the middle ages, especially in light of Maimonides' exposition, in addition to incorporating commentaries to various daily, weekly, and yearly liturgies. In his Introduction to the work, Wolfson notes how Maimonides' *Sefer ha-Mitzvot* functioned as de León's literary model, even though the latter did not adhere strictly to the former's classification.[11]

His dissertation clearly reveals a number of issues that will carry through much of his subsequent work. For one thing, it shows his interest in examining the intersection between philosophy and mysticism in the medieval tradition. This interest in philosophy, as we shall see shortly, never left Wolfson, and even his most technical studies of Jewish mysticism are informed by philosophical hermeneutics. Secondly, his dissertation shows his interest in the literary structure of the *Zohar*, a feature that had received but scant attention prior to him.[12] Indeed, Wolfson sought to uncover the various literary axes upon which the zoharic understanding of various themes central to Judaism (e.g., creation, revelation, exile, redemption) turn. The *Zohar*, as so much of Wolfson's subsequent work will show, generates meaning through paradox, in which the fragility of antinomies (right-left; creation-destruction; revelation-obfuscation) reveal their apophatic renunciation, that is their invocation by denial. As he frames it in one of his earliest articles, the

> ideal of human perfection that is found in the Zohar according to which one must incorporate evil, even the demonic side, into one's spiritual path. I will suggest that there are two distinct typologies in the Zohar, one positive and the other negative, that both assume this to be the case. In the one case appropriation of the demonic is viewed only as a means for purgation and refinement, whereas in the other it is a means for containment and unification. Common to both is the assumption that one can achieve holiness only through the unholy, that one can see the light only through darkness.[13]

---

[11] E.g., Wolfson, *The Book of the Pomegranate*, 30–31; see further Elliot R. Wolfson, "Mystical Rationalization of the Commandments in *Sefer ha-Rimmon*," *Hebrew Union College Annual* 59 (1987): 217–51.

[12] Wolfson's first published article is on precisely this feature. See his "Left Contained in the Right: A Study in Zoharic Hermeneutics," *Association for Jewish Studies Review* 11 (1986): 27–52.

[13] Elliot R. Wolfson, "Light Through Darkness: The Ideal of Human Perfection in the Zohar," *Harvard Theological Review* 81 (1988): 73–95, at 76.

The play of opposites reveals the silence behind language and how an imageless God appears, paradoxically, through the mediation of visual symbolic imagery. This vision, as his work on the imaginative faculty will clearly show, and which I shall discuss shortly, hovers on and around the borders of a language that speaks as it simultaneously un-speaks, through a disclosure that appears through an act of disappearance and that disappears through its appearance. It is the space in-between—between language and un-language, between disclosure and hiddenness—that signals Wolfson fascination with language and its limits. Moreover, it is the imaginative faculty, a faculty to which Wolfson would devote his first book-length monograph, that, for the kabbalists and the Neoplatonic philosophical sources upon which they drew, would function as the palace of images and, by extension, the locus of incarnation and dematerialization or the removal of matter from form.

After completing his dissertation, Wolfson taught for a year at Cornell University in Ithaca, New York, before joining the faculty of the Skirball Department of Hebrew and Judaic Studies at New York University in 1987, and he was subsequently appointed as the Abraham Lieberman Professor. Wolfson has been the recipient of several academic honors and awards. He has, for example, served as the Regenstein Visiting Professor in Jewish Studies at the Divinity School, University of Chicago (1992); Visiting Professor in the Russian State University in the Humanities (1995); a fellow at the Institute for Advanced Study, Princeton (1996); the Shoshana Shier Distinguished Visiting Professor, University of Toronto (1998); a fellow at the Institute for Advanced Studies, the Hebrew University of Jerusalem (2000, 2008–2009); the Crown-Minnow Visiting Professor of Theology and Jewish Studies, University of Notre Dame (2002); Brownstone Visiting Professor of Jewish Studies, Dartmouth College (2003); Visiting Professor in the Humanities Center, Johns Hopkins University (2005); Professor of Jewish Mysticism in Shandong University, Jinan, China (2005); the Lynette S. Autrey Visiting Professor, Humanities Research Center, Rice University (2007); and a Fellow at the Center for Advanced Jewish Studies at the University of Pennsylvania (2012). He has also taught at Cornell University, Queens College (CUNY), Princeton University, Jewish Theological Seminary of America, Reconstructionist Rabbinical College, Hebrew Union College, Bard College, and Columbia University. Wolfson is also a fellow of the American Academy of Arts and Sciences (AAAS), the American Academy of Jewish Research (AAJR), and the American Society for the Study of Religion (ASSR).

Wolfson, a prolific thinker, is the author of over 12 volumes (several of which have been translated into other languages), 5 edited volumes, and well over 150 book chapters and articles. He is also the author of two books of poetry,[14] and has had a gallery showing of his paintings. As I mentioned earlier, it is important not simply to see the poetic and artistic works of Wolfson as avocational; on the contrary, both represent alternative attempts to encounter an imageless god through the mediation of symbolic imagery. His painted canvases communicate the paradox of vision that takes place at the intersection of appearance and disappearance and of disclosure and hiddenness. Like his linguistic work, the quest of his visual oeuvre is both to ruminate on and to seek to provide form to the formless.

In like manner, Wolfson's poetry seeks to present his philosophical reflection in another language, "a language beyond language" as he tells us in the interview that appears near the end of this volume. Like his work on philosophy and on kabbalah, it revels in language and the overcoming of traditional binaries through the process of chiasmus. In a poem called "darkening," for example, we read:

> how much darker can darkness become
> before it is no longer dark?
> i test the limit here in the center,
> where flesh melts and fire freezes,
> from the waiting that waits for those who wait,
> while those who wait are weighed
> on the scale without balance
> in the absence of wait,
> uttering the inescapable truth,
> something is even if it is nothing,
> empty fullness,
> silence of senseless chatter
> that reverberates against
> impenetrable membrane
> her sacred veil[15]

The poem illustrates similar themes shared by Wolfson's poetry and his prose, though the former eschews the often technical nature of the latter.

---

[14] Elliot R. Wolfson, *Pathwings: Philosophic and Poetic Reflections on the Hermeneutics of Time and Language* (Barrytown, NY: Barrytown/Station Hill Press, 2004). This volume includes sixty poems that appear with a selection of his essays. The second collection is *Footdreams and Treetales: 92 Poems* (New York: Fordham University Press, 2007). A study of Wolfson's poetic work may be found in Galli, *On Wings of Moonlight*.

[15] Elliot R. Wolfson, "darkening," in *Pathwings*, 72.

Wolfson's books, many of which will make more detailed appearances below, have won numerous prestigious awards, further attesting to the deep respect his work has garnered in the academy. His *Through a Speculum That Shines* (1994) received the American Academy of Religion's Award for Excellence in the Study of Religion in the Category of Historical Studies, in addition to the National Jewish Book Award for Excellence in Scholarship. His *Language, Eros, Being* (2005) received the National Jewish Book Award for Excellence in Scholarship. And his *Dream Interpreted within a Dream* (2011) received the American Academy of Religion's Award for Excellence in Constructive and Reflective Studies. Clearly the discipline of religious studies has acknowledged Wolfson's outstanding contribution to the field.

In 2014, Wolfson was appointed to the Marsha and Jay Glazer Chair in Jewish Studies in the Department of Religious Studies at the University of California, Santa Barbara. This appointment is significant because it signals his departure from working and teaching within the context of a Jewish studies department, where he has spent most of his adult life, to a new intellectual environment, one that will see him work and train graduate students in the context of religious studies, particularly in the subfields of postmodern hermeneutics and the phenomenology of religion.

The Palace of the Imagination

Wolfson's first book-length monograph after the publication of his dissertation was entitled *Through a Speculum That Shines: Vision and Imagination in Medieval Jewish Mysticism* (1994). It is a revolutionary study that examines the visionary impulse and the simultaneous prohibition (e.g., Deut. 4:16–19) against iconic representation of the divine within Jewish mysticism and, by extension, within monotheism more generally. Without such an impulse, God is but a distant deity, aloof from the mundane affairs of humanity. Yet, if God is portrayed in human form, God risks becoming little more than a god with human frailties not unlike those found in the Greek pantheon. This paradox proves to be one of the tensions endemic to the monotheistic enterprise, something that Wolfson will pick up on again, albeit from a different angle, in his *Giving Beyond the Gift* (2014). One of the traditional ways of dealing with this tension in the scholarly literature is to posit that Greek culture is visual and that Hebraic is somehow auditory or nonvisual. Unlike the towering figure of the previous generation of scholarship on Jewish mysticism, Gershom Scholem, who used such civilizational reifications, Wolfson eschews them in favor of the acknowledgment that one cannot paint entire civilizations with the same ontological brush. Rather Greek and Jew, Jew and Greek, comingle in such a manner that their histories and their destinies become virtually impossible to unravel, one from the other. It is because of this comingling—for example, Heidegger's seminars on Plato, who was also a source of medieval Jewish philosophy and mysticism; or the kabbalah's influence on Jakob Böhme (1575–1624) and Friedrich Schelling (1775–1854), who were important in Heidegger's intellectual development—that Wolfson has no hesitation, despite the objection of his critics, of reading medieval Jewish texts and postmodern philosophical ones together.

Certainly the archeological record is full of examples in which various images appear on synagogue walls and floors; however, physical images are not Wolfson's concern. Rather, he has decided to focus on *mental* images of God in which the individual mystic "wrestled with the conflict of experiencing an almost tangible object of his or her vision, on the one hand, and with the stated normative belief that God in his true nature is incorporeal and hence invisible, on the other."[16] These images, in other words, do not exist apart from the structures of an individual's consciousness. The philosophical issues that drive his analysis, then, are primarily phenomenological (i.e., what are the structures of consciousness that permit the individual to experience the world from his or her own point of view) and ontological (i.e., what is the nature of the image that makes this possible). The key, for Wolfson, is the imagination, "the vehicle for the contemplative ascent to the spiritual realm and the ultimate conjunction of the individual and the intelligent forms, the reunion or reunification of the soul and its spiritual root."[17] Given his interests, it should be clear that *Through a Speculum That Shines* cannot be a simple historical study, one of anticipations and influences. On the contrary, using a hermeneutic that guides all his work, namely, that "by digging deep into one tradition, one finds the paths to other traditions,"[18] he seeks to show how medieval Jewish (and, by extension, other monotheistic) philosophers and mystics, in addition to contemporary Continental philosophers, given all their diverse linguistic and cultural expressions, nevertheless shared a common epistemic heritage that pivots around, but is not subsumed by binaries such as veiling/

---

[16] Elliot R. Wolfson, *Through a Speculum That Shines: Vision and Imagination in Medieval Jewish Mysticism* (Princeton, NJ: Princeton University Press, 1994), 3–4.

[17] Ibid., 297.

[18] See the interview near the end of this book for more on this topic in Wolfson's own words.

unveiling, revelation/concealment, and appearance/disappearance. This certainly does not mean that he is looking for a universal truth that manifests itself in the various philosophical or religious traditions that he studies, but it does mean that these traditions may possess certain common discourses in which sameness and difference appear. It is not Wolfson's goal to point out such features in a simplistic or reductive fashion; rather, through investigation into the semantic registers of original texts (in their original languages), Wolfson, as a textual archaeologist, seeks out subterranean and untrammeled paths between a variety of traditions.

For Wolfson, it was the visionary texts of the Bible that inspired all later iterations of Jewish mysticism. At the heart of the biblical heritage is the simultaneous affirmation that God could assume a visual form and the rejection that He could be iconically represented. This means that the tension of aniconism (i.e., the avoidance of images) on the one hand, and the impulse to visualize the divine on the other is essential to all subsequent varieties of Jewish mysticism. Even in this early work, Wolfson articulates an important aspect of his subsequent methodology, which is a mistrust of historical reductionism in favor of a more nuanced phenomenological approach that, while certainly appreciative of what historicism has to offer, does not slavishly follow it. To understand Jewish mysticism in a sophisticated manner, however, Wolfson argues that it is necessary to examine "the myths, symbols, and deep structures that have informed the life experiences of Jewish mystics through the ages."[19]

The methodological approach in this work gets to the heart of Wolfson's skill as a scholar: his textual expertise and sensitivity to linguistic expression necessarily means that he reads texts carefully and closely; he possesses a masterful knowledge of the manuscript tradition that grants him access to a wealth of unpublished material; and he is a voracious reader of scholarship from numerous disciplines. He puts these skills in the service of an interpretive framework that eschews a strict historicism that simply or neatly confines the past to its immediate contexts. Rather, his approach permits access into the ahistorical imaginal world about which he writes so articulately in the historical mystics that he studies. This is why Wolfson's work in kabbalah risks being misunderstood. On one level, it certainly tells us about the categories and mentalité of Jewish mysticism in its many historical iterations, but on a much deeper level it is a polyphonic and cosmopolitan conversation with a host of philosophical, psychological, and

---

[19] Wolfson, *Through a Speculum That Shines*, 393.

literary ideas, which even the most passing glimpse at his footnotes and bibliography clearly reveals.

Central to Wolfson's analysis in *Through a Speculum That Shines*, as we have already seen at several junctures in this essay, resides the imagination, which he characterizes as "the divine element of the soul that enables one to gain access to the realm of incorporeality by transferring or transmuting sensory data and/or rational concepts into symbols."[20] Invoking the language of Henry Corbin, the late scholar of Islamic mysticism, Wolfson employs the term "imaginal," to indicate a realm serving as a symbolic intermediary that allows for the imaging of the imageless God, who can paradoxically be seen as an anthropos or human figure. This revealed God, according to Wolfson, allows us to understand his concealment that necessarily makes his revelation possible. It is the imagination, he argues, that "produces symbols of the spiritual entities that act as interpretive filtering screens through which these entities appear in human consciousness."[21] These images, neither totally corporeal nor totally spiritual, permit us (and I think that Wolfson has more than medieval mystics in mind) access to the realm of incorporeality through their very corporeality.

But Wolfson goes even further than this. Influenced by the work of a number of French feminists, most notably the philosopher and psychoanalyst Luce Irigaray, he contends that the visionary experience, what he calls the ocularcentrism, of the Jewish mystics both emerges from and is indicative of larger rabbinic phallomorphic culture, that is, a culture in which the phallus is regarded as the ultimate marker of gender identity. The mystical eroticism associated with this, he argues, puts the phallus at the center of the visual encounter. This should not necessarily surprise us because kabbalistic texts were, after all, written by and for males, and as a result they necessarily portray sexuality from a male perspective. In terms of the kabbalistic imagery associated with the sefirotic world of the divine pleroma this means that the male kabbalists identified with and were fascinated by the ninth sefirah, which signifies the divine phallus. This homoerotic impulse subsequently denigrated the feminine (both earthly and cosmic), which functions as little more than an instrument, a speculum, through which the mystic visualizes the phallus. The act of contemplation, the reading of Torah, an act that can only be carried out by circumcised males, thus becomes an attempt to remove the veils that cover the divine

---

[20] Ibid., 8.
[21] Ibid., 62.

phallus. This is not to say that the mystics engaged in visionary experiences were homosexuals. Statistically speaking, some, of course, would have been, but Wolfson's point is more rarefied. He argues, on the contrary, that the homoerotic bonding of males theosophically symbolizes and even actualizes the union of male and female in the Godhead.[22] It is a point, moreover, that should also silence those who want to see in the *Shekhinah* an unequivocal adulation of the feminine side of God, an early prototype for Jewish feminism.[23]

It is also worth noting that *Through a Speculum That Shines* makes an important contribution to introducing the study of Jewish mysticism into the realm of religious studies. Wolfson, as we have seen, has not only read broadly and widely in this larger field, but his study has articulated and thus contributed to our understanding of the tensions inherent to monotheism. It is for this reason that it received a much larger audience than traditional technical studies on Jewish mysticism. The book received, as mentioned, an AAR Award of Excellence, which shows that his work was read not only among those in Jewish studies, but spoke to those in the larger discipline of religious studies more generally.

Hermeneutics and Temporality

Since Wolfson has always approached kabbalah from the perspective of contemporary hermeneutics, it is perhaps only natural that his work would gradually begin to take on an even greater philosophical hue. Certainly his earlier analyses were, as we have just seen, in conversation with Continental philosophy, especially the tradition of French feminism. However, in his subsequent work, we see a turn (*die Kehre*) so that philosophical issues come increasingly to the foreground. Much of this subsequent work is pure philosophy in which the texts of Jewish mysticism—zoharic, Lurianic, Chabad—intertwine with texts from other religious traditions—Christian, Muslim, Hindu, Buddhist—in the service of an increasing interest in philosophical issues such as time, temporality, death, and the poetic ontology of language. We now see on full display Wolfson's indebtedness to and

---

[22] Ibid., 371 n. 155.

[23] Wolfson is particularly interested in the gendered terminology found in kabbalistic and other Jewish sources that is used to image God. Feminism, thus, becomes a way to critique and destabilize the traditional Jewish use of gender categories. See, for example, his *Circle in the Square: Studies in the Use of Gender in Kabbalistic Symbolism* (Albany: State University of New York Press, 1995).

struggle with the thought of Martin Heidegger, one of the most important philosophers of the twentieth century.

Given Heidegger's political leanings, it is perhaps necessary to address, but certainly not apologize for, Wolfson's invocation and use of this thinker. Although arguably the most important modern philosopher after Kant, Heidegger's political views and vile anti-Semitism have caused many of his modern detractors simply to discredit his work.[24] Some are also bothered by the fact that Jewish thinkers find Heidegger's ideas to be worthy of engagement. How, they fallaciously reason, can a Jewish philosopher employ the vocabulary and categories of such a person, especially when such categories either emerge out of or seemingly endorse anti-Semitism? Wolfson has steadfastly refused to enter into this futile debate, preferring to avoid the contingent political reverberations and instead show how Heidegger's *philosophical* thinking illumines medieval texts. This will come out clearly in the interview with Wolfson that appears near the end of this volume. Suffice it to say in the meantime, however, that some have been critical of Wolfson's use of Heidegger, confusing, it would seem, the man with the thinking. Wolfson writes, "I do not naively assume that Heidegger's thought can be entirely divorced from its historical context nor do I condone him for his moral failings. At the same time, I would not subscribe to the view that his thought can be reduced simply to his political engagement with Nazism."[25]

Instead of waging political debates over Heidegger, Wolfson prefers to engage him as the iconoclastic thinker that he was. He is particularly attracted to the later Heidegger, the one who denied that Being can be represented accurately in scientific or pseudoscientific prose and who, concomitantly, forged a new pathway for another kind of thinking, a poetic thinking that seeks to respond to Being in language. The notion of dwelling (*Wohnen*) as poetic habitation sees and uses language as a form of disclosure that disrupts the intransigence of our quotidian existence. *Poesis* now becomes that activity, for Wolfson as for Heidegger, that reconciles thought with time, and functions as that which tears the fabric of the everyday.

It is certainly not Wolfson's intention to either rationalize or excuse Heidegger's rhetoric, but to get to the core of his thinking, a core that is

---

[24] This gained renewed impetus in recent months owing to the publication of Heidegger's intellectual diaries, entitled *Black Notebooks* (*Schwarze Hefte*), that he kept during the 1930s and 1940s, and that seem to show that Heidegger never ceased to be a Nazi. Without wanting to exonerate him for his failings, however, it is important not to reduce all of Heidegger's thought to this dimension.

[25] Wolfson, *Language, Eros, Being*, 420 n. 241.

untouched by political expediencies. Wolfson also responds forcefully to critics who want to know how someone who works on medieval texts can anachronistically use twentieth-century philosophical thought. As should be clear by now, one response is that, although Wolfson has worked on medieval texts, these texts are but points of departure for thinking about universal themes and concepts. And, as we have already seen, another, perhaps more chronistic minded, response, is that Heidegger's own work on the Greek philosophers means that Heidegger is certainly thinking with the same kinds of categories that medieval philosophers and mystics were. Wolfson does not rule out a kabbalistic influence on Heidegger that would have been derived, again historically, by way of intermediaries such as Böhme and Schelling.[26] Indeed, Wolfson sees a basic similarity between Heidegger's critique of Western rationalism and that proposed by medieval kabbalah. Even more provocatively, Wolfson argues that, not unlike the kabbalists, Heidegger privileges a particular destiny (for him, that of the German Volk) and a particular language (German) that potentially undermines and devalues the Other.[27] For ultimately Heidegger believed, not unlike the kabbalists with respect to the Jewish people, that a particular ethnos was destined to carry out a monumental spiritual mission, which was nothing less than to transform Being, to show the path from instrumental technology to poetic dwelling. This is an important topic, and my own sense is that it will increasingly preoccupy Wolfson's philosophical thinking in the years to come.

We begin to see an even clearer intersection between kabbalistic materials and modern philosophy in Wolfson's thinking in two important books that came out in relative quick succession. *Language, Eros, Being* (2005) and *Alef, Mem, Tau* (2006) are extensive and wide-ranging meditations on the nature of time and, by extension, on the coordinates of life, death, and the nature of existence between them. At the beginning of *Language, Eros, Being*, Wolfson provides a theoretical justification that illumines much of his scholarly activity. It is meant, on one level, as a philosophical response to historical positivists that want to claim that one cannot read medieval

---

[26] Even Scholem had noted the influence of kabbalah on Schelling. See Gershom Scholem, *Major Trends in Jewish Mysticism* (New York: Schocken, 1954), 409 n. 19 and 412 n. 77.

[27] Wolfson discusses this issue in the interview with Aubrey Glazer, "What Does Heidegger's Anti-Semitism Mean for Jewish Philosophy?" *Religion Dispatches*, April 3, 2014, available at http://religiondispatches.org/what-does-heideggers-anti-semitism-mean-for-jewish-philosophy/. Wolfson talks at length about the xenophobic and racialist dimensions of kabbalah in his *Venturing Beyond: Morality and Law in Kabbalistic Mysticism* (Oxford: Oxford University Press, 2006).

thinkers through modern and/or postmodern lenses. Using insights from physics, philosophy, and literature, among other disciplines, to argue that the telling of time cannot be distinguished from the time of telling, Wolfson offers philosophical justification for his project. At the epicenter of this justification is what he calls the "timeswerve": "Time reversal, therefore, does not, theoretically, imply a mechanical retracing of previous moments by circumabulating the curve, going back to the future and arriving at the past."[28] Or, as he subsequently puts it, "the past may not, after all, extend monodirectionally into the present, which was its future, but rather may swerve its way curvilinearly, future awaiting its past, past becoming its future."[29] The succession of time means that the "now" is both past and future and, thus, not now, thereby imploding any neat or traditional notion of succession. Time, linearly, but especially when conceived of circularly or curvilinearly, returns us to the place we have never been; a return in which we find ourselves, simultaneously again and anew, within the palace of the imagination, the place where the simulacrum of reality transforms reality into a simulacrum.

The heart of *Language, Eros, Being*—L, E, B = *lev* = heart, the seat of the imaginative faculty—is poetics and how, once again, the imagination functions as the sine qua non of human cognition. Poetic language is that which manifests the silence, thereby giving concealment its disclosure, and the formless its form. Once again, as in *Through a Speculum That Shines*, Wolfson shows us how inherent to kabbalistic texts is a tension between asceticism and eroticism, a tension that pivots around the erotically configured visionary imagination. For Wolfson, as the essays collected below reveal, there can be no form that is not embodied and it is the imaginative faculty, as so much of his work has shown in both poetic and philosophical detail, that is responsible for this activity. In his own words:

> The symbol is a fusion of "opposite equals" (in Whitman's telling phrase) held together in the sensible experience of transcendence that the symbol elicits. The experience of transcendence irrupts ecstatically at the limit of the temporal horizon and is thus accessible only through a web of symbolic deflections; by nature, therefore, the symbol reveals and conceals concurrently. What is envisioned in mystical enlightenment is experienced and interpreted in symbols drawn from our shared phenomenological sensibilities, but what we experience in the everyday world alludes semiotically to the imaginal world of poetic prisms.[30]

---

[28] Wolfson, *Language, Eros, Being*, xvii.
[29] Ibid., xx.
[30] Ibid., 127.

For the kabbalists, for the poets, for Wolfson, indeed for all those with sensitivity to see within and beyond, the symbolic dreamscape of the imaginal realm and the phenomenological nature of the mundane world are brought together—fragilely, ephemerally—through the power of language and the poetic imagination that recognizes the encounter. It is here again that Wolfson finds the work of Heidegger, especially the later Heidegger, to be so important. The dual function of the sign, to conceal and reveal, is what, in Heidegger's words, makes untruth the very nature of truth.[31] According to Heidegger, "Truth is un-truth, insofar as there belongs to it the reservoir of the not-yet uncovered, the un-covered, in the sense of concealment. In unconcealedness, as truth, there occurs also the other 'un-' of a double restrain or refusal. Truth occurs as such in the opposition of clearing and double concealing."[32] By untruth, of course, neither Heidegger nor Wolfson mean "lie" or "falsehood." Rather, they mean that all that is revealed is by the act of its very revelation concealed. It is precisely this simultaneity that Wolfson's prose seeks to reveal/conceal. "What better way to articulate the inadequacy of words," Wolfson writes, "but with words written to articulate the inadequacy of words."[33] It is the paradox of language that Wolfson seeks to mine, trying, I would argue, to find the silence from which language arises. Here, it is important to note, that Wolfson's thought is also indebted to the work of Franz Rosenzweig, for whom language, silence, and *poesis* form the building blocks of creation, revelation, and redemption.

Another aspect that we see in *Language, Eros, Being* is a comparative dimension with other religious traditions, specifically Islam and Buddhism. His reasoning behind this, as he makes clear in the preface to his *Open Secret* (2009), is again philosophical. In examining texts from other religious traditions, he writes that it is possible "to find confirmation of my hermeneutic belief that by digging into the soil of a specific cultural matrix one may uncover roots that lead to others."[34] This hermeneutic enables Wolfson to "seek points of affinity" between what he considers to be "disparate spiritual orbits." This is what enables him, for example, to ascertain similarities between medieval kabbalists and Sufi thinkers, such as Ibn Arabi, on the nature of the veil and unveiling; and, in *Open Secret*, a work I shall discuss presently, to show how the notion of emptiness in Mahayana Buddhism

---

[31] E.g., Martin Heidegger, *Poetry, Language, Thought*, trans. Albert Hofstadter (New York: Harper and Row, 1971), 54. For Wolfson's discussion of this Heideggerian motif, see, for example *Giving Beyond the Gift*, 45–54.

[32] Heidegger, *Poetry, Language, Thought*, 60.

[33] Wolfson, *Language, Eros, Being*, 20.

[34] Wolfson *Open Secret*, xiii.

illumines the Lubavitch notion of what he calls apophatic embodiment, a term that alludes to the fact that, framed somewhat differently, the unseen can only be seen through the seen.

The concern with temporality finds further expression in his *Alef, Mem, Tau* (2006), a book-length study on the nexus between time, truth, and death, again using kabbalistic texts as his point of departure. Wolfson employs these three letters which are the first, middle, and final letters of the Hebrew alphabet—and that, when put together spell *emet* (truth)—as semiotic signposts of the three tenses of time: past, present, and future. Indebted to the phenomenologist Edmond Husserl, Wolfson sets out in this work to think about the paradox of time: how the essential structures of consciousness make possible the unified perception of an object that occurs across successive moments. How, in other words, can consciousness that is constituted by time account for the persistence of the contents of consciousness? These three letters, in other words, disclose the time of truth that, he argues, is concealed in the truth of time.

Reading numerous kabbalistic sources, Wolfson seeks to offer an ontology of time that is, at the same time, a grammar of becoming. "The correlation of truth and divinity," he writes,

> underscores that truth, which embodies in its semiotic constellation the triadic structure of temporality, is the mark of the divine eternally becoming in time—a formulation that is still too dichotomous, as the divine becoming is not an event in time but the eventuality of time, an eventuality instantiated in the momentous eruption of the moment wherein life and death converge in the coming to be of that which endures everlastingly and the endurance of that which comes to be provisionally.[35]

Rather than conceive of the beginning, the middle, and the end as linear points, Wolfson, returning to the concept of the timeswerve that he articulated in *Language, Eros, Being*, sees them—to invoke the language of Heraclitus—as shared points on the circumference of the circle. The very points that mark time, framed somewhat differently, now conquer time. The beginning, for example, cannot be a beginning on this circumference because there is nothing, no time, for it to begin. In like manner, the end cannot be the end on this timeswerve because it holds out the possibility for rebirth. Between this endless beginning and beginningless end is the presentless present, the present that always succumbs to the past and the future.

---

[35] Wolfson, *Alef, Mem, Tau: Kabbalistic Musings on Time, Truth, and Death* (Berkeley: University of California Press, 2006), 175.

Secrecy and Comparison

Wolfson has always been interested in secrecy, especially as it relates to its opposite, openness.[36] Only by breaking the seal of the secret, he maintains, is it possible to realize the nature of secrecy for without knowing what the secret is we do not know that it is a secret. The secret thus needs its disclosure for us to know that it was a secret in the first place. Every disclosure of a secret, framed somewhat different, is also its simultaneous covering that retains the secrecy. There can, paradoxically, be no secrecy because we need to know the secret, the open secret, before we can ascend/assent to it. In his *Open Secret* (2009), Wolfson examines the paradox of secrecy by subjecting the textual tradition associated with Chabad, particularly those of its seventh Rebbe, Menachem Mendel Schneerson, to close scrutiny. To phrase this paradox in Wolfson's own words:

> Not only is the broadcasting of the esoteric seen as a propadeutic to accelerate the redemption, but redemption is depicted as the wholesale dispersion of the mysteries of the Torah, an overt breaking of the seal of esotericism. But it is precisely with respect to the explicit claims about the disclosure of secrets that the scholar must be wary of being swayed by a literalist approach that would take the seventh Rebbe at his word. There is no suggestion of willful deceit on the part of Schneerson, of an intention to falsify, but there is an appeal to the wisdom of the tradition pertaining to the hermeneutic duplicity of secrecy: the secret will no longer be secret if and when the secret will be exposed to have been nothing more than the secret that there is a secret. To discover the secret that there is no secret is the ultimate secret that one can neither divulge without withholding nor withhold without divulging.[37]

As in his other work, Wolfson invokes Buddhist and Hindu texts to illumine and be illumined by those of Judaism, in this case Chabad. Wolfson writes of his "dabbling in Buddhist texts, including the presentation of the messianic ideal as attaining—through negation—the consciousness that extends beyond consciousness, crossing beyond the river to the shore of nondiscrimination, the shore where there is no more need to speak of the shore."[38] It is at this point that Wolfson brings in his discussion of Buddhist texts, particularly from the Mahayana tradition. Here, he is most interested

---

36 Earlier studies include Elliot R. Wolfson, "Occultation of the Feminine and the Body of Secrecy in Medieval Kabbalah," in *Rending the Veil: Concealment and Revelation of Secrets in the History of Religion*, ed. E. R. Wolfson (New York and London: Seven Bridges Press, 1999), 113–54. This essay is reprinted below.

37 Wolfson, *Open Secret*, 247–48.

38 Ibid., xiii.

in the notion of *madhyamaka* (the middle way), that I discussed earlier, and that is a form of logic that "posits the identity of opposites in the opposition of their identity."[39] Wolfson elaborates:

> The logic to which I refer is based on the tetralemmic scheme: S is P; ~P; both P and ~P; neither P nor ~P. The middle of the four-cornered logic, which some scholars consider to be the core of Buddhist philosophy, should not be conceived of as a meridian point situated equidistantly between extremes, the venerated golden mean between excess and privation in the Western philosophical tradition, but as *the indeterminate space that contains both and neither of the extremes, the absent present that is present as absent, the lull between affirmation and negation, identity and nonidentity, the void that cannot be avoided. In this middle excluded by the logic of the excluded middle, purportedly contradictory properties are attributed and not attributed to the (non)substance at the same time and in the same relation, whence it follows that the propositions $(A \cdot \sim A)$ and $\sim(A \cdot \sim A)$ converge in the point of their divergence.*[40]

I have put these last couple of sentences in italics because they get to the heart of Wolfson's work. His thought, in all of its manifestations, is an attempt to arrive at this indeterminate space, a space that, to repeat, "contains both and neither of the extremes, the absent present that is present as absent, the lull between affirmation and negation, identity and nonidentity, the void that cannot be avoided."

Comparison, for Wolfson, is not facile. It is based neither on simplistic notions of influence nor chronistic renderings. It is, on the contrary, based on the notion that, despite semantic and conceptual discrepancies, there are real *philosophical* reasons for applying concepts from Buddhist logic to, say, modern texts associated with Chabad. I also note here that in earlier studies, Wolfson had used modern philosophers associated with the Continental tradition to illumine medieval texts; in *Open Secret*, however, he reverses this process and uses medieval Buddhist (and Hindu and Muslim) texts to send light on modern Jewish texts. Using this comparative model, Wolfson argues that the very notion of messianic liberation is to be released from all conceptual limitations, including the very notion of being emancipated from liberation. He writes:

> The ultimate legacy of the seventh Rebbe's messianic aspiration, the encrypted message he wished to bequeath to future generations, lies in proffering an understanding of salvation as the expanded consciousness of and

---

[39] Ibid., 109.
[40] Ibid., 109.

reabsorption in the inestimable essence, whose essence it is to resist essentialization, the moment of eternity for which we await in its fully temporalized sense, the advent of the absolute (non)event. True liberation, on this score, would consist of being liberated from the very need to be liberated.[41]

Dreams, Oneiropoiesis, and the Chiasmic Structure of Reality

More recently, Wolfson has turned his attention to dreams. However, as a product of the imaginative faculty, this interest again returns him to the beginning. For Wolfson, dreams incarnate, once again, the paradox of reality because the authenticity of the dream is ultimately judged by its artificiality, its dreamlike quality, just as the dream's truth is not undermined by its deception. As in his previous analyses, Wolfson works on the notion that opposites are the same by virtue of being opposite. The dream and reality, in other words, represent two modes of existence that ultimately need one another and subsequently give definition to its opposite. In his *A Dream Interpreted within a Dream: Oneiropoiesis and the Prism of Imagination* (2011), Wolfson sets out to "think the matter of the dream from inside the contours of the dream."[42] In typical fashion, he reads far and wide, in numerous disciplines and traditions, as he seeks to leave no stone unturned in his quest to elucidate a concept. Invoking neuroscience, for example, he claims:

> In my way of thinking, the cerebral activity of dreaming should be considered exemplary of the increased aptitude for abstraction and ratiocination that developed in the hominid brain as a consequence of the multimodal sensory integration. Through a process of evolutionary selection, this augmented apperception, enhanced intelligence, and the ensuing refinement of the nervous system formed what has legitimately been called the *numinous mind*, a degree of mentation typified above all by the symbolic cognition that has endowed us with myriad incompatible traits, including the proclivity to imagine the unimaginable.[43]

From here, Wolfson moves through a vast array of sources—biblical, rabbinic, kabbalistic, philosophic—and a panoply of theoretical frameworks—psychoanalytic, phenomenological, neuroscientific—to simultaneously celebrate and interrogate the dreamworld and the world of the dream. In

---

[41] Ibid., 300.
[42] Elliot R. Wolfson, *A Dream Interpreted within a Dream: Oneiropoiesis and the Prism of Imagination* (New York: Zone Books, 2011), 15.
[43] Ibid., 20.

this world, to use Wolfson's locution, "the time of dreaming is to be ascertained from the dreaming of time, but the dreaming of time can be calibrated only in the time of dreaming."[44]

For Wolfson, the dream is a masterpiece. Although the dream must by necessity take place within the purview of the individual, that is, the particular, it is ultimately something with universal, that is, cultural significance. Here Wolfson repeats a theme that we have seen throughout this introduction: the particular must always be indexical of the universal. Dreams become for Wolfson reality, a mytho-logic that permit, both unapologetically and repeatedly, a concurrence of what "wakefulness" constructs as incongruent and contradictory. Wolfson seeks to carve out space in this volume, in the dreamscape of its vision, a space that will permit philosophers and scholars of religion to examine the religious claims of the believer that neither revert to simplistic claims of theism or atheism, idealism or materialism, and transcendence or immanence. This is because the dream makes possible the impossible by its very act of being possible. For Wolfson,

> The invisible, accordingly, is not an excess of the real, the limitless positivity of the possible impossibility positioned outside the symbolic, but rather the signifier of lack, the delimited negativity of the impossible possibility inherent in the symbolic. The real, if we continue to avail ourselves of this nomenclature, is sustained by the multitude of appearances it maintains by disrupting them repeatedly, rendering them visible in their invisibility and invisible in their visibility, without, however, professing the existence of a noumenal core that persists as the same beneath the semblance of the phenomenal—no face behind the mask that is not itself a mask.[45]

Wolfson, framed somewhat differently, asks us to understand the texture of the divine world through the structure of the dream without either appealing to or summoning a supernatural or metaphysical transcendence. Rather than take the dream for granted, he celebrates its creativity while he simultaneously shows its significance for thinking about transcendence, immanence, and experience. The end of *A Dream Interpreted within a Dream* finds Wolfson at his most intellectually playful as he weaves together Moses de León, Shankara, Rumi, and Nagarjuna in order to show how the spiritual insights from these diverse, temporally unconnected traditions, nevertheless hold the dream up as the locus of enlightened consciousness. Using the words of the late Michel Foucault, Wolfson speaks of these convergences as

---

[44] Ibid., 21.
[45] Ibid., 41.

the last stage of the "great mythology of the dream, the fantastic cosmogony of the dream where the whole universe seems to conspire at a momentary and vacillating image."[46] It is here that Wolfson returns to the image: "It is the speculum through which we grasp that the world is like a dream, that there is no way to access truth in this world except through the dissimilitude of the image."[47] He concludes the book in typical poetic fashion:

> In the dreamless dream, the dream before the dream, one dreams the dream that is dreamt as the dream one no longer dreams. By interpreting that dream, the dream within the dream, we edge ever closer to waking from the dream that we are dreaming that we are waking from the dream.[48]

The Gift

At many times in this introductory essay, I have tried to situate Wolfson against the backdrop of some of the thinkers he has thought with. One such thinker that has figured rarely in this introduction, but has been an important catalyst in so much of Wolfson's work, is Franz Rosenzweig, perhaps the most important Jewish philosopher in the twentieth century, though he himself resisted the locution. Rosenzweig is also someone whose work, like Wolfson's, is full of penetrating philosophical insight and literary creativity. Indeed, it safe to say that of all those who inhabit the traditional canon of Jewish philosophy, it is Rosenzweig more than anyone who has influenced Wolfson. This is certainly not to say that Rosenzweig is an easy inheritance for Wolfson. In the conclusion to his *Alef, Mem, Tau*, for example, Wolfson seeks to build creatively on Rosenzweig's notion of temporality. For Rosenzweig, the disavowal of time by the eternal people (i.e., the Jewish people) enables them to surpass time by experiencing the fullness of time. This leads to a concept of temporality wherein past, present, and future "converge in an absolute that is all-in-all."[49] For Wolfson, however, the concept of time-being as existing in being-time, especially as found in esoteric tradition associated with kabbalistic materials, militates against such an approach because inherent to it is the hope, the promise of retrieval, restoration, and return.

---

[46] Ibid., 273.
[47] Ibid., 267.
[48] Ibid., 274.
[49] Wolfson, *Alef, Mem, Tau*, 176, 177.

Wolfson again struggles with the Jewish philosophical canon in his recent *Giving Beyond the Gift* (2014). In this monograph, he seeks to explicate the theolatrous impulse that resides at the very heart of monotheism. It is a difficult work that grapples "with the extent to which the discernment that the final iconoclastic achievement of monotheism calls for destroying the idol of the very God personified as the deity that must be worshipped without being idolized."[50] If previous works had seen kabbalah providing him with a "repository of texts," *Giving Beyond the Gift* now sees him using modern Jewish philosophers as his repository. Wolfson argues that many of these philosophers, the luminaries of modern Jewish thought—Hermann Cohen, Martin Buber, Franz Rosenzweig, and Emmanuel Levinas—were, despite the fact that they were aware of the pitfalls of scriptural theism and the desire on the part of the human imagination to create false representations of transcendence, nevertheless guilty of personifying transcendence. The only two contemporary Jewish thinkers, on Wolfson's reading, that were able to resist this were Jacques Derrida and his former teacher, Edith Wyschogrod, both of whom, to use a quotation that I used earlier in another context, "were prepared to thrust aside the authority of tradition, and, as a consequence, they accepted the fate of social dislocation and political estrangement, occupying a place that is no place, nomadically adrift without any discernible lifeline to be reanchored in a specific community."[51]

Once we remove all images from God, as monotheism would seem to imply, what is left? "To deplete God of the anthropomorphic and anthropopathic embellishments," Wolfson warns us, "decisively curtails the imagination's ability to concoct the deity in personalist terms."[52] Religion, including monotheist religion, Wolfson argues, is ultimately dependent upon idolatry. This, needless to say, has major ramifications for the belief, liturgical, and ritualistic structures of Judaism: "All propositional utterances about God, even apophatic statements of what God is not, are not only ambiguous and hyperbolic but, literally speaking, fictitious as they attempt to describe linguistically the indescribable and to delimit conceptually the illimitable."[53] The way to overcome this problem, for many postmodern theologians, is to posit a form of negative theology, a religion without

---

[50] Wolfson, *Giving Beyond the Gift*, xvii.
[51] Ibid., xviii.
[52] Ibid.
[53] Ibid.

religion, as it were. For Wolfson, however, such an approach is not radical enough because negative theologians still retain a metaphorical vocabulary that reinscribes precisely what they have sought to avoid.

In order to try to find a way out of this dilemma, Wolfson proposes the concept of a deep-rooted and far-reaching apophasis (i.e., affirmation through denial). Rather than choosing to go down a path that resembles Thomas J. J. Altizer's Christian a-theism, or Death of God theology, Wolfson posits an "apophasis of the apophasis," a form of triple negation wherein theology and transcendence collapse, but leave a trace of something. This something, for Wolfson, is not the unknowable One, but a fullness/emptiness—what Wolfson calls a "pleromatic abyss" at the core of reality's being. It is within this context that Wolfson invokes the philosophical metaphor of "the gift," or what happens when someone (including God) gives something to someone else. However, Wolfson simultaneously critiques and offers an alternative to the Christocentrism found in the work of Jean-Luc Marion, one of the most influential figures writing today on the metaphor of the gift. Wolfson, however, argues that Marion's belief that the phenomenological nature of the gift as that which appears in the giving of the Eucharist and the Parousia is problematic and presupposes a Christian bias and, as a result, is not purely phenomenological.

In the place of Marion's obfuscation of the line between phenomenology and theology, Wolfson offers an alternative. For him, "What gives just gives, not as a gift but as the inevitable consequence of there being something rather than nothing, the fundamental datum of existence that remains inexplicable in spite of the most imaginative efforts on the parts of philosophers and physicists to explain it."[54] It is the notion of givenness, not the gift, that is important because in the concept of givenness all notions of giver and givenness, even the gift itself, disappear. The gift, as it were, has now been ungifted. According to Wolfson,

> We would say that the something that is given is the very nothing that gives, and hence that something is nothing to the extent that nothing is something... in the giving, there is giving—nothing more, nothing less. Just as the rose blooms because it blooms, so the giving gives, not as gift but as giving, without will, intention, or design. Both object and subject, the given and the giver, are subsumed in the giving, which is indistinguishable from givenness.[55]

---

54 Ibid., 257.
55 Ibid., 357.

In conclusion, Wolfson's work as the essays below will show in greater detail, spans many idioms and exists on many disciplinary registers. His contributions, accordingly, are many. He has, for one thing, opened up the study of kabbalah to issues of relevance to the academic study of religion, including, but not limited to, gender analysis and poetics. In so doing, he has contributed, in ways that few others have, Jewish material to larger analytical frameworks supplied by philosophy, religious studies, and comparative literature within the larger context of the humanities. And, in terms of philosophy, Wolfson has used kabbalistic texts to think about and contribute to larger conversations such as the phenomenology of the imagination, the dialectic relationship between immanence and transcendence, the limits of temporality, and, most recently, the notion of the gift. In all of his many contributions, Wolfson's thinking comes full circle—ending whence it began, beginning where it ends—the place where language, being, and time dance in the imagination's silhouette.

The Essays That Follow

The first essay, "Occultation of the Feminine and the Body of Secrecy in Medieval Kabbalah," finds Wolfson engaging a topic that, as we have seen above, has intrigued him throughout his career, namely, the nature of secrecy.[56] Wolfson argues that although the exoteric and esoteric dimensions of the text are distinguishable from one another, according to the medieval kabbalists, each is paradoxically expressed by and through the other. The exoteric sense of the Torah, in other words, sustains its esoteric sense by masking it in the guise of what it is not. "In the final analysis," writes Wolfson, "the hermeneutical position adopted in *Zohar* is such that there can be no unveiling of naked truth, for truth that is stark naked—divested of all appearance—is mere simulation. If the secret is the truth that is completely disrobed, then the secret is nothing to see."[57] This link between concealment and disclosure leads Wolfson to posit a connection between esotericism and eroticism, which in zoharic literature is connected to the phallic aspect of the divine. The uncovering of secrecy is thus linked, for Wolfson, to a phallocentric eroticism. Indeed, it is the subsequent

---

[56] Elliot R. Wolfson, "Occultation of the Feminine and the Body of Secrecy in Medieval Kabbalah," in *Rending the Veil: Concealment and Revelation of Secrets in the History of Religion*, ed. E. R. Wolfson (New York and London: Seven Bridges Press, 1999), 113–54 (below, pp. 35–68).

[57] Ibid., 116 (below, p. 37).

occultation of the feminine that becomes the symbol par excellence of zoharic secrecy, something that must be uncovered through the male gaze.

The second essay, "Iconicity of the Text: Reification of the Torah and the Idolatrous Impulse of Zoharic Kabbalah," shows Wolfson using kabbalistic texts to think philosophically by exploring the phenomenological texture and hermeneutical presuppositions of the kabbalah.[58] The essay pivots around another two central themes that reappear in much of his writings: the imagination and the idolatrous impulse that resides at the heart of monotheism. The thrust of this essay is the kabbalistic desire to reify the Torah in the imaginative faculty as the incarnate form of the divine. Phenomenologically, this is important because it means that the image is that of which has no image. For Wolfson, "the enduring quest to attain a vision of the image of that which has no image may be termed the impulse for idolatry. This impulse has been fed by the paradox that the God seen is the invisible God."[59]

The third essay, "Iconic Visualization and the Imaginal Body of God: The Role of Intention in the Rabbinic Conception of Prayer," challenges the assumption that Judaism has rejected incarnationism.[60] If we opt not to buy into this assumption, however, we are presented with acknowledging "the common ground and the uniqueness of this doctrine in the two religious cultures."[61] For Wolfson, as for Jacob Neusner, incarnation is related to the topic of anthropomorphism; unlike Neusner who takes incarnation to be metaphorical, however, Wolfson argues that the concept necessarily means God can be embodied. As a result he uses "the word 'incarnation' to refer to the ontic presencing of God in a theophanic image."[62]

To make his argument, he examines the notion of *kawwanah* (intention) in rabbinic theology as it relates to prayer, which becomes one of the primary ways to access the incarnated body of the divine. Through the proper intention in prayer, Wolfson claims that the devotee's heart "becomes the throne upon which God dwells at the same time that God is transformed into the throne upon which the devotee dwells."[63] Wolfson argues that

---

[58] Elliot R. Wolfson, "Iconicity of the Text: Reification of the Torah and the Idolatrous Impulse of Zoharic Kabbalah," *Jewish Studies Quarterly* 11 (2004): 215–42 (below, pp. 69–96).

[59] Ibid., 221 (below, p. 74).

[60] Elliot R. Wolfson, "Iconic Visualization and the Imaginal Body of God: The Role of Intention in the Rabbinic Conception of Prayer," *Modern Theology* 12 (1996): 137–62 (below, pp. 97–126).

[61] Ibid., 138 (below, p. 98).

[62] Ibid., 139 (below, p. 100).

[63] Ibid., 140 (below, pp. 101–102).

philologically *kawwanah* is derived from the root *kwn*, which implies a turning, as in a facing representing a form of mental concentration. This concentration entails, in some rabbinic sources, "conjuring a mental image of God."[64] The locus of such imagining is the imaginative faculty. This means that the devotee is required to represent the divine presence by imaging God in human form, something that becomes, in prayer, connected to the visualization of the holy, celestial Temple.

The fourth and final essay, "Not Yet Now: Speaking of the End and the End of Speaking," which is previously unpublished, clearly reveals many of the philosophical issues that I have raised above.[65] It is a richly textured and deeply poetic-philosophical meditation on "the end," the end of language and of temporality; the end, in other words, that is death, which must necessarily be connected to its opposite, birth and the beginning that it engenders. The finality of death, for Wolfson, is not a matter of extinction but hope—hope for, what Levinas calls, the "promise of transcendence," and what Wolfson here calls desire for "the relentless becoming of the future that signals the end that never ends in virtue of its being the consummate end."[66] Wolfson envisages death as "not the deficiency of no more but the surplus of not yet," by which he means that the moment of death functions as the "mirror-image" of the beginning, "and thus we can say of it that *its point of departure is contained in its point of arrival*, and much like the beginning, the end is a withdrawal in the very heart of the present."[67] But if the moment of birth is the creation of self, the moment of death is the creation of another, which alludes to the ethical implications of his thought.

This means that, for Wolfson, in conversation with the likes of Heidegger and Merleau-Ponty, we know that we die, but we never experience our death. Death becomes "quintessentially the nonevent of the terminus delimited as the limit always to be delimited," writes Wolfson, " the limit beyond which there is no limit, and hence the limit of what cannot be delimited, the threshold that may be crossed only by not-crossing."[68] Wolfson then brings this discussion into conversation with some of the key terms of Judaism, interpreted through the lens of Rosenzweig, for whom redemption is in

---

[64] Ibid., 141 (below, p. 105).
[65] Elliot R. Wolfson, "Not Yet Now: Speaking of the End and the End of Speaking," pp. 127–93 in this volume. A version of the paper was originally presented at a symposium entitled "Jews and the Ends of Theory" that took place at Duke University (Durham, North Carolina) on April 30–May 1, 2013.
[66] Wolfson, "Not Yet Now," below, p. 129.
[67] Ibid., below, p. 139.
[68] Ibid., below, p. 141.

the future but in such a manner that it retrieves the past and ruptures the present, "thereby bending the timeline such that not-yet is already-there insofar as already-there is not-yet."[69] It is also important to note that Wolfson does not slavishly follow Rosenzweig here, but uses the thought of Walter Benjamin, Theodor Adorno, and Ernst Bloch to read against him. Redemption, framed somewhat differently, is not the end, but that which is always possible, always in the process of coming-to-be. Wolfson then threads in traditional Jewish sources to reinforce his philosophical point: "The Messiah is the one that comes by not-coming, the one that is present by being absent. Waiting for the end is the adjournment of time that occasions the fostering of time."[70]

Taken together, these four essays clearly show the breadth and scope of Wolfson's poetic thinking.

---

[69] Ibid., below, p. 153.
[70] Ibid., below, p. 156.

OCCULTATION OF THE FEMININE AND THE BODY OF SECRECY IN MEDIEVAL KABBALAH*

Elliot R. Wolfson

> Perhaps truth is a woman
> who has reasons
> for not letting us see her reasons?
> Friedrich Nietzsche, *The Gay Science*

Dis/Closing the Secret Secretly

The occult tradition of Judaism, which by the High Middle Ages is referred to most frequently by the generic term *kabbalah*, literally, "that which has been received," is usually studied under the rubric of mysticism. A far better term, however, to capture the nature of this phenomenon is *esotericism*. Indeed, as I have argued elsewhere, the mystical dimensions expressed in Jewish sources—and here I extend the scope to include more than just kabbalistic texts—are contextualized within the hermeneutical framework of esotericism.[1] Here it is relevant to recall as well that in the first of his ten unhistorical aphorisms on the history of kabbalah, Gershom Scholem duly noted the central concern with the issue of secrecy in the kabbalistic sources. He remarked that the fundamental problem that presents itself is that, on the one hand, the kabbalists presume that truth is transmitted from generation to generation, but on the other hand, the truth of which they speak is secretive and thus cannot by nature be fully transmitted. In his inimitable style of ironic paradox, Scholem wrote, "Authentic tradition (*echte Tradition*) remains hidden; only the fallen tradition (*verfallende Tradition*) falls (*verfällt*) upon an object and only when it is fallen does its greatness become visible."[2] The truly esoteric knowledge cannot be divulged if it is to remain

---

* This article was first published as Elliot R. Wolfson, "Occultation of the Feminine and the Body of Secrecy in Medieval Kabbalah," in *Rending the Veil: Concealment of Revelation of Secrets in the History of Religion* (New York and London: Seven Bridges Press, 1999), 113–154.
  [1] E. R. Wolfson, "Beyond the Spoken Word: Oral Tradition and Written Transmission in Medieval Jewish Mysticism," to be published in the proceedings of a conference on orality held at the University of Pennsylvania, May 1996.
  [2] The original German text and translation are cited from D. Biale, "Gershom Scholem's Ten Unhistorical Aphorisms on Kabbalah," in *Gershom Scholem*, ed. H. Bloom (New York, 1987), pp. 103–104.

esoteric, and thus a secret tradition that is transmitted is by definition a fallen (as opposed to an authentic) tradition.

The fascination with secrecy, which has held great power over the Jewish imagination through the generations,[3] is often linked exegetically to the verse, "To investigate the matter is the glory of kings, but to conceal the matter is the glory of God" (Ps. 25:2). It is not an exaggeration to say that the words of the psalmist served as an oracle posted on the walls of the small elitist circles wherein specific secrets pertaining to both symbols and rites have been transmitted orally and in writing. This is true even though the eventual proliferation of the latter usually posed a challenge to the explicit injunction against disclosing secrets publicly. To be sure, not every written exposition of occult knowledge is in defiance of this injunction, for there were kabbalists who mastered the art of concealing secrets by revealing them. This, in my mind, is exemplified in the zoharic literature, wherein mysteries of Torah are disclosed through being hidden, an exegetical pattern that the zoharic authorship discerns in the Torah itself.[4] The exoteric and esoteric layers are distinguishable, but one can only be expressed through the other. The way to the secret is through the letter of the text, not by discarding it. One passage worth particular mention is a text wherein

---

[3] On the centrality of esotericism in the history of Jewish mysticism, consider the perceptive remarks of W. T. Stace, *Mysticism and Philosophy* (London, 1960), p. 57: "The degrees in which mystics tend thus to cloak their experiences from the public view vary with individual temperaments and also with the traditions of the particular culture, religion, or society. The most extreme secrecy was observed ... among Jewish mystics."

[4] On the hermeneutical play of concealment and disclosure evident in the zoharic orientation toward secrets, see Y. Liebes, *Studies in the Zohar*, trans. A. Schwartz, S. Nakache, and P. Peli (Albany, 1993), pp. 26–30. The point is expressed in any number of zoharic contexts, but perhaps nowhere as poignantly as in *Zohar* 2:98b–99b, which includes the exposition of the parable of the maiden without eyes. For an extended discussion of the hermeneutical implications of this parable, see E. R. Wolfson, "Beautiful Maiden without Eyes: *Peshaṭ* and *Sod* in Zoharic Hermeneutics," in *The Midrashic Imagination: Jewish Exegesis, Thought, and History*, ed. M. Fishbane (Albany, 1993), pp. 155–203; idem, *Through a Speculum That Shines: Vision and Imagination in Medieval Jewish Mysticism* (Princeton, 1994), pp. 384–387. Needless to say, this parable has been discussed by a number of scholars. To mention here some of the relevant references: G. Scholem, *On the Kabbalah and Its Symbolism*, trans. R. Manheim (New York, 1965), pp. 55–56; I. Tishby, *The Wisdom of the Zohar*, trans. D. Goldstein (Oxford, 1989), pp. 1084–1085; F. Talmage, "Apples of Gold: The Inner Meaning of Sacred Texts in Medieval Judaism," in *Jewish Spirituality: From the Bible Through the Middle Ages*, ed. A. Green (New York, 1986), pp. 316–318; M. Idel, *Kabbalah: New Perspectives* (New Haven, 1988), pp. 227–229; Y. Liebes, "Zohar and Eros," *Alpayyim* 9 (1994): 87–98 (Hebrew); M. Oron, "'Place Me As a Seal Upon Your Heart': Reflections on the Poetics of the Author of the *Zohar* in the *Section of Sabba de-Mishpaṭim*," in *Massu'ot: Studies in Kabbalistic Literature and Jewish Philosophy in Memory of Prof. Ephraim Gottlieb*, ed. M. Oron and A. Goldreich (Jerusalem, 1994), pp. 1–24 (Hebrew); and P. Giller, "Love and Upheaval in the Zohar's Sabba de-Mishpaṭim," *Journal of Jewish Thought and Philosophy* 7 (1997): 31–60.

the hermeneutical dissimulation is framed in ontological terms: just as the name of God is both hidden and revealed, the former corresponding to YHWH and the latter to Adonai, so the Torah, which is identical with the name,[5] is concurrently concealed and disclosed. Indeed, all the matters of this world and the supernal world are hidden and revealed.[6] The example of the name illumines the impenetrable depth of the paradox: ultimately there are not two names, but one name, for the very name that is written YHWH is pronounced Adonai. The articulation of the name YHWH as Adonai, therefore, is precisely that which preserves the ineffability of the name. The inexpressibility of the inexpressible is preserved only through that which is expressed. Analogously, the exoteric sense of Torah sustains the esoteric meaning by masking it in the guise of that which it is not. In the final analysis, the hermeneutical position adopted in *Zohar* is such that there can be no unveiling of naked truth, for truth that is stark naked—divested of all appearance—is mere simulation. If the secret is the truth that is completely disrobed, then the secret is nothing to see.[7] By contrast, the truth that is apparent is disclosed in and through the garment of its enclosure.[8] The tension between the formless glory and the image

---

[5] Regarding this hermeneutical principle in medieval kabbalah, see Scholem, *On the Kabbalah and Its Symbolism*, pp. 37–44; Tishby, *Wisdom of the Zohar*, pp. 283–284, 292–295, 1079–1082; and M. Idel, "The Concept of Torah in Hekhalot Literature and Its Metamorphosis in Kabbalah," *Jerusalem Studies in Jewish Thought* 1 (1981): 23–84, esp. 49–58 (Hebrew).

[6] *Zohar* 2:230b.

[7] See J. Derrida, *Glas*, trans. J. P. Leavey, Jr., and R. Rand (Lincoln and London, 1986), p. 50: "The Jewish *Geheimnis*, the hearth in which one looks for the center under a sensible cover [*enveloppe*]—the tent of the tabernacle, the stone of the temple, the robe that clothes the text of the covenant—is finally discovered as an empty room, is not uncovered, never ends being uncovered, as it has nothing to show." For an illuminating discussion of the notion of the secret in Derrida's philosophical reflections, see J. D. Caputo, *The Prayers and Tears of Jacques Derrida: Religion without Religion* (Bloomington and Indianapolis, 1997), pp. 101–112.

[8] A possible alternative to the view that I have attributed to the zoharic text may be found in a vivid parable employed by Joseph Gikatilla, *Sha'arei Orah*, ed. J. Ben-Shlomo (Jerusalem, 1981), 1:195–199 in an effort to explicate the relationship of the Tetragrammaton, which is equated with the Torah (see op. cit., p. 48; and references to the scholarly treatment of this topic given above in n. 5), to the rest of the names and appellations: There is a progressive disrobing on the part of the king, which is proportionate to those who are in his company, until the point that he takes off all of his clothing when he is alone with the queen. The garments here represent the other names and appellations by means of which the Tetragrammaton, which is the ontological name, governs the world. In a second passage from this work (op. cit., pp. 205–206), Gikatilla returns to this parabolic image, but in that context the disrobing on the part of the king and the subsequent union between the king and his wife is related symbolically to God's relationship to the spiritual elite of the Jewish males, that is, the pious, ascetics, and pure ones. See E. R. Wolfson, "Eunuchs Who Keep the Sabbath: Becoming Male and the Ascetic Ideal in Thirteenth-Century Jewish Mysticism," in *Becoming Male in the Middle Ages*, ed. J. J. Cohen and B. Wheeler (New

endowed with form accounts for what may be called the erotics of dressing in zoharic literature, which is predicated on the paradox that nudity is the ultimate veil and the veil, the ultimate nudity: the naked body is the garment that obstructs the gaze, whereas the garment renders the body naked in its transparency.[9]

The full force of this dialectic can be ascertained only if one bears in mind the implicit gender signification of this symbolism:[10] For the medieval kabbalist, the concealed name is correlated with the masculine, and the revealed name, with the feminine. Consequently, the feminine is assigned the paradoxical role of representing that which cannot be represented. Representation in this case does not denote a representing of that which is eclipsed from the field of vision, but the making present of that which forever alludes presence,[11] the representation of the masculine absence that is known as absent only in its specula(riza)tion through the mirror of the feminine.[12] The value of the feminine from the androcentric standpoint adopted by the male kabbalists lies exclusively in the fact that she is the speculum that refracts the nonrepresentable image of the masculine glory, an ocularcentric conception that can be expressed in auditory terms as the revealed name through which the concealed name is articulated.[13] In a similar manner, the *peshat*, the outer sense of the text,

---

York, 1997), pp. 172–174. Although it might seem that Gikatilla, in contrast to the zoharic authorship, embraces the notion of a naked truth, which would be expressed symbolically by the image of the king removing all of his clothes, the fact is that for Gikatilla as well there is always a garment, for the king who stands naked is the name itself, the Tetragrammaton, which is the ultimate garment. One might say that there is no nakedness beyond the attire of the four-letter name.

[9] See M. Perniola, "Between Clothing and Nudity," in *Fragments for a History of the Human Body, Part Two*, ed. M. Feher with R. Naddaff and N. Tazi (New York, 1989), pp. 237–265.

[10] Beyond the specific instance of the kabbalistic literature it is evident that the issue of revealing and concealing is often linked to the eroticized body, a point that has been made by many writers from different theoretical perspectives. For recent discussion along these lines, see A. L. Brown, *Subjects of Deceit: A Phenomenology of Lying* (Albany, 1998), pp. 90–127.

[11] See endnote 1.

[12] My analysis here is greatly indebted to L. Irigaray, *Marine Lover of Friedrich Nietzsche*, trans. G. C. Gill (New York, 1991), pp. 83–85. Although Irigaray does not deal at all with the symbolic orientation of the medieval kabbalists, her incisive remarks can be fruitfully applied to this world. Lest one protest that this is not a justifiable application on my part, it should be remembered that Irigary's insights relate to the Western philosophical tradition of which the kabbalists are an integral part.

[13] See Wolfson, *Through a Speculum That Shines*, pp. 306–317. The convergence of the visual and auditory modes of symbolization related particularly to the role of the *Shekhinah* as the garment that makes the masculine glory both visible and audible is well captured in the summary account in Moses Cordovero, *Pardes Rimmonim* (Jerusalem, 1962),

serves as the sheath through which the *sod*, the secret, is disclosed. One obtains the covering of *peshaṭ* through the exegetical act of uncovering.[14] Later in this essay I shall return to this paradox of the mirror/garment, the cognizance of which is fundamental to the ecstatic experience underlying the hermeneutical orientation of zoharic kabbalah.

The matter of putting down secrets implicates the kabbalist in a process of esoteric writing, which is predicated on the notion that written allusions to secrets become themselves secrets that require decipherment at the hands of an interpreter. In this manner, the subtle interplay of revelation and concealment fosters a rhetoric of secrecy based on the interface of orality and writing as it pertains to the dissemination of esoteric knowledge. The hermeneutical circle thus created by the paradox of the secret as that which is disclosed in its concealment and concealed in its disclosure has preserved the essentially esoteric nature of this enterprise even in textual communities (such as the fraternity surrounding the *Zohar* in late-thirteenth-century Castile or the mystical fellowship clustered around Isaac Luria in sixteenth-century Safed) that have advocated a fuller written expression of secrets. These secrets, whose authenticity presumably is linked to their having been transmitted in a continuous chain, retain something of their secret nature even when committed to writing. Indeed, the zoharic image of the book of concealment (*sifra di-ṣeni'uta*),[15] that is, the book that conceals the secrets it reveals,[16] captures the paradoxical nature

---

Chap. 23, s.v. *imrat*: "Thus the *Shekhinah* is a garment (*levush*) and a palace (*heikhal*) in relation to *Tif'eret*, for the Tetragrammaton is not mentioned except in his palace, which is 'Adonai. And she is called by the term *imra* insofar as she is the diadem (*aṭarah*) on the head of her husband." Regarding the implications of this symbolism in the writings of Cordovero as it relates to the phallic transformation of the *Shekhinah* in her elevation, see E. R. Wolfson, "Coronation of the Sabbath Bride: Kabbalistic Myth and the Ritual of Androgynisation," *Journal of Jewish Thought and Philosophy* 6 (1997): 335–339.

[14] There is obviously a play on the words *peshaṭ*, the external sense, and *lehafshiṭ*, to strip away. The *peshaṭ*, which is the garment, is uncovered by an act of covering. Alternatively expressed, the unveiling of meaning appears through the veil of the text.

[15] This literary unit, which is likely itself a composite of discrete textual strands, appears in *Zohar* 2:176b–179a.

[16] The ontological implication of the zoharic expression is underscored in the postscript to the textual unit wherein the "book of concealment," *sifra di-ṣeni'uta*, is identified with the "concealment of the King," *ṣeni'uta de-malka*. The process of divine autogenesis, the unveiling of that which is veiled, is concomitantly the composition of the esoteric book, the text that reveals the secret by concealment. This idea is captured in the formulation used in a number of the relevant zoharic passages, *ṣeni'uta de-sifra*, the "concealment of the book," which conveys the idea that the book hides in its very disclosure. See *Zohar* 2:176a; 3:128a, 130a, 130b, 131a, 133a–b, 135a, 138b, 139a–b, 141a, 142a–b, 143a–b, 146b, 289a. On the poetic underpinning of this textual unit, which is related to the creativity of the divine, see Liebes, "Zohar and Eros," pp. 78–79. For a more general characterization of poetry as the utilization of the language of mystery to reveal the secret that must be concealed, see

of secrecy more overtly than a purely oral form of discourse: the secret as such must be exposed if it is to be a secret, but being a secret precludes its being exposed.

Still, we are intrigued by the phenomenon of secrecy in the history of kabbalah, and we ask, what is it about secrets that is so compelling and seductive? Why is it that kabbalists have continuously fostered the notion of mysteries that cannot be openly disclosed even, and perhaps especially, in the context of written disclosure? The esotericism cultivated in kabbalistic fraternities does not simply involve the hiding of information from others. Quite the contrary, an important aspect of secrecy is clearly the investiture of power to those who seek to disseminate the secrets they possess, but in such a way that the hidden nature of the secret is preserved. To state the obvious, a secret presupposes the concomitant transmission and withholding on the part of the one in possession of the secret.[17] If I possess a secret and transmit it to no one, the secret has no relevance. By the same token, if I readily divulge that secret without discretion, the secrecy of that secret is rendered ineffectual. What empowers me as the keeper of a secret is not only that I transmit it to some and not to others but that in the very transmission, I maintain the secret by holding back in my advancing forward. From that vantage point, therefore, the secret is a secret only to the extent that it is concealed in its disclosure, but it may be concealed in its disclosure only if it is disclosed in its concealment.[18]

The confluence of concealment and disclosure underscores another essential element in the nature of secrecy expressed in the history of kabbalah. I refer to the link between esotericism and eroticism, which is related more specifically to the insight that transmission of secrets requires the play of openness and closure basic to the push and pull of eros. The erotics of esoteric disclosure is a particular application of the more general perception that reading, which is marked by the dialectic of knowing and not knowing, is an act of desire.[19] Alternatively expressed, the motif of

---

the poignant discussion in N. O. Brown, *Apocalypse and/or Metamorphosis* (Berkeley, 1991), pp. 3–4.

[17] This insight lies at the basis of the analysis of F. Kermode, *The Genesis of Secrecy: On the Interpretation of Narrative* (Cambridge, MA, and London, 1979).

[18] Consider George Simmel's notion of the triadic structure of secrecy discussed by H. G. Kippenberg and G. G. Stroumsa, "Introduction: Secrecy and Its Benefits," in *Secrecy and Concealment: Studies in the History of Mediterranean and Near Eastern Religions*, ed. H. G. Kippenberg and G. G. Stroumsa (Leiden, 1995), pp. xiii–xiv.

[19] The erotic nature of reading is especially salient in the notion of textuality offered by Roland Barthes in *The Pleasure of the Text* and *A Lover's Discourse. Fragments*. See the pertinent reflections in the introduction to *Sexuality and Masquerade: The Dedalus Book of Sexual Ambiguity*, ed. E. Wilson (Cambridge, 1996), pp. 4–5.

passing on secrets, which we may refer to as the generative nature of esoteric knowledge, is associated in the kabbalistic tradition with the dynamic
of flow and containment, the (male) master who bestows and the (male)
disciple who receives. In the receiving, however, there is as much, if not
more, power than in the bestowal, another facet that renders the use of the
image of the (homo)erotic perfectly apt to characterize the process of communication of esoteric traditions.[20]

On this score, it is of interest to remark that in one of his works, Jacques
Derrida notes in passing that the genealogy of secrecy is also a history of
sexuality.[21] Derrida's formulation seems to me to apply especially well to
Jewish esotericism. In my own work, I have argued that the history of Jewish
mysticism can be viewed as a progressive disclosure of the secret that is
contextualized in the phallic aspect of the divine.[22] This is not to deny
that secrets operate on many different levels in Jewish mystical literature.
However, my thesis is that (1) the structure of secrecy as such involves the
uncovering of the sign that by nature must be concealed, and that (2) in the
relevant sources (penned through the ages by male Jews), but especially
conspicuous in the medieval kabbalah, this is related to a phallocentric
eroticism.

My claim is based on two assumptions, which in my judgment are well
attested in the primary texts of kabbalistic literature: the phallus is the
mark of signification that by nature must be concealed.[23] The signifier,
however, has the task of disclosing that which is signified. The convergence
of these two factors yields the contradictory nature of secrecy: to reveal
itself, the phallus must be veiled. From that vantage point, each explication of a secret is compared phenomenologically in kabbalistic literature
to the primordial exposure of the phallus, or more specifically, the aspect
of the phallus that is exposed through the rite of circumcision, the sign of
the covenant, which is linked anatomically to the corona (*aṭarah*). Given
the centrality of the covenant of circumcision in rabbinic Judaism (based
on biblical precedent) as the marker of Jewish identity,[24] it should come as
no surprise that kabbalists would interpret the foundational ceremony as

----

20 See Wolfson, *Through a Speculum That Shines*, pp. 368–372. See also endnote 2.
21 J. Derrida, *The Gift of Death*, trans. D. Wills (Chicago and London, 1995), p. 3.
22 Wolfson, *Through a Speculum That Shines*.
23 In this matter, I have been especially influenced by the Lacanian notion that the
phallus as signifier can play its role only when masked. See A. Lemaire, *Jacques Lacan*,
trans. D. Macey (London, 1977), pp. 87–88.
24 Many have written on circumcision, but particularly pertinent for our discussion of
the kabbalistic androcentrism is the work of L. A. Hoffman, *Covenant of Blood: Circumcision and Gender in Rabbinic Judaism* (Chicago and London, 1996).

the paradigm for an esoteric hermeneutic based on the unmasking of the mystery that is concealed.[25] Circumcision is the sacrament through which the Jew enacts the role of dissimulation by cutting away the foreskin to create the sign, the presence that is represented through its own absence.[26] The paradox is fully expressed in the insistence on the part of kabbalists that it is forbidden to gaze on the corona that is laid bare.[27] In the disclosure is the concealment, for the marking of the sign occasions the erasure of the name.[28]

The primacy accorded the phallocentric orientation in kabbalistic symbology is based on the larger assumption that sexual imagery is the principal linguistic field to which all others are related by way of euphemism or displacement. Indeed, the primary works of theosophic kabbalah proffer the view that language itself, in both its verbal and graphic forms, is an expression of God's erotic impulse, which seeks closure in the narcissistic coincidence between the will of desire and its object.[29] In an ontological system that recognizes one ultimate reality, there is no genuine other;[30] hence, the underlying logic of the mythical structure is such that heterosexual eros is transmuted into the homoerotic, which in the final analysis is an expression of the autoerotic.[31] From a psychoanalytic perspective, this

---

[25] See E. R. Wolfson, "Circumcision, Vision of God, and Textual Interpretation: From Midrashic Trope to Mystical Symbol," *History of Religions* 27 (1987): 189–215, reprinted with some slight modifications in idem, *Circle in the Square: Studies in the Use of Gender in Kabbalistic Symbolism* (Albany, 1995), pp. 29–48, and notes on pp. 140–155.

[26] The point is well understood by Irigaray, *Marine Lover*, pp. 81–82, who thus contrasted castration (the obliteration of the masculine to constitute the feminine as essential lack) and circumcision: "Now the Jewish operation, despite what is cut away, lies in the realm of the sign. What is cut away is only cut away in order to make a sign. It is 'true' that it is also in the realm of the body. But almost the reverse of castrating, this excision is what marks the body's entry into the world of signs.... And rightly so, moreover: circumcision attests to a specialist's expertise in the field of signs. Should the rest of the stage be transformed into a protesting chorus, in the name of castration no less, that changes, in fact, nothing. The spot left by the Jew is still there. To make him play it over again as a simulacrum is worth more. Provided he is made to pass as other. And without a veil? The thing taken from him was (only) a blind. Though a necessary one. His role will therefore be to enact dissimulation."

[27] See Wolfson, *Through a Speculum That Shines*, pp. 339–345.

[28] I refer here to a process that elsewhere I have called the erasing of the erasure. See *Circle in the Square*, pp. 49–78.

[29] See my study referred to in the previous note.

[30] See E. R. Wolfson, "Woman—The Feminine as Other In Theosophic Kabbalah: Some Philosophical Observations on the Divine Androgyne," in *The Other in Jewish Thought and History: Constructions of Jewish Culture and Identity*, ed. by L. Silberstein and R. Cohn (New York, 1994), pp. 166–204.

[31] See Wolfson, "Eunuchs Who Keep the Sabbath," pp. 169–171.

may strike the ear as a form of reductionism, but from the standpoint of symbolic discourse, the claim is expansionist in the extreme, for all forms of experience relate to the erotic, which is the most appropriate way to express the creative potency of the divine. The nexus of eroticism and esotericism in the kabbalistic worldview is predicated on the presumption that the deepest ontology of religious experience embraces the erotic.

I am in full agreement, therefore, with a position articulated by a number of scholars regarding the use of erotic imagery to characterize the experience of the sacred. Matters pertaining to the spiritual realm can be depicted in erotic terms because there is a presumption with respect to the nature of divine sexuality, which is reflected in human sexuality.[32] My contention that kabbalists perceived the erotic, and more specifically phallic, element in the very texture of being is not equivalent to reducing everything in a simplistic fashion to the crude phallocentrism of the pornographic imagination, as some of my critics have mistakenly claimed.[33] On the contrary, as I have argued explicitly in several studies, the phallocentric eroticism of the kabbalistic tradition is predicated ideally on an ascetic renunciation of heterosexual carnality and the concomitant affirmation of the homosocial rapture of mystical ecstasy,[34] which are expressed in the zoharic text itself in terms of erotic passion that binds the members of the fraternity.[35]

---

[32] I will list only a few representative studies that affirm the confluence of the spiritual and the erotic: J. Evola, *Eros and the Mysteries of Love: The Metaphysics of Sex* (Rochester, Vermont, 1983); B. Z. Goldberg, *The Sacred Fire: The Story of Sex in Religion* (New York, 1958); G. Bataille, *Death and Sensuality: A Study of Eroticism and the Taboo* (New York, 1962); W. Doninger O'Flaherty, *Asceticism and Eroticism in the Mythology of Siva* (London and New York, 1973); J. Kripal, *Kali's Child: The Mystical and the Erotic in the Life and Teachings of Ramakrishna* (Chicago, 1995). See also the collection of essays in *Sexual Archetypes, East and West*, ed. B. Gupta (New York, 1987), and on the relationship of mystical experience and the language of passion in medieval Christendom, see D. de Rougemont, *Love in the Western World*, trans. M. Belgian (Princeton, 1983), pp. 141–170.

[33] M. Verman, "Kabbalah Refracted: Review Essay," *Shofar* 14 (1996): 129; A. Green, "Kabbalistic Re-Vision: A Review Article of Elliot Wolfson's 'Through a Speculum That Shines,'" *History of Religions* 36 (1997): 272 n. 16.

[34] See Wolfson, "Eunuchs Who Keep the Sabbath"; idem, "Asceticism and Eroticism in Medieval Jewish Philosophical and Mystical Exegesis of the Song of Songs," to be published in the proceedings of the conference "With Reverence for the Word: Medieval Scriptural Exegesis in Judaism, Christianity, and Islam," May 11–14, 1997, University of Toronto. For a parallel insight that the celebration of the homosocial bonding between God and Christian men rests upon an unequivocal rejection of homosexual deviance, see E. B. Keiser, *Courtly Desire and Medieval Homophobia: The Legitimation of Sexual Pleasure in Cleanness and Its Contexts* (New Haven and London, 1997), pp. 165–200.

[35] Although in his discussion of the messianic theosophy of the *Idrot* sections of zoharic literature (*Studies in the Zohar*, pp. 37–43) Liebes recognizes the importance of the motif of love that binds together the members of the mystical fraternity, in his discussion

In this essay I will explore one particular theme related to the larger nexus of eroticism and esotericism in medieval kabbalah. Previously, as I have already intimated, I have investigated the phallocentric dimension of kabbalistic esotericism, epitomized by the identification of the phallic potency of the divine anthropos as the ontological root of secrecy; this theme is underscored by the verbal assonance between the words *sod*, "secret," and *yesod*, "foundation," the term used most frequently to name the ninth of the ten attributes of the Godhead, which corresponds to the phallus. The complex of motifs to be discussed here has forced me to refocus my gaze, for I will reexamine the theme of secrecy in the kabbalistic tradition from the specific vantage point of the body of the feminine. As I shall demonstrate, however, the link between the feminine and the notion of secrecy affirmed by the kabbalists involved in the production of the zoharic literature is contingent on the occultation of the former. Simply put, my thesis is that the trope of the hidden woman, the female that must be veiled, functions as a symbolic depiction of the body of secrecy in the poetic discourse espoused by the zoharic authorship. In the complex gender orientation evident in the literary strands of the *Zohar*, the image of the woman as mystery entails the dissimulation that hides itself, for the secret that is unveiled in the pretense of not-showing is the masculine transvaluation of the feminine, the female specularized through the gaze of the male.

Secrecy Unveiled in the Veil of Femininity

The most poignant illustration of the motif of truth as the concealed woman in the zoharic corpus is the parabolic image spoken by the mysterious

---

of the *tiqqun* (rectification) through erotic union (op. cit., pp. 71–74) he privileges heterosexual activity as the only form of eros that has redemptive value. The homoerotic relation that pertains between Simeon ben Yoḥai and the other members of the fraternity is explored by Liebes in "Zohar and Eros," pp. 104–112, but in that context as well he assigns priority to heterosexuality as the means to bring about the messianic repair of the primal sin of celibacy. In my judgment, however, celibacy is not rectified simply by affirming and engaging in heterosexual intercourse. The matter is more complex inasmuch as the erotic bond of the members of the fraternity is predicated on the (temporary) abrogation of carnal sexuality. The *tiqqun* for celibacy, therefore, is attained dialectically through abstinence from physical sex between the kabbalist and his spouse, which facilitates the erotic bonding of the male mystics in their textual community. As I put the matter in "Eunuchs Who Keep the Sabbath," p. 165, the symbolic worldview of the *Zohar* entails the insight that "homoeroticism is the carnality of celibate renunciation." See also my brief criticism of Liebes in *Through a Speculum That Shines*, p. 371 n. 155, and my more extensive remarks in "Constructions of the *Shekhinah* in the Messianic Theosophy of Abraham Cardoso, With an Annotated Edition of *Derush ha-Shekhinah*," *Kabbalah: Journal for the Study of Jewish Mystical Texts* 3 (1998): 46–51.

elder (*sabba*)[36] concerning the beautiful maiden without eyes, which is applied to the Torah.[37] This parabolic utterance is elucidated by means of another parable regarding the beautiful beloved who is hidden within her palace, whence she discreetly reveals herself to her lover in a sequence of disclosures that culminates with the face-to-face encounter between the lover and the beloved, the enlightened sage and the Torah. The parable itself is introduced by the hermeneutical claim that God hides all the secrets within the "garments" of the Torah, which refers to the literal words of the text.[38] The sage, who is described in contrast to the maiden/Torah as the one full of eyes, sees the mystery through the garment in which it is hidden. The secret, then, is garbed in the covering of the plain sense, but by means of that very covering it is revealed, but only to the one who has the eyes to see through the veil.[39]

---

[36] In the concluding postscript of the relevant section, *Zohar* 2:114a, the elder is identified by name as R. Yeiva Sabba, who appears elsewhere in the zoharic narrative. See *Zohar* 1:55a, 59a, 225a; 2:135a. In a number of contexts, we read of the "book of R. Yeiva Sabba" (1:47a, 117b; 2:6a, 60b, 206b; 3:7b, 155b), or of the "book of legends (*aggadah*) of R. Yeiva Sabba" (3:289a, 293a, 295a), or simply the "legend (*aggadah*) of R. Yeiva Sabba" (3:290a, 290b). It is possible that the identification of the elder in the section on Mishpaṭim as R. Yeiva reflects a later redactional accretion to the base text.

[37] *Zohar* 2:95a, 99a–b. For scholarly treatments of the parable, see references supplied above, n. 4.

[38] *Zohar* 2:98b. Regarding the use of the image of the garment to describe the status of the literal sense of Torah, see D. Cohen-Aloro, *The Secret of the Garment in the Zohar* (Jerusalem, 1987), pp. 45–49 (Hebrew).

[39] For elaboration of this point, see Wolfson, "Beautiful Maiden," pp. 186–187. (The original version of this paper was written for a one-day assembly of scholars who addressed various aspects of the "midrashic condition," a meeting that was held at Brandeis University in January 1991. The revised version was submitted to the editor for publication in the fall of that year.) Liebes, "Zohar and Eros," p. 97 n. 182, criticizes my understanding of the image of the beautiful maiden without eyes as a reference to the fact that the text in and of itself is blind, that is, without sense. Liebes did not comprehend the dialectical force of my argument. Thus he refers only to the part of my study that would seem to support his criticism and he neglects to cite the continuation of my argument that not only undermines his criticism but clearly indicates that my position is closer to what he presents as his own view. I argued that the hermeneutical theory implied in the zoharic parable is that in bestowing meaning on the text the interpreter draws meaning out from the text. From that perspective it is difficult to distinguish in a clear way between eisegesis and exegesis. It is curious that Liebes does not at all refer to a second passage in "Beautiful Maiden" (pp. 171–172) wherein I state explicitly that interpretation in the *Zohar* is an unfolding of the infinite meaning within the text. For the sake of setting the record straight, I will cite the relevant portion of my argument: "The movement of zoharic hermeneutics may be thus compared to a circle, beginning and ending with the text in its literal sense. For the *Zohar* the search for the deepest truths of Scripture is a gradual stripping away of the external forms or garments until one gets to the inner core, but when one gets to that inner core what one finds is nothing other than the *peshaṭ*, i.e., the text as it is. To interpret, therefore, from the perspective of the *Zohar*, is not to impose finite meaning on the text, but to unfold the infinite meaning within the text." In that context, moreover, I make use of

Interestingly enough, the zoharic author inserts this hermeneutical discussion regarding the meaning of the text in the context of a complicated deliberation on the nature of the soul of the convert.[40] I cannot enter here into a full discussion of what is arguably one of the most intricate and convoluted sections of the zoharic text. For the purposes of this analysis, I will streamline the argument. The analogy is drawn in the following manner: just as God conceals the secrets of Torah in the cloak of the letters of the text, the soul of the Jew (or, more specifically, the *neshamah*, which originates in the gradation of *Binah*) in its descent from the supernal Garden of Eden (that is, *Malkhut*) to this world is cloaked in the soul of the convert. For the sage, the task is to set his interpretative glance on the Torah, which is the beautiful maiden without eyes, so that he may discern the secret hidden beneath the letter of the text, but there is no way for him to apprehend that esoteric meaning except through the garment of the literal sense. In the same manner, the mystery of the convert is such that the Jewish soul is temporarily garbed in the body of a Gentile.

The mystery of the convert is thus related exegetically to the verse "If a priest's daughter marries a layman" (Lev. 22:12): the "priest's daughter" (*bat kohen*) refers symbolically to the holy soul of the Jew, for the latter emanates from its ontological source in *Binah*, the great mother of the sefirotic gradations. When the spirit (or breath) of *Ḥesed*, "lovingkindness," which is allied symbolically with the priest, blows, the soul settles in the "concealment of the Tree of Life," that is, within the phallic gradation of *Yesod*, whence it enters the repository of the Garden of Eden, which is the feminine *Malkhut*. When the male Jew below transgresses sexually by engaging in intercourse with the Gentile woman, he draws down the force of the evil inclination, and the Jewish soul inhabits the "layman" (*ish zar*), the body of the non-Jew, in which it is trapped until the moment of conversion.[41] The interpretation of this verse as a reference to the phenomenon of conversion is buttressed by the symbolic association of the priest and *Ḥesed*, and the further association of the latter with the patriarch Abraham, who is

---

Ricoeur's term "appropriation" to convey the idea that interpretation is a recovery of what is latent in the text. It is lamentable that the judgmental ire of the scholarly critique was not tempered by a more careful assessment of my argument.

[40] See J. H. A. Wijnhoven, "The Zohar and the Proselyte," in *Texts and Responses: Studies Presented to Nahum N. Glatzer on the Occasion of His Seventieth Birthday by His Students*, ed. M. A. Fishbane and P. R. Flohr (Leiden, 1975), pp. 120–140, especially 130–131.

[41] *Zohar* 2:95a–b. See also endnote 3.

described in the *Zohar* (on the basis of an older rabbinic source)[42] as the "first of the converts" (*qadma'ah la-giyyorin*).[43]

The full implication of the zoharic text may be gained if we heed more attentively the import of the biblical idiom *ish zar*, which should be translated as the "foreign man," for the term *zar* in zoharic literature denotes the ontological sense of otherness linked to the demonic potency.[44] Thus, elsewhere in the *Zohar*, the offspring that results from the intercourse of the male Jew and the female Christian are considered "alien children," *banim zarim*, born from the one who has broken faith with God (Hos. 5:6).[45] The conjugal relationship between the Jewish man and the Christian woman sets the stage for the zoharic version of the ancient Gnostic myth. This myth is reworked in the medieval kabbalistic source in distinctively ethnocentric terms, for the alienation of spirit is not related to the general condition of human embodiment but rather to the particular embodiment of the Jewish soul in the Christian body, which results from the transgressive act. There is, however, another possibility embraced by the zoharic authorship and related, as well, to the verse concerning the marriage of the priest's daughter and the strange man. In this case, the conversion comes about when the Christian soul desires to become Jewish, a desire that brings about the ontological transformation of the demonic soul into a spark of divinity. Moses de León succinctly expressed the matter in one of his Hebrew compositions:

> You must know that the uncircumcised nations have no soul except from the side of impurity, for they are immersed in the foreskin, and on account

---

[42] According to a statement attributed to Rava in Babylonian Talmud, Sukkah 49b (and repeated in Ḥagigah 3a), Abraham is assigned the title *teḥilah la-gerim*, the "first of the converts." On the rabbinic portrait of Abraham as a proselyte (in some passages related to his own circumcision at the age of ninety-nine according to Gen. 17:24) or as one who (together with Sarah) was engaged in the process of converting others (derived exegetically from Gen. 12:5), see G. G. Porton, *The Stranger Within Your Gates: Converts and Conversion in Rabbinic Literature* (Chicago and London, 1994), pp. 58, 91, 139, 197, 211, 217, 224 n. 45, 256 n. 85, 262 n. 142, 319 n. 310.

[43] *Zohar* 2:95a. See *Zohar* 1:95a; Wijnhoven, "Zohar and the Proselyte," pp. 125–127.

[44] The demonic potency is thus designated in several passages in the *Zohar* by the biblical idiom (Ps. 81:10) *el zar*, "strange god." In some contexts, this locution is related specifically to the male potency of the demonic realm as opposed to the feminine, which is designated *el nekhar*, the "foreign god." See *Zohar* 1:161b; 2:182a, 243a, 263b, 268a; 3:13a, 106a–b. On the use of the term *zar* to refer to the demonic potency, see *Zohar* 2:133b; 3:7a, 55a, 73b, 297a. The nexus between idolatry, sexual misconduct, and the demonic is emphasized repeatedly in the zoharic corpus. See *Zohar* 1:131b; 2:3b, 61a, 87b, 90a; 3:84a, 142a; Tishby, *Wisdom of the Zohar*, pp. 461–462, 1365; Wolfson, *Circle in the Square*, p. 140 n. 2.

[45] *Zohar* 1:93a, 204a; 2:87b, 90a. See also *Zohar* 1:131a–b.

> of this their spirits are impure.... When they remove from themselves this
> filth, which is the foreskin, their impurity departs from them, and they
> approach their purity by means of the true justice (*ha-ṣedeq ha-amiti*).
> Thus the convert is called the righteous convert (*ger ṣedeq*), for this is the
> gradation of the covenant (*madregat ha-berit*), and this is the secret of the
> covenant (*sod ha-berit*) and the eternal life (*ḥei ha-olam*), which is the secret
> of Sabbath (*sod shabbat*).[46]

Conversion thus entails an ontological transubstantiation, for the soul of
the convert divests itself of its demonic character and enters into the divine
realm of holiness. The point of access, and the grade to which the converted
soul is attached, is the last of the sefirotic emanations, which is referred to
in the above passage by several names, to wit, justice, the secret of the covenant, eternal life, and the secret of Sabbath. In the language of the *Zohar*, the
convert separates from the Other Side and enters beneath the wings of
the *Shekhinah*. The technical name of the convert *ger ṣedeq* derives from
the fact that the divine presence, the divine attribute to which the convert
is conjoined, is referred to as Justice (*ṣedeq*).[47]

In order for this radical metastasis to take place, it is also necessary for
the divine to inhabit the foreign body of the demonic. The soul of the convert is described accordingly by the zoharic authorship: "Woeful is the holy
soul that belongs to the 'foreign man' and who emanates upon the proselyte
that converts, and who flies to him from the Garden of Eden in a concealed
way, upon the edifice that is constructed from the impure foreskin."[48] The
latter clearly refers to the body of the Christian, which derives from the side
of the foreskin and thus stands in opposition to the covenant, the aspect of
holiness that corresponds to Israel. The convert is described further as the
"soul that belonged to the Other Side, the foreign man, and she is oppressed
by him."[49] There is a glaring disparity, therefore, in the life of the convert,
for prior to the conversion, the soul of the potential convert is a Christian
on the outside but secretly a Jew. Dissimulation lies at the core of the identity of the would-be convert: he is what he is not for he is not what he is.

---

[46] J. H. A. Wijnhoven, "*Sefer ha-Mishkal*: Text and Study," Ph.D. dissertation, Brandeis
University, 1964, p. 132.

[47] *Zohar* 1:13a–b, 96a.

[48] *Zohar* 2:98b.

[49] *Zohar* 2:95b. I have explored the demonization of Christianity in the zoharic literature in "Re/membering the Covenant: Memory, Forgetfulness, and the Construction of History in the *Zohar*," to appear in *Jewish History and Jewish Memory: Yerushalmi Festschrift*,
ed. E. Carlebach and D. S. Myers, pp. 214–246.

Tellingly, the zoharic author refers to this mystery as the "secret that is higher than all the rest."[50] Given the widely accepted view expressed in kabbalistic literature with respect to the origin of the Jewish soul in the sefirotic realm,[51] it seems reasonable to conclude that the allusion here is to the fact that the embodiment of the Jewish soul in the Christian corresponds symbolically to the exile of the pneumatic spark of God. The esoteric significance of the soul being cloaked in a foreign garment is the displacement of an aspect of God from the pleroma of light, expressed in the mythical language of the estrangement of the daughter from the father. In a manifestly androcentric manner, the banished and disenfranchised aspect of the divine, which creates a blurring of identity in the social sphere, is linked especially to the female gender.[52] The point is made explicitly in the elder's interpretation of the verse, "If he marries another, he must not withhold from this one her food, her clothing, or her conjugal rights" (Exod. 21:10), in light of the verse, "And the dust returns to the earth as it was, and the spirit returns to God who bestowed it" (Eccles. 12:7):

> What is [the meaning of] "and the spirit returns?" This is the *Shekhinah*, which is the holy spirit. When the *Shekhinah* sees in the ten sojourns that she must take that Israel does not want to return in repentance before the blessed holy One, the Other Side rules over the holy land, as it has been established by the comrades. Come and see: The spirit of a man who is worthy is crowned in the image in the Garden of Eden below, and every Sabbath and new month the spirits are crowned, and they are divested [of the body] and they ascend above. Just as the blessed holy One acts in relation to the supernal, holy soul above, so too he acts in relation to that spirit below in the Garden of Eden below, which rises before him. He says, "This is the spirit of the body of so-and-so." Immediately, the blessed holy One crowns that spirit in several crowns, and he delights in her.[53]

In the specific example of the potential convert, one might say that prior to the conversion, the Jew is alienated in the other that mirrors the soul, as the soul that mirrors the other. The sense of dislocation is correlated with

---

[50] *Zohar* 2:95b.

[51] For an extensive discussion of the zoharic treatment of the soul, see Tishby, *Wisdom of the Zohar*, pp. 677–722.

[52] It goes without saying that this (dis)orientation is not unique to the medieval kabbalah, but it has roots in much older phases of the Jewish religion, indeed stretching back to ancient Israel. For an enlightening study of the theme of concealment and the blurring of identity, see T. K. Beat, *The Book of Hiding: Gender, Ethnicity, Annihilation, and Esther* (London and New York, 1997).

[53] *Zohur* 2:97b. See also endnote 4.

the duality of good and evil woven into the very fabric of being. This ontological presumption is related in the zoharic context by the poetic image of
the rotating scale (*tiqla*),[54] which is described as the "pillar that stands in
balance in the air that blows" (*amuda de-qayyama letiqlin go awira de-
nashvat*). The weight comprises scales of justice (*mo'znei ṣedeq*) on the
right and scales of deceit (*mo'znei mirmah*) on the left, the force of holiness
and the force of impurity.[55] In conjunction with this scale, the souls are
said to "rise and descend, depart and return." However, when the right side
is oppressed by the left, a condition that is tied exegetically to the phrase,
"when a man rules over a man to treat him unjustly," *et asher shalaṭ ha-adam
be-adam le-ra lo* (Eccles. 8:9),[56] the daughter of the priest can be wed to the
foreign man, the alien one who stems from the other side. Thus, the verse in
question is related by the zoharic authorship to the mystery of the oppression of the Jewish soul in the body of a Christian. The world is governed by
the Tree of Knowledge of Good and Evil. Consequently, when those of the
world behave in accordance with the side of goodness, the scale is tipped
to the right side, but when they behave in accordance with the side of evil,
it is tipped to the left. The Jewish souls, which are in the scale at the time
that the evil force dominates, are oppressed by the demonic side.[57] What
may be called the ontological possibility for conversion, therefore, involves
the suffering and oppression of the Jewish soul in the body of the Christian,
which is manifest in the historical domination of Jacob by Esau. Beyond

---

[54] My translation of the word *tiqla* as "rotating scale" is an attempt to combine the
two salient connotations of this term as it is employed in the zoharic text. See *Zohar*
1:109b–110a; 2:99b; and the lengthy discussion of this term in Y. Liebes, *Sections on the
Zohar Lexicon* (Jerusalem, 1976), pp. 327–331 (Hebrew).

[55] See Liebes, *Sections*, pp. 331–332.

[56] As Liebes, "Zohar and Eros," p. 87 n. 126, points out, this is a unique occurrence in the
body of the *Zohar* wherein both the force of holiness and that of impurity are designated
by the term *adam*, a usage that is found in the later strata of zoharic literature to contrast
Samael, the evil man (referred to as *adam beliyya'al* on the basis of Prov. 6:12), and the holy
One, the good man (*adam ṭov*, which is also designated by the title *yisra'el*). See *Tiqqunei Zohar*, ed. R. Margaliot (Jerusalem, 1978), sec. 67, 98b; *Zohar Ḥadash*, ed. R. Margaliot
(Jerusalem, 1978), 106d (*Tiqqunim*). In the main body of *Zohar*, the contrast between the
divine and the demonic is often framed in terms of the philological point that only the former is referred to by the term *adam*, an anthropological approach indebted to the rabbinic
notion that Jews, in contrast to idolaters, are called by the name *adam*. See Babylonian
Talmud, Yevamot 61a; Baba Meṣi'a 114b; Keritut 6b; *Zohar* 1:20b, 28b, 1:35b; 2:25b (*Piqqudin*),
86a, 120a (*Ra'aya Meheimna*), 162b, 275b; 3:125a (*Ra'aya Meheimna*), 143b, 219a, 238b (*Ra'aya
Meheimna*); *Zohar Ḥadash*, 37b; "*Sefer ha-Mishkal*," p. 130; Liebes, *Sections*, pp. 30, 46–47,
54–55. On a key passage wherein the demonic force is represented as *ish* (as opposed to
adam), see *Zohar* 3:48b, analyzed in E. R. Wolfson, "Light Through Darkness: The Ideal of
Human Perfection in the Zohar," *Harvard Theological Review* 81 (1988): 81 n. 29.

[57] *Zohar* 2:95b.

the historical plane, moreover, this oppression signifies the anguish of the divine spark trapped in the shell of the demonic.

Immediately preceding the discussion regarding the concealment of secrets in the Torah, further mysteries regarding the convert are disclosed, but in this case in relation to the laws pertaining to the sale of an Israelite woman by her father into slavery (Exod. 21:7–11). The daughter refers symbolically to the Jewish soul, and the father, to God. In light of the complexity of the zoharic exegesis, the reader would be best served if I translate the relevant passage in full:

> All the souls of the converts fly out from the Garden of Eden in a concealed manner. When the souls, which [the converts] inherit from the Garden of Eden, depart from this world, to what place do they return? It has been taught:[58] The one who takes and holds on to the property of converts at the outset merits them. So too all those supernal, holy souls that the blessed holy One prepares below, as we have said.... all of them issue forth at appointed times and ascend in order to take delight in the Garden of Eden. They encounter the souls of the converts, and those souls who hold on to them grasp them and merit them, and they are garbed in them, and they ascend. All of them exist in this garment, and they descend to the Garden in this garment, for in the Garden of Eden nothing exists without the garment of those who exist there. If you say that on account of this garment these souls are deprived of all the pleasure they had at first, it is written, "If he marries another, he must not withhold from this one her food, her clothing, or her conjugal rights" (Exod. 21:10). In the Garden they exist in the garment that they initially seized and merited. When they ascend above they are divested of it, for there they exist without a garment.... When these holy souls descend to this world so that each one will dwell in its place, which is appropriate for human beings, all of them descend garbed in these souls [of the converts] of which we spoke, and thus they enter the holy seed, and in this garment they are enslaved by them in this world. When these garments draw on matters of this world, those holy souls are sustained from the scent emitted by these garments.[59]

It is reasonable to conclude that the proximity of the above citation and the discussion of God's hiding secret matters in the Torah underscores the fact that in the mind of the zoharic authorship, the ontological account of the convert, which entails the garbing of the holy seed of the Jewish soul in the Christian body, sheds light on the hermeneutical notion of secrets being cloaked in the letters of Torah. Indeed, just as in the case of the convert, the external garment conceals the inner soul revealed therein, so in the

58 Babylonian Talmud, Baba Batra 52b.
59 *Zohar* 2:98b.

case of Torah, the literal sense is the covering that hides but also reveals the secret meaning. Accordingly, the task of reading does not necessitate the complete discarding of the garments for the soul to be disclosed. On the contrary, as I have already noted in passing, the language of the *Zohar* is very precise: The wise ones, who are full of eyes, see the hidden matter only through the garment (*mi-go levushah*).[60] After having established the general hermeneutical point, the zoharic authorship returns to the specific example of the convert:

> In several places the blessed holy One gave a warning about the convert so that the holy seed will be forewarned regarding him, and afterward the concealed matter comes out from its sheath. When it is revealed, it returns immediately to its sheath wherein it is garbed. In every place that he gave a warning about the convert, the matter came out from its sheath and was revealed, and it says, "You know the soul of the convert" (Exod. 23:9). Immediately it entered its sheath, and returned to its garment wherein it was concealed, as it is written [in the continuation of the verse], "For you were converts in the land of Egypt." Scripture thought that since it was immediately garbed, there was no one taking heed of it. Through the soul of the convert the holy soul knows of the matters of this world and derives pleasure from them.[61]

In this most extraordinary passage, the zoharic authorship reveals the mystical intent of the biblical assertion that the Israelites were "strangers," *gerim*, in Egypt, a historical reflection that is meant contextually to legitimate the moral prescript not to oppress the stranger. From the vantage point of the author of the zoharic passage, the rationale for the ethical injunction to act kindly toward the convert is the historical claim that the Israelites were converts themselves. But this is a secret that must be concealed. Most remarkable is the literary intent assigned to Scripture itself: "since it was immediately garbed, there was no one taking heed of it." The operative notion of the secret espoused by the medieval kabbalists, epitomized by this zoharic text, involves the doubling of mystery: the Torah hides the secret it hides.[62] That is, the ultimate dissimulation of Torah lies in the pretense that there is no secret. So profound is the mystery of conversion that the secret conceals its own secrecy; the dissimulation hides itself in the mirror of the text.[63] To reveal the secret, the concealment must

---

[60] I am here repeating and expanding my argument in "Beautiful Maiden," pp. 169–170.

[61] *Zohar* 2:98b–99a.

[62] An even profounder level of dissimulation is the secret that is never kept.

[63] My formulation here is indebted to the description of truth as the feminine in Irigaray, *Marine Lover*, p. 89. On the trope of the book as a mirror in historical perspective, see H. Grabes, *Speculum, Mirror und Looking-Glass* (Tübingen, 1973), pp. 101–102.

be concealed, and thus the Torah seeks to hide the fact that the ancient Israelites were converts. But, of course, the zoharic author (that is, the kabbalistic luminary) knows better, and thus he uncovers the secret by bringing forth the hidden matter from beneath its sheath. In so doing, the secret no longer conceals its own secrecy in the masquerade of truth that is image. In the game of hide-and-seek, the mystic interpreter dis/covers the secret hiding beneath the garment. The selling of the Israelite maiden into slavery and the marriage of the priest's daughter to a stranger, the two scriptural accounts related to the fate of the convert, both signify the displacement of the divine spark in a foreign body. To uncover the mystery that the ancient Israelites were converts is to understand the ultimate ontological truth that is predicated on the paradoxical coincidence of opposites: just as the soul of the Jew is embodied in the personhood of the Christian, so the divine inhabits the form of the demonic. To reveal this secret, moreover, has soteriological value inasmuch as the investiture of the esoteric sense in the letters of Torah is understood as the exile of the divine. The interpretative activity of the kabbalist, which is primarily the unveiling of the mystical import of Scripture, reveals the secret garbed in the cloak of the text and thereby redeems the aspect of God imprisoned in the form of the incarnate Torah.[64]

Enclosure of the Feminine:
Secrecy, Modesty, and the Mystery of Redemption

From other passages in the *Zohar*, one must conclude that the process of disclosure is indicative of the exilic condition when the feminine is dispersed amongst the nations, whereas the concealment of the mystery is characteristic of redemption, a state wherein the feminine is enclosed securely within her spatial boundaries.[65] The uncovering of secrets, which involves the disrobing of the text, is cast primarily in messianic terms as the means to bring about the union of male and female, but the consummation of that union results in the concealment of that which has been unveiled. The re/covery is portrayed geometrically as the centering of the point within the circle. *Prima facie*, it would seem that the depiction of redemption in terms of the concealment of the feminine is a reverse of the current situation described in a number of passages in zoharic literature: during the six weekdays the feminine is closed, but on the Sabbath she is

---

[64] See endnote 5.
[65] *Zohar* 1:84b, 115b–116a; 2:170b–171a; 3:125b.

open to receive the overflow from the masculine potency,[66] a process that is brought to fruition by the conjugal intercourse on the part of the kabbalist with his wife on Friday evening.[67] Closer inspection of the relevant sources reveals that there is no contradiction, for the opening of the feminine to receive from the masculine is the initial stage of the redemptive process. However, the culminating phase results in the reintegration of the feminine to the masculine, which is depicted in a number of images, including the elevation of the feminine to the position of the crown on the masculine[68] or the centering of the feminine as the point within the circle. Both of these symbolic images are related in zoharic literature to the ontological stabilization of the *Shekhinah* on the Sabbath, which is a prolepsis of the final redemption.[69]

Let us probe more deeply into the symbolic representation of the enclosure of the feminine within the masculine. I begin with a zoharic passage, which is an interpretation of the verse, "O my dove, in the cranny of the rocks, hidden by the cliff" (Song of Songs 2:14):

> "O my dove," this is the Community of Israel. "In the cranny of the rock," this is Jerusalem, for it rises above the rest of the world. Just as a rock is supernal to and stronger than everything, so Jerusalem is supernal to and stronger than everything. "Hidden by the cliff," this is the place that is called the Holy of Holies, the heart of all the world. Therefore, it is written "hidden by the cliff," for there the *Shekhinah* is hidden like the woman who is modest (*ṣenuʿah*) in relation to her husband, and she does not depart from the house to the outside, as it is written, "Your wife should be as a fruitful vine within your house" (Ps. 128:3). Similarly, the Community of Israel does not rest outside of her place, the hiddenness of the gradation,[70] except in the time of exile.[71]

---

[66] *Zohar* 1:75b; 2:204a; *Tiqqunei Zohar*, sec. 19, 38a; see Tishby, *Wisdom of the Zohar*, pp. 438–439, 1226–1227; E. K. Ginsburg, *The Sabbath in the Classical Kabbalah* (Albany, 1989), pp. 115–116, 292–293; Wolfson, "Coronation of the Sabbath Bride," pp. 315–316.

[67] For a recent discussion of this motif, see Wolfson, "Eunuchs Who Keep the Sabbath," pp. 159–162.

[68] See Wolfson, *Circle in the Square*, pp. 116–117; idem, "*Tiqqun ha-Shekhinah*: Redemption and the Overcoming of Gender Dimorphism in the Messianic Kabbalah of Moses Hayyim Luzzatto," *History of Religions* 36 (1997): 322–332.

[69] See Wolfson, "Coronation of the Sabbath Bride," pp. 315–324.

[70] The Aramaic idiom *setiru de-darga*, which I have translated the "hiddenness of the gradation," is an exact rendering of the biblical expression *be-seter ha-madregah*, "hidden by the cliff." According to the zoharic interpretation, this term refers to the gradation wherein the *Shekhinah* is hidden in the time of redemption.

[71] *Zohar* 1:84b.

Following the position articulated in the classical rabbinic corpus, the zoharic author affirms that the dispersion of the *Shekhinah* amongst the nations was in order to protect her children. Deviating from the rabbinic position, however, the kabbalist notes that such a state is precarious, for the *Shekhinah* is exposed and thus open to the pernicious effect of the demonic forces. Indeed, according to another passage in the *Zohar*, the destruction of the Jerusalem Temple is described from the vantage point of the separation of the Matrona from the King, resulting in the exposure of the genitals of the former. Conversely, the construction of the Temple below as the place of dwelling for the divine glory parallels the unification above between the masculine and the feminine aspects of the divine, the blessed holy One and the *Shekhinah*. When the Temple stands and there is unity above and below, then the feminine is stabilized in her permanent habitation. Transgression on the part of Jewish males severs the bond between male and female, and the latter is driven from her dwelling. This banishment and consequent homelessness are depicted in the image of her being unclothed: "The King separates from the Matrona, and the Matrona is driven from her Temple, and consequently she is naked with respect to all, for the matter of the exposure of the genitals does not apply to the King without the Matrona or to the Matrona without the King, and thus it is written, 'Do not uncover the nakedness of your father and the nakedness of your mother' (Lev. 18:7)."[72]

Exile entails separation of male and female, which in turn results in the exposure of the genitals, a situation that is especially dangerous for the feminine inasmuch as she is subject to the potential encroachment of the demonic force of Samael. The prohibition against illicit sexual relations, referred to by the idiom *gilluy arayot*, the uncovering of the nakedness, is linked in zoharic literature to the warning regarding the improper disclosure of the secrets of Torah.[73] It follows that if the exilic condition is one that is marked by the uncovering of the genitals, esoteric knowledge cannot be fully revealed. In the state of redemption, by contrast, the *Shekhinah* will be concealed within the rebuilt Temple like a woman who is compared metaphorically to the fruitful vine hidden within the house. The spatial enclosure within the confines of the Temple symbolically depicts the concealment of the feminine that is appropriate to her unification with the masculine. In the moment of *hieros gamos*, the *Shekhinah*

---

[72] *Zohar* 3:74b.
[73] Liebes, *Studies in the Zohar*, p. 25.

is obviously fully exposed vis-à-vis her masculine consort—an intimacy that is conveyed in the zoharic text by the image of the face-to-face encounter[74]—but in the same moment she must be concealed to protect herself against the possible intrusion of the demonic power.[75] Thus, the biblical locution interpreted as a reference to the Holy of Holies is *be-seter ha-madregah*, which should be rendered according to the theosophic symbolism deployed in the zoharic context as "in the secrecy of the gradation." The place wherein the *Shekhinah* is hidden is the locus of occult wisdom, the divine gradation that is identified as the ontological root of secrecy. The matter of esotericism, therefore, is related directly to the erotic interpretation of the sacrificial cult of the Temple.

In another zoharic context, the matter is expressed specifically as an interpretation of the verse "A garden locked is my sister the bride, a fountain locked, a sealed-up spring" (Song of Songs 4:12): "R. Isaac said: When the holy King remembers Israel on account of his name, and the Matrona returns to her place, it is written 'When he goes in to make expiation in the Shrine, nobody else shall be in the Tent of Meeting until he comes out' (Lev. 16:17). Thus when the priest entered to unify the holy name, to make atonement in holiness, to unite the King and the Matrona, it is written 'nobody else shall be in the Tent of Meeting'."[76] Entry into the sacred space of the Tabernacle, which is symbolically equivalent to the Temple, is prohibited because the cultic activity of the priest fosters the union of the masculine and the feminine aspects of the divine, a union that must be concealed. The necessity for concealment is tied to the female, who must be hidden within the erotogenic zone wherein the holy coupling takes place. The intrinsic hiddenness of the feminine is exegetically linked to the verse from the Song wherein the sister/bride is compared poetically to the images of a locked garden, a locked fountain, and a sealed-up spring.[77] To cite a third passage from the *Zohar* where the point is further elaborated:

---

[74] Ibid., pp. 68–69.

[75] In some zoharic passages, the concealment of the feminine from the masculine is given a negative valence. In this hiding, which is occasioned by the transgressions of Israel below, the divine feminine is compared to a woman in her menstrual period in which she is forbidden to have physical contact with her husband. See *Zohar* 1:61a.

[76] *Zohar* 3:66b. Consider the words of Blake from *Jerusalem* in *The Complete Poetry and Prose of William Blake*, ed. D. V. Erdman, commentary by H. Bloom (Berkeley and Los Angeles, 1982), p. 193: "In Beulah the Female lets down her beautiful Tabernacle;/ Which the Male enters magnificent between her Cherubim:/ And becomes One with her mingling condensing in Self-love/ The Rocky Law of Condemnation & double Generation, & Death."

[77] The verse from the Song is applied in a number of passages in zoharic literature to the feminine *Shekhinah*. The opening of the closed woman is facilitated by the male or

R. Jose began his discourse: "Your wife should be as a fruitful vine within your house; your sons, like olive saplings around your table" (Ps. 128:3). "Your wife should be as a fruitful vine," all the time that your wife is inside the house and does not go out she is modest (ṣenu'ah), and it is proper for her to give birth to righteous offspring. "As a fruitful vine," just as the vine is not planted in another species but only in its own, so the worthy woman does not produce seedlings in another man, and just as there is nothing grafted unto the vine from another tree, so too in the case of the worthy woman.... From this we learn that when the *Shekhinah* is hidden (ṣen'ia) in her place as is appropriate for her, as it were, "your sons, like olive saplings," this refers to Israel when they are dwelling in the land. "Around your table," for they eat, drink, offer sacrifices, and are joyous before the blessed holy One, and the supernal and lower beings are blessed on account of them. When the *Shekhinah* departs, Israel are exiled from the table of their father and they are amongst the nations. They scream every day and there is none who hears them but the blessed holy One, as it is written, "Yet, even then, when they are in the land of their enemies, [I will not reject or spurn them so as to destroy them, annulling My covenant with them: for I the Lord am their God]" (Lev. 26:44).[78]

The concealment of the *Shekhinah* in her appropriate dwelling, which is reflected below in the edifice of the Temple, marks the ideal situation wherein the divine androgyny is perfectly constituted. The word ṣenu'ah, which is applied to the feminine *Shekhinah* in this citation and in the other relevant contexts, has the double connotation of "hidden" and (sexually) "modest."[79] The philological point underscores the attitude cultivated by the traditional male kabbalist with respect to female sexuality and the notion of secrecy more generally: the eschatological condition of the *Shekhinah* reflects and is reinforced by the sexual modesty of Jewish women, who

---

is said to occur as a result of the masculine potency. See *Zohar* 1:32b, 262b; 2:4a; *Tiqqunei Zohar*, Introduction, 12b; sec. 19, 38a (see above, n. 66), 39a (in this context, the image of the locked garden is explicitly linked to the virgin); sec. 21, 60b, 61a; sec. 28, 72b; sec. 29, 72b–73a.

[78] *Zohar* 1:115b–116a.

[79] The double connotation of the term ṣenu'ah applied to the *Shekhinah* has its basis in a passage in *Sefer ha-Bahir*. See *The Book Bahir: An Edition Based on the Earliest Manuscripts*, ed. D. Abrams (Los Angeles, 1994), § 104, pp. 187–189. In the effort to explain the divine potency referred to as the west, which clearly refers to the *Shekhinah* (given the well-established tradition concerning the location of the latter in the west), the following parable is offered: "[This may be compared to] the prince who has a beautiful bride and she is hidden (ṣenu'ah) in his chamber, and he would take great wealth from the house of his father and bring it to her, and she would take everything, and constantly hide (maṣna'at) it and mix everything until the end of days." On the implicitly (and, in some cases, explicitly) erotic relation that pertains between father, daughter, and son adopted in several bahiric passages, see E. R. Wolfson, "Hebraic and Hellenic Conceptions of Wisdom in *Sefer ha-Bahir*," *Poetics Today* 19 (1998): 156–167.

ideally should remain within the home so that the upper covenant, the sign of which is inscribed on the male organ, is not forgotten or damaged. Thus, reflecting on why Jonah fled to Tarshish, the zoharic authorship comments:

> The *Shekhinah* does not dwell outside the land of Israel, and thus in order for the *Shekhinah* not to dwell upon him, he fled from the land of Israel. The *Shekhinah* dwells there, as it says, "Your wife should be as a fruitful vine within your house" (Ps. 128:3). "A fruitful vine," this refers to the *Shekhinah*. Just as the *Shekhinah* was hidden within the Holy of Holies, so too a wife must be modest and not go out from her house.[80]

A link is thus forged between sexual modesty and the occultation of the feminine.[81] This occultation, in turn, is related specifically to the concealment of secrets even though from the traditional kabbalistic perspective it is clearly the male to whom the secrets are entrusted. Not only is it exclusively to the male that the secrets are concomitantly revealed and concealed, but only to the male who is sexually pure, for the locus of the secret is in the gradation that corresponds to the phallus. Nevertheless, the female plays an instrumental role in this process since the sexual modesty of the male is dependent on her, just as above the concealment of secrets is dependent on the enclosure of the feminine potency within the proper spatial boundaries of the idealized Holy of Holies. The point is made explicitly by the sixteenth-century kabbalist Moses Cordovero, reflecting on the verse, "When men began to increase on earth and daughters were born to them" (Gen. 6:1):

> It says "daughters" and not "sons" because the essence of sexual modesty (*ṣeniʿut*) depends on the feminine, for [women] must be modest, and by means of this the men will be modest and the children will emerge with a disposition of modesty. Therefore, the beginning of the damage sprouted from the licentiousness of the daughters, and thus it says "and daughters were born to them." And from here the sexual immorality (*periṣut*) began to produce a bad result, estranged children.... The explanation for the blessed copulation is related to the fact that the holy soul is garbed within it, and it must be like the supernal copulation, for just as the supernal copulation is hidden in secrecy, such that no created being can experience it, so too the

---

[80] *Zohar* 2:170b–171a.

[81] On the correlation of secrecy and sexual modesty, see E. R. Wolfson, "From Sealed Book to Open Text: Time, Memory, and Narrativity in Kabbalistic Hermeneutics," in *Interpreting Judaism in a Postmodern Age*, ed. S. Kepnes (New York and London, 1996), p. 157. See ibid., p. 173 n. 57, where I mentioned that a similar nexus between mystery and modesty, which is connected to the feminine in particular, is essential to the thought of Emmanuel Levinas.

lower copulation must be in concealment (*ṣeni'ut*) such that it is not known by any creature in the world. Consequently, the holy soul, which is made from the supernal copulation, will descend, but when the copulation is in the open and in public no supernal holiness dwells there.[82]

Sexual modesty, *ṣeni'ut*, is related to the concealment of the feminine, whereas licentiousness, *periṣut*, is related to the exposure of the feminine. Cordovero's remarks highlight the androcentric dimension of the kabbalistic symbolism, already implicit in the earlier sources, including the passages from the *Zohar* to which I have referred. The disclosure of the feminine reflects an ontologically defective state, albeit one that has an impact on the phenomenological accessibility of the divine. In his commentary on Ezekiel's chariot vision, Moses de León connects this idea exegetically to the words that inaugurate the prophetic epiphany, "the heavens opened and I saw visions of God," that is, in the exilic state, "that which was concealed is disclosed," *mah she-hayah satum nir'eh*, for there is no shelter or covering protecting the *Shekhinah*. The geographical dispersion of the exile is the symbolic intent of the heavens opening up, which signifies a rupture in the divine, "everything was a single unity that was bound in a sturdy bond in the secret of the heavens," *hayah ha-kol yiḥud meyuḥad mequshar be-qesher amiṣ be-sod shamayim*. Most interestingly, the visions of God are here related directly to this state of disclosure that is associated with exile, a point that is related exegetically to the fact that the word for visions, *mar'ot*, is presumed by the author to have been written in the defective form (without the letter *waw*). In the state of exile, therefore, the *Shekhinah* is likened to the mirror (*mar'eh*) in which the image is seen, whereas in a more perfect state of redemption, she would be hidden: "That which was concealed 'as a fruitful vine within your house' (Ps. 128:3) went outside, and she was seen and revealed in another land in this day; she descended to Babylonia outside her boundary, and she was made visible there."[83]

A better understanding of the nexus of spatial delimitation and the occultation of the feminine will indicate even more clearly how deep the chord of androcentrism strikes in the kabbalistic literature. Above I noted in passing that the enclosure of the feminine within the masculine is portrayed in the geometric image of the midpoint of the circle. In a separate study, I have argued that the symbolization of the *Shekhinah* as the point

---

[82] *Zohar 'im Perush Or Yaqar* (Jerusalem, 1963), 2:233.

[83] *R. Moses de León's Commentary to Ezekiel's Chariot*, critically edited from manuscript and introduced by A. Farber-Ginat, and edited for publication by D. Abrams (Los Angeles, 1998), p. 58 (Hebrew).

in the center of the circle signifies the aspect of the female that is anatomically homologous to the male.[84] Without rehearsing all of the technical arguments and textual examples that I put forth in support of my position, let me simply reiterate that the application of the symbol of the point to the feminine implies a gender transformation of the feminine. When the feminine potency is concentrated in the center of the circle, she is described in overtly phallic terms such as the foundation stone whence all entities derive or the spring that overflows and sustains all things. It is particularly important for this study that the symbol of the midpoint is also associated with the image of the enclosed female. The one as the other is meant to convey the symbolic intention regarding the phallic nature of the feminine.

The implications of this symbolism for the role of gender in the theosophic kabbalah should be fairly obvious. The concealed feminine represents the body of secrecy, but in that occultation she has been transposed into an aspect of the male. Given the structural affinity between the phallic potency and the rhetoric of secrecy, it should come as little surprise that for the exclusively male kabbalists, the locus of secrets should be in the female envisioned as part of the male. We are now in a better position to understand the parabolic image of the Torah as the beautiful maiden without eyes to which I referred above. To sum up the previous discussion: the esoteric meaning is garbed in the exoteric in the same manner that the existential situation of the convert involves the dissimulation of the Jewish soul and the donning of the garment of a Christian. On the surface, the two would appear to be diametrically opposed. But for the wise one who has eyes to see, the two are not radically distinct at all, for the truth of the internal is beheld precisely from the external covering. In the case of the convert, as I have also noted above, the zoharic authorship relates the secret to the verse, "You shall not oppress a stranger, for you know the feelings of the stranger, having yourselves been strangers in the land of Egypt" (Exod. 23:9). Taking the word *ger* to refer to the religious convert rather than to the ethnic stranger, the kabbalistic interpretation of the verse proffered by the zoharic authorship is that the Israelites themselves were converts. The seemingly ontological wedge separating Jew and non-Jew is thus substantially narrowed by this realization, which arises exegetically from the implicit meaning covered by the sheath of the explicit text. As the continuation of that passage indicates, the one to whom the secrets are revealed comprehends not only that contextual sense is an allusion to inner truth,

---

[84] Wolfson, "Coronation of the Sabbath Bride," pp. 319–324.

but that the allusion is the veil through which the unveiling is veiled in the veil of unveiling.

The hermeneutical relationship can be framed as well in gendered terms. Thus, for example, in one zoharic context, the divine is portrayed in the dichotomy of that which is hidden and that which is revealed (*satim we-galya*): "We have learnt that the blessed holy One is hidden and revealed. The revealed relates to the courthouse below and the concealed to the place whence all blessings emerge."[85] To decode this relatively straightforward passage, it will be noted that the hidden aspect is related to the male, or more precisely to *Yesod*, the wellspring of all blessings, and the revealed aspect is related to the female, or the *Shekhinah*, the attribute of limitation referred to symbolically as the lower courthouse, that is, the place whence judgment is issued. As I noted above, in other zoharic passages, the Torah is delineated in the same manner, for it is emphasized that the Torah is hidden and revealed because it is identical with the name, which is itself hidden and revealed. We are justified, therefore, in utilizing this formulation to disclose something fundamental about the zoharic attitude toward the hermeneutics of esotericism. Indeed, in the continuation of the aforementioned passage, the zoharic authorship draws the obvious hermeneutical principle as it emerges from the theosophical notion of the concomitant concealment and disclosure of the divine: "Therefore [to the extent] that all the words of a person are in secrecy, blessings dwell upon him, and if they are disclosed, it is a place upon which the courthouse rests on him. Since it is a place that is disclosed, that which is called the evil eye governs it. Everything is in the supernal mystery in the pattern of that which is above."[86]

Secrecy is contextualized in the phallic component of the divine, but in the moment of union, the female itself is transposed into part of the male. The reunion of male and female in the theosophic kabbalah is a process of reintegration of the female in the male or, to put the matter somewhat differently, insofar as the female provides the space to contain the male, she may be considered the extended phallus.[87] On the essential role of the female to contain the male, I mention here one example from the text of

---

[85] *Zohar* 1:64b.

[86] Ibid.

[87] *Circle in the Square*, pp. 92–98. The correlation of the feminine and space is a motif that has been well noted in feminist criticism. As an illustration of this insight, see C. Keller, *Apocalypse Now and Then: A Feminist Guide to the End of the World* (Boston, 1996), pp. 140–180.

the *Zohar*, which involves the interpretation of the expression *aron ha-berit*, "ark of the covenant," as a reference to the *Shekhinah* that contains the mystery of the "image of the holy body" (*raza diyoqna de-gufa qaddisha*) of the divine anthropos, which is also depicted as the "secret of the Torah" (*raza de-oraita*).[88] In this context, the "holy body" refers more specifically to the phallus, which is the aspect of the divine anatomy wherein the mystery of Torah is localized. Indeed, it is stated explicitly in that passage that only one who is careful with respect to the phallus, which is referred to as the "sign of the holy covenant" (*ot qayyama qaddisha*), is considered to be in the category of the human (*adam*) in the fullest sense,[89] an anthropological classification that effectively dehumanizes both Jewish women and non-Jews, for the ontological status of the complete human is imparted exclusively to Jewish males. In that context, moreover, this symbolic nexus is applied to the custom of placing the corpse of the righteous man in a coffin, for he alone is worthy of such an honor since he was careful with respect to the "sign of the holy covenant." The biblical paradigm is Joseph, of whom it says that "he was embalmed and placed in a coffin in Egypt" (Gen. 50:26). Commenting on the double *yod* in the word *vayyisem*, the author of this zoharic passage writes:

> The covenant was joined to the covenant, the secret below in the secret above, and he entered the coffin. What is the reason? For he guards the holy covenant and it is established in him. Thus it was appropriate for him to enter into the coffin, for only the righteous one, who knows and is aware of the fact that he has never sinned with respect to that phallus, the sign of the holy covenant, can enter into the coffin.... The coffin is not joined except to the righteous one who guards the sign of the holy covenant.[90]

The mystical valence attributed to the placing of Joseph in the coffin involves the sacred union of the divine phallus—appropriately personified by Joseph, inasmuch as his righteousness is related to the fact that he was scrupulous in sexual matters pertaining especially to the phallus—and the feminine, symbolized by the casket. The symbolic image conveys the philosophical principle of the feminine as the empty space that contains the

---

[88] *Zohar* 2:214b.

[89] The exact words of the zoharic text (2:214b) are *u-ma'an ihu de-qa'im be-raza de-adam ma'an de-natir ot qayyama qaddisha*, which translate literally as "and who is the one who exists in the secret of Adam? The one who guards the sign of the holy covenant." In light of such statements, it is astonishing that my critics have accused me of reading the phallocentric orientation into the *Zohar* and other kabbalistic sources that espouse a similar viewpoint.

[90] *Zohar* 2:214b.

phallic potency. The choice of this particular image is also important insofar as it underscores the nexus of eros and thanatos.[91] The ultimate symbol
of death is transformed into a potent image for eros. What may be gathered
from this specific example is the more general claim that the "othering"
of the feminine, which entails the psychic projection of the feminine as
other, is to be evaluated strictly from the point of view of the male. The
phallocentric dimension of the zoharic imagery is well captured in the following account of Lacan's theory of signification, given by Judith Butler:
"This is an Other that constitutes, not the limit of masculinity in a feminine alterity, but the site of a masculine self-elaboration. For women to 'be'
the Phallus means, then, to reflect the power of the Phallus, to signify that
power, to 'embody' the Phallus, to supply the site to which it penetrates,
and to signify the Phallus through 'being' its Other, its absence, its lack,
the dialectical confirmation of its identity."[92] The contemporary feminist
reflection is an entirely apt portrayal of the underlying assumption of the
theosophic symbolism embraced by the members of the zoharic circle and
other kabbalists.

From this perspective, one can comprehend that the zoharic portrayal
of the body of secrecy is related in several key passages to the motif of
the occultation of the feminine. The hidden woman is the modest wife
secluded in the house, which parallels the enclosure of the *Shekhinah* in
the Holy of Holies. In this state, the female is united in secrecy with the
male, and as a result of that union she becomes the fruitful vine, an image
that clearly conveys the act of bestowal and fruition, traits that are generally associated with the masculine and, more specifically, with the phallus.
Indeed, the woman who is sealed up in the house becomes the fruitful vine,
for she is transformed into the male, and the power that receives becomes
the power that bestows. The ultimate secret, the mystery that marks the
path of secrecy, centers around the fact that the occluded feminine is one
whose femininity is no longer ontologically distinct from the male. For the
kabbalists, this secret lies at the core of the mystical insight that brings
about messianic redemption. In the case of the *Zohar* and related kabbalistic literature, however, the secret did not involve esoteric knowledge that
had to be suppressed for political reasons. Rather, the erotic nature of the

---

[91] See H. Marcuse, *Eros and Civilization: A Philosophical Inquiry into Freud* (Boston,
1974), pp. 222–237.

[92] Judith Butler, *Gender Trouble: Feminism and the Subversion of Identity* (New York,
1990), p. 44. In my study, "Re/membering the Covenant," I cited the words of Butler. I repeat
them here on account of their clarity and incisiveness of expression.

union necessitated the concealment of that which was exposed, which again underscores the fact that concealment and disclosure are inseparably linked in dialectical tension. By contrast, in modern scholarship, this secret has assumed another connotation, for it has become dangerous to uncover that which is hidden in the symbol of the concealed woman.[93] Alas, in what can only be called hermeneutical revenge, the secret has hid itself precisely from the very scholars who have undertaken the systematic exposure of the mysteries of the tradition. The disclosure of this secret on my part has not been without a price, but it is a price that must be paid if the notion of secrecy in kabbalistic esotericism is to be properly understood.

Endnotes

1. I will take this opportunity to respond to the criticism of my work made by Y. Liebes, "Judaism and Myth," *Dimmuy* 14 (1997): 15 n. 5 (Hebrew). (I thank Gil Anidjar for drawing my attention to this essay.) In the body of his study (p. 7), Liebes makes the point that Jewish mystics have embraced the paradox that the vision of God is occasioned by not seeing, which he relates to the quality of humility. In the note, Liebes signals out my book, *Through a Speculum That Shines*, as an illustration of not grasping this point. This is a rather remarkable claim inasmuch as countless times in that work, as well as in other studies (not at all mentioned by Liebes), I have noted the ultimate paradox with respect to the vision of God in the history of Jewish mysticism engendered by the concomitant affirmation of presence and absence. Repeatedly, I have emphasized that the God who is visible to Jewish mystics is the invisible God, and that which is revealed is revealed in its concealment. Indeed, on the very first page of the book, I write: "The theological tension between vision and invisibility provides the narrative context to articulate the esoteric dialectic of concealment and disclosure so characteristic of the various currents of Jewish mysticism. To see the God who is hidden—or, more precisely, the aspect of God that is hiddenness as such—is the destiny of the Jewish mystic, bestowed upon him by the name Israel, which, as some ancient authors playfully proposed, signifies the one who sees God" (p. ix). In the conclusion of the book, I reiterate the point: "The tension between aniconism, on the one hand, and visualizing the deity, on the other, is an essential component of the relevant varieties of Jewish mystical speculation.... In all of the mystical sources dealt with in this study there is a tension between disclosure and concealment of the divine form. This tension, I believe, is related to the fact that the ultimate object of vision is the phallus that must be hidden. The unveiling of the veiled phallus in the visionary encounter necessitates language that is paradoxical and contradictory" (pp. 394–396). Leaving aside for a moment the correctness of my assumption that the phallus is the site of mystical vision, it is evident that I embrace the paradoxical notion that the vision is of that which is invisible. That is the force of my locution that the object of vision is that which must be hidden. In terms of the zoharic text itself, I say the following: "The *Zohar* thus embraces the paradox that the divine phallus is both concealed and revealed" (p. 343). I thus go on to speak of the "essential feature of the mystic vision as a seeing of the veiled phallus." Again, one may quibble with my phallic interpretation, but one would have to admit that my thesis is predicated on accepting the paradox that the mystical vision is a seeing of that which must be veiled. Indeed, already in my

---

93   See endnote 6.

dissertation "Sefer ha-Rimmon: Critical Edition and Study," Brandeis University, 1986, p. 23, I touch upon this paradox when I note that Moses de León, whom I considered at the time to be the sole author of the *Zohar*, was influenced by the Maimonidean hermeneutic of esotericism, which is predicated on "letting that which is hidden appear and that which appears remain hidden. The teaching of truth, like truth itself, is characterized by a hide-and-seek dialectic: the concealed is disclosed as the disclosed is concealed." The criticism by Liebes is nothing more than a cavalier dismissal of my work that unfortunately does not measure up to the standard of legitimate academic dispute.

2. An interesting formulation of the implicit homoerotic dimension of the transmission of secrets from the master to his disciples seems to be implied in the following remark of Joseph Angelet, *Livnat ha-Sappir* (Jerusalem, 1913), 60b–c: "You already know that the justice above, which is in the Jerusalem that is constructed, is the Tree of life, and it is called 'Lord,' in the secret of 'the ark of the covenant of the Lord of all the earth' (Josh. 3:11). . . . and it is called male. The Community of Israel, which receives from him, is called by the name woman (*ishshah*), the 'fire of the Lord' (*'esh h'* [the individual *he* is a standard scribal circumlocution for the Tetragrammaton], which are the same letters that make up the word *ishshah*). Since Rashbi, may peace be upon him, would cause his wisdom and Torah, which was called the Tree of Life, to overflow to the sages, he too was called the 'Tree of Life' and the 'Lord' in this manner in relation to the lower beings who receive the Torah and wisdom from his mouth. This is proven from the Idra [the zoharic section that relates to the gathering of R. Simeon and the rest of the comrades to discourse about the most recondite theosophic secrets], for he set forth the arrayments (*tiqqen tiqqunim*) of the Tree of Life. . . . and the rest of the sages explicated the arrayments, each one in accordance with the level that he comprehended. If you comprehend the secret of 'For in his image did God make the perfect man' (Gen. 9:6, with the author's addition of the word 'perfect'), you will comprehend the great principle in the Torah that was explicated by Ben Azzai, and this is the great principle regarding 'You shall love your neighbor as yourself' (Lev. 19:18), and this is a secret concealed for the wise of heart, for by means of their arousal below the holy power is aroused above." Let me note that Angelet's reference to Ben Azzai, probably cited from memory, is a distortion of the relevant rabbinic source according to which Aqiva's choice of the verse "You shall love your neighbor as yourself" (Lev. 19:18) as indicative of the "great principle" (*kelal gadol*) of Torah is opposed by Ben Azzai's comment that the verse "This is the record of Adam's genealogy: On the day that God created Adam, he made him in the image of God" (Gen. 5:1) is an even greater principle (*zeh kelal gadol mi-zeh*). See *Sifra, Qedoshim* 4:12. The order is inverted in *Genesis Rabbah* 24:7, ed. J. Theodor and Ch. Albeck (Jerusalem, 1967), pp. 236–237. The main point for our purpose, however, is Angelet's citation of the obligation to love one's fellow man in the context of casting the process of transmission of secrets by the master, Simeon ben Yoḥai, to his colleagues. The master who imparts corresponds to the phallic potency of the Tree of Life, which overflows to the feminine receptacle, represented symbolically by the comrades who receive and explicate the words arrayed by the master. Together they constitute the perfect human, the androgynous Adam in whose image humanity was created. For a similar pattern in the body of *Zohar*, see Wolfson, *Through a Speculum That Shines*, pp. 371–372 n. 155. It is also of interest to note that Angelet describes Simeon ben Yoḥai's rhetorical activity in the dissemination of secrets in terms of the erotically charged verse, "Like an apple tree among the trees of the forest, so is my beloved among the young boys" (Song of Songs 2:3): The beloved is Simeon and the young boys the rest of the comrades. On the relationship of Angelet to the zoharic circle, see Liebes, *Studies in the Zohar*, pp. 134, 224–225 n. 298. For a more extensive discussion of some elements in the writings of this kabbalist, see I. Felix, "Chapters in the Kabbalistic Thought of R. Joseph Angelet," M.A. thesis, Hebrew University, 1991 (Hebrew).

3. Compare the use of the expression *guf zar*, "alien body," in *Zohar* 1:127a (*Midrash ha-Ne'lam*). In that context as well it is clear that the word *zar* refers more specifically to the non-Jew. I would thus respectfully take issue with Giller's assertion, "Love and Upheaval," p. 36, that *ish zar*, the "nonpriest," symbolizes the physical body in an apparently generic sense.

Giller himself notes that throughout this zoharic section the "images of ascent and descent are employed to underscore the strained relationships between Jews and Gentiles." The more nuanced interpretation of *ish zar* as a reference to the body of a non-Jew, or specifically that of a Christian, supports his claim regarding the underlying tension of this literary unit. The alienation to which the zoharic authorship alludes in this case is not the generic imprisonment of the soul in the physical body, but it relates more precisely to the entrapment of the Jewish soul in a Christian body. In this respect, one might contrast the zoharic myth of the alienation of the Jewish soul in the body of the Christian from the Gnostic myth of the estrangement of the soul in general in the body, which has its roots in Platonic thought. In spite of the many important developments in scholarly research on the phenomenon of Gnosticism in its multivalent nature, one of the most articulate formulations of this basic element in Gnostic myth remains H. Jonas, *The Gnostic Religion: The Message of the Alien God and the Beginnings of Christianity*, 2nd ed. (Boston, 1963), pp. 48–99. Many scholars have noted the Platonic element of Gnosticism in its classical expression. For a review of this relationship, with reference to many of the relevant studies, see B. A. Pearson, *Gnosticism, Judaism, and Egyptian Christianity* (Minneapolis, 1990), pp. 148–164. One might consider the kabbalistic orientation an ethnocentric application of the more generic philosophic position that lies at the core of the Gnostic worldview, and this applies even to those Gnostic texts that seem to be based on the notion of the fall of Sophia, which may be related in part to the Hellenistic Jewish speculation on wisdom (*hokhmah*). See G. MacRae, "The Jewish Background of the Gnostic Sophia Myth," *Novum Testamentum* 12 (1970): 86–101.

4. On the motif of the exile of *Shekhinah* in the zoharic corpus, see Tishby, *Wisdom of the Zohar*, pp. 382–385. The psychical application of this theme is much older in kabbalistic sources. Indeed, the nexus of the dispersion of the *Shekhinah* and the transmigration of the Jewish souls seems to be implied already in a passage in *Sefer ha-Bahir*. See G. Scholem, *On the Mystical Shape of the Godhead: Basic Concepts in the Kabbalah*, trans. J. Neugroschel and ed. J. Chipman (New York, 1991), pp. 203–204. The possible Gnostic background to the bahiric myth of the lower wisdom who falls from the realm of light was already noted by G. Scholem, *Origins of the Kabbalah*, trans. A. Arkush and ed. R. J. Zwi Werblowsky (Princeton, 1987), pp. 93–95. In this context, it is noteworthy that the depiction of the feminine in the ancient Gnostic works seems to me more equivocal than in the medieval kabbalistic sources. That is, in the former there is a genuine ambivalence such that one finds both positive and negative images, whereas in the case of the latter, positive elements are associated only with the masculinized feminine. Regarding the ambivalence of gender imagery in Gnostic sources, see M. A. Williams, "Uses of Gender Imagery in Ancient Gnostic Texts," in *Gender and Religion: On the Complexity of Symbols*, ed. C. W. Bynum, S. Harrell, and P. Richman (Boston, 1986), pp. 196–227; idem, "Variety in Gnostic Perspectives on Gender," in *Images of the Feminine in Gnosticism*, ed. K. L. King (Philadelphia, 1988), pp. 2–22. On the variance of the Gnostic image of the feminine in particular, see J. J. Buckley, "Sex, Suffering, and Incarnation: Female Symbolism in Gnosticism," in *The Allure of Gnosticism: The Gnostic Experience in Jungian Psychology and Contemporary Culture*, ed. R. A. Segal, J. Singer, and M. Stein (Chicago and La Salle, 1995), pp. 94–106. In my judgment, the textual evidence of the kabbalistic material yields a far more monolithic picture inasmuch as the kabbalists were operating with a clear-cut principle of gender transformation rooted in an unambiguous androcentric perspective. In my work, I have referred to the containment of the female in the male, the left in the right, as the principle of the male androgyne, which is the key to understanding the kabbalistic idea of androgyny. With respect to the divine and the demonic, the male is ontologically privileged. However, the prioritizing of the masculine in both realms demands a double transposition of gender, the male into female and the female into male. In terms of the divine realm, the transformation of the male into female (enacted through the assimilation of the male kabbalist into the divine feminine) is to facilitate the metamorphosis of the female into the male (that is, to transpose the gender of the divine feminine so that she is restored to the male). The ideal of androgyny implied in the imaginal symbol of the divine anthropos (as refracted through the prism of the medieval male kabbalists) is thus one in

which the primal androgyne is reconstituted (and still not beyond embodiment) when the female is reintegrated in the male. In terms of the demonic, the transposition of the male into female, that is, the male who is female, involves the image of the emasculated male, which is represented in the zoharic text by the symbol of the seven Edomite kings whose weapons were not found. The transposition of the female into male entails the symbol of the warrior queen, the phallic princess who wages war and avenges wrong, the quality of punitive judgment. Translated into sexual terms, the male Samael is the castrated god, who is emulated below by the Christian clergy who adopt celibacy as the ultimate spiritual ideal; the female Lilith is the prostitute arrayed in royal garments of seduction, the temptress who torments the male Jew in the guise of the Gentile woman. The insistence on the part of my critics that I have imposed an androcentric (and even worse phallocentric) reading on the kabbalistic sources is empty rhetoric that fails to engage in a sustained reading of either the primary materials or my analysis.

5. The sense of suffering on the part of God in his giving the Torah (personified in distinctively erotic terms as the feminine entity in which the male glory takes delight) to Israel is implied in a number of rabbinic statements, for example, Babylonian Talmud, Shabbat 89a; *Exodus Rabbah* 33:1. Particularly the latter passage, which entails the parabolic image of God being sold together with the Torah to Israel, had an important impact on a parable in *Sefer ha-Bahir*, which in turn influenced subsequent kabbalists. See Scholem, *Origins of the Kabbalah*, p. 170; and Wolfson, *Circle in the Square*, pp. 11–12. See especially the commentary of Naḥmanides to Exod. 25:3. The esoteric significance, which Naḥmanides marks by his signature expression "by way of truth" (*al derekh ha-emet*), of the offering (*terumah*) is related to the wisdom that God gave to Solomon, i.e., the feminine attribute of the *Shekhinah* that is imparted as a gift by the father (or the upper wisdom) to the son. In the context of alluding to this mystery, Naḥmanides refers explicitly to the aggadic comment in *Exodus Rabbah* 33:1, to which he adds the following interpretative gloss: "For the gift (*terumah*) will be for me and I am with her, in the manner of 'My beloved is mine and I am his' (Song of Songs 2:16), and thus it says 'Exactly as I show you' [*ke-khol asher ani mar'eh otkha*] (Exod. 25:9), for the I (*ani*) is the vision (*mar'eh*)." For a brief discussion of this passage, see Wolfson, *Circle in the Square*, pp. 15–16. Naḥmanides is thus alluding to the fact that the *Shekhinah*, which is designated by the first person pronoun, is the speculum through which the divine appears, a speculum that is related as well to the Torah, which is the wisdom bestowed as a gift upon Israel by God. The nexus of the Torah as the prism by means of which the divine light is refracted and the exile of *Shekhinah* is also implicit in the zoharic parable according to my reading. This notion of the incarnation of the *Shekhinah* in the form of the Torah, which entails the suffering of God exiled in the letters of the material scroll, is a foundational aspect of Naḥmanides' overall hermeneutical approach, which, unfortunately, has not been appreciated by most scholars who have worked on his admittedly complex and multidimensional thought. For a preliminary discussion of the symbolic identification of Torah and the feminine *Shekhinah* in Naḥmanides, see Wolfson, *Circle in the Square*, pp. 15–16. I intend to elaborate someday on the theme that I have mentioned in this note. On the incarnational aspect of Naḥmanides' theosophy, see E. R. Wolfson, "The Secret of the Garment in Naḥmanides," *Da'at* 24 (1990): 25–49 (English section); idem, *Through a Speculum That Shines*, pp. 63–64.

6. This is particularly evident in Green, "Kabbalistic Re-vision." Green claims that my understanding of gender symbolism in the theosophic kabbalah has set aside "the truly important role occupied by the female, especially in the Zoharic sources" (p. 270). He then proceeds to offer a litany of images used to characterize the *Shekhinah*, including, queen of the lower worlds, hind of the dawn, mother that nourishes the universe, city, temple, holy of holies, kingship (*malkhut*, which Green perplexingly renders in the neutral term "realm") that exerts dominion, governance, and judgment over existence. After going through this list, Green concludes: "The Zohar is at least as fixed with celebration of the female as it is with the male. . . . Wolfson's dismissal of this entire world of symbols through his single insight concerning *atarah*. . . . produces a significantly distorted picture of kabbalistic eros."

Anyone truly familiar with the range of my work would readily discern that the notion that I have dismissed this entire world of symbols characterizing the *Shekhinah* is grossly misleading and unfair. The real issue that emerges from my work, which is simply ignored by Green, is that these positive characteristics of the *Shekhinah* are predicated on a gendered axiology that kabbalists shared with other men living in medieval European cities, enhanced as well by biblical and rabbinic sources. In fact, I have argued that ostensibly female images are valenced as masculine in the androcentric culture of the kabbalists. Indeed, the androcentricism is so pervasive that female biological traits are appropriated as masculine. Thus even birthing and lactation are seen as masculine traits, for in the dominant kabbalistic symbology when a woman gives birth or nurses she assumes the gender value of a male. I have not ignored these obvious feminine attributes, as Green claims, but what I have done is contextualize them in a more sophisticated analysis of gender as a hermeneutical category. See especially "Crossing Gender Boundaries in Kabbalistic Ritual and Myth," in *Circle in the Square*, pp. 79–121, and extensive notes on pp. 195–232. Regrettably, Green does not relate to this aspect of my work, which is in fact my singular contribution, and thus his criticisms consistently miss the point. Those who wish to ignore my emphasis on the phallocentric androcentrism that characterizes this tradition may find comfort in the alleged alternative presented by Green, but in my mind I do not see any real option being offered here that truly responds to my scholarship. One can only hope that intelligent readers will see through the glass darkly and understand that these barbs in no way pose a serious intellectual challenge to my thesis. My detailed response to Green's review can be found in *"Tiqqun ha-Shekhinah."* See also "Coronation of the Sabbath Bride."

ICONICITY OF THE TEXT: REIFICATION OF TORAH AND THE IDOLATROUS IMPULSE OF ZOHARIC KABBALAH*

Elliot R. Wolfson

> Among the precepts of Mosaic religion is one that has more significance than is first obvious. It is the prohibition against making an image of God, which means the compulsion to worship an invisible God.... If this prohibition was accepted, however, it was bound to exercise a profound influence. For it signified subordinating sense perception to an abstract idea; it was a triumph of spirituality over senses; more precisely, an instinctual renunciation accompanied by its psychologically necessary consequences.
>
> Sigmund Freud, *Moses and Monotheism*

In a diary entry dated January 16, 1922, Franz Kafka described his writing as "an assault upon the border," which "might have developed quite easily into a new esoteric doctrine, a Kabbala."[1] Several scholars, including Gershom Scholem, have examined Kafka's penchant for the paradoxical nature of language and experience from the particular vantage point of the history of kabbalah,[2] but none has captured the matter as well as Kafka himself in the aforementioned passage. Our task is not to dwell on the literary works of Kafka, but to think through the image of assaulting the border in an effort to understand the phenomenological texture and hermeneutical presuppositions of the kabbalah. More specifically, we will be examining the question of assault on the border from the perspective of the iconicity

---

* This article was first published as Elliot R. Wolfson, "Iconicity of the Text: Reification of the Torah and the Idolatrous Impulse of Zoharic Kabbalah," *Jewish Studies Quarterly* 11 (2004): 215–242. Printed with permission from Mohr Siebeck, Tübingen.

[1] Text cited in Judith Glatzer Wechsler, "Eli Lissitzky's 'Interchange Stations': The Letter and the Spirit," in *The Jew in the Text: Modernity and the Construction of Identity*, edited by Linda Nochlin and Tamar Garb (London, 1995), p. 190. Karl E. Grözinger, *Kafka and Kabbalah*, translated by Susan H. Ray (New York, 1994), uses this citation from Kafka's diaries as the opening quote of his book.

[2] For a review of the scholarly discussion surrounding this issue, see Philip Beitchman, *Alchemy of the Word: Cabala of the Renaissance* (Albany, 1998), pp. 159–164. See also Grözinger, *Kafka and Kabbalah*, pp. 187–188. On the link between the symbolic nature of language in kabbalah and the symbolism of Kafka, see the remark of Adorno to Scholem in a letter dated April 4, 1939, cited in Theodor W. Adorno, *Beethoven: The Philosophy of Music*, edited by Rolf Tiedemann, translated by Edmund Jephcott (Stanford, 1998), p. 245 n. 305.

of the text and the idolatrous impulse to reify the Torah as the incarnate form of the divine.[3] This particular example will afford us the opportunity to evaluate Kafka's insightful remark concerning the essential connection between kabbalah as a cultural phenomenon and the attack on the borders of tradition.

Before proceeding to this issue let me make a preliminary observation with respect to the taxonomy of the term "kabbalah." In the study of the multifaceted forms of esoteric wisdom and praxis that converged and surfaced in the High Middle Ages, one must surely be on guard against reductionism. A monolithic reading that flattens all differences will not do justice to the rich legacy of kabbalists through the ages. There is a tendency in contemporary scholarship, which is a further development of the previous generation of scholars, to emphasize two main typological categories, theosophic and ecstatic, in order to control the overwhelming number of texts that one must study in the pursuit of understanding the nature of this complex phenomenon.[4] I surely would not deny the need to be mindful of concrete details in the study of kabbalah, and thereby avoid the temptation to speak of abstract generalities. I am reminded of the contrast that Abraham Isaac Kook made between "rationalist contemplation," which submerges particularities within the "universal insight," and "esotericism," which seeks to penetrate into the most minute details of the particularities.[5] Leaving aside the cogency of the distinction between philosophy and mysticism, one familiar with kabbalistic compositions cannot argue with Kook's depiction of the exacting quality of esotericism, *ha-raziyyut ha-peraṭit*.

Notwithstanding this cautionary stance, I would argue that it is still possible, indeed necessary, to isolate structural elements that are not only recurrent through generations, but which cut across typological boundaries as well.[6] Hereuistically, it has been beneficial to both professors and

---

[3] It is of interest to recall here the discussion in Maurice Blanchot, *The Space of Literature*, translated with an introduction by Ann Smock (Lincoln and London, 1982), pp. 82–83, regarding the nexus between art and idolatry, which is understood as the struggle against the imaginary, in the work of Kafka.

[4] The typological classification was employed by Gershom Scholem and it has been developed further by Moshe Idel. See Hava Tirosh-Rothschild, "Continuity and Revision in the Study of the Kabbalah," *AJS Review* 16 (1991): 174–176.

[5] Abraham Isaac Kook, *Orot ha-Qodesh*, edited by David Kohen (Jerusalem, 1969), 1: 105.

[6] For further elaboration, see Elliot R. Wolfson, *Abraham Abulafia—Kabbalist and Prophet: Hermeneutics, Theosophy, and Theurgy* (Los Angeles, 2000), pp. 1–8. The typological classification between ecstatic and theosophic kabbalah has also been challenged by reference to specific issues in the work of Ḥaviva Pedayah. See, for instance, "'Possessed by Speech:' Towards an Understanding of the Prophetic-Ecstatic Patterns among Early Kabbalists," *Tarbiz* 65 (1996): 565–636 (Hebrew); idem, "The Divinity as Place and Time and the Holy Place in Jewish Mysticism," in *Sacred Space: Shrine, City, Land: Proceedings of*

students to adopt the typological distinction between theosophic and ecstatic kabbalah, but careful study of the relevant material suggests that this classification may collapse under the weight of its own textual specificity. This is surely the case with respect to the focus of this study. I will be concentrating on zoharic literature, considered the classical example of theosophic kabbalah, which in all likelihood began to crystallize in the last decades of the thirteenth century and in the early decades of the fourteenth, but I am of the opinion that with respect to the issue before us, we can speak of an orientation shared by theosophic and ecstatic kabbalists, not to mention countless other mystics and masters of secret doctrine who do not fit neatly into either of these scholarly categories. To grasp the impulse for idolatry and the reification of Torah as an iconic object of visual contemplation is a key to appreciating the religious sensibility that informed the kabbalistic masters behind the composition of zoharic literature.

What, then, do I mean by the idolatrous impulse? Clearly, by the time classical works of kabbalah were being composed and redacted, idolatry in the technical scriptural sense of worshipping material images of other or strange gods was of no great concern; nor was the more specific rabbinic application of this term to worship of images of the stars and constellations a burning issue.[7] This is not to deny that medieval astrological ideas, and even the more pertinent astral magic, were influential in the ideational development of kabbalah.[8] Indeed, in the opinion of several medieval rabbinic authorities, which were undoubtedly known by the kabbalists, magical practices of this sort were considered idolatrous and therefore prohibited by biblical law.[9] My point is, however, that the issue of *avodah zarah*, "foreign worship," was not related primarily to astral magic in the minds of kabbalists from the period of the composition of *Zohar*.

By the term "idolatry" I wish to convey the figural envisioning of the divine, and especially the configuration of God in anthropomorphic images.[10] My assessment of zoharic texts leads me to the conclusion that

---

the International Conference in Memory of Joshua Prawer, edited by Benjamin Z. Kedar and R.J. Zwi Werblowsky (Hampshire and London, 1998), pp. 84–111.

[7] See José Faur, "The Biblical Idea of Idolatry," *Jewish Quarterly Review* 69 (1978–79): 1–15; Ephraim E. Urbach, "The Rabbinical Laws of Idolatry in the Second and Third Centuries in Light of Archaeological and Historical Facts," *Israel Exploration Journal* 9 (1959): 149–165, 229–245.

[8] For a comprehensive study of this topic, see Dov Schwartz, *Astral Magic in Medieval Jewish Thought* (Ramat-Gan, 1999), pp. 125–144 (Hebrew).

[9] Schwartz, *Astral Magic*, pp. 24, 68–72, 94–103, 136, 177–178.

[10] See Moshe Halbertal and Avishai Margalit, *Idolatry*, translated by Naomi Goldblum (Cambridge, MA, and London, 1992), pp. 37–66; Kenneth Seeskin, *No Other Gods: The Modern Struggle Against Idolatry* (West Orange, 1995), pp. 31–49.

for kabbalists in this Castilian fraternity "idol" may refer to an image, an abstract, immaterial likeness, rather than a pictorial representation or sculpted form.[11] Many scholars have noted the centrality of anthropomorphism in kabbalistic lore, which in great measure is indebted to older esoteric sources wherein the corporeal depiction of God is discernible.[12] My own contribution to this discussion has been the attempt to articulate in somewhat more elaborate phenomenological terms that the locus of these images is the human imagination.[13] That is, from the kabbalists' perspective, the divine anthropos is a symbolic image envisioned within the imaginative faculty. Just as the specular image seen in the mirror is not identical to the object of which it is an image, so the intangible image of God seen in the mirror of imagination is not identical to God. In the latter case, however, the matter is rendered far more paradoxical by the fact that for kabbalists the image is of that which has no image.[14] To say, therefore, that for kabbalists it is only through the imagination that the image of the divine anthropos is perceived is to indicate that, epistemologically, they occupy a position between the extremes of naïve realism (God is literally a body) and

---

[11] On the relationship between immaterial images and idolatry, see the pertinent remarks of William J. T. Mitchell, *Iconology: Image, Text, Ideology* (Chicago and London, 1986), pp. 31–36.

[12] I will not cite here all of the relevant sources, but let me mention the still valuable essay on the anthropomorphic depiction of God in the history of Jewish mysticism by Gershom Scholem, *On the Mystical Shape of the Godhead: Basic Concepts in the Kabbalah*, translated by Joachim Neugroschel, edited and revised by Jonathan Chipman (New York, 1991), pp. 15–55. The extent to which the anthropomorphic symbolism of the medieval kabbalah, which is based in great measure on the older *shi'ur qomah* speculation that attributed corporeal dimensions to the divine form, continues to vex the minds of contemporary scholars can be gauged from Moshe Hallamish, *An Introduction to the Kabbalah*, translated by Ruth Bar-Ilan and Ora Wiskind-Elper (Albany, 1999), p. 141: "The fact that the Kabbalists frequently felt compelled to defend the institution of *shi'ur komah* indicates that they had not abandoned the possibility of anthropomorphization. Thus, without believing in it, the Kabbalists present extensive descriptions and fantastic images of the Divine based upon parts of the human body." Why must we assume that the kabbalists did not believe in the anthropomorphic descriptions of the divine that they actively promoted? Surely, what Hallamish intended was that we could not say that the kabbalists believed that God literally has a physical body. His formulation reveals the persistent difficulty in dealing with this salient part of the tradition. The notion of the imaginal body that I have employed offers a way to get beyond the dichotomy of allegorically removing the force of the anthropomorphic speculations, on the one hand, and naïvely accepting them at face value, on the other.

[13] Elliot R. Wolfson, *Through a Speculum That Shines: Vision and Imagination in Medieval Jewish Mysticism* (Princeton, 1994).

[14] For a fascinating psychoanalytic study on the image of the mirror as mediating symbol, see Pierre Legendre, *Dieu au miroir: étude sur l'institution des images* (Paris, 1994), and the relevant material extracted from this work in *Law and the Unconscious: A Legendre Reader*, edited by Peter Goodrich, translated by Peter Goodrich with Alain Pottage and Anton Schütz (New York, 1997), pp. 211–254.

allegorical reductionism (in no way can we meaningfully attribute corpo-reality to God). God is a body paradigmatically, that is, the body in which God can be imaged is the hyperliteral pattern of the corporeal body, a body composed of the letters of the name YHWH.

It would be well to recall that in one context Scholem, reflecting both the influence of the positive philosophy of mythology enunciated by Schelling[15] and the thinking-in-images (*Bilddenken*) of Benjamin,[16] remarked that there is an inescapable conflict between "conceptual thinking" and "sym-bolic thinking" based on concrete mythical images. In the history of kab-balah, one can find evidence of both modes of thought, although, according to Scholem, the primary and dominant phenomenon is the latter. As he puts it, "The discursive thinking of the Kabbalists is a kind of asymptotic process: the conceptual formulations are an attempt to provide an approxi-mate philosophical interpretation of inexhaustible symbolic images, to interpret these images as abbreviations for conceptual series. The obvious failure of such attempts shows that images and symbols are nothing of the sort."[17] In another context, Scholem similarly speaks of two basic tenden-cies in the kabbalah, the "mystical direction expressed in images and sym-bols whose inner proximity to the realm of myth is often very striking," and the "speculative" attempt to assign "ideational meaning to the symbols." Regarding the latter, Scholem writes:

> The speculative expositions of kabbalistic teaching largely depended on the ideas of neoplatonic and Aristotelian philosophy, as they were known in the Middle Ages, and were couched in the terminology customary to these fields. Hence the cosmology of the Kabbalah is borrowed from them and is not at all original, being expressed in the common medieval doctrine of the separate intellects and the spheres. Its real originality lies in the problems that transcend this cosmology.[18]

---

[15] See Edward A. Beach, *The Potencies of Gods: Schelling's Philosophy of Mythology* (Albany, 1994), pp. 1–2, 6–13, 25–45, 226–230. On the role of imagination in Schelling's privileging of the mythopoeic over the philosophical, see John Llewelyn, *The HypoCritical Imagination: Between Kant and Levinas* (London and New York, 2000), pp. 50–68.

[16] See Sigrid Weigel, *Body- and Image-Space: Re-reading Walter Benjamin*, translated by Georgina Paul with Rachel McNicholl and Jeremy Gaines (London and New York, 1996), pp. ix–xvii, 8–11, 21–22, 49–60, 80–83. The influence of both Schelling and Benjamin on Scholem has been noted by Andreas Kilcher, *Die Spachtheorie der Kabbala als Ästhetisches Paradigma: Die Konstruktion einer Ästhetischen Kabbala Seit der Frühen Neuzeit* (Stuttgart and Weimar, 1998), pp. 45–46.

[17] Gershom Scholem, *On the Kabbalah and Its Symbolism*, translated by Ralph Manheim (New York, 1969), p. 96.

[18] Gershom Scholem, *Kabbalah* (Jerusalem, 1974), pp. 87–88. See ibid., p. 117, where Scholem concludes that the philosophers did not deal at all with the divine emanations, although the kabbalists were influenced by philosophical cosmology when discussing the

Bracketing the validity of Scholem's attempt to contrast medieval Jewish philosophy and kabbalah on these grounds, it is instructive that he expressed
himself here, in contrast to other places in his work,[19] in such a way that
images are privileged in the kabbalistic orientation. I have expanded this
approach by arguing that, by and large, kabbalists considered imagination
the divine element of soul that enables one to gain access to the invisible
by transferring or transmuting sensory data and/or rational concepts into
symbols. The primary function of imagination may be viewed as hermeneutical. Through images within the heart, the locus of imagination, the
divine, whose pure essence is incompatible with all form, is nevertheless
manifest as an imaginative presence. The enduring legacy of the prophetic
tradition that has informed and challenged Judaism as a religious culture
through the ages is that the God who cannot be depicted iconically appears
to human beings in multiple images, including, most significantly, that of
an anthropos. Moreover, the role of the imaginal, which serves as a symbolic intermediary allowing for the imaging of the imageless, is a tradition
that has its roots in biblical and rabbinic texts, although it is developed and
articulated most fully in the various strands of medieval mystical literature, including the esoteric works of the Rhineland Jewish Pietists,[20] the
theosophic kabbalah, especially zoharic literature,[21] and the prophetic kabbalah elaborated by Abraham Abulafia and his disciples.[22] The enduring
quest to attain a vision of the image of that which has no image may be
termed the impulse for idolatry. This impulse has been fed by the paradox
that the God seen is the invisible God.[23]

---

world below the last of the *sefirot*. This statement must be qualified, however, in light of
the fact that some of the early kabbalists identified either the *sefirot* collectively with the
separate intellects or one of the *sefirot* (usually the second or the tenth) with the Active
Intellect.

[19] See, for instance, *Kabbalah*, p. 370, and discussion in Wolfson, *Through a Speculum
That Shines*, pp. 278–279.

[20] Wolfson, *Through a Speculum that Shines*, pp. 188–269; idem, "Sacred Space and
Mental Iconography: Imago Templi and Contemplation in Rhineland Jewish Pietism," in *Ki
Baruch Hu: Ancient Near Eastern, Biblical, and Judaic Studies in Honor of Baruch A. Levine*,
edited by Robert Chazan, William W. Hallo, Lawrence H. Schiffman (Winona Lake, 1999),
pp. 593–634.

[21] Wolfson, *Through a Speculum That Shines*, pp. 326–392.

[22] Gershom Scholem, *Major Trends in Jewish Mysticism* (New York, 1954), pp. 138–142;
Moshe Idel, *The Mystical Experience in Abraham Abulafia* (Albany, 1988), pp. 95–105, 116–
119; Wolfson, "Sacred Space," pp. 599–600 n. 15; idem, *Abraham Abulafia*, pp. 207–209.

[23] The paradox is well captured by Edmond Jabès, *The Book of Questions*, vol. 2,
translated by Rosemarie Waldrop (Hanover and London, 1991), p. 277: "God is invisible. I

Iconic Visualization of God in Theosophic Kabbalah

Due to the limitations of space, I cannot enter into all of the complex issues related to the iconic visualization of God in the varied currents of Jewish mysticism, let alone in the more limited history of the trend of mystical speculation known in scholarly parlance as theosophic kabbalah. As I have already intimated, I am focusing on these matters as they are treated in the main body of zoharic literature, itself an immense undertaking that cannot be dealt with adequately in an essay of this length. To speak in a generalization that seems to me textually warranted, central to zoharic kabbalah is the ecstatic experience of enlightenment, that is, the visual contemplation of the divine in imagistic pictures related symbolically to the *sefirot*, the ten luminous emanations. The term *sefirot*, first employed in *Sefer Yeṣirah*, whose provenance is still a matter of scholarly dispute, is notoriously difficult to translate. Indeed, there is no consensus regarding the lexical meaning of the term. Etymologically, one may presume that the word *sefirot* derives from the root *sfr*, which can be vocalized as *sefer*, "book," but it also may be associated with the word *sappir*, "sapphire." Additionally, the root *sfr* can be vocalized as *safar*, "to count." No single word in English can adequately account for the range of semantic meaning linked to the term *sefirot*, which denotes concurrently luminosity (*sappir*), speech (*sefer*), and enumeration (*sefar*). The ecstatic experience attested in kabbalistic sources is marked by the convergence of these three fields of discourse: The divine potencies are visualized as translucent letters enumerated within the book written by God. This book, which is identified further as the most sacred of divine names, YHWH, is the text that can also be envisioned as limbs of the divine body. Alternatively expressed, the Torah, which is composed of multiple names contained within the one name, is the mirror in which the image of the imageless God appears as it is reflected in the mirror of the mystic's imagination.[24] The double mirroring aptly describes the hermeneutical condition that oriented the zoharic kabbalists on the path of poetic thinking: The text is a mirror that reflects the translucency of the reader's imagination and the reader's imagination a mirror that reflects the translucency of the text.

---

have often seen Him such as He could appear to me. All appearance manifests something invisible at the edge of horizons, which we seize by its legitimate desire to be."

[24] On the image of the double mirror, see Wolfson, "Sacred Space," p. 597. See the citation from Jabès below in n. 33.

As I have already noted, central to this trend of kabbalah is the emphasis on the pictorial configuration of the *sefirot* in the shape of an anthropos. In *Sefer ha-Bahir*, one of the earliest documents that remains a key for contemporary scholars who seek to uncover what some of the roots of the occult tradition may have been, it is presumed in an unqualified way that the potencies (*middot*) of God or the forms (*surot*) relate to the limbs of a human body; the theosophical claim is linked exegetically to the biblical notion of the divine image in which Adam was created.[25] That is, the image of God is interpreted in distinctively somatic terms. The significance of this dimension of the kabbalistic outlook is underscored in the following explanation of the fundamental commandment of Jewish monotheism, to know that there is a God, offered by Joseph of Hamadan: "The rationale for this commandment by way of kabbalah is that one should know the property of the body (*tekhunat ha-guf*) as Scripture says 'And God created Adam in his image' (Gen 1:27) so that man should know the matter of the chariot, the matter of the *sefirot*, which is the property of the body, and he should bind them for they are one form."[26]

Needless to say, many other examples could have been cited, but this one reference will suffice to make the point that the corporeal interpretation of the divine image is a basic tenet of medieval kabbalistic theosophy.[27] In the subsequent development of this literature, especially in the

---

[25] Daniel Abrams, *The Book Bahir: An Edition Based on the Earliest Manuscripts* (Los Angeles, 1994), sec. 55, p. 151, and sec. 116, p. 200 (Hebrew). For discussion of the divine forms in bahiric symbolism, see Gershom Scholem, *Origins of the Kabbalah*, edited by R. J. Zwi Werblowsky, translated by Alan Arkush (Princeton, 1987), pp. 139–142; idem, *On the Mystical Shape*, pp. 43–45; Moshe Idel, *Kabbalah: New Perspectives* (New Haven, 1988), pp. 122–128. For an analysis of this mythical symbol from a gender perspective, see Elliot R. Wolfson, "Woman—The Feminine as Other in Theosophic Kabbalah: Some Philosophical Observations on the Divine Androgyne," in *The Other in Jewish Thought and History: Constructions of Jewish Culture and Identity*, edited by Laurence J. Silberstein and Robert L. Cohn (New York and London, 1994), p. 171; idem, "Hebraic and Hellenic Conceptions of Wisdom in *Sefer ha-Bahir*," *Poetics Today* 19 (1998): 166–167.

[26] Menachem Meier, "A Critical Edition of the *Sefer Ta'amey ha-Mitzwoth* ('Book of Reasons of the Commandments') Attributed to Isaac Ibn Farhi/Section I—Positive Commandments/ With Introduction and Notes," Brandeis University, Ph. D. dissertation, 1974, p. 3.

[27] This is not to deny that in medieval kabbalistic literature we cannot find qualifications regarding the somatic interpretation of the divine image. In some sources, the rationalist standpoint, which is articulated most emphatically by Maimonides, is adopted. For instance, see *R. Moses de Leon's Sefer Sheqel ha-Qodesh*, edited by Charles Mopsik (Los Angeles, 1996), pp. 2–3 (in Hebrew); Joseph Gikatilla, *Sha'arei Orah*, edited by Joseph Ben-Shlomo, 2 vols. (Jerusalem, 1981), 1:49–51; Menaḥem Recanaṭi, *Be'ur al ha-Torah* (Jerusalem, 1961), 37b–c. See Boaz Huss, "R. Joseph Gikatilla's Definition of Symbolism and its Versions in Kabbalistic Literature," *Jerusalem Studies in Jewish Thought* 12 (1996): 157–176, esp. 160–165 (Hebrew).

fraternities of male kabbalists active in the second half of the thirteenth century in northern Spain, the anthropomorphism of the earlier tradition was articulated in more systematic or, at the very least, in more elaborate fashion. Two points that are essential to my reflections: First, the preponderant utilization of anthropomorphic imagery to depict the divine on the part of the kabbalists is predicated on the presumption that the Hebrew letters assigned to each of the relevant limbs constitutes the reality of the body on both the human and divine planes of being. For kabbalists, therefore, the use of human terms to speak about matters divine is not simply understood in the philosophical manner as an approximate way to speak of God, a concession to the inevitable limitations of embodied human beings who desire to speak of that which is disembodied.[28] On the contrary, when examined from the kabbalistic perspective, the examples of anthropomorphism in the canonical texts of the tradition employed to describe God indicate that the nature of human corporeality can only be understood in light of divine corporeality, but the body of God is constituted by the letters of the Hebrew alphabet, which are all contained in or derive from the Tetragrammaton.[29] Theosophic and prophetic kabbalists agree that the four-letter name is the root-word, the origin of all language, the mystical essence of Torah, which is envisioned concurrently in the bodily image of a human form.[30] A recurrent feature of medieval Jewish esotericism is the tradition that Torah, which is the imaginal body of God, is composed of letters of the name.[31] At a subsequent stage of this analysis I will return to the secret of this image, but suffice it here to note that the kabbalistic tradition yields a notion of a literal body, that is, a body made up of letters. This image of body transforms the corporeality of that which is incorporeal into an icon of that which is not visible.[32]

My second observation concerns the presumption that the anthropomorphic shape of the divine is configured within the imagination of the

---

[28] See David B. Burrell, *Knowing the Unknowable God: Ibn-Sina, Maimonides, Aquinas* (Notre Dame, 1986).

[29] For a fuller exploration of this theme, see Elliot R. Wolfson, "Anthropomorphic Imagery and Letter Symbolism in the *Zohar*," *Jerusalem Studies in Jewish Thought* 8 (1989): 147–181 (Hebrew).

[30] See discussion in Wolfson, *Abraham Abulafia*, pp. 56–73.

[31] The notion of body as text has to be seen against the larger philosophical background regarding verbal images. See Mitchell, *Iconology*, pp. 19–31.

[32] My formulation is indebted to the phenomenology of the invisible within the visible articulated in Jean-Luc Marion, *La croisée de visible* (Paris, 1991), as cited in Graham Ward, "The Gendered Body of the Jewish Jesus," in *Religion and Sexuality*, edited by Michael A. Hayes, Wendy Porter, and David Tombs (Sheffield, 1998), p. 176 n. 16.

mystic, primarily in the context of contemplative prayer and Torah study. The experience of union, which is so often designated as the distinctive mark of mystical experience, is affirmed in the relevant kabbalistic sources only to the extent that one cleaves to the form of God that one has visualized in one's imagination. In this state of consciousness, the phenomenal boundaries of inside and outside dissolve, for only by means of the internal image does one experience the divine as external.[33] Through the proper visual comprehension the mind or heart of the devotee becomes the throne upon which God dwells at the same time that God is transformed into the throne upon which the devotee dwells. The meeting point of the two, the holy of holies, is the nakedly garbed Torah. Through the garments of Torah, the letters that constitute the limbs of the textual body, the enlightened exegete sees the hidden light of God, which is identified as the secret in the double sense of inner reality and esoteric meaning. The critical aspect of contemplation in zoharic literature, therefore, is not union with God per se, but the anthropomorphic representation and visual apprehension of God that ensues from the state of mystical conjunction, *devequt*. I am not suggesting that the idea of *devequt* in zoharic symbolism does not relate at all to unitive experiences that could be explained both on the basis of Aristotelian epistemology and Neoplatonic ontology. My point is, rather, that the experience of union serves the ultimate goal of inducing mystical consciousness, which involves the visual comprehension of the immediate and direct presence of God as the imaginal body, a body composed of the four letters of the name, which splinter into the twenty-two letters of Torah.

My understanding of mystical contemplation as the imaginal visualization of God contrasts sharply with Scholem's characterization of meditation as it appears in kabbalistic literature from the middle of the thirteenth century as "contemplation by the intellect, whose objects are neither images nor visions, but non-sensual matters such as words, names, or thoughts."[34] I note, parenthetically, that this characterization conflicts with the view that Scholem expressed elsewhere, which I mentioned above, regarding the nature of kabbalah as a symbolic thinking based on images in contrast to the discursive thinking of philosophy based on concepts. No one could

---

[33] One is here reminded of the poetic formulation of the philosophical point offered by Edmond Jabès, *The Book of Questions*, vol. 1, translated by Rosmarie Waldrop (Hanover and London, 1991), p. 203: "'A double mirror,' he said, 'separates us from the Lord so that God sees Himself when trying to see us, and we, when trying to see Him, see only our own face.'"

[34] *Kabbalah*, p. 369, and for other relevant references in Scholem's publications, see Wolfson, "Sacred Space," p. 600 n. 16.

argue with the claim that the *sefirot*, the spiritual entities that make up the divine pleroma, constitute the ultimate object of meditation in theosophic kabbalah. The important point, however, is that these entities, whatever their ontological status vis-à-vis the infinite Godhead (the kabbalists offered two conceptual possibilities, the *sefirot* are the essence of God or they are instruments by means of which God expresses his creative potency), are phenomenally experienced only insofar as they are configured in particular sentient forms within human consciousness. Contemplation of the linguistic structures mentioned by Scholem—words, names, and thoughts—is itself dependent on imaginative visualization of these very structures. Can we in any meaningful way distinguish the verbal and visual?

One must raise questions about Scholem's sweeping attempt to contrast Christian and kabbalistic doctrines of meditation on the grounds that "in Christian mysticism a pictorial and concrete subject, such as the suffering of Christ and all that pertains to it, is given to the meditator, while in Kabbalah, the subject given is abstract and cannot be visualized, such as the Tetragrammaton and its combinations."[35] The textual evidence from kabbalists indicates just the contrary: The divine names, and especially the Tetragrammaton, serve as the object of contemplation only to the degree that they assume morphic (and, in many instances, anthropomorphic) shape in the mind of the mystic. One of the fundamental ways that this is achieved is through envisioning God's form, a basic tenet in theosophic and prophetic kabbalah. The contemplative gaze is precisely what lies at the heart of the kabbalistic conception of *kawwanah* in prayer. Indeed, some of the earliest kabbalistic documents suggest that *kawwanah*, the intentionality required in liturgical worship, was predicated on the representation of the *sefirot* as an anthropomorphic shape configured as the letters of the name YHWH within the imaginative faculty—here again we note the convergence of anthropomorphic imagery and linguistic symbolism.[36] To be sure, the conjured image is not the portrait of the suffering Christ, as Scholem remarks, but it is an anthropomorphic form that is no less graphic.

Countless examples could have been cited to support my claim, but I will mention one brief passage from a section of *Zohar* known as *Idra Zuṭa*, the "Small Gathering," which appears (undoubtedly as a consequence of the redactional process) in the culmination of the zoharic text as the final meeting of Simeon ben Yoḥai and the members of the fraternity that results

---

[35] *Kabbalah*, p. 371.
[36] Wolfson, *Through a Speculum That Shines*, pp. 288–304.

in the master's death. The relevant passage, which is cited as a quotation from the aggadah of R. Yeiva Sabba, is a mystical reflection on the name of the third emanation, *Binah*, "understanding," the mother that comes forth from and is united with the second emanation, *Ḥokhmah*, "wisdom," the father. From the union of these two emanations comes forth *Tif'eret*, "beauty," which is also depicted as the son who contains within himself *Malkhut*, "royalty," the daughter who becomes the bride of the brother/son. In the four letters of the name *Binah*, there is a reference to the quaternity of divine potencies: The *yod* and *he* refer respectively to *Ḥokhmah* and *Binah*, and the remaining consonants, *bet* and *nun*, spell *ben*, which is the son, but the latter is androgynous (in the pattern of Adam according to the first chapter of Genesis) and thus contains *bat*, the daughter, within himself. Although not stated explicitly, from other zoharic passages it is reasonable to assume that the son and daughter, *Tif'eret* and *Malkhut*, may also be symbolically marked by the last two letters of the Tetragrammaton, *waw* and *he*. The four letters of the name, therefore, correspond to the father, mother, son, and daughter. The sensitive nature of this disclosure and the implied manner of visualizing the divine is underscored by a remark contained in the zoharic text itself after the matter is brought to light: "These words cannot be revealed except to the supernal holy ones who have entered and exited and who know the ways of the blessed holy One, and they do not deviate to the right or to the left.... Praiseworthy is the lot of one who merits to know his ways, and who does not deviate from them or err with respect to them, for these matters are concealed, and the supernal holy ones are illumined by them like the one who is illumined from the flame of the candle. These words are not transmitted except to one who has entered and exited."[37]

This one example is illustrative of a larger point affirmed by the kabbalists whose opinions are preserved in the zoharic corpus as well as scores of other kabbalists who lived before and after the dissemination of this composition: The visionary imagination is informed by a confluence of letter and anthropomorphic symbolism.[38] There is no justification to Scholem's claim that in the kabbalistic approach to contemplation, in contrast to the

---

[37] *Zohar* 3:290a.

[38] The correlation of the anatomical forms and different permutations of the Tetragrammaton is especially prominent in the contemplative exercises promulgated in the name of Isaac Luria. See Lawrence Fine, "The Study of Torah as a Rite of Theurgical Contemplation in Lurianic Kabbalah," in *Approaches to Judaism in Medieval Times*, vol. 3, edited by David R. Blumenthal (Atlanta, 1988), pp. 29–40.

Christian, the "subject given is abstract and cannot be visualized, such as the Tetragrammaton and its combinations." A proper grasp of the kabbalistic material necessitates the understanding that in this contemplative practice the name is visualized in strikingly concrete and embodied terms as an anthropos, which is the incarnational form of the Torah.[39]

In the aforecited passage from *Zohar*, one is introduced as well to another critical dimension of the pictorial representation of God in somatic terms: Only one who transforms the physical body into a spiritual body—a transformation that is presented in the relevant texts as an angelification of the mystic—is capable of imaging the divine form in bodily images.[40] This is the implication of the zoharic claim that the words concerning the portrayal of God as father, mother, son, and daughter can be revealed only to the "supernal holy ones" who have entered and exited. The kabbalists who have undergone the ecstatic experience of visual contemplation in a successful manner with their faith and mental capacity intact—a point that is underscored by the use of the technical expression "to enter and to exit"[41]—are called supernal holy ones, a term that usually designates angelic beings. The application of this expression to the kabbalists signifies their transfiguration, which is expressed as well in the image of illumination. Other passages in the zoharic corpus emphasize that this transfiguration ensues from the adoption of an austere lifestyle and the consequent curtailment

---

[39] A bold formulation of the kabbalistic interpretation of Torah as the incarnate form of God is found in Menaḥem Recanaṭi, *Ṭa'amei ha-Miṣwot*, MS Vatican 209, fol. 1b: "The holy One, blessed be he, is not something apart from the Torah and the Torah is not distinct from him, and he is not something distinct from the Torah. Thus the sages of kabbalah say that the holy One, blessed be he, is the Torah." For a slightly different and, in my view, inferior version of this text see the printed edition of Recanaṭi's *Ṭa'amei ha-Miṣwot*, edited by Simḥah Lieberman (London, 1962), p. 2.

[40] Underlying the mystical conception of angelification is the kabbalistic acceptance of a much older belief regarding the notion of an astral or aetheral body. For discussion of this motif connected especially to the biblical notion of the divine image, see Scholem, *On the Mystical Shape*, pp. 251–273. See, for example, the kabbalistic fragment cited by Scholem, *Origins*, p. 291, according to which the sacred body of the righteous is said to be woven by the angels in contrast to the body of the sinner, which is said to be woven by angels of destruction. The interpretation of the plural form in the verse "Let us make Adam in our image" (Gen. 1:26) reflects the exegesis of R. Jonathan reported by R. Samuel ben Naḥman in *Genesis Rabbah*, edited by Julius Theodor and Chanoch Albeck (Jerusalem, 1965), 8:8, pp. 61–62.

[41] On this technical expression see Elliot R. Wolfson, "Forms of Visionary Ascent as Ecstatic Experience in the Zoharic Literature," in *Gershom Scholem's Major Trends in Jewish Mysticism 50 Years After: Proceedings of the Sixth International Conference on the History of Jewish Mysticism*, edited by Peter Schäfer and Joseph Dan (Tübingen, 1993), p. 211 and other references cited in n. 11 *ad locum*.

of physical desire.[42] Simply put, the ascetic negation of the physical body allows for the ocular apprehension of God's imaginal body. The mindfulness achieved by meditative ascent affirmed in zoharic texts is not a state of abstract emptiness, a peeling away of all material form from consciousness to attain the illumination of formless absorption. It is quite the opposite: Contemplation eventuates in the polishing of the mind so that reflected therein is the image of the divine anthropos.[43] From that vantage point, the mystical tradition expressed in *Zohar* retrieves the iconic representation of the divine, albeit located in the imagination.

Imaging the Imageless and the Prohibition on Pictorial Representation

On the basis of the previous discussion it may be argued that the contemplative practice, which has informed the worldview of kabbalists in a relatively persistent manner, is the visual imaging of the being to whom no image may be attributed. In the mystical vision, the imagelessness of God is not called into question. On the contrary, as I have already noted, the visual experience of kabbalists affirms the paradox that the God who is seen is invisible, for the concealed cannot be revealed unless it be revealed as the concealed that is revealed. Alternatively expressed, the *sefirot* reveal the luminous darkness of the infinite dark light, but only in such a manner that the dark light continues to be concealed as the luminous darkness.[44]

---

[42] The ascetic orientation in zoharic literature is discussed briefly by Isaiah Tishby, *The Wisdom of the Zohar*, translated by David Goldstein (Oxford, 1989), pp. 764–765, and in more detail in Elliot R. Wolfson, "Eunuchs Who Keep the Sabbath: Becoming Male and the Ascetic Ideal in Thirteenth-Century Jewish Mysticism," in *Becoming Male in the Middle Ages*, edited by Jeffrey J. Cohen and Bonnie Wheeler (New York, 1997), pp. 151–185.

[43] The point, which is so basic to understanding the phenomenological underpinning of the hermeneutical experience depicted in countless zoharic passages, is expressed concisely and clearly by the fifteenth-century Italian kabbalist, Judah Ḥayyat, in his commentary to *Ma'arekhet ha-Elohut* (Jerusalem, 1963), 143a, an anonymous treatise, probably written in Spain in the early part of the fourteenth century: "The lower anthropos is a throne for the supernal anthropos, for the physical limbs that are in him allude to the spiritual limbs above, which are the divine potencies, and not for naught does it say 'Let us make Adam in our image' (Gen. 1:26). Inasmuch as this image is the image of the spiritual, supernal anthropos, and the prophet is the physical man who, in the moment of prophecy, is almost transformed into a spiritual entity, and his external senses almost depart from him, he sees the image of an anthropos, just as he sees his image in a glass mirror."

[44] I have discussed the hermeneutical dialectic of secrecy in various publications. See, for example, Elliot R. Wolfson, "Occultation of the Feminine and the Body of Secrecy in Medieval Kabbalah," in *Rending the Veil: Concealment and Secrecy in the History of Religions*,

Kabbalistic theosophy rests on the assumption that the limitless assumes the form of the limited, and thus kabbalists understood that one of their primary religious obligations (indebted to ancient esoteric speculation, which is preserved in the *shi'ur qomah* texts, based on the ascription of corporeal dimensions to the body of the Creator) consisted of attributing measure to the Infinite (*ein sof*) by means of visually contemplating the imaginal form of the divine anthropos (*adam qadmon*). The point is made explicitly in one of the more recondite sections of the zoharic text, which deals with the entity known as the measuring-line (*qav ha-middah*), the instrument by means of which the delimiting of the limitless takes place, the emanation of the Infinite into the imaginal form that is imaged concurrently as light, letter, and limb:

> The *ayin* and *dalet* [of Deut 6:4] are enlarged, [for they spell the word] *ed* [witness] to attest about the secret of secrets, to bring forth a measure that measures the secret of faith. The one who knows this secret knows the secret of his master and inherits the two worlds, this world and the world-to-come. This measure is called the line-of-measure, and this was given to the holy, supernal sages who know the secret of their master and are occupied with his glory... and they are the true righteous ones in whom is the secret of the upper Faith. To them is given to know and to contemplate for they do not turn right or left.... The one who knows the secret of wisdom can comprehend and can produce a measure in all aspects, until he knows the supernal secrets, the secrets of his master, the secrets of wisdom so that he may know and comprehend. Fortunate is the portion of one that knows and contemplates in this world and in the world-to-come, for by means of this principle a person should arrange his feet such that he enters [from behind] the curtain and walks in a straight way. Fortunate is he in this world and in the world-come.[45]

The esoteric gnosis, which is the distinctive possession of the supernal sage who knows the secret of God, is portrayed as the process of mapping out the divine body, a process that is referred to in the above citation as the "measure that measures the secret of faith." The spiritual enlightenment of the kabbalist below parallels an ontological process above by means of which the infinite darkness is illuminated through the emanation of the sefirotic potencies. By knowing the measure by which the imaginal body of

---

edited by Elliot R. Wolfson (New York and London, 1999), pp. 113–121, and further references supplied on pp. 148–149 n. 1.

[45] *Zohar Ḥadash*, edited by Reuven Margaliot (Jerusalem, 1978), 57a. For fuller citation and analysis of this passage, see Elliot R. Wolfson, *Circle in the Square: Studies in the Use of Gender in Kabbalistic Symbolism* (Albany, 1995), pp. 72–74.

God is measured the kabbalist apprehends the secret of faith, a technical expression employed in zoharic literature to depict the divine pleroma, and related especially to the sacred coupling of male and female. It is surely not inconsequential that this task is linked exegetically to the utterance of the *shema* (Deut 6:4), the liturgical expression of the monotheistic foundation of Judaism. The kabbalist who measures the divine form through visual contemplation gives witness to the unity of God—the mystical intent of the word *ed*, "witness," which is spelled by the orthographically enlarged *ayin* of *shema* and *dalet* of *eḥad*—precisely in his discernment of the multiple powers that make up the divine realm.

What is so extraordinary about kabbalists through the generations, hardly altered by differences in time or place, is their resolute aversion to depict pictorially the symbolic images that they articulated in such overt language. In spite of the very explicit anthropomorphic nature of their reflections on the Godhead, at times embracing intense erotic imagery, kabbalists have consistently upheld the injunction against representing God graphically in bodily terms. To be sure, one finds in kabbalistic texts, both in manuscript and in print, diagrams of the divine potencies usually in the form of what has become known as the *illan ha-sefirot*, the tree of the emanations. In the wake of the spread of the complex theosophy of Lurianic kabbalah in the sixteenth and seventeenth centuries, these diagrams grew increasingly more intricate. The striking feature about these diagrams, however, is the conspicuous absence of the very anthropomorphic detail that is so prevalent in the verbal depiction of the divine that accompanies the diagrams. Typically, instead of pictures of an explicit corporeal nature, kabbalists drew abstract geometric forms, usually consisting of circles and lines, to depict the symbolic language that is patently anthropomorphic in nature. This is not to deny that there are exceptions to the rule, which indicate that certain kabbalists (or scribes who copied the relevant sources) thought it perfectly reasonable to use the outline of a human form to represent the sefirotic potencies. On the whole, however, kabbalistic sources demonstrate a remarkable reluctance to portray the divine in corporeal images, and this in spite of the fact that the symbolic language employed by kabbalists to describe God is overwhelmingly anthropomorphic in tone. For the most part the iconotropic representations were expressed in the symbolic language of imagination.

Once more we come upon an intriguing irony: The very tradition that so steadfastly preserved the prohibition against figural representation fostered a highly intense and complex anthropomorphic and sexually nuanced sketching of the divine. Abstract shapes used to depict the divine pleroma on occasion accompany kabbalistic texts, and often enough these shapes are implicitly anthropomorphic. To be more precise, the geometric shapes of the circle and line allude symbolically to the feminine and masculine potencies, and this is so both in terms of the linguistic description of these shapes and their graphic representation. The attribution of gender characteristics to the letters of the Hebrew alphabet, which is a repeated motif in kabbalistic literature, is itself predicated on the assumption that the contours of physical bodies allude to aspects of the divine body, which is always engendered in its literal embodiment.[46] Indeed, in the final analysis, the concreteness of corporeality consists in the ability to discern the semiotic underpinning of body. The example that best illustrates the convergence of anthropomorphic imagery and letter symbolism is the kabbalistic understanding of Torah as the embodied form of God to which I have already referred. The process of uncovering the form that is hidden can never be terminated for that which is uncovered has no image. The uncovering of the imageless comes by way of conjuring the image that comprises multiple images. Analogously, the disclosing of the secret ensues through a continual process of covering by producing different layers of meaning, the *levushei oraita*, "garments of Torah," according to the noteworthy locution of one zoharic passage.[47]

It may be concluded, therefore, that the unusually daring portrayal of God in anthropomorphic terms on the part of zoharic kabbalists did not seem to implicate them in crossing the line set by the traditional ban on iconic representation of the divine. On the contrary, as I have already intimated, the paradox consists of the fact that it is precisely the injunction against iconic figuration of God that unleashed such a powerful visual imagination on the part of kabbalists in their effort to chart the contours and dimensions of the divine body. There are, however, occasional indications

---

[46] See Elliot R. Wolfson, "Letter Symbolism and Merkavah Imagery in the *Zohar*," in *Alei Shefer: Studies in the Literature of Jewish Thought Presented to Rabbi Dr. Alexandre Safran*, edited by Moshe Hallamish (Ramat-Gan, 1990), pp. 195–236, esp. 215–224 (English section).

[47] *Zohar* 3:152a. In the zoharic text, the actual expression is "garment of Torah," *levusha de-oraita*, but I have taken the liberty to use the plural form. See also *Sefer Me'irat Einayim by Isaac of Acre: A Critical Edition*, edited by Amos Goldreich (Jerusalem, 1981), p. 110 (in Hebrew): "You must know that the verses, that is, the words and letters, that a man sees with his eyes are like the garment of a man that covers his body. The contextual interpretations and the commentaries are the body and the true kabbalah, the potencies, and the great and wondrous secrets that emerge from the Torah are the soul, and this is the import of what is written 'From my flesh I shall see God' (Job 19:26)." For a creative discussion of this zoharic motif, see Michael Fishbane, *The Garments of Torah: Essays in Biblical Hermeneutics* (Bloomington and Indianapolis, 1989), pp. 33–46.

that kabbalists behind the composition of *Zohar* themselves were aware of the fact that they were pushing the limit of theological discourse to the point of brushing up against the edges of idolatry.[48] It is certainly not coincidental that towards the beginning of *Idra Rabba*, the "Great Gathering," a section of zoharic literature wherein the anthropomorphic language is particularly bold, Simeon ben Yoḥai is said to have begun his exposition with the verse, "Cursed be the man who makes a sculptured or molten image, abhorred by the Lord, a craftsman's handiwork, and sets it up in secret" (Deut 27:15).[49] From the vantage point of those not illumined with mystical insight it might seem that theosophic descriptions of the divine anthropos constitute a form of idol-making, and thus the master begins his exposition with the moral exhortation against making an idol and setting it up in secret, *we-sam ba-sater.* When viewed from the perspective of the enlightened kabbalists, however, not only is the anthropomorphic representation not to be confused with idol worship in secret, but it constitutes the disclosure of the secret on the mystical path. To craft the image of God in the imagination is the paramount act of devotion that unifies the divine nature and thereby sustains the world. It would seem that it is for this reason that Simeon ben Yoḥai is adamant in his warning to members of the fraternity that they should not set up an idol in secrecy, that is, they should not reify the anthropomorphic images of God conjured within the imagination.[50] The ironic intent of this admonition, however, is that disclosure of secrets about the divine anthropos is a form of erecting an idol carved not from stone but from images in the mind. One who iconically envisions the secret must be mindful of not placing the idol in secret.

The scriptural admonition against setting up the idol in secret is transformed in the zoharic text into the exhortation to expose secrets of God on the part of the master and disciples bonded together in the mystical fraternity. R. Simeon's words are profoundly ironic, for the ostensible safeguarding of the biblical prohibition is a transvaluation of the law against idolatry.

---

[48] It must be pointed out that historically kabbalists were attacked for promoting an idolatrous theology inasmuch as the unity of God was supposedly challenged by a theosophic doctrine of multiple divine potencies and the theurgical notion of prayer based on the idea that intentionality had to be directed to different potencies. See Tishby, *Wisdom of the Zohar*, pp. 240–241.

[49] *Zohar* 3:127b–128a.

[50] Reflecting on this zoharic passage, Tishby, *Wisdom of the Zohar*, p. 287, wrote, "to take the symbols literally as denoting the actual essence of God is considered to be a form of idolatry." My own analysis agrees in part with Tishby, but I have emphasized an ironic element that overturns the verse by affirming an acceptable form of idolatry related to the anthropomorphic configuration of the divine within the imagination.

The iconic depiction of God is the decisive expression of piety. The import of the theme of idolatry in this context is elucidated by another passage wherein the inappropriate explication of secrets by uttering words of Torah that one has not understood or that one has not received from a teacher is also interpreted as a form of worshipping an idol.[51] Beyond this we may posit that the symbolic thinking of kabbalists, which involves the mythopoeic figuration of God in human form, is potentially a kind of idol-making aligned with the demonic other side. Support for this may be derived from a passage in the introduction to *Tiqqunei Zohar* wherein the admonition of Deut 27:15 is applied explicitly to one who forms a mental image of the one who has no image, not even the image of the letters or the vowel-points.[52] Idolatry is transferred from the production of material images to that of mental images that serve as the iconic representation of God. But in the aforementioned zoharic context this process is looked upon negatively as a breach with what is ritually required. What is so extraordinary about the previously cited passage from the beginning of *Idra Rabba* is the fact that the intent of the biblical injunction is turned on its head, for the seemingly idolatrous activity of the imaginative depiction of God in overtly anthropomorphic terms is presented as true worship of God in the heart, *avodah she-ba-lev*, the rabbinic idiom for liturgical service. To worship God in the heart is transmuted in the mystical tradition of zoharic kabbalah to forming a contemplative image of God in the imagination.[53]

To appreciate the exegetical impudence exemplified by this text, it is important to recall that in zoharic literature idolatry is connected symbolically to the demonic other side.[54] I will cite one critical passage from *Tiqqunei Zohar* that illumines this symbolic nexus:

---

[51] *Zohar* 2:87a.

[52] *Tiqqunei Zohar*, Introduction, 6b.

[53] As stated, one can perceive the gap separating the zoharic ideal of imaginal contemplation and the contemplative ideal proffered by Maimonides, which necessitates a gradual stripping away of all images to the point of intellectual conjunction. Maimonides himself, however, recognized the ultimate necessity of the imagination, and his use of the parable of the king's palace towards the end of the *Guide* (III.51) to depict various social groups and their relationship to God suggests that he, too, could not rid himself of the imagination in the effort to communicate what he considered to be religious truth. The parable as figurative trope depends on imagination. See José Faur, *Homo Mysticus: A Guide to Maimonides's Guide for the Perplexed* (Syracuse, 1999), pp. 55–88; Lenn E. Goodman, "Maimonides and the Philosophers of Islam: The Problem of Theophany," in *Judaism and Islam Boundaries, Communication and Interaction: Essays in Honor of William M. Brinner*, edited by Benjamin H. Hary, John L. Hayes, and Fred Astren (Leiden: Brill, 2000), pp. 279–301.

[54] This idea is expressed in pre-zoharic kabbalistic sources. See, for instance, the interpretation of *elohim aherim* given by Naḥmanides in his commentary to Exod 20:3, in *Perush ha-Ramban al ha-Torah*, edited by Ḥayyim D. Chavel, 2 vols. (Jerusalem, 1984), 1:390:

The spine is called back (*aḥor*) from the side of the moon, but from the side of the middle pillar it is called front (*qedem*). The secret of the matter is "You formed me from before and behind" (Ps 139:5), and in the exile "He has withdrawn his right hand in the presence of the foe" (Lam 2:3). Who is the foe? This is Samael, for all other gods (*elohim aḥerim*) are from behind (*le-aḥor*). In order not to gaze upon *Shekhinah* in the west, which is the back (*aḥor*), one must place her to the right. Therefore, it is forbidden to pray to the west, which is the back, for other gods are there, and Saturn is there, the elixir of death. Because she was first in the west and then turned to the right, the other gods inquire of her, "Saturn (*shabbetai*), where is Sabbath (*ayyeh shabbat*)?" The letters of *shabbetai* are *ayyeh shabbat.*[55]

The place of the *Shekhinah* is in the west,[56] which is the back (*aḥor*), but this is also the region of the other gods (*elohim aḥerim*), the demonic potencies led by Samael. The latter is identified as Saturn, a planet that is frequently depicted in malevolent terms, the astrological maleficus.[57]

"Know that in every place that Scripture mentions 'other gods' the intent is to those other than the glorious name (*shem ha-nikhbad*)." Inasmuch as the "glorious name" refers to *elohim*, which is the name associated with *Shekhinah* (for references see Elliot R. Wolfson, "By Way of Truth: Aspects of Naḥmanides' Kabbalistic Hermeneutic," *Association for Jewish Studies Review* 14 [1989]: 142 n. 109), it stands to reason that Naḥmanides intends that the other gods denote the demonic powers extrinsic to the divine presence. Naḥmanides alludes to this kabbalistic secret in the continuation of this passage, op. cit., p. 391: "By way of truth, understand the secret of the face (*panim*), and Scripture exhorted with respect to this revelation 'The Lord spoke to you face to face' (Deut 5:4), and know the secret of the word 'others' (*aḥerim*), and the whole verse can be understood according to its literal and plain sense." The face of God denotes the unity of male and female, a mystery conveyed more patently by the expression "face to face," *panim be-fanim*, whereas the back, *aḥor*, relates to other gods, *elohim aḥerim*, demonic forces that stand outside the realm of holiness. Halbertal and Margalit, *Idolatry*, pp. 194–195, explain the interpretation of "other gods" in Naḥmanides as a reference to the sin of separating the divine potencies into autonomous powers. See citation of Isaac of Acre below at n. 75. While it is certainly true that there is an intricate relationship between the activity of cutting the shoots and empowering the demonic realm, I think the reader would have been better served had Halbertal and Margalit at least noted that Naḥmanides is also hinting at the notion of a force of impurity that can act autonomously or at least in opposition to the force of purity. The allusion to a demonic force is also apparent in the interpretation of the scapegoat to Azazel that Naḥmanides offers in his commentary on Lev 16:8, in *Perush ha-Ramban al ha-Torah*, 2:88–91. On the attribution of traditions concerning the demonic to Naḥmanides, see Scholem, *Origins*, p. 297 n. 192, and reference cited there to one of his earlier studies. For a less dualistic approach, see Chayim Henoch, *Nachmanides Philosopher and Mystic: The Religious Thought of Nachmanides From His Exegesis of the Mitzvot* (Jerusalem, 1978): 414–427 (Hebrew).

[55] *Tiqqunei Zohar*, sec. 21, 56b.

[56] Babylonian Talmud, Baba Batra 25a.

[57] The negative connotations of Saturn are attested in the astrological ruminations preserved in older rabbinic sources. For example, see *Pesiqta Rabbati*, edited Meir Friedmann (Vienna, 1880), 20, 96a. In that context, Saturn is associated with the view that in the future the nations of the world would rule over Israel. Louis Ginzberg, *The Legends*

The letters of the Hebrew name for this planet, *shabbetai*, can be transposed into the expression *ayyeh shabbat*, "where is Sabbath?" This play on words denotes that the demonic force of Saturn is the antithesis of the holy force of Sabbath.[58] Given the identification of Samael as the archon of Esau,[59] and the further identification of Esau as Christianity in medieval rabbinic sources,[60] it is reasonable to surmise that implicit in this passage is the presumption that Saturn is Jesus, the demonic power that is the ontological source of idolatry. If my surmise is correct, then it stands to reason that the position adopted here is one of radical dichotomization of the holy and the impure, Sabbath and Sabbatai. According to another zoharic passage, however, the word for idol, *pesel*, is interpreted as the "refuse of

---

of the Jews, 6 vols. (Philadelphia, 1968), 5:405 n. 72, mentions a legend reported by a number of medieval rabbinic sources according to which Moses chose Saturday as the day of rest since this is presumed to be the unlucky day of Saturn. On the negative portrayal of Saturn, see also *Baraita de-Mazzalot*, in *Battei Midrashot*, edited by Solomon Wertheimer, 2 vols. (Jerusalem, 1980), 2: 35. Interestingly, there are astrological sources from antiquity and the middle ages wherein the "black star" of Saturn, identified as well in some contexts as the abode of the devil, is depicted as the star of Israel, a view enhanced by the fact that the Jewish Sabbath is on Saturday, which is Saturn's day. See sources and discussion in Carl G. Jung, *Aion: Researches into the Phenomenology of the Self*, translated by R. F. C. Hull, second edition (Princeton, 1979), pp. 74–76. The tradition that Saturn is the patron of Israel is found in Samuel ibn Zarza; see Schwartz, *Astral Magic*, p. 164. It must be pointed out, however, that the same author preserves the negative portrayal of Saturn as a destructive force; see op. cit., p. 149. See also op. cit., pp. 277–278. On the nexus between Saturn and the disclosure of secrets, see the passage of ibn Zarza cited by Schwartz, op. cit., p. 119. A link between Saturn and Sabbath is also found in some medieval kabbalistic texts such as the anonymous *Sefer ha-Temunah*. See Ḥaviva Pedayah, "Sabbath, Saturn, and the Diminution of the Moon—The Sacred Conjunction: Sign and Image," *Eshel Beer-Sheva* 4 (1996): 143–191 (Hebrew). On the link between Saturn and the moon, see sources cited and discussed by Carl G. Jung, *Mysterium Coniunctionis: An Inquiry into the Separation and Synthesis of Psychic Opposites in Alchemy*, translated by R. F. C. Hull, second edition (Princeton, 1970), p. 175 n. 358. On the destructive and melancholic power of Saturn combined with the messianic character of this planet, which were assigned especially to Sabbatai Ṣevi, see Moshe Idel, "Saturn and Sabbatai Tzevi: A New Approach to Sabbateanism," in *Toward the Millennium: Messianic Expectations From the Bible to Waco*, edited by Peter Schäfer and Mark R. Cohen (Leiden, 1998), pp. 173–202; idem, *Messianic Mystics* (New Haven and London, 1998), pp. 192–195.

58 For an elaborate account of the dark side of Saturn, see *Zohar* 3:227b (*Ra'aya Meheimna*). The antithesis of Samael and Sabbath is emphasized elsewhere in zoharic literature. For example, see *Zohar* 3:243a (*Ra'aya Meheimna*).

59 For references to this motif in rabbinic and zoharic sources, see Elliot R. Wolfson, "Re/membering the Covenant: Memory, Forgetfulness, and the Construction of History in the *Zohar*," in *Jewish History and Jewish Memory: Essays in Honor of Yosef Hayim Yerushalmi*, edited by Elisheva Carlebach, John M. Efron, and David M. Myers (Hanover and London, 1998), pp. 237 n. 40.

60 See Gerson D. Cohen, *Studies in the Variety of Rabbinic Culture* (Philadelphia, 1991), pp. 243–269, esp. 259–260.

holiness" (*pesolet di-qedushah*), which is the secret of the other gods.[61] By identifying the object of idol worship in this manner, there is an attempt to avoid positing an absolute metaphysical dualism, for the demonic force is perceived as the dross of the holy realm rather than an autonomous, sinister power.[62] To be sure, this very term demarcates the difference between the two realms, for one who worships idols is involved with the refuse of holiness and not with the spark of holiness itself. Nevertheless, the notion of the refuse of holiness problematizes the hard and fast polarization of the two realms.[63]

What, then, does it mean for a Jewish male to give way to his temptation for idol worship by occupying himself with the dregs of the sacred? To understand this it is necessary to recall that the nexus between idolatry and the demonic in zoharic literature is expressed as well in terms of sexual deviancy, which is related more specifically to the Jewish male entering the holy covenant inscribed on the penis into the unholy space of the Gentile woman, the embodiment of the feminine aspect of the demonic who assumes the posture of the seductress.[64] Indeed, the biblical command against turning toward idols (Lev 19:4) is interpreted in one zoharic passage as a prohibition of gazing upon the women of the nations lest the Jewish male become sexually aroused.[65] Based on the biblical linkage of idolatry as the worship of a foreign god and adultery as having intercourse with the woman from the other nations, in *Zohar* we find an unequivocal description of idolatry as the lust for the forbidden woman.[66] In another part of the aforecited passage from *Tiqqunei Zohar*, the desecration of Sabbath by carrying into the public domain (*reshut ha-rabbim*) is equated with having intercourse with the prostitute and thereby defiling the sign of

---

[61] *Zohar* 2:91a.

[62] The less dualistic approach to *elohim aḥerim* is accentuated in Gikatilla, *Sha'arei Orah*, 2:17–19. On Gikatilla's view regarding the nature of evil, see Scholem, *On the Mystical Shape*, pp. 78–81; Ephraim Gottlieb, *Studies in the Kabbala Literature*, edited by Joseph Hacker (Tel-Aviv, 1976), pp. 278–279 (Hebrew); Ben-Shlomo, "Introduction," in Gikatilla, *Sha'arei Orah*, 1:34–39.

[63] On the tension between the monistic and dualistic approaches to the problem of evil in zoharic kabbalah, see Tishby, *Wisdom of the Zohar*, pp. 450–458.

[64] *Zohar* 1:38b; 2:87b; Tishby, *Wisdom of the Zohar*, pp. 461, 468–469. In *Zohar* 3:42a, the ingestion of forbidden foods on the part of a Jew is considered to be idolatry since the line separating holy and demonic is crossed in a manner that is analogous to a Jewish man having sexual relations with a Gentile woman.

[65] *Zohar* 3:84a.

[66] *Zohar* 1:38b; 2:90a.

the covenant by placing it in the domain of the other power.[67] Insofar as Sabbath is on a par with all Torah, an older rabbinic dictum utilized in this later kabbalistic work,[68] the point of this comment is to underscore the extent to which the worship of the false god is intertwined with the Jewish male's lust for the harlot, which in this context is limited more specifically to a Gentile woman whose soul derives from the demonic.[69] Moreover, inasmuch as the zoharic kabbalists, in line with a number of medieval rabbinic authorities, considered Christianity as opposed to Islam idolatrous,[70] it makes perfectly good sense for the misguided eros to be associated more specifically with the desire of the male Jew for the Christian woman. Fornication with a Christian woman has the same effect as sexual intercourse with one's wife during her menstrual period, for the holy covenant is defiled and the offspring of such a union partakes ontologically of the impure spirit.[71] Promiscuous sexual behavior and idolatrous religious practices were thus understood as forms of seduction by the serpentine feminine impurity that lead to the desecration of the male body of the Jew made in the image of God.[72]

Another dimension of the nexus between idolatry and the erotic yearning for the demonic other in zoharic literature (attested in other kabbalistic sources) is the view of idol worship as creating a separation of the male and female within the Godhead. The act of separation is understood more precisely as an expression of the impulse to reify *Shekhinah*, the feminine aspect of the divine.[73] A significant aspect of kabbalistic symbolism, which

---

[67] *Tiqqunei Zohar*, sec. 21, 57a–b. On the utilization of the rabbinic category of *reshut ha-rabbim* as a sign for the alienation of exile, see Pinchas Giller, *The Enlightened Will Shine: Symbolization and Theurgy in the Later Strata of the Zohar* (Albany, 1993), p. 41.

[68] Palestinian Talmud, Berakhot 1:7, 3c; Nedarim 3:14, 38b; *Exodus Rabbah* 25:12.

[69] In *Zohar* 1:38b, idolatry is designated the "foreign fear" and is identified further as the prostitute (*eshet zenunin*). See also *Zohar* 2:148b, 245a.

[70] *Mishnah im Perush Rabbenu Mosheh ben Maimon: Seder Nezikin*, edited by Joseph Kafiḥ (Jerusalem, 1965), Avodah Zarah 1:3, p. 225; *Mishneh Torah*, Avodat Kokhavim 9:4.

[71] *Zohar* 1:131b; 2:87b; Moses de León, *Mishkan ha-Edut*, MS Berlin, Staatsbibliothek Or. Quat. 833, fols. 26a–27a; *The Book of the Pomegranate: Moses de León's Sefer ha-Rimmon*, edited by Elliot R. Wolfson (Atlanta, 1988), pp. 212–213; Wolfson, "Remembering the Covenant," pp. 216–224.

[72] The *Zohar* repeatedly links sexual relations with Gentile women and idolatry (understood as the worship of the other god of the demonic realm). For references, see Wolfson, "Re/membering the Covenant," p. 235 n. 33. On the worship of idols as a contamination of the Jewish male body, see *Book of the Pomegranate*, pp. 268–269.

[73] According to the formulation adopted by some kabbalists, informed by the statement in *Sefer Yeṣirah* regarding the ten *sefirot* "ten and not nine, ten and not eleven" (1:4), one must be careful not to cut off the first of the *sefirot, Keter*, just as one must be careful not to

is not always appreciated by contemporary scholars and especially those who want to assuage the androcentricism of the tradition, is the following asymmetry: Even though the unity of God is repeatedly pitched as the union of male and female, only the worship of the female in exclusion of the male is portrayed as idolatry. Foreign worship, *avodah zarah*, consists of venerating *Shekhinah* in isolation from the rest of the sefirotic emanations.[74] The point is captured succinctly in a remark by Isaac of Acre, a kabbalist more or less contemporary with the zoharic circle. In his effort to explain the kabbalistic intent of the commentary of Naḥmanides on the verse "You shall have no other gods besides me" (Exod 20:3), Isaac writes: "I say with all the paltriness of intellect that is in me that all the effort of the master was to allude in the secret of 'You shall have no other gods besides me' that one should not cut the shoots and not separate [the attribute of] *Aṭarah* in thought, and one should not direct intention to her alone through sacrifices or prayer, but only in the unity of the edifice (*yiḥud ha-binyan*)."[75] The "strange worship" of idolatry is interpreted as the estrangement of the female (designated by the term *aṭarah*, literally, the diadem) from the rest of the emanations, the reification of the feminine potency as an object of liturgical worship. One must not offer sacrifice or prayer to *Shekhinah* when she is detached from the rest of the *sefirot*, which are referred to as *binyan*, the edifice.[76] The kabbalistic perspective on idolatry, Naḥmanides explained, is that it is an act of heresy, a "cutting of the shoots" that creates a rupture in the letters of the divine name, a theme that is related to the major accounts of sin in the biblical text, including the eating of the fruit of the Tree of Knowledge in the Garden of Eden, the building of the Tower of Babel, and the creation of the Golden Calf.[77] The danger connected to the idolatrous act centers around the male need to worship the female in isolation. To appreciate the psychological element implicit in this reification,

---

isolate the last of them, *Shekhinah*. See, for instance, the commentary of Azriel of Gerona to the relevant passage in *Sefer Yeṣirah* in *Kitvei Ramban*, edited by Ḥayyim D. Chavel, 2 vols. (Jerusalem, 1982), 2:454.

[74] A sustained discussion of this theme is found in *sha'ar ha-harisah*, the chapter on heresy, in *Ma'arekhet ha-Elohut*, 113a–134a.

[75] *Sefer Me'irat Einayim*, p. 105.

[76] To appreciate the kabbalistic application of the term *binyan* to the totality of the *sefirot*, one must bear in mind that this edifice is shaped by the fourfold structure of the letters of the name. For a perceptive insight regarding the relationship of the Tetragrammaton to the fourfold cosmological pattern, see Pedaya, "Divinity as Place and Time," pp. 89–90.

[77] See Tishby, *Wisdom of the Zohar*, pp. 374–376; Halbertal and Margalit, *Idolatry*, pp. 190–201.

one must bear in mind that *Shekhinah* is viewed as the focal point of *tefillah*, worship,[78] and *qiyyum miṣwot*, fulfillment of ritual obligations.[79] A common denominator thus exists between pious devotion and idolatrous worship inasmuch as both acts are directed toward the feminine potency. The key difference lies, however, in the insistence that piety as opposed to idolatry involves the mystery of faith, which is dependent on maintaining the unity of the masculine and feminine aspects of God. I have argued in a number of studies that this unity ultimately entails the ontic restoration of the female to the male, an ontological principle linked exegetically to the scriptural notion (attested in the second account of creation) that the female is constructed out of the male body, an androcentric conception that defies logic and experience.[80] Nevertheless, to achieve this state of restoration it is necessary to unite the female and male. Idol worship is predicated on keeping these forces separate.

The lust for the other is the thread that ties together the two explanations of idolatry, to wit, the worship of the feminine aspect of holiness alienated from the masculine, on the one hand, and the worship of the feminine aspect of the demonic as a goddess worthy of obeisance, on the other. The theosophical significance of idolatry, therefore, is the reification of the feminine, which expresses itself in one of the two ways that I have mentioned. When the matter is examined in this way, one may conclude that there is no substantial difference between *Shekhinah* and Lilith, the female on the side of holiness and the female on the side of impurity.[81] Any attempt to treat the feminine in isolation from the masculine is heresy, an infringement on the monotheistic mystery of faith. The idolatrous reification of the feminine as an autonomous power can be applied as well to Torah, which is depicted in several key passages in *Zohar* (based on much earlier sources) as the female persona of the divine.[82] The ontic identification

---

[78] See Elliot R. Wolfson, "Mystical-Theurgical Dimensions of Prayer in *Sefer ha-Rimmon*," in *Approaches to Judaism in Medieval Times*, vol. 3, edited by David R. Blumenthal (Atlanta, 1988), pp. 41–79, esp. 52–56.

[79] *Book of the Pomegranate*, pp. 59–62 (English introduction).

[80] For a representative sampling of some of my studies that have dealt with this topic, see "Woman—The Feminine as Other," *Circle in the Square*, pp. 79–121; "Tiqqun ha-Shekhinah: Redemption and the Overcoming of Gender Dimorphism in the Messianic Kabbalah of Moses Ḥayyim Luzzatto," *History of Religions* 36 (1997): 289–332; "Constructions of the Feminine in the Sabbatian Theology of Abraham Cardoso, with a Critical Edition of *Derush ha-Shekhinah*," *Kabbalah: A Journal for the Study of Jewish Mystical Texts* 3 (1998): 11–143.

[81] Tishby, *Wisdom of the Zohar*, pp. 376–379.

[82] On the female imaging of Torah in rabbinic and kabbalistic sources, see Wolfson, *Circle in the Square*, pp. 1–28, and notes on pp. 123–140; idem, *Through a Speculum That Shines*, pp. 385–386.

of Torah and God, a basic hermeneutical axiom uniformly posited by kab-balists, has the potential to foster the tendency on the part of Jewish men to treat the scroll of Torah as a fetishist object of erotic imagination. As a consequence of this desire, Torah would be turned into an idol, a *pesel*,[83] a piece cut off from the whole.[84] In the following remark, Joseph of Hamadan underscores the intricate nexus between idolatry as the exclusive worship of the feminine and the idealization of Torah:

> Know that this matter "You shall have no other gods besides me" (Exod 20:3) corresponds to *Ze'eir Anpin*, the attribute of *Malkhut*, which is the secret of the bride, for one should not separate her from the bridegroom, the king, Lord of hosts. One should not make of it a form unto itself or a god unto itself, and one should not cut the shoots... and the one who worships this attribute and makes of her a thing unto itself worships idolatry. Concerning this the verse says "You shall have no other gods besides me." And it is written "You shall not make for yourself a sculptured image (*pesel*) or any likeness" (ibid., 20:4), that is, one should not decree (*yifsol*) in one's mind to worship anything but the unique name (*shem ha-meyuhad*).... This is what Jeremiah, may peace be upon him, alluded to in his book, "The children gather sticks, [the fathers build the fire, the mothers knead dough, to make cakes] for the queen of heaven" (Jer 7:18), [the expression *milekhet ha-shamayim*] is missing an *alef*,[85] [for this alludes to] the queen of heaven, which is the second cherub, the secret of the bride, the community of Israel, for their intention was to worship this attribute and it was considered as if they worshipped idols. This is the secret that when the Torah was given to Moses our master, peace be upon him, it was said "do not go near a woman" (Exod 19:15), this is *Shekhinah*, and corresponding to this it says "For you must not worship the other god, for the Lord, whose name is jealousy, is a jealous God" (ibid. 34:14). Not for naught is [the word] "jealousy" (*qanna*) used here, for jealousy (*qin'ah*) is found in relation to a man's wife.[86]

Idolatry, or the worship of other gods, is interpreted as the veneration of the bride, referred to by the technical terms *Ze'eir Anpin* and *Malkhut*,[87]

---

[83] It is of interest to consider the description of the first tablets inscribed by the finger of God (Exod 32:16) in *Zohar* 2:84b.

[84] On the feminine figure of the divine, with specific reference to the iconic representation bordering ostensibly on idolatry, see Charles Mopsik, *Le Zohar: Lamentations* (Paris, 2000), pp. 36–46, esp. 41–42.

[85] The assumption is that the correct spelling should be *mele'khet*, the constructive form of the nominative *mela'khah*, which signifies "work" or "labor."

[86] MS Paris, Bibliothèque Nationale, héb. 817, fol. 141b.

[87] In the works of Joseph of Hamadan, the expression *ze'eir anpin*, the "smaller countenance," refers symbolically to the feminine *Shekhinah*, in contrast to zoharic literature where it refers to the masculine potency, either *Tif'eret* or the emanations from Ḥokhmah to Yesod. See Idel, *Kabbalah: New Perspectives*, pp. 134–135; Yehuda Liebes, *Studies*

separated from the bridegroom. In a fascinating inversion, the notion of an idol, *pesel*, is related to the mandate to craft in mind (*yifsol be-maḥashavto*) the true object of supplication, the *shem meyuḥad*, YHWH, for this name signifies the masculine potency that contains the feminine within itself. Joseph of Hamadan perceptively interprets the biblical account that at Sinai the Israelite men were prohibited from touching a woman as a warning against worshipping *Shekhinah* in isolation from the male. There is an implicit spiritual danger in the revelation of Torah, for it can lead to the reification of the feminine as a distinct object of idolization. Kabbalists were especially cognizant of this peril since their contemplative envisioning was so tied up with the feminine potency. It will be recalled that in the celebrated parable of the beautiful maiden in the *Zohar*, the ultimate stage of interpretation, revealing the secret, is depicted as a face to face union of lover and maiden, exegete and Torah.[88] Hence, the dramatization of Torah as an erotic object does not yield reification of the feminine isolated from the masculine, for the ideal calls for unification of feminine with masculine. That this union is thoroughly androcentric, however, is attested by the fact that the exegete is called the "husband of Torah" and "master of the house," terms that suggest that the feminine Torah is subordinate to the masculine exegete after she has successfully enticed him to know her face to face.[89]

By way of summary, it may be said that looming in the center of the zoharic kabbalists' worldview is the visual contemplation of the image of that which has no image, the doubling of vision that renders visible the invisible in the invisibility of the visible, a revelation that reveals itself in the laying bare of that which is withheld. Just as the name of God is both hidden and revealed, the former corresponding to YHWH and the latter to Adonai, so the Torah, which is identical with the name, is concurrently concealed and disclosed.[90] Indeed, all the matters of this world and the supernal world are hidden and revealed. The example of the name illumines the impenetrable depth of the paradox: ultimately there are not two names, but one name, for the very name that is written YHWH is pronounced Adonai. Analogously, the images by which the imageless God is manifest preserve

---

in the Zohar, translated by Arnold Schwartz, Stephanie Nakache, and Penina Peli (Albany, 1993), pp. 105–107; Charles Mopsik, *Les Grands textes de la Cabale: les rites qui font dieu* (Paris, 1992), p. 214 n. 34.

[88] Several scholars have discussed this section of zoharic literature. For a selective list of some of the relevant sources, see Wolfson, "Occultation of the Feminine," p. 115 n. 4.

[89] See Wolfson, *Through a Speculum That Shines*, p. 388.

[90] *Zohar* 3:159a, 230b.

the imagelessness of the divine reality just as the exoteric sense of Torah sustains the esoteric meaning by masking it in the guise of that which it is not. The image conjured in the imagination is the medium through which that which has no image appears in the image of the truth that preserves the truth of the image. It would seem that it is for this reason that Simeon ben Yoḥai was adamant in his warning to members of the fraternity that they should not set up an idol in secrecy, that is, they should not reify the anthropomorphic images of God that are invoked within the imagination in the effort to envision the form of that which has no form. Disclosure of secrets is itself a form of fashioning an icon of the divine anthropos from mental images that is to be distinguished from erecting an idol carved from material stones. One may not build an idol in secrecy, but secrecy demands that one construct an icon in the imagination.

ICONIC VISUALIZATION AND THE IMAGINAL BODY OF GOD: THE ROLE OF INTENTION IN THE RABBINIC CONCEPTION OF PRAYER*

Elliot R. Wolfson

God Incarnate: Beyond the Rhetoric of Anthropomorphic Representation

The general impression that one gets from historians of religion is that Judaism has officially rejected incarnation as a legitimate theological position. Indeed, a commonplace in scholarly literature, reflected as well in popular consciousness, is that one of the critical theological differences between Judaism and Christianity lies precisely in the fact that the latter officially adopted (after the middle of the third century) as a central tenet the belief in the incarnation of God in the body of Jesus. As stated in the council of Nicaea in 325, Jesus Christ, the only Son of God, is "of the same substance" (*homoousios*) as God the Father. Whatever Judaic elements helped give shape to the early formation of Christianity, it is presumed that this particular dimension of the nascent religion could not have been derived from Judaism inasmuch as the latter rejects the corporeal imaging of God and the more radical claim that God can inhabit a body.[1] Judged from the Judaic perspective, therefore, the Christological doctrine of incarnation, which Gregory of Nyssa aptly called the "mystery of our faith,"[2] is a scandalous blasphemy that undermines scriptural monotheism.[3]

---

* This article was first published as Elliot R. Wolfson, "Iconic Visualization and the Imaginal Body of God: The Role of Intention in the Rabbinic Conception of Prayer," *Modern Theology* 12 (1996): 137–162.

[1] This is not, of course, the perception of all Christian authorities for some located the roots of the Christological doctrines in Judaism and thus tried to support their arguments with scriptural prooftexts. See R. L. Wilken, *The Myth of Christian Beginnings* (Notre Dame, 1980), pp. 87–94; J. Herrin, *The Formation of Christendom* (Princeton, 1987), pp. 96–97. Other thinkers maintained that the truth of incarnation depended on faith alone, even if the doctrines of the divine Logos and of the Holy Spirit were based on Hebrew Scripture. See J. Pelikan, *Christianity and Classical Culture: The Metamorphosis of Natural Theology in the Christian Encounter with Hellenism* (New Haven, 1993), pp. 187 and 318.

[2] See Pelikan, *Christianity and Classical Culture*, pp. 119, 264–267, 284–285.

[3] See, for example, H. J. Schoeps, *The Jewish-Christian Argument: A History of Theologies in Conflict* (New York, 1963), pp. 23–25; M. Wyschogrod, *The Body of Faith Judaism*

Thus far the stereotypical characterization of Judaism and Christianity. Like most stereotypes there is a measure of truth to this one, but it is grossly oversimplified. While it may be valid to conclude that the particular expression of incarnation in Christianity has neither precedent in the ancient Israelite religion nor parallel in any of the varieties of Judaism in late antiquity that were contemporaneous with the emerging religion, this does not mean that the doctrine of incarnation in general is antithetical to Judaism. On the contrary, as Jacob Neusner has observed, the idea of incarnation unique to Christianity should be viewed as the "particular framing" of the conception of incarnation that was idiomatic to various Judaic authors.[4] By reclaiming the significance of incarnation in the history of Judaism, therefore, one can simultaneously acknowledge the common ground and the uniqueness of this doctrine in the two religious cultures.

To appreciate the place that the concept of incarnation occupies in the spiritual economy of Judaism, one must relate this particular issue to the larger problem of anthropomorphism, the figural representation of God in human terms. In his book on the incarnation of God in formative rabbinic Judaism, Neusner begins with this obvious point: "Anthropomorphism forms the genus of which incarnation constitutes a species."[5] In the history of Judaism the problem of anthropomorphism has been directly related to the question of iconic representation.[6] According to a growing consensus in biblical scholarship, textual and archaeological evidence indicates that for the ancient Israelites the issue was not God's corporeality, but the problem of materially representing the divine in corporeal images.[7] The official cult, already in the early monarchic period, was aniconic, but this aniconism did not imply the incorporeality of God. Recently it has even been suggested that the prohibition of iconic representation was related to the

---

as Corporeal Election (New York, 1983), pp. xv, 11, 95, 113, 138, 212–213; S. S. Schwarzschild, "De Idololatria," in Procedings of the Academy for Jewish Philosophy, ed. D. Novak and N. M. Samuelson (Lanham, 1992), pp. 223–225.

[4] J. Neusner, The Incarnation of God: The Character of Divinity in Formative Judaism (Philadelphia, 1988), p. 6.

[5] Ibid., p. 11.

[6] See E. R. Wolfson, Through a Speculum That Shines: Vision and Imagination in Medieval Jewish Mysticism (Princeton, 1994), pp. 33–51. In the history of Christianity as well, the doctrine of incarnation was the ultimate justification for the iconic representation of Christ in human form. See Herrin, Formation of Christendom, pp. 333, 344–345.

[7] See J. Glen Taylor, "The Two Earliest Known Representations of Yahweh," in Ascribe to the Lord: Biblical and Other Studies in Memory of Peter C. Craigie, ed. L. Eslinger and G. Taylor (Sheffield, 1988), pp. 557–566.

taboo of seeing and portraying God's phallus.[8] Of late a variety of scholars have also reexamined the centrality of anthropomorphic representation in the mythic imagination of the rabbis.[9] Although it is premature to speak of a scholarly consensus in this area, we may refer to a new paradigm that is emerging with respect to our appreciation of the mythopoeic nature of rabbinic theological pronouncements.

But what of the notion of incarnation itself: Is there any evidence that belief in divine incarnation is part and parcel of the patrimony of ancient Israelite faith, which served in turn as the basis for subsequent developments in the history of Judaism? The scholar who has dealt with this question in the most systematic way is Neusner, to whose work I have already referred. Yet, as I pointed out in my review of Neusner's monograph,[10] the word "incarnation" is used by him to refer to the representation of God in human form.[11] Incarnation is thus reduced to a rhetorical trope, for to speak

---

[8] See H. Eilberg-Schwartz, "The Problem of the Body for the People of the Book," in *People of the Body: Jews and Judaism from an Embodied Perspective*, ed. H. Eilberg-Schwartz (Albany, 1992), pp. 17–46, and idem, *God's Phallus and Other Problems for Men and Monotheism* (Boston, 1994). Independently, I have explored the phallomorphic nature of the visionary encounter with God in Jewish mystical literature, based in great measure on the earlier biblical and rabbinic sources. See reference to my book given in n. 6.

[9] See M. Idel, *Kabbalah: New Perspectives* (New Haven, 1988), pp. 38–39, 113–122, 128–136, 156–172; idem, *Golem Jewish: Magical and Mystical Traditions on the Artificial Anthropoid* (Albany, 1990), pp. 27–43; D. Boyarin, *Intertextuality and the Reading of Midrash* (Bloomington, 1990); idem, *Carnal Israel: Reading Sex in Talmudic Culture* (Berkeley, 1993); M. Fishbane, "Some Forms of Divine Appearance in Ancient Jewish Thought," in *From Ancient Israel to Modern Judaism: Intellect in Quest of Understanding: Essays in Honor of Marvin Fox*, ed. J. Neusner, E. S. Frerichs, and N. M. Sarna (Atlanta, 1989), 2:261–270; idem, "The 'Measures' of God's Glory in the Ancient Midrash," in *Messiah and Christos: Studies in the Jewish Origins of Christianity Presented to David Flusser on the Occasion of His Seventy-Fifth Birthday*, ed. I. Gruenwald, S. Shaked, and G. G. Stroumsa (Tübingen, 1992), pp. 53–74; idem, "The Well of Living Water: A Biblical Motif and its Ancient Transformation," in *Sha'arei Talmon: Studies in the Bible, Qumran, and the Ancient Near East Presented to Shemaryahu Talmon*, ed. M. Fishbane and E. Tov (Winona Lake, 1992), pp. 3–16; idem, "Arm of the Lord: Biblical Myth, Rabbinic Midrash, and the Mystery of History," in *Language, Theology, and the Bible: Essays in Honour of James Barr*, ed. S. E. Balentine and J. Barton (Oxford, 1994), pp. 271–292; E. R. Wolfson, "Images of God's Feet: Some Observations on the Divine Body in Judaism," in *People of the Body: Jews and Judaism from an Embodied Perspective*, pp. 143–181; Y. Liebes, "De Natura Dei: On the Development of the Jewish Myth," in *Studies in Jewish Myth and Jewish Messianism*, trans. B. Stein (Albany, 1993), pp. 1–64; M. Bar-Ilan, "The Hand of God: A Chapter in Rabbinic Anthropomorphism," in *Rashi 1040–1990: Hommage à Ephraim E. Urbach*, ed. G. Sed-Rajna (Paris, 1993), pp. 321–335; A. Goshen-Gottstein, "The Body as Image of God in Rabbinic Literature," *Harvard Theological Review* 87 (1994) pp. 171–195. Cf. also the study of Eilberg-Schwartz cited in preceding note and that of David Stern in n. 13.

[10] *Jewish Quarterly Review* 81 (1990): pp. 219–222.

[11] Neusner, *Incarnation of God*, pp. ix, 1–2, 4, 11–12, 168, passim.

of the body of God means depicting God metaphorically in embodied terms. Thus, according to Neusner, the incarnation of God reaches its most perfect expression in the Babylonian Talmud because God is represented in that literary compilation as a "fully spelled out and individual personality: divinity in the form of humanity."[12]

The textual evidence adduced by Neusner does not amount to proof of a conception of incarnation distinguished from anthropomorphic figuration. Describing God as one who wears phylacteries or as a sage wrapped in a prayer shawl are striking examples of the rabbinic utilization of anthropomorphic expressions to convey religious truths, but they are a far cry from positing an incarnational theology predicated on the notion that God can assume a physical appearance or that he/she can be manifest in the flesh.[13] Phenomenologically, the doctrine of incarnation is not merely a rhetorical matter, for it implies an ontological transubstantiation. To say that God is incarnate is to claim something more than that God can be represented metaphorically as a human being. Incarnation is not merely a way to speak of God; it implies that the divine is embodied, whether we understand that embodiment veridically or docetically, a philosophical issue that divided Christian interpreters from an early period.[14]

In this study I examine one example of an incarnational doctrine in rabbinic theology related to the topic of *kawwanah*, intentionality in prayer. I will suggest that *kawwanah*, at least according to one trajectory that can be traced in rabbinic writings, entailed a visual apprehension of the divine predicated on the belief that God can assume an incarnate form. Thus, I am using the word "incarnation" to refer to the ontic presencing of God in a theophanic image. Underlying the rabbinic discussions on intentionality in prayer is the notion of God's imaginal body. By "imaginal body" I wish to convey the idea that the somatic form of God inheres in the human imagination as a symbolic configuration.[15] Within the aniconic framework of classical Judaism, only such a body could be ascribed to God. This does not mean, however, that the rabbinic texts that speak of God's body are to

---

[12] Ibid., p. 120, and cf. pp. 165–197, 201–230.

[13] A similar position is taken by D. Stern, "*Imitatio Hominis*: Anthropomorphism and the Character(s) of God in Rabbinic Literature," *Prooftexts* 12 (1992): pp. 151–174.

[14] See H. A. Wolfson, *The Philosophy of the Church Fathers: Faith, Trinity, Incarnation* (Cambridge, MA, 1970), pp. 364–493. See also M. Werner, *The Formation of Christian Dogma* (Boston, 1965), pp. 128–129, 147–149; U. B. Muller, *Die Menschwerdung des Gottessohnes: Fruhchristliche Inkarnationsvorsteeungen und die Anfange des Doketismus* (Stuttgart, 1990).

[15] My use of terminlogy has been influenced by the work of Henry Corbin. See *Through a Speculum That Shines*, pp. 8, 61–63, and pertinent notes.

be deciphered as merely allegorical or metaphorical. On the contrary, the language of the texts points to an experience of divine embodiment. One of the key ways to access that body in the symbolic imagination is through prayer.

Prayer and the Iconic Visualization of God's Body

Scholars have generally agreed that the rabbinic idea of *kawwanah*, as it pertains particularly to the recitation of the *Shema* and the *Amidah*, entails primarily mental focus or directing the heart to God so that all potentially diverting thoughts are impeded.[16] What has not been sufficiently explored in the scholarly analyses, however, has been the iconic dimension of *kawwanah* and the role of the imagination.[17] Specifically, the thesis that I shall put forth is that the intention implied by this *terminus technicus* in several key rabbinic passages involves the formation of an iconic image of God within the mind (or heart).[18] The term *kawwanah*, therefore, refers to an internal state of consciousness by means of which the worshiper creates a mental icon of God, the function of which is to locate the divine presence in space. In this state of consciousness the phenomenal boundaries of inside and outside dissolve, for only by means of the internal image does the worshiper experience the divine as external. Through the proper *kawwanah* the heart of the devotee becomes the throne upon which God

---

[16] See H. G. Enelow, "Kawwana: The Struggle for Inwardness in Judaism," in *Studies in Jewish Literature Issued in Honor of Professor Kaufmann Kohler on the Occasion of His Seventieth Birthday* (Berlin, 1913), pp. 84–88; G. F. Moore, *Judaism in the First Centuries of the Christian Era: The Age of the Tannaim* (Cambridge, MA, 1927), 2:223–225; E. E. Urbach, *The Sages: Their Concepts and Beliefs*, trans. I. Abrahams (Jerusalem, 1975), p. 397; T. Zahavy, "Kavvanah for Prayer in the Mishnah and Talmud," in *New Perspectives on Ancient Judaism, Volume One: Religion, Literature, and Society in Ancient Israel, Formative Christianity and Judaism*, ed. J. Neusner, P. Borgen, E. S. Frerichs, and R. Horsley (Lanham, 1987), pp. 37–48; idem, *Studies in Jewish Prayer* (Lanham, 1990), pp. 39–40, 111–119.

[17] One scholar who has paid attention to the role of symbolic images in the rabbinic idea of *kawwanah*, compared especially to the intuitive state of poetic consciousness, has been Zahavy, *Studies in Jewish Prayer*, pp. 112–116.

[18] My discussion is of necessity limited to the rabbinic texts wherein the word *kawwanah*, or one of its grammatical conjugations, is used in a liturgical context. I will not be discussing the rabbinic application of *kawwanah* to other contexts, most notably the observance of religious rituals in general (cf. B. Berakhot 13a, Eruvin 95b, Pesaḥim 114b). Moreover, I am focusing on one particular theme related to prayer in the rabbinic corpus of the formative period, principally Mishnah, Tosefta, Palestinian and Babylonian Talmuds. I am not claiming that my particular focus is the exclusive or even the most recurring meaning assigned to the term *kawwanah*, although I would argue that it has a certain priority.

dwells at the same time that God is transformed into the throne upon which the devotee dwells.[19]

The phenomenological assonance of this rabbinic term can be gauged from a proper attentiveness to its philological ground. The word *kawwanah* is derived from the word *kiwwen* (from the root *kwn*), which means "to turn" or "to face a particular direction" (the word for direction is *kiwwun*). Whatever layers of signification and hermeneutical transformations the term has assumed in rabbinic sources through different historical periods, something of its etymological foundation is retained, for at the core *kawwanah* in prayer involves a turning of the head in a given direction. This intentional facing underlies the ideal of mental concentration, the setting and focusing of the mind on a fixed object and the blocking out of all distracting thoughts.[20] Thus the Mishnah apodictically declares, "One should not rise to pray [the *Amidah*] save through heaviness of the head."[21] The state of mind referred to as *koved ro'sh*, which I have translated as "heaviness of the head," is achieved by means of proper mental concentration.[22]

---

[19] See A. Goldberg, "Service of the Heart: Liturgical Aspects of Synagogue Worship," in *Standing Before God: Studies on Prayer in Scriptures and in Tradition with Essays in Honor of John M. Oesterreicher*, ed. A. Finkel and L. Frizzel (New York, 1981), pp. 195–211.

[20] Consider the tradition reported in P. Berakhot 2:5, 5a, regarding Ḥiyya the Great's meditational practice, which consisted of thinking about the Persian hierarchy. In the same passage, Samuel is described as someone who improved his mental focus during prayer by counting birds or clouds, whereas Bun bar Ḥiyya used to count stones for this purpose. See S. Lieberman, *Texts and Studies* (New York, 1974), pp. 59, 276–277; Zahavy, "*Kavvanah* for Prayer in the Mishnah and Talmud," p. 44. The idiom *kiwwen libbo* also has the connotation of directng the mind to a specific task at hand. Cf. M. Berakhot 2:1, T. Berakhot 2:3, B. Berakhot 13a. For a different explanation of the dictum in the Tosefta, see S. Lieberman, *Tosefta Ki-Fshutah, Order Zera'im, Part I*, second edition (Jerusalem, 1992), p. 15 (Hebrew). According to Lieberman, the intent of this remark is simply that the one reciting the *Shema* must direct his heart to God.

[21] M. Berakhot 5:1. Cf. *Tanḥuma*, Wayyera, 9, ed. S. Buber (Vilna, 1885), 45b; *Midrash Tehillim* 108:1, ed. S. Buber (Vilna, 1891), 232a. The sentiment of the mishnaic ruling is captured in one of the teachings reportedly transmitted by R. Eliezer to his students when he was ill: "When you pray, know before whom you stand, and on account of that you will merit the life of the world-to-come" (B. Berakhot 28b). A slightly different version of this passage appears in *Avot de-Rabbi Natan*, version A, ch. 19, ed. S. Schechter (Vienna, 1887), p. 70, and in the medieval composition, *Orḥot Ḥayyim*, § 18, cited in *Oṣar Midrashim*, ed. J. D. Eisenstein (New York, 1956), p. 29.

[22] In a number of medieval commentators, the expression *koved rosh* is associated with awe, submission, and humility, and, in some cases, it is linked to the teaching of Simeon the Pious regarding the need to imagine the *Shekhinah*. Cf. *She'iltot de-Rav Ahai Ga'on* (Jerusalem, 1961), Lekh lekha, § 8, p. 45; D. Hedegård, *Seder R. Amram Gaon: Hebrew Text with Critical Apparatus, Translation with Notes and Introduction* (Lund, 1951), ch. 34, p. 79 (Hebrew text on p. 32); Rashi's commentary to B. Berakhot 30b, s.v. *koved rosh; Perush ha-Tefillot le-Rabbenu Shelomo*, included in *Sefer ha-Pardes*, ed. H. L. Ehrenreich (Budapest, 1924), p. 298; *Siddur Rashi*, ed. S. Buber (Berlin, 1911), § 25, pp. 18–19; Abraham ben Isaac

It is clearly for this reason that, immediately after the aforecited dictum, the redactor(s) of the Mishnah placed the tradition about the ancient pietists who used to wait one hour before they began their prayers "in order to direct their hearts to God," *kede she-yikhawwenu et libbam la-maqom*.[23] The case of the ancient pietists provides a particular example of the general rule established in the opening remark. The point is further underscored in the concluding comment of this section of the Mishnah, "even if a king asks about his welfare, he should not respond, and even if a serpent is clinging to his heel, he should not stop." The worshiper's concentration must be so intense that nothing—neither king nor serpent—should divert his attention.

There is a recognition on the part of some rabbis that such a state must be fostered by preparatory mental exercises. Thus, according to another rabbinic dictum, "one should not rise to pray out of conversation, play, or lightheadedness, but only out of words of wisdom."[24] The reference to "words of wisdom," *devarim shel ḥokhmah*, which in a parallel text appears as *davar shel torah*, "word of Torah,"[25] signifies that engagement with intellectual matters helps focus the mind. Study thus prepares the individual for worship. The need for undivided mental concentration is also conveyed in a teaching attributed to R. Eliezer: "A person should always ascertain with

---

of Nabonne, *Sefer ha-Eshkol*, ed. Z. B. Auerbach (Halberstaadt, 1868), Hilkhot Tefillah, § 9, p. 18; *Mishnah im Perush Rabbenu Mosheh ben Maimon*, ed. Y. Kafaḥ (Jerusalem, 1963), Seder Zeraʻim, p. 41; Asher bar Saul of Lunel, *Sefer ha-Minhagot*, in *Sifran shel Ri'shonim*, ed. S. Assaf (Jerusalem, 1935), p. 130; Ṣedeqiah ben Abraham, *Shibbole ha-Leqeṭ ha-Shalem*, ed. S. K. Mirsky (New York, 1966), § 17, p. 182; Judah ben Yaqar, *Perush ha-Tefillot we-ha-Berakhot*, ed. S. Yerushalmi (Jerusalem, 1979), pt. 1, p. 55; Eleazar of Worms, *Sefer ha-Roqeaḥ* (Jerusalem, 1967), p. 214; Jacob ben Asher, *Ṭur*, Oraḥ Ḥayyim, § 93; Isaac ben Moses, *Or Zaruʻa* (Zhitomir, 1862), § 100, 19b; Joseph Karo, *Shulḥan Arukh*, Oraḥ Ḥayyim, § 93:1. The possibility that *koved ro'sh* denotes the bodily gesture of bowing the head is raised by Nathan ben Yeḥiel, *Aruch Completum*, ed. A. Kohut, 4:193, s.v. *koved*. See also *Perushe Rabbenu Ḥananel le-Masekhet Berakhot*, ed. D. Metzger (Jerusalem, 1990), p. 68.

23 M. Berkhot 5:1. According to another tradition, the ancient pietists waited one hour before their prayers and one hour after their prayers. Cf. P. Berakhot 5:1, 8d; B. Berakhot 32b; Maimonides, *Mishneh Torah*, Hilkhot Tefillah 4:16. In *Sefer Ḥasidim*, ed. J. Wistinetzki with introduction by J. Freimann (Frankfurt am Main, 1924), § 451, the talmudic tradition is rendered as "the ancient pietists would wait one hour during their prayers, for they would wait before every word. So with respect to each and every blessing, they were silent until they directed their hearts; this is the foundation of prayer from the outset." On silence as a means to invoke the proper intention of the heart during worship, cf. ibid., §§ 456, 1605.

24 T. Berakhot 3:21. On the prohibition of acting with lightheadedness (*qallut ro'sh*) in the synagogue, cf. T. Megillah 2:11; P. Megillah 3:4, 74a.

25 P. Berakhot 5:1, 8d. In B. Berakhot 31a, the expression *halakhah pesuqah*, "decided law," appears in place of *davar shel torah* or *devarim shel ḥokhmah*. According to another tradition recorded in that context, the "joy of ritual," *simḥah shel miṣwah*, is presented as the condition that prepares one for worship.

respect to himself, if he can direct his heart, then he should pray, but if not, then he should not pray."[26] Intentionality, according to this viewpoint, is not only desired, it is absolutely required, for without the proper focus of mind one cannot pray. Less extreme, and perhaps eminently more practical, opinions have been espoused by different rabbinic authorities over the ages, but it would have been universally agreed in the rabbinic academies, as one may deduce from the preserved written documents, that prayer as a matter of halakhic necessity demands mental attention.[27] That the internal state of *kawwanah* is related, moreover, to specific external gestures seems to be implied by the tradition, reported by R. Judah, regarding R. Aqiva's excessive kneelings and prostrations when he prayed alone.[28] At the very least, this is how the redactor of this section understood the import of this tradition and thus it is placed right after the general rabbinic statement that the worshiper must direct his heart to heaven.[29] Another physical gesture related to cultivating the proper intention is the general standing posture required by prayer (based on biblical precedent and the posture required in the sacrificial rite) and more specifically to the need to keep one's feet together.[30]

---

[26] B. Berakhot 30b. Cf. *Midrash Le-olam*, in *Bet ha-Midrash*, 3:110: "A person should always focus his attention (*le-olam yekhawwen adam et aṣmo*), if he can direct his heart, then he should pray, but if not, then he should not pray."

[27] According to a baraita in B. Berakhot 32b, the practice of waiting one hour before and one hour after prayer is presented as a proscription for every worshiper. Cf. Maimonides, *Mishneh Torah*, Hilkhot Tefillah 4:16; Asher bar Saul of Lunel, *Sefer ha-Minhagot*, p. 130; Jacob ben Asher, *Ṭur*, Oraḥ Ḥayyim, § 93; *Shulḥan Arukh*, Oraḥ Ḥayyim, § 93:1. In light of this, as well as other textual considerations that cannot be pursued here, I cannot agree with the argument of I. Elbogen, *Jewish Liturgy: A Comprehensive History*, trans. R. P. Scheindlin (Philadelphia, 1993), pp. 205 and 285–286, that the rabbinic interest in *kawwanah* as an inward, spiritual ideal is expressed only in works of aggadah and not in codes of halakhah. An examination of the rabbinic sources indicates that this dichotomization is not appropriate. On the contrary, the issue of *kawwanah* has a direct impact on halakhic regulations. Cf. B. Berakhot 34b; Maimonides, *Mishneh Torah*, Hilkhot Tefillah 10:1; *Ṭur*, Oraḥ Ḥayyim, § 101; *Shulḥan Arukh*, Oraḥ Ḥayyim, § 101:1. For a more measured approach to this question, see M. Kadushin, *The Rabbinic Mind* (New York, 1952), pp. 208–209.

[28] B. Berakhot 31a.

[29] For discussion of the role of kneelings and prostrations in Jewish prayer according to talmudic and medieval sources, see E. Zimmer, "Poses and Postures During Prayer," *Sidra* 5 (1989): pp. 109–116 (Hebrew); U. Ehrlich, "Modes of Prayer and Their Significance in the Time of the Mishnah and the Talmud," Ph.D. thesis, Hebrew University, 1993, pp. 27–66 (Hebrew).

[30] P. Berakhot 1:1, 2c; B. Berakhot 10b. See Zimmer, "Poses and Postures During Prayer," pp. 107–116; Ehrlich, "Modes of Prayer," pp. 9–26. On hand gestures related to liturgical worship, see Zimmer, op. cit., pp. 95–107; Ehrlich, op. cit., pp. 119–128. In a variety of medieval texts, related especially to pietistic groups in France and Germany, the custom of swaying or shaking the body during worship is emphasized, a practice linked exegetically to Ps. 35:10 and reported on the basis of an older homiletical (*midrash*) or esoteric work (*ma'aseh*

The aforecited statements epitomize the attitude about prayer prevalent in the rabbinic circles, reflected in one of the key terms used to refer to prayer, *avodah ba-lev* (or, alternatively, *avodah she-ba-lev*), "worship of the heart."[31] Based principally on the proximity of the words *avodah* and *lev* in the verse, "to love the Lord your God and to serve Him with all your heart" (Deut. 11:13), the rabbis coined the idiom *avodah ba-lev* to underscore that prayer must be a heartfelt and mindful experience.[32] The rabbinic ideal of *kawwanat ha-lev* connotes in a general sense mental concentration and contemplative focus, a practice referred to occasionally in the Babylonian Talmud as *iyyun tefillah*, "meditation in prayer."[33] I suggest, moreover, that, according to some rabbinic authorities, this directing of the heart entailed conjuring a mental image of God, which serves as the object of prayer. Concentration is thus achieved through the faculty of the imagination, a motif that is developed at length in medieval mystical and devotional sources. This is implied, for instance, in the teaching attributed to Simeon the Pious, reported by Ḥana ben Bizna: "The one who prays must see himself as if the *Shekhinah* were opposite him, as it says, 'I have set the Lord always before me' (Ps. 16:8)."[34] The essential thought underlying the teaching of Simeon the Pious is that prayer is predicated on the imaginary presencing of God, a process referred to in the idiomatic rabbinic Hebrew, *ha-mitpallel ṣarikh she-yir'eh aṣmo ke'illu shekhinah kenegdo*.[35] The term *ke'illu*, "as if,"

---

merkavah). See Abraham ben Nathan of Lunel, *Sefer ha-Manhig*, ed. Y. Raphael (Jerusalem, 1978); 1:85, and other sources cited in n. 19 ad locum. For additional sources and an analysis of the evolution of this custom, see Zimmer, op. cit., pp. 116–127.

[31] P. Berakhot 4:1, 7a; B. Ta'anit 2a; *Sifre on Deuteronomy*, 41, ed. L. Finkelstein (New York, 1969), p. 88 (see S. D. Fraade, *From Tradition to Commentary: Torah and Its Interpretation in the Midrash Sifre to Deuteronomy* [Albany, 1991], pp. 89–92); *Midrash Tehillim* 66:1, 157b; *Midrash Samuel*, 2:10, ed. S. Buber (Cracow, 1893), 25b.

[32] That proper intention of the heart, *kawwanat ha-lev*, has an effect on the acceptability of prayer by God is emphasized in the statement attributed to R. Samuel ben Naḥman in P. Berakhot 5:5, 9d. Cf. *Leviticus Rabbah* 16:9, ed. M. Margulies (New York, 1993), pp. 366–367, and see n. 5 *ad locum*; *Midrash Tehillim* 10:7, 49a, 108:1, 232a; *Pesiqta Rabbati* 47, ed. M. Friedmann (Vienna, 1880), 198b; *Tanḥuma*, Naso, 18, ed. Buber, 17b; *Numbers Rabbah* 11:4. In other rabbinic passages it is emphasized that prayer must be a spontaneous event surging from the heart or flowing from the mouth, an ideal that in part contrasts with the notion of deliberate intentionality implied in the statements about *kawwanah*. Cf. M. Avot 2:13, M. Berakhot 4:3–4 and 5:5, T. Berakhot 3:3. For a recent study of these and other related passages, see S. Naeh, "'Creates the Fruit of Lips': A Phenomenological Study of Prayer According to Mishnah *Berakhot* 4:3, 5:5," *Tarbiz* 63 (1994): pp. 185–201 (Hebrew).

[33] Cf. B. Berakhot 55a, Shabbat 118b (and cf. Tosafot, s. v. *iyyun tefillah*), 127a (cf. commentary of Rashi, s. v. *we-iyyun tefillah*), Baba Batra 164b.

[34] B. Sanhedrin 22a.

[35] The point was well understood by the Aramaic translator of Ps. 16:8, the verse cited as a prooftext in the dictum attributed to Simeon the Pious, "I will place the Lord before me constantly because His presence rests upon me, and I will not stir." See A. Goldberg,

resonates with semiotic vibrancy, signifying that the worshiper must imaginatively represent the *Shekhinah* in iconic form.[36] The hypothetical "as if"

Untersuchungen uber die Vorstellung von der Schekhinah in der Fruhen Rabbinischen Literatur (Berlin, 1969), p. 425. Compare also the paraphrase of the dictum of Simeon the Pious in *She'iltot de-Rav Ahai Ga'on*, Lekh lekha, § 8, p. 45: "The one who prays must see himself as if the *Shekhinah* were dwelling opposite him (*sheruyyah kenegdo*), as it says, 'I have set the Lord always before me' (Ps. 16:8)." Cf. *Hilkhot Rav Alfasi*, Tractate Berakhot, 22b. The additional word *sheruyyah* lends emphasis to the ontic presencing of God's imaginal body implied by the original talmudic statement. Cf. B. Tamid 32b. The rabbinic idiom *shekhinah kenegdo* thus parallels the biblical expression *nokhah pene adonai*, and it is obvious that it signifies the dwelling of the Presence. Thus in the commentary of Rashi, *ad locum*, the words *shekhinah kenegdo* are rendered as *shekhinah sheruyyah alaw*, the "Presence dwells upon him."

[36] The idea that I am attributing to Simeon the Pious bears a resemblance to the doceticism espoused by some early Christian thinkers. The connection of Simeon the Pious and Jewish-Christians may be suggested by the tradition preserved in B. Keritot 6b concerning Simeon's insistence that if the "sinners of Israel" (*posh'e yisra'el*) do not fast on a particular day that day cannot be considered an official fast. A. Marmorstein, *Studies in Jewish Theology*, ed. J. Rabbinowitz and M. S. Lew (London, 1950), pp. 183–184, 207, 215, argued that in this context the term *posh'e yisra'el* refers to Jewish-Christians. See also M. Simon, *Verus Israel: A Study of the Relations Between Christians and Jews in the Roman Empire* (135–425), trans. H. McKeating (Oxford, 1986), pp. 256–258, 408–409. The term "sinner of Israel," *poshe'a yisra'el*, seems to be used as a description of Jesus in B. Gittin 56b–57a. See J. Z. Lauterbach, *Rabbinic Essays* (New York, 1973), pp. 502–503, 508. For a recent survey of the historical presence of Jewish-Christians in Palestine in the first two centuries, see J. E. Taylor, *Christians and the Holy Places: The Myth of Jewish-Christian Origins* (Oxford, 1993), pp. 1–47. The presumed priestly lineage of Simeon the Pious may have had an impact on the centrality of the visionary dimension in his understanding of *kawwanah*. The priestly pedigree of Simeon the Pious is implied by T. Kelim 1:6 wherein he boasts that once he entered the sacred space of the Temple (between the altar and the porch) without washing his hands and feet. See L. Finkelstein, *The Pharisees: The Sociological Background of Their Faith* (Philadelphia, 1966), pp. cvii–cix, 85. The particular link between the priests and visionary experience is related, of course, to the fact that the Temple was viewed as the sacred site in which visions could occur. See Wolfson, *Through a Speculum That Shines*, pp. 17–18, and references to other scholarly material given on p. 18 n. 28. It is also of interest to consider the tradition reported in the name of Simeon the Pious by Hana ben Bizna in B. Berakhot 7a, "the Holy One, blessed be He, showed Moses the knot of the phylacteries." The tradition regarding the knot of God's head phylacteries is found in a passage in one of the key textual units of the Hekhalot literature. See G. Scholem, *Jewish Gnosticism, Merkabah Mysticism, and Talmudic Tradition* (New York, 1965), p. 105, and *Synopse zur Hekhalot Literatur*, ed. P. Schafer et al. (Tübingen, 1981), § 500; a translation is found in M. D. Swartz, *Mystical Prayer in Ancient Judaism: An Analysis of Ma'aseh Merkavah* (Tübingen, 1992), p. 229. For alternative translations and analyses, see P. Schafer, *The Hidden and Manifest God: Some Major Themes in Early Jewish Mysticism*, trans. A. Pomerance (Albany, 1992), p. 87, and Wolfson, *Through a Speculum That Shines*, p. 98. It is likely that the motif of the head phylacteries is related to the image of the crown that is also found in Jewish esoteric literature and in Karaitic polemics against rabbinic anthropomorphism. See M. Bar-Ilan, "The Idea of Crowning God in Hekhalot Mysticism and the Karaitic Polemic," *Jerusalem Studies in Jewish Thought* 6:1–2 (1987): pp. 221–233 (Hebrew). Perhaps the statement ascribed to Simeon the Pious should be located within the spectrum of esoteric Jewish beliefs, which may also have some connections to the priestly phenomenon.

has the power to bridge the ontic chasm that separates different spheres of being or the historical chasm that separates two periods of time.[37] The *ke'illu* functions, therefore, as the hermeneutical key that opens the mind onto the horizon of myth, which is neither true nor false, but a symbolic construct that blurs the distinction between imagined and real. Indeed, the imaginal world of the "as if" is in some sense more real than the empirical and historical realm of space and time.

In the particular case that I am discussing, the *ke'illu* homologizes the act of prayer and the visionary representation of the *Shekhinah*. Prayer is ritually transformed by the formulaic *ke'illu* into the mental imaging of the divine. The iconic representation, which involves ascribing anthropomorphic characteristics to God, is related by Simeon the Pious to the verse, "I have set the Lord always before me," *shiwwiti yhwh lenegdi tamid.* Once again, philology can enhance our phenomenological sensibility: *shiwwiti,* which is derived from *shawah,* "to make equal," conveys the analogical function of the imaginal symbol,[38] which allows the inexpressible to be

---

S. C. Reif, *Judaism and Hebrew Prayer: New Perspectives on Jewish Liturgical History* (Cambridge, 1993), p. 105, discusses this tradition ascribed to Simeon the Pious in conjunction with the tannaitic remark regarding the meditational practice of the "early pietists." He notes the mystical nature of both pietistic traditions. See also Kadushin, *The Rabbinic Mind*, p. 208. Other traditions reported in the name of Simeon the Pious link him either to mystical or magical speculation; cf. B. Berakhot 3b (parallel text in Sanhedrin 16a), Yoma 77a, Sukkah 52b, Yevamot 60b, Sotah 10b and 36b, Sanhedrin 91b.

[37] The hermeneutical function in midrashic sources of the "as if" to create a "time-shift" from the biblical past to the historical present has been noted by M. Bregman, "Past and Present in Midrashic Literature," *Hebrew Annual Review* 2 (1978): pp. 47–49. I have discussed this hermeneutical term in rabbinic sources in "The Mystical Significance of Torah Study in German Pietism," *Jewish Quarterly Review* 84 (1993): p. 60, and again in "The Face of Jacob in the Moon: Mystical Transformations of an Aggadic Myth," in *The Seductiveness of Jewish Myth Challenge or Response?*, ed. S. Daniel Breslauer (Albany, 1996), p. 236. See also M. Fishbane, *The Kiss of God: Spiritual and Mystical Death in Judaism* (Seattle, 1994), pp. 87–91, repeated with slight variations in idem, "The Imagination of Death in Jewish Spirituality," in *Death, Ecstasy, and Other Worldly Journeys*, ed. M. Fishbane and J. J. Collins (Albany, 1995), pp. 184–189.

[38] On the analogical function of the term *shawah* (conjugated as *shiwwah* or *hishwah*), cf. Isa. 38:13, 40, 25, 45:5, Hosea 10:1, Lam. 2:13. Particularly relevant is the expression *shaweh li* placed in the mouth of God. Cf. *Tanḥuma*, Wayyera, 14 (ed. Buber, 32, 53a); Beḥuqotai, 4 (ed. Buber, 6, 56a); *Pesiqta Rabbati* 42, 175a. (Michael Fishbane, who kindly called my attention to this expression in midrashic souces, is presently working on this trope as part of his full-scale study on the mythic creativity of classical midrash.) In these contexts the import of the expression is clearly that one becomes like or equal to God, which is precisely the underlying meaning in the statement of Simeon the Pious discussed in the body of this paper. Cf. *Leviticus Rabbah* 30:2, p. 693, where Ps. 16:8 is used as a prooftext for the idea that scribes and teachers of young children will stand to the right of God in the future. In this midrashic context as well, the analogical function of the symbol seems to be implied in the interpretation of the verse *shiwwiti yhwh lenegdi tamid.* By contrast, in

expressed and the nonrepresentable to be represented.[39] The Psalmist's utterance, *shiwwiti yhwh lenegdi tamid*, can be converted semantically to "I form an image in my mind constantly." This is exactly what is implied in the aphorism of Simeon the Pious: the worshiper must symbolically represent the divine presence by imagining God anthropomorphically, for in the absence of this imaginary form there is no image and without an image there is nothing to worship.[40] It is plausible that reflected in the statement of Simeon the Pious is an actual praxis performed by a fraternity of pietists to which he belonged. I suspect, moreover, that imaginative visualization is implied in the tradition recorded in the Mishnah regarding the ancient pietists to which I referred above. The specific context in which this tradition appears suggests that the issue of directing the heart to God involved total concentration. Beyond that, however, I conjecture that this act involved the imaging of God as an anthropomorphic presence, the phenomenological condition that makes prayer in a theistic sense possible.

Imago Templi and the Localization of God's Body in Sacred Space

From other passages in the rabbinic corpus one may deduce that *kawwanah* entailed in a primary sense the imaginal localization of God in space. One may distinguish two main approaches in the relevant rabbinic comments regarding the precise place wherein God is localized through the imagination.[41] According to one line of thinking, the Holy of Holies, the inner sanctum of the Temple in Jerusalem, is the object of mental intention. This view is based on the biblical conception of the Temple as the building wherein the imageless God of Israel, who could not be represented in material shape, assumed a visible form. The Jerusalem Temple lacked

---

Midrash Tehillim 119:5, 246b, Ps. 16:8 is applied to a state of living in God's presence without any overt iconic dimension.

[39] See my discussion of the symbol in *Through a Speculum That Shines*, pp. 61–63, 67–73.

[40] The point was well understood by G. van der Leeuw, who aptly called his chapter on the phenomenology of prayer, "Endowment With Form In Worship." See *Religion in Essence and Manifestation*, trans. J. E. Turner, with new foreword by N. Smart (Princeton, 1986), pp. 447–453.

[41] The spatial orientation connected with human intentionality in prayer is also evident in B. Baba Batra 25b: "R. Isaac said: The one who wants to become wise should face south [when he prays] and the one who wants to become wealthy should face north. A sign for you is that the table was in the north and the candelabrum in the south. R. Joshua ben Levi said: One should always face south because by becoming wise one becomes wealthy, as it says, 'In her right hand is length of days, in her left, riches and honor' (Prov. 3:16)." The implications of the orientation of the face in the rabbinic notion of worship have recently been explored by Ehrlich, "Modes of Prayer," pp. 20–22, 67–108.

any central cult image, an icon of the deity, but within its spatial confines God could be imaged, especially as an anthropomorphic figure seated upon the throne in the palace-shrine of the Holy of Holies.[42] Moreover, it is evident from a number of biblical verses that the Temple was perceived (both within and outside the geographical boundaries of the land of Israel) as the central locality to which prayers were directed.[43] In light of the fact that the Holy of Holies was understood to be the locus of theophany and the primary place to which prayers were addressed, one can well understand why the rabbis continued to think of that place in particular as the space wherein the divine could be imaginatively visualized through a process of mental concentration associated with liturgical worship.[44] The rabbinic attitude is typified in the anonymous remark, "Whoever prays in that place in Jerusalem it is as if he prayed before the throne of glory, for the gateway to heaven is there and an opening is opened for prayer to be heard, as it says, 'for this is the gateway to heaven' (Gen. 28:17)."[45] The significance of praying at the site of the Temple is linked to the fact that it

---

[42] See B. Goldman, *The Sacred Portal: A Primary Symbol in Ancient Judaic Art* (Detroit, 1966), pp. 34–38; J. D. Levenson, "Jerusalem Temple in Devotional and Visionary Experience," in *Jewish Spirituality From the Bible Through the Middle Ages*, pp. 32–61. Needless to say, the ancient Israelite belief, cultivated in the period of the Second Temple as well, regarding the visionary status of the Temple is the basis for the Christological notion of the Temple as either the visible form of God in the body of Christ or the symbolic prefiguration of the Church. See Y. M. J. Congar, *Le Mystère du temple ou l'Économie de la Présence de Dieu à sa créature de la Genèse à l'Apocalypse* (Paris, 1963), pp. 139–180; R. J. Mckelvey, *The New Temple: The Church in the New Testament* (Oxford, 1969); S. Ferber, "The Temple of Solomon in Early Christian and Byzantine Art," in *The Temple of Solomon: Archaeological Fact and Medieval Tradition in Christian, Islamic and Jewish Art*, ed. J. Gutmann (Missoula, 1976), pp. 21–43; J. B. Chance, *Jerusalem, the Temple, and the New Age in Luke–Acts* (Macon, 1988); A. F. Segal, *Paul the Convert: The Apostolate and Apostasy of Saul the Pharisee* (New Haven, 1990), pp. 168–169. For a new approach to the story of Jesus from within the framework of cultic activities of the Pharisees during the last decades of the Second Temple period, see B. Chilton, *The Temple of Jesus: His Sacrificial Program Within a Cultural History of Sacrifice* (University Park, 1992).

[43] The directing of prayers from outside the land to the Temple in Jerusalem is affirmed in 1 Kings 8:48–49 and Dan. 6:11. That the Temple was perceived as the favored setting for prayer is affirmed in any number of biblical passages, especially in the book of Psalms. This motif is clearly related to the comparison of the Temple to the Tent of Meeting, which served as the meeting-point of God and human. See Congar, *Le Mystère du temple*, pp. 115–119, 279–293; C. R. Koester, *The Dwelling of God: The Tabernacle in the Old Testament, Intertestamental Jewish Literature, and the New Testament* (Washington DC, 1989).

[44] See Urbach, *The Sages*, pp. 57–58; Ehrlich, "Modes of Prayer," pp. 18–22.

[45] I have followed the reading of this dictum preserved in *Pirqe Rabbi Eliezer* (Warsaw, 1852), ch. 35, 82b. For a different reading, cf. *Midrash Tehillim* 91:7, 200b: "Whoever prays in Jerusalem it is as if he prayed before the throne of glory." The passage from *Pirqe Rabbi Eliezer* is cited according to this reading by a number of medieval commentators. Cf. Naḥmanides' commentary to Gen. 28:12; Israel ibn al-Nakawa, *Menorat ha-Ma'or*, ed. H. G. Enelow (New York, 1930), 2:110.

is the gateway to heaven through which prayers are received. The earthly Temple is assigned this role because of the ontic correspondence between it and the celestial Temple.[46] More specifically, the ark that is within the Holy of Holies corresponds to the throne of glory, and just as the *Shekhinah* above assumes material shape upon the throne, so below the *Shekhinah* can be imaged in tangible form upon the ark. By praying in the place of the Temple, therefore, one is imaginatively transported to the celestial realm, *kol ha-mitpallel be-maqom ha-zeh bi-yerushalayim ke'illu mitpallel lifne kisse ha-kavod.* We note, again, the hermeneutical power of the *ke'illu* to effect the imaginary transport across ontological boundaries, in this case from the Temple in Jerusalem to the glorious throne in heaven.

That the presence of God in the Temple was viewed by the rabbis as an object of visual contemplation in a cultic context is implied in the mishnaic description of the water-drawing ceremony on the second night of the festival of Sukkot. When the procession of celebrants reached the gate leading eastward, they turned to the west and said, "Our ancestors who were in this place, 'their backs were to the Temple of the Lord and their faces to the east; they were bowing low to the sun in the east' (Ezek. 8:16). But we are [turned] to the Lord and our eyes are [turned] to the Lord."[47] In contrast to the idolatrous worship, which consisted of prostrating the body in the direction of the sun in the east, the legitimate liturgical worship was dependent on the physical gesture of facing west, an act that facilitated the ocular apprehension of the divine within the spatial confines of the Temple. The westward orientation of the Temple ritual was applied in other passages to prayer, as we find, for example, in the following dictum transmitted in the name of R. Joshua ben Levi: "We must be grateful to our forefathers for they informed us of the place of worship, as it says, 'and the host of heaven prostrate themselves before You' (Neh. 9:6)."[48] Just as the host of heavenly bodies, including the sun, move from east to west and thus prostrate themselves before God in the west, so, too, the Jewish people must direct their

---

[46] On the parallelism between the earthly Temple and its celestial counterpart, see V. Aptowitzer, "The Celestial Temple as Viewed in the Aggadah," in *Tarbiz* 2 (1931): pp. 137–153, 257–277 (Hebrew, abridged English translation in *Binah: Studies in Jewish History, Thought, and Culture*, vol. 2, ed. J. Dan [New York, 1989], pp. 1–29); R. Patai, *Man and Temple in Ancient Jewish Myth and Ritual* (Toronto, 1947), pp. 130–132. For a different approach to this material, see E. E. Urbach, "The Lower Jerusalem and the Supernal Jerusalem," in idem, *The World of the Sages: Collected Studies* (Jerusalem, 1988), pp. 376–391 (Hebrew).

[47] M. Sukkah 5:4. The connection of this statement and the tradition about directing the heart to God in prayer was previously noted by Lieberman, *Tosefta Ki-Fshutah, Order Zera'im, Part I*, p. 44 n. 65. See also Urbach, *The Sages*, pp. 59–60; Ehrlich, "Modes of Prayer," pp. 100–105.

[48] B. Baba Batra 25a.

prayers in that direction. The implicit theological presumption here, which also had an impact on the architectural planning and construction of synagogues from Late Antiquity,[49] is stated succinctly in another maxim, attributed alternatively to R. Abbahu and to R. Joshua ben Levi, "the *Shekhinah* is in the west."[50]

This orientation is epitomized in the rabbinic dictum that those outside the land of Israel must direct their concentration during worship to the land, those in the land to Jerusalem, those in Jerusalem to the Temple, and those standing on the Temple mount to the Holy of Holies.[51] That the

---

[49] Cf. T. Megillah 3:22: "The entrances to the synagogues are only made on the east for thus we find that the Temple was open on the east as it says, 'Those who were to camp before the Tabernacle, in front—before the Tent of Meeting, on the east' (Num. 3:38)." See Urbach, *The Sages*, p. 62. On the question of the Jerusalem-orientation in the architectural structure of synagogues in the land of Israel and the Diaspora, see A. R. Seager, "Ancient Synagogue Architecture An Overview," in *Ancient Synagogues: The State of Research*, ed. J. Gutmann (Ann Arbor, 1981), pp. 39–47, esp. 41; L. I. Levine, "The Form and Content of the Synagogue in the Second Temple Period," in *Synagogues in Antiquity*, ed. A. Kasher, A. Oppenheimer, and U. Rappaport (Jerusalem, 1987), p. 16.

[50] B. Baba Batra 25a. This view is set against the idea that the *Shekhinah* is in every place, an opinion attributed to R. Ishmael and R. Hoshaya. Urbach, *The Sages*, pp. 61–62, raised the possibility that the tendency to eliminate the fixed prayer-orientation on the grounds that the Presence is ubiquitous may be seen as a reaction to Judeo-Christians who emphasized that prayer must be directed to Jerusalem (regarding this possibility, see S. Lieberman, *Tosefta Ki-Fshutah, Order Mo'ed, Part V* [Jerusalem, 1992], p. 1200 n. 82–83). Urbach also notes that by the third century it became a universal practice amongst Christians to face east in prayer. As he further observes (pp. 62–63), a polemic against such liturgical practices is clearly operative in the statement in B. Baba Batra 25a attributed to R. Sheshet that one can direct prayer to all directions except east because the heretics give instruction to face in that direction during their worship. On the prohibition of facing west during prayer on account of the presence of the demonic force in that place, cf. *Tiqqune Zohar* 21, ed. R. Margaliot (Jerusalem, 1978), 56b. Interestingly, this medieval kabbalist accepts the talmudic tradition regarding the location of the *Shekhinah* in the west, but he suggests that because of the impure powers that are attached to that place, it is necessary for the Jews to relocate the *Shekhinah* in the south, which is the right side of mercy. Needless to say, the practice in countries west of the land of Israel is to face east, as a number of traditional commentators point out. Cf. Tosafot to B. Berakhot 30a, s. v. *le-talpiyyot*; Moses ben Jacob of Coucy, *Sefer Miṣwot Gadol* (Jerusalem, 1983), positive commandments, 19, 10d; *Ṭur*, Oraḥ Ḥayyim, § 94; Menaḥem ben Solomon Meiri, *Beit ha-Beḥirah al Massekhet Berakhot*, ed. Samuel Dickman (Jerusalem, 1965), p. 106; Israel ibn al-Nakawa, *Menorat ha-Ma'or*, 2:110; the note of Moses Isserles to the *Shulḥan Arukh*, Oraḥ Ḥayyim, § 94:1. In his marginal gloss, Isserles remarks that the place of the ark and the precise spot to which the prayers are directed is not the place where the sun rises because that would appear to be worship of the sun, which is the "way of the heretics." This is obviously an effort to deal with the statement of R. Sheshet discussed above and the contemporary practice of facing east during prayer. See also the commentary of Moses Isserles, *Darkhe Mosheh*, to Joseph Karo's *Bet Yosef* on the *Ṭur*, Oraḥ Ḥayyim, § 94.

[51] T. Berakhot 3:15–16; P. Berakhot 4:5, 8b–c; B. Berakhot: 30a; *Sifre on Deuteronomy*, 29, p. 47; *Song of Songs Kabbah* 4:11, ed. S. Dunansky (Jerusalem, 1980), p. 110; *Pesiqta Rabbati* 33, 149b; *Tanḥuma*, Wayyishlaḥ, 21, ed. Buber, 87b; the fragment of *Tanḥuma* published by L. Ginzberg, *Genizah Studies in Memory of Doctor Solomon Schechter* (New York, 1969),

mental intention here manifests itself kinetically is evident from a careful scrutiny of the language employed in the relevant passages. The version of this dictum in the Tosefta (Berakhot 3:15) begins, *ha-omdim be-ḥuṣah la-areṣ mekhawwenin et libbam keneged ereṣ yisra'el*, and, similarly, the Babylonian Talmud (Berakhot 30a) reads, *hayah omed be-ḥuṣ la-areṣ yekhawwen et libbo keneged ereṣ yisra'el.*[52] By contrast, the version in the Palestinian Talmud (Berakhot 4:5) begins, *ha-omdim u-mitpallelin be-ḥuṣah la-areṣ hofkhin et penehen kelappe ereṣ yisra'el*, and, similarly, *Sifre Devarim* reads, *ha-omdim be-ḥuṣah la-ares hofkhim penehem keneged ereṣ yisra'el.*[53] In my view, the semantic variant is negligible, for the directing of one's heart, which lies at the basis of *kawwanah*, is fundamentally a turning of the face. The progressively narrowing focus of the spatial orientation serves the purpose of unifying the people of Israel, for all prayers are to be directed ultimately to the one place that was perceived to be the cosmic navel, the Holy of Holies in the Temple of Jerusalem.[54] The mandate to orient prayer towards Jerusalem underlies the following maxim reported by R. Ḥiyya bar Abba in the name of R. Yoḥanan: "A person should only pray in a house that has windows, as it says, 'in the upper chamber he had windows facing Jerusalem [and three times a day he knelt down, prayed, and made confession to his God]' (Dan. 6:11)."[55] The scriptural prooftext clearly reveals that the necessity of placing windows in a house of worship is to allow the one who prays to emulate Daniel who directed his prayers to Jerusalem.[56]

The sociological function of this orientation is evident in two other rabbinic rulings, the first concerns the worship of one who is riding on an ass and the second the worship of one who is riding on a boat, a wagon, or a

---

1:99–100 (Hebrew). Needless to say, the rabbinic ideas are based on motifs expressed in Scripture. See Urbach, *The Sages*, pp. 58–59.

[52] A similar form is found in the versions found in *Pesiqta Rabbati* and *Tanḥuma*. For references, see previous note.

[53] *Sifre on Deuteronomy*, 29, p. 47. Virtually the same formulation is found in *Song of Songs Rabbah* 4:11, p. 110.

[54] Smith, "Earth and Gods," pp. 112–115.

[55] B. Berakhot 34a. A slightly different version of this dictum, also attributed to R. Ḥiyya bar Abba, appears in B. Berakhot 30a.

[56] Cf. Maimonides, *Mishneh Torah*, Hilkhot Tefillah 5:6, *Sefer Miṣwot Gadol*, positive commandments, 19, 10d; Joseph Karo, *Bet Yosef* to the *Ṭur*, Oraḥ Ḥayyim, § 90, s. v. *we-ṣarikh she-yiheyu ḥalonot*; idem, *Shulḥan Arukh*, Oraḥ Ḥayyim, § 90:4; Israel ibn al-Nakawa, *Menorat ha-Ma'or*, 2:113. By contrast, in his commentary to B. Berakhot 34b, Rashi explains that the windows "cause a person to direct his heart for he looks [through them] toward heaven and his heart is humbled." Jacob ben Asher, *Ṭur*, Oraḥ Ḥayyim, § 90, cites the explanation of Rashi from which he draws the following conclusion: "According to this it is necessary that [the windows] should be opened to the very direction towards which one prays." See Ehrlich, "Modes of Prayer," pp. 117–118.

raft. According to the mishnaic formulation of the first case, the individual is directed to dismount the animal in order to recite his prayer, but if he cannot do so, he should turn to face Jerusalem, and if he cannot do that, he should direct his thoughts to the Holy of Holies in the Temple.[57] The language of the version of this dictum preserved in the Tosefta is slightly different: if one is available to hold the ass, the person should dismount and pray, but if not, then he should pray in his place, i.e., while mounted on the animal. According to the opinion of R. Judah, referred to simply as "Rabbi," whether there is someone to hold the ass or not, the person can pray while still being mounted on the animal provided that his heart is properly focused.[58] In the Palestinian Talmud the teaching of Rabbi Judah has the following textual variant: the one mounted on the ass should pray from that position "for in that way his heart is settled."[59] Another version of the Tosefta is cited in the Babylonian Talmud as a baraita of the rabbis. In that case the statement of R. Judah is that one who is riding on an ass should pray from that position because "his mind is not settled."[60] R. Judah is not presenting a theoretical alternative to the demand that the worshiper must have the Temple of Jerusalem in mind. On the contrary, I presume that the Tosefta preserves the best reading: the physical position of the worshiper is immaterial, for the essential thing is that he direct his heart to the place that is considered sacred. According to the variant readings, the main issue is a purely practical one: the traveler will be more relaxed if he does not have to dismount the beast of burden.[61]

In a manner consonant with the dictum regarding one who is riding an ass, the theological principle underlying the law pertaining to one who is riding on a boat, a wagon, or raft is that the Holy of Holies is the focal point of religious devotion and piety.[62] The selection of the Holy of Holies as the object of visual contemplation is related to the larger nexus established in rabbinic writings between prayer and sacrifice, synagogue worship and Temple service. As a variety of scholars have noted, in the Second Temple period prayer began to occupy a more central place in the religious lives of Jews as the significance of sacrifices diminished; indeed, we are justified in speaking of the use of prayers in the Temple even if it is likely that the

---

[57] M. Berakhot 4:5.
[58] T. Berakhot 3:18.
[59] P. Berakhot 4:5, 8b.
[60] B. Berakhot 30a.
[61] The point is made clear in a later reworking of the rabbinic text in *Tanḥuma*, Ḥayye Sarah, 1.
[62] M. Berakhot 4:6.

obligatory prayer of the synagogue service evolved independently.[63] It is thus incorrect to view the institution of prayer as a sudden attempt on the part of the rabbis to compensate for the cultural castration brought on by the destruction of the Temple,[64] but it is nonetheless clear that this event helped catalyze the institutionalization of statutory and fixed prayer as a communal activity. Furthermore, the rabbis consciously modeled the structure and rites of liturgy on the basis of the sacrificial cult. The particular issue of the worshiper's directing his intention to the Holy of Holies is one example of the deep symbolic affinity between Temple and Synagogue.[65] Just as one made a sacred pilgrimage to the holy site of the Temple where sacrifices were offered and the divine Presence was visually encountered, so in the moment of prayer one contemplates and imagines the form of God in that very site.[66]

The determinative factor for the rabbis, however, is not the physical existence of the Temple, but the valorization of the ground where it once stood as sacred. Presumably, the gesture of facing the Temple during prayer applies even after it has been destroyed.[67] Thus, we find the following

---

[63] See Elbogen, *Jewish Liturgy*, pp. 187–199; J. Heinemann, *Prayer in the Talmud: Forms and Patterns* (Berlin, 1977), pp. 122–155; L. I. Levine, "The Second Temple Synagogue: The Formative Years," in *The Synagogue in Late Antiquity*, pp. 7–31; idem, "The Form and Content of the Synagogue in the Second Temple Period," in *Synagogues in Antiquity*, pp. 11–29; E. Fleischer, "On the Beginnings of Obligatory Jewish Prayer," *Tarbiz* 59 (1990): pp. 397–441 (Hebrew); S. Reif, "On the Earliest Development of Jewish Prayer," *Tarbiz* 60 (1991): pp. 677–681 (Hebrew), and the rejoinder by Fleischer in *Tarbiz* 60 (1991): pp. 683–688 (Hebrew).

[64] This topic has been discussed by many scholars. I offer here some representative treatments: J. R. Brown, *Temple and Sacrifice in Rabbinic Judaism* (Evanston, 1963); R. Goldenberg, "The Broken Axis: Rabbinic Judaism and the Fall of Jerusalem," *Journal of the American Academy of Religion* 45 (1977): pp. 869–882; idem, "Early Rabbinic Explanations of the Destruction of Jerusalem," *Journal of Jewish Studies* 33 (1982): pp. 518–525; B. M. Bokser, "Rabbinic Responses to Catastrophe: From Continuity to Discontinuity," *Proceedings of the American Academy of Jewish Research* 50 (1983): pp. 37–61; D. W. Nelson, "Responses to the Destruction of the Second Temple in the Tannaitic Midrashim," Ph.D. dissertation, New York University, 1991.

[65] See S. J. D. Cohen, "The Temple and the Synagogue," in *The Temple in Antiquity*, ed. T. G. Madsen (Provo, 1984), pp. 151–174; S. Safrai, "The Temple and the Synagogue," in *Synagogues in Antiquity*, pp. 31–51.

[66] On the role of the pilgrimage to the holy site of the Temple in Judaism, Christianity, and Islam, see F. E. Peters, *Jerusalem and Mecca: The Typology of the Holy City in the Near East* (New York, 1986), pp. 80–122. For a recent review of the role of pilgrimage and sacred places in the phenomenology of religious experience, see C. C. Park, *Sacred Worlds: An Introduction to Geography and Religion* (London, 1994), pp. 245–285.

[67] It is likely that underlying these dicta is the view, expressed for example by R. Eleazar ben Pedat, that the divine Presence did not depart from the site of the Temple even after it had been destroyed. R. Samuel bar Naḥman, by contrast, expressed the view that as a result of the destruction God removed his Presence to heaven. See Urbach, *The Sages*, pp. 56–57.

expansion in the Palestinian Talmud on the tannaitic statement that all of Israel direct their prayers to one place, *kol yisra'el mitpallelin le-maqom eḥad*:[68]

> It follows that all of Israel pray to one place, as it is written, "For My house shall be called a house of prayer for all peoples" (Isa. 56:7). R. Joshua ben Levi said [this may be derived from the verse], "the front part of the house," *hu ha-heikhal lifnay* (1 Kings 6:17), [which should be decoded as] inside the house to which all faces are turned (*lifnim heikhal she-kol ha-panim ponim lo*). [This makes sense] during the time that it was built, but from where do we know [that this is so] after it is destroyed? R. Abun said [it may be derived from the verse] "built to hold weapons," *banuy le-talpiyyot* (Song of Songs 4:4) [this refers to] the hill towards which all mouths pray (*tel she-kol ha-piyyot mitpallelin alaw*).[69]

The Temple is designated the "hill towards which all mouths pray," or, according to the variant in the Babylonian Talmud, the "hill towards which all mouths are turned,"[70] even after it has been destroyed for it retains its function as the locus of visionary intention in worship. The memory of the Temple's existence is sufficient to endow the space where it once stood with sacred significance. Alternatively expressed, the injunction to face the Temple may be another example of the rabbinic authorities behaving as if the Temple were standing so that liturgical worship could assume the ritual efficacy of the sacrificial cult.[71] Far from fading from the spiritual economy of the Jews, the Temple is transformed symbolically into a ritual space in which there is a convergence of physical and virtual reality. In more conventional phenomenological terms, it may be said that the space of the Temple is sacred because the worshiper endows it with meaning by noetically directing his prayers to it. The demand that prayer is principally oriented towards the Temple, even after its destruction, and the related theological claim that the *Shekhinah* does not depart from that place, do not necessarily entail an implicit messianic hope.[72] On the contrary, the claims for the enduring sanctity of the Temple as the locus for the imaginary visualization of God betoken that the messianic expectation has given way to a pietistic quietism according to which proper intention in prayer

---

68 T. Berakhot 3:16.

69 P. Berakhot 4:5, 8c.

70 B. Berakhot 30a. Cf. *Pesiqta Rabbati* 33, 149b: *tel she-kol ha-peniyyot ponim bo; Song of Songs Rabbah* 4:11, p. 10: *heikhal she-kol ha-piyyot mitpallelot bo*.

71 See Bregman, "Past and Present in Midrashic Literature," pp. 53–54.

72 As suggested by Urbach, *The Sages*, p. 708 n. 94.

more than adequately fulfills the spiritual function of the Temple and its sacrificial cult.

According to the second line of thinking expressed by rabbinic authorities, the object of *kawwanah* is not the earthly Temple but the celestial one. Such a view is consistent with those who maintained that the ultimate purpose of *kawwanah* is to direct one's attention to God, believed by the rabbis to occupy a throne in heaven. Thus, for example, in the Palestinian Talmud there is the following explanation of the mishnaic ruling, referred to above, that if one is riding on an ass he should descend before he prays, and if he cannot descend he should turn his head toward the Temple, and if he cannot turn his head physically he should direct the concentration of his heart to the Temple: "To which Temple? R. Ḥiyya the Great said the Temple above, and R. Simeon ben Ḥalafta said the Temple below. R. Pineḥas said there is no disagreement between them for the Temple below parallels the Temple above."[73] According to R. Ḥiyya, the worshiper, who is at a distance from the earthly Temple, must direct his mind to the heavenly Temple because the latter is the true locus of visionary devotion. It is possible that the opinion of R. Ḥiyya is a tacit rejection of, or at least an open alternative to, the practice of visionary ascensions to the heavenly Temple cultivated by apocalyptic and/or mystical fraternities.[74] That is to say, R. Ḥiyya's position implies that the way to make contact with God in the celestial abode is through proper mental concentration rather than by means of an ascent, whether in or out of body. R. Simeon ben Ḥalafta, in contrast to R. Ḥiyya, is of the opinion that the physical locality of the earthly Temple must be the object of one's *kawwanah*. Even in the absence of the Temple one must direct one's mental concentration to the place where the Temple stood. The Palestinian amora, Pineḥas bar Ḥama, ostensibly resolves the dispute between the two tannaim by affirming the parallelism between the celestial and terrestrial Temples: by directing attention to the one the worshiper is concomitantly directing his attention to the other.[75]

---

[73] P. Berakhot 4:5, 8c. Cf. parallel in *Song of Songs Rabbah* 4:11, p. 110.

[74] A similar argument has been advanced by Fraade, *From Tradition to Commentary*, pp. 93–94.

[75] The point was well understood by Lieberman, *Tosefta Ki-Fshutah, Order Zera'im, Part I*, p. 43: "These are the two details that are operative for every worshiper, that he should imagine as if his prayer passes by way of the Holy of Holies to the *Shekhinah*." See also L. Ginzberg, *A Commentary on the Palestinian Talmud: A Study of the Development of the Halakah and Haggadah in Palestine and Babylonia, Berakhot IV* (New York, 1971), 3:402–403 (Hebrew).

The shift from physical to imaginal space is clearly evident in another tannaitic ruling: a blind person and someone who cannot orient himself in space, and therefore cannot discern the direction of Jerusalem, must direct the attention of their hearts to God in heaven when they pray, *mekhawwenin et libbam keneged avihem she-ba-shamayim u-mitpallelin*.[76] The logical implication of this halakhic injunction is clear: the real object of intention is the divine Presence and thus those who cannot visually orient themselves in the spatial world (even to the degree of blindness) must concentrate their mental focus on the heavenly abode of God. The point is driven home in the second statement attributed generically to the rabbis: "The worshiper must direct his heart to [God who is in] heaven. Abba Saul said, a sign for this matter [can be found in the verse] 'You will make their hearts firm. You will incline Your ear' (Ps. 10:17)."[77] The implication of the dictum, *ha-mitpallel ṣarikh she-yikhawwen et libbo la-shamayim*, is that the obligation to pray is only fulfilled when the one who prays has directed his heart to God, here referred to metonymically by the term *shamayim*, for it is assumed that heaven is the permanent location of the divine.[78] Mental iconography (realized in imaginal space) replaces physical geography. One might argue that the example of the blind person mitigates against my view that *kawwanah* entails a visionary element or an iconic depiction of God. But the understanding of blindness in this particular context does not necessitate or validate such a claim. On the contrary, the supposition is that the blind person, much as the one who cannot find his bearings in space, can still visually direct the mind's eye to God in the heavenly chamber. The heterogeneity of the invisible to the visible is challenged by the fact that the invisible itself enters the realm of the spectacle inasmuch as the task assigned to the human imagination is to form an image by means of which the invisible is seen.[79] Indeed, the rationale for pairing the blind person and the one who cannot determine spatial directions is that in both cases physical sight, which proves to be of no avail in the process of worship, is replaced by mental vision and the object of intention is God in heaven

---

[76] T. Berakhot 3:14. Cf. P. Berakhot 4:5, 8b; B. Berakhot 30a; compare B. Yoma 76a.

[77] B. Berakhot 31a. Cf. T. Berakhot 3:6; *Tanḥuma*, Ḥayye Sarah, 1.

[78] The underlying principle here, that God occupies a place in the celestial Temple even when the earthly Temple is destroyed, is the position affirmed most frequently in rabbinic sources. One text that stands in marked contrast is the dictum attributed to R. Yoḥanan in B. Ta'anit 5a: "The Holy One, blessed be He, said, I will not enter Jerusalem above until I enter Jerusalem below." Cf. *Midrash Tehillim* 122:4, 254b.

[79] My language here reflects the discussion in J. Derrida, *Memoirs of the Blind: The Self-Portrait and Other Ruins*, trans P.-A. Brault and M. Naas (Chicago, 1993), p. 45.

rather than the glory in the Temple. The transference of the scopic field from the earthly to the celestial only underscores that *kawwanah* in its originary sense entailed the visual representation of the divine as a spectacular object.[80]

The displacement of which I speak is implied as well in the tradition attributed to R. Yose, "the one who prays should cast his eyes below and his heart above."[81] Contextually, this opinion is presented as a compromise between the opposing views of R. Ḥiyya and R. Simeon ben Judah ha-Nasi, for according to the latter the one who prays must cast his eyes below to the earthly Temple, a view linked exegetically to the verse, "My eyes and My heart shall ever be there' (1 Kings 9:3), whereas according to the former the one who prays must direct his heart above to the heavenly Temple,[82] a position supported by the verse, "Let us lift up our hearts with our hands to God in heaven" (Lam. 3:40). R. Yose's opinion fosters a split consciousness predicated on the ontological assumption that the Temple above parallels the Temple below. The worshiper can simultaneously look in the direction of the Temple below and contemplate the Temple above because there is perfect symmetry between the two. According to various medieval Talmudic commentators, the instruction of R. Yose is removed from any

---

[80] Cf. Menahem ben Solomon Meiri, *Beit ha-Beḥirah al-Massekhet Berakhot*, p. 106: "Regarding the fact that we turn to the east, it is not because the essence of prayer is toward the east, but because we are standing to the west of Jerusalem and we direct our intention to the Temple and to the glory of God that dwells within it." Meiri's remark is a comment on the tannaitic decree that a worshiper who is blind or who cannot orient himself in space should direct the intention of the heart to God in heaven. On the textual level there is an obvious difference between the directive to focus one's attention on the earthly Temple and the instruction to focus one's attention on God in heaven; indeed, the latter possibility is upheld as the alternative approach adopted by those who cannot fulfill the former. Yet, for Meiri, the two positions are completely homologized, for the point of facing Jerusalem is to direct one's attention to the place where God appears, which is the ultimate purpose of directing one's prayers to God in his heavenly abode. Ezekiel Landau, *Ṣelah ha-Shalem he-Ḥadash* (Jerusalem, 1995), 1:23, notes that all worshipers must face the Holy of Holies because "through there one's prayer would ascend." The ruling that a blind person or one who cannot determine spatial directions should direct his attention to God in heaven also refers to the Holy of Holies "because there is the tabernacle of his Father in heaven." On the special significance of the synagogue, cf. idem, *Derushe ha-Ṣelah* (Warsaw, 1886), 33c.

[81] B. Yevamot 105b.

[82] In the printed text, as well as some manuscripts, the reading is one who prays must cast one's eyes above, which contrasts with the opinion that one who prays must cast one's eyes below. My paraphrase reflects the textual emendation suggested by Isaac Alfasi and Asher ben Yeḥiel; both authorities are cited in *Ein Ya'aqov* to B. Yevamot 105b. See also Lieberman, *Tosefta Ki-Fshutah, Order Zera'im, Part I*, p. 43. Ehrlich, "Modes of Prayer," pp. 110–111, has argued that the better reading is the standard one.

specific reference to the Temple, that is, the contrast is between physically looking down and mentally directing one's heart above.[83] Other commentators, by contrast, well understood that the gestures recommended by R. Yose are related more specifically to the image of the Temple on the earthly and heavenly planes. Thus, commenting on the words "his eyes below," Solomon ben Isaac (Rashi) remarks: "towards the land of Israel because the *Shekhinah* exists there." An attempt to synthesize the two interpretative positions is found in the statement of Jacob ben Asher, although it is evident that he recognized that the primary meaning followed the orientation of Rashi:

> He should bend his head down a bit so that his eyes will be below toward the ground, as it says, "My eyes and My heart shall ever be there" (1 Kings 9:3), and we pray facing the Temple. Therefore, he must cast his eyes below corresponding to it, and it will be considered as if he were standing in it and praying, and with his heart he should concentrate above, as it says, "Let us lift up our hearts with our hands to God in heaven" (Lam. 3:40).[84]

The import of R. Yose's statement, as Jacob ben Asher's explanation makes clear, is that proper intention in prayer demands the split consciousness of which I spoke above, that is, looking with the eyes towards the Temple in Jerusalem and contemplating with the heart the Temple in heaven. In an even more dramatic vein, Jonah ben Abraham Gerondi, in the commentary compiled by one of his disciples on Isaac ben Jacob Alfasi's register of laws and customs derived from Berakhot, relates to the talmudic claim that the worshiper "must cast his eyes below and his heart above" a twofold imaginative process:

---

[83] Cf. *Sefer Halakhot Gedolot*, ed. E. Hildesheimer (Jerusalem, 1971), 1:34: "He who prays must look below and direct his mind above." According to a variant reading of this passage recorded in n. 74 *ad locum*, "when one prays one should lower one's face to the ground and one's heart should be [turned] to heaven." The latter reading (with slight variation) is found in *Sefer Halakhot Gedolot* (Jerusalem, 1992), p. 56. A similar explanation is adopted by Maimonides, *Mishneh Torah*, Hilkhot Tefillah 5:4. See also *Sefer ha-Orah* (attributed to Rashi), ed. S. Buber (Lemberg, 1905), p. 7; Simḥah ben Samuel, *Maḥzor Viṭry*, ed. S. Hurwitz (Nurnberg, 1923), p. 15. Zimmer, "Poses and Postures During Prayer," p. 90, follows this line of interpretation. By contrast, Ehrlich, "Modes of Prayer," p. 110, notes that the correct interpretation is the orienting of the eyes towards the Temple.

[84] *Ṭur*, Oraḥ Ḥayyim, § 95. Cf. *Shulḥan Arukh*, Oraḥ Ḥayyim, § 95:2. This is one of a variety of examples that demonstrate Karo's propensity to follow earlier Ashkenazi customs and rites, especially when they buttress his mystical leanings. See I. Ta-Shema, "Rabbi Joseph Karo Between Spain and Germany," *Tarbiz* 59 (1990): pp. 153–170 (Hebrew).

He should contemplate in his heart as if he were standing in heaven, and he removes from his heart all delights of this world and all pleasures of the body, in the manner that the ancients said, "when you wish to focus [the mind] you should strip your body from your soul."[85] After he has attained this thought, he should also contemplate as if he were standing in the Temple that is below, for by means of this his prayer is more pleasing to God.[86]

This passage, which the disciple of R. Jonah transmitted as a direct (and perhaps oral) tradition "from the mouth of my teacher, the rabbi," affirms that *kawwanah* requires that the worshiper imagine that he is standing, initially, in the heavenly Temple and, secondarily, in the earthly Temple. The mystical pietism of R. Jonah, in my opinion, is consonant with the symbolic intent of the *imago templi* operative in R. Yose's teaching. Furthermore, it is clear that with respect to this issue, as in several others, R. Jonah's view reflects an orientation that is in full accord with the esoteric teaching of Ḥaside Ashkenaz,[87] which I have discussed at length elsewhere.[88]

God's Imaginal Body and the Sanctity of the Synagogue

From the detailed analysis of the rabbinic texts that I have offered in the previous section, it may be concluded that the rabbis themselves, both

---

[85] The idea of *kawwanah* expressed here, reported as a tradition of the ancients (*qadmonim*), bears a phenomenological resemblance to the notion of *devequt* developed by Provençal and Geronese kabbalists, which likewise emphasized the separating of mind from body. On the relationship of Jonah Gerondi to the kabbalists, see G. Scholem, "A New Document on the History of the Beginning of Kabbalah," in *Sefer Bialik*, ed. J. Fichman (Jerusalem, 1934), pp. 141–162, esp. 143–144 (Hebrew); idem, *Reshit ha-Qabbalah* (Tel-Aviv, 1948), pp. 155–156; idem, *Origins of the Kabbalah*, ed. R. J. Zwi Weblowsky and trans. A. Arkush (Princeton, 1987), p. 392; J. Dan, *Jewish Mysticism and Jewish Ethics* (Seattle, 1986), pp. 32–38; idem, "The Cultural and Social Background of the Emergence of Traditional Ethical Literature," *Jerusalem Studies in Jewish Thought* 7 (1988): pp. 239–264, esp. 250–252 (Hebrew).

[86] *Hilkhot Rav Alfasi*, Tractate Berakhot, 22b. The passage is cited by Isserles, *Darkhe Mosheh*, to the *Bet Yosef* on the *Ṭur*, Oraḥ Ḥayyim, § 95. R. Jonah's interpretation of R. Yose's statement is based on the symbolic homology between the sacrificial cult of the Temple and the liturgical rite of the Synagogue. Cf. R. Jonah's comment on M. Avot 1:2 in *Perush Rabbenu Yonah mi-Gerondi al Massekhet Avot* (Jerusalem, 1969), p. 4.

[87] See I. Ta-Shema, "Ashkenazi Hasidism in Spain: R. Jonah Gerondi—the Man and His Work," in *Exile and Diaspora: Studies in the History of the Jewish People Presented to Professor Haim Beinart on the Occasion of His Seventieth Birthday*, ed. A. Mirsky, A Grossman, and Y. Kaplan (Jerusalem, 1988), pp. 165–194 (Hebrew); E. Kanarfogel, *Jewish Education and Society in the High Middle Ages* (Detroit, 1992), pp. 77–78, and references to other scholarly literature on p. 176 n. 78.

[88] See *Through a Speculum That Shines*, pp. 195–214, and "Sacred Space and Mental Iconography: Imago Templi and Contemplation in Rhineland Jewish Pietism," to appear in the *festschrift* honoring Baruch Levine.

within and outside the land of Israel, presumed that the transcendent and imageless God could be manifest in a visible, tangible form through prayer. Even though the rabbis clearly would not have articulated an incarnational theology of the kind affirmed by Christianity, they attempted in their own way to keep alive the theophanic traditions attested in Scripture. The effort to mediate between the aniconic and iconic tendencies resulted in the positing of what I have called the "imaginal body." I have focused, moreover, on prayer, which is one of the key ways affirmed by the rabbis to access that body. Indeed, a central phenomenological feature of the rabbinic understanding of intentionality in liturgical worship is the localization of the divine Presence in space.

If one begins from the theological premise that God is omnipresent, then it would follow that wherever one prayed, the Presence would be there. Yet, rabbinic authorities insisted on the importance of circumscribing prayer within the spatial confines of the synagogue. "R. Abba [in the name of] R. Ḥiyya in the name of R. Yoḥanan said: A person must pray in a place that is designated for prayer... R. Tanḥum bar Ḥanina said: A person must designate a place within the synagogue to pray."[89] The mandate to establish a fixed place of worship within the synagogue generated a variety of ethical and pietistic teachings,[90] but the essential point for the purposes of this analysis is to note that the distinctiveness of the synagogue is related to the assumption that the presence of God is found in that space.[91] The point is accentuated in a statement attributed to R. Abbahu: "'Seek the Lord while He can be found' (Isa. 55:6). Where is He found? In the houses of worship and the houses of study."[92] In another statement, ascribed to R. Isaac, the same idea is derived from the verse, "God stands in the divine assembly" (Ps. 82:1), i.e., the gathering of worshipers is compared to a divine assembly, *adat el*, in which God is found.[93] The synagogue is viewed, like the Tabernacle and the Temple, as a sacred site wherein God dwells. It is preferable, therefore, to pray in the synagogue, an opinion that is expressed

---

[89] P. Berakhot 4:5, 8b. The requirement to establish a permanent place in the synagogue for prayers was widely accepted in the standard codes of Jewish law and ritual. Cf. Maimonides, *Mishneh Torah*, Hilkhot Tefillah 5:6, 8:1, *Ṭur*, Oraḥ Ḥayyim, § 90; *Shulḥan Arukh*, Oraḥ Ḥayyim, § 90:19. See also the responsum against individuals who worship while standing on the outside of the synagogue in *Teshuvot Rav Natronai ben Hilai Gaon*, ed. J. Brody (Jerusalem, 1994); 1:131–132.

[90] P. Berakhot 5:1, 8d; B. Berakhot 6b and 7b.

[91] Cf. *Midrash Tehillim* 90:10, 196a; *Pirqe Rabbi Eliezer*, ch. 35, 82a; *Bereshit Rabbati*, ed. C. Albeck (Jerusalem, 1940), p. 188; *Midrash ha-Gadol on Genesis*, ed. M. Margulies (Jerusalem, 1975), p. 498; Israel ibn al Nakawa, *Menorat ha-Ma'or*, 2:43–44.

[92] P. Berakhot 5:1, 8d.

[93] B. Berakhot 6a.

hyperbolically in the dictum attributed to Abba Benjamin: "The prayer of a person is not heard except in the synagogue, as it says, '[Yet turn, O Lord my God, to the prayer and supplication of Your servant,] and hear the cry and prayer [that Your servant offers before You this day]' (1 Kings 8:28), in the place where there is crying there is prayer."[94] The underlying rationale here is the homology that the rabbis made between the Temple and the synagogue: just as the former was the permanent place of God's dwelling, so, too, the latter. It is thus not coincidental that the interpretation (attributed to R. Isaac) of the expression "diminished sanctuary" (*miqdash me'at*) in Ezek. 11:16 as referring to "the houses of worship and the houses of study in Babylonia" is contextualized in B. Megillah 29a after Abbaye's statement that the *Shekhinah* in Babylonia was limited to two well-known synagogues. The statement of Abbaye is itself placed by the redactor of the text after the dictum attributed to R. Simeon ben Yoḥai that the *Shekhinah* accompanies Israel in all of their exiles. The position of Abbaye is a modification of the more general claim of R. Simeon ben Yoḥai: the *Shekhinah* is present with the Jewish people, but only within the sacred space of select synagogues. The comment of R. Isaac similarly qualifies the viewpoint of R. Simeon ben Yoḥai, but in a more expansive way than Abbaye, for he maintains that the *Shekhinah* is present in all synagogues and academies in Babylonia.

The portrayal of the synagogue as a *miqdash me'at* has had a great impact on liturgical practices that evolved through the generations.[95] Related to this motif is the assumption that within the space of the synagogue God's imaginal body can be visualized by means of the proper intentionality. This feature of the rabbinic phenomenology of prayer is well captured in a comment made by Hai ben Sherira Gaon, head of the talmudic academy in Pumbedita. Reflecting on the dictum attributed to R. Joshua ben Levi, "it is forbidden for one to sit within four cubits of prayer,"[96] Hai comments as follows:

---

94 Ibid. The word that I have translated as crying is *rinnah*. Biblically, this can connote either a ring of weeping or more joyful singing.

95 See I. Ta-Shema, "Synagogal Sancity—Symbolism and Reality," in *Knesset Ezra Literature and Life in the Synagogue: Studies Presented to Ezra Fleischer*, pp. 351–364 (Hebrew). In this study, Ta-Shema investigates two specific rituals, the lighting of the perpetual light (*ner tamid*) in the synagogue and the prohibition of the ritually impure entering into the sanctuary, which are related to the symbol of the synagogue as a *miqdash me'at*. The attitude of Jews through the generations is well summarized by Israel ibn al-Nakawa, *Menorat ha-Ma'or*, 2:39: "The one who enters the synagogue, even when it is not the time of prayer, must behave with dignity because the *Shekhinah* dwells there and it is called a 'diminished sanctuary.'"

96 B. Berakhot 31b.

When a person rises to pray, it is forbidden for another to sit within four cubits in proximity to the worshiper because this is a place of the Presence (*maqom shekhinah*). A proof of this is that, when a person finishes his prayer, he must take three steps backwards and afterward offer a parting farewell. If he does not do so, it is as if he has not prayed. Why is this so? Because of the glory of the Presence (*kevod shekhinah*),[97] and thus it is established that the "four cubits of prayer" are the place of the Presence.[98]

The expression *maqom shekhinah* conveys the idea that through prayer the divine Presence is contained and localized in the sacred space of the synagogue. That this expression should not be understood in a merely figurative way is evident from the halakhic issue to which Hai Gaon relates this idea, viz., it is prohibited for a person to sit idly within four cubits of the one who is worshiping because the latter is standing in the company of the somatic presence of the *Shekhinah*. To appreciate the full import of this text, it is necessary to note that in Hai Gaon's religious philosophy the *Shekhinah* refers to the amorphous light of the divine that is configured in particular shapes within the human imagination. In my opinion, the term "imaginal body" is an appropriate way to describe Hai's ontological assumption regarding the *Shekhinah*, for the body of the *Shekhinah* is constituted by the imaginative faculty.[99] Hence, an idle person is forbidden to sit within four cubits of one engaged in prayer because the space within which one prays is the place wherein the *Shekhinah* resides. The visual form of the divine inheres in the imagination, but the visualization can take place only within a specific space that is designated as holy.[100] Moreover, Hai mentions a custom that is specified in another talmudic discussion: the one who prays must formally depart from the prayer by the gesture of taking three steps backwards and offering a farewell by bowing to the right and

---

[97] On the gesture of taking three steps as a sign of respect and honor for God, cf. *Song of Songs Rabbah* 3:3, p. 84; *Ruth Rabbah* 2:15; *Tanḥuma*, Ki Tissa, 5; *Pesiqta de-Rav Kahana*, 2:7, ed. B. Mandelbaum (New York, 1962), 1:24. Cf. also *Tanḥuma*, Shemot, 15 (ed. Buber, 13).

[98] Cited in *Shibbole ha-Leqeṭ ha-Shalem*, § 25, pp. 203–204; *Sefer ha-Pardes*, p. 327; Israel ibn al-Nakawa, *Menorat ha-Ma'or*, 2:121–122; B. Lewin, *Otzar ha-Gaonim: Thesaurus of the Gaonic Responsa and Commentaries* (Jerusalem, 1984), 1:74 (Hebrew).

[99] See my discussion of Hai's thought in *Through a Speculum That Shines*, pp. 144–148, and 157–158.

[100] Consider the interpretative gloss in *Perushe Rabbenu Ḥananel le-Massekhet Berakhot*, p. 10, on the talmudic statement, "whence do we know that the Holy One, blessed be He, is found in the synagogue?" (B. Berakhot 6b): "That is, whence do we know that the glory of the Holy One, blessed be He, is found [in the synagogue]"? Cf. Eliezer ben Nathan of Mainz, *Sefer Raban*, ed. S. Z. Ehrenreich (New York, 1958), Berakhot, § 126.

to the left.[101] To appreciate the mythic force of this ritual (transmitted in the name of R. Joshua ben Levi) one must bear in mind the larger talmudic context from which this passage is extracted. The general principle underlying this particular gesture is found in the mishnaic ruling (M. Yoma 5:1) that the High Priest must exit from the Holy of Holies the way that he came in, *yaṣa u-va lo be-derekh beit kenisato*, i.e., he exists by walking backwards with his face turned south and the ark to his left. Clearly, the gesture of taking three steps backward when one completes the *Amidah* is an application of this principle, for just as the High Priest could not turn his back on the Holy of Holies, so, too, the worshiper must walk backwards in order not to turn his back on the *Shekhinah*, who dwells within the ritualized space of prayer. Inasmuch as prayer occasions the ontic presencing of the divine, it follows that departure from prayer requires a physical rite that facilitates the psychic transition from the sacred to the mundane. Thus we read in another geonic responsum:

> You have asked what is the reason why after prayer we take three steps backwards. It is because when a person stands in prayer he stands in a place of holiness and the *Shekhinah* is on top of his head, as it says, 'I have set the Lord always before me' (Ps. 16:8), and within four cubits from the place of his standing it is [considered] a place of holiness. Whence [is this known]? For thus the sage said, "it is forbidden for one to sit within four cubits of prayer"... when a person departs from his prayer he must take three steps backwards, for he is going out of a holy place and he will stand in a profane place. Proof of this matter is that when we go back three steps we bid farewell to one [side] and to the other, that is to say, up to this point we were in a place of holiness and now we have gone out to a profane place.[102]

This text is extraordinary for many reasons, not least of which because it presents in lucid terms how the ritualized behavior reflects the mythic structures operative in the rabbinic understanding of prayer. When one rises to recite the *Amidah*, the *Shekhinah* rests atop one's head,[103] an

---

[101] B. Yoma 53b. Cf. Maimonides, *Mishneh Torah*, Hilkhot Tefillah, 5:10–11, *Ṭur*, Oraḥ Ḥayyim, § 123.

[102] B. Lewin, *Otzar ha-Gaonim Thesaurus of the Gaonic Responsa and Commentaries*, 6:24; cf. *Shibbole ha-Leqeṭ ha-Shalem*, § 18, p. 191, and H. Taubes, *Otzar ha-Gaonim le-Massekhet Sanhedrin* (Jerusalem, 1984), 13:164.

[103] It is probable that the same mythical notion underlies the custom to cover one's head during prayer. Cf. *Sefer ha-Orah*, p. 7; Maimonides, *Mishneh Torah*, Hilkhot Tefillah 5:5; *Ṭur*, Oraḥ Ḥayyim § 91; *Shulḥan Arukh*, Oraḥ Ḥayyim § 91:5. In B. Shabbat 118b a tradition is recorded regarding R. Huna ben Joshua who did not walk four cubits with his head uncovered. In B. Qiddushin 31a this tradition is reiterated, but in that context the rationale given for this custom is that the *Shekhinah* is on top of one's head. Cf. Maimonides, *Mishneh Torah*, Hilkhot Deʿot 5:6; *Guide of the Perplexed* III:52; Jonah ben Abraham Gerondi,

experience that is exegetically linked to Ps. 16:8, for in the moment of worship one mentally conjures an image of the divine. Even though the locus of the iconic form is in the mind, it has the power to transform the physical space of the worshiper from profane to sacred and thus one who is not praying must distance himself in an adequate manner from the worshiper. At the completion of the prayer there is a reverse transition from the sacred to the profane, and this, too, must be marked by the specific rites of taking three steps backwards and bowing the head to the right and the left side.

The geonic texts analyzed above render explicit what is implied in the rabbinic material: prayer necessitates the iconic visualization of God, for in order to pray, one must stand in the continual presence of God, but that is achieved only through the formation of a mental image of the divine body within the sacred space of the synagogue. The point is articulated clearly by Solomon ben Abraham ibn Adret. Commenting on the talmudic dictum that one must establish a fixed place for worship within a synagogue, ibn Adret remarked that the "awesomeness of the place causes the One who is sought there to be standing before his eyes and at his right side all day, and from this he will come to the attributes of piety and modesty, and his heart will not stir from his intentions, as it says, 'I have set the Lord always before me; He is at my right hand, I shall never be shaken' (Ps. 16:8)."[104] The synagogue provides the physical space wherein the imaginary vision of the divine body can take place.

To sum up: In the history of Judaism, unlike Christianity, belief in incarnation never attained the status of dogma. On the contrary, in rabbinic texts there are clear polemical statements against the Christological

---

Sefer ha-Yir'ah (Brooklyn, 1974), p. 2; *Tur,* Orah Hayyim § 2; *Shulhan Arukh,* Orah Hayyim § 2:6; *Zohar* 3:122b (*Piqqudin*), 187a. It is likely that this is the reason why the medieval commentators included the custom to pray with one's head covered in their list of bodily postures required for prayer. See, in particular, Israel ibn al-Nakawa, *Menorat ha-Ma'or,* 2:122: "It is necessary that his head be covered during the time of prayer because of the glory of the *Shekhinah* before whom he prays." Regarding this custom, see E. Zimmer, "Men's Headcovering: The Metamorphosis of This Practice," in *Reverence, Righteousness, and Rahamanut: Essays in Memory of Rabbi Dr. Leo Jung,* ed. J. J. Schachter (Northvale, N.J., 1992), pp. 325–352. On the possibility that Paul polemicized against this ritual, see Segal, *Paul the Convert,* pp. 152–156. On covering the head as an external sign of the fear of God, cf. B. Shabbat 156b. Finally, it is worth mentioning that in kabbalistic sources the tradition about not walking four cubits with an uncovered head is merged with the rabbinic statement that the covering of the head was restricted to those who are married (B. Qiddushin 29b), for the obvious reason that, according to the kabbalists, the *Shekhinah* rests only on the head of one who is married. Cf. *The Book of the Pomegranate: Moses de Leon's Sefer ha-Rimmon,* ed. E. R. Wolfson (Atlanta, 1988), p. 224 (Hebrew section).

104 *Commentary on the Legends in the Talmud,* ed. L. A. Feldman (Jerusalem, 1991), p. 6 (Hebrew).

doctrine, and in medieval philosophical literature one of the recurring tenets viewed as basic to Judaism was the claim that God is not a body. However, in rabbinic Judaism of the formative and the medieval periods, based on biblical precedent, an anthropomorphic conception of God is affirmed. These anthropomorphic characterizations are not to be taken figuratively. Underlying the rhetoric of representation is the eidetic presumption that God can be experienced in a tangible and concrete manner. Prayer, according to the rabbis, is one of the key ways that God is so experienced. Proper intentionality in prayer is predicated on the iconic visualization of the divine within the imagination. In the physical space delimited by the liturgical rites, the imaginal body of God assumes incarnate form. It may be concluded, therefore, that the rabbinic notion of incarnation embraces the paradox that God's body is physical only to the extent that it is mental and it is mental only to the extent that it is physical.

NOT YET NOW: SPEAKING OF THE END AND THE END OF SPEAKING

Elliot R. Wolfson

> Where the future is concerned: Expectation is directed
> toward the future; it is merely anticipatory, and like all
> anticipation, it can be deceptive. But life is living on,
> and the law of time also attributes an apodictic con-
> tent to expectation.
>
> Edmund Husserl, *Analyses Concerning Passive and
> Active Synthesis: Lectures on Transcendental Logic*

The theme of this chapter intimates both profound risk and uncertainty, ensuing, as it does, from the ominous realization that to speak of the end one must venture to the limits of both language and temporality. Phenomenologically, we experience all sorts of endings—indeed, as philosophers have long noted, we are constantly beleaguered with the menacing sense that ephemerality is the enduring aspect of time, that the only true permanence is impermanence—but I trust that most would concur that the ending par excellence, the end of endings, as it were, is death. It is for this reason that I will commence my reflections on the discourse of the end with an analysis of death as the futural anterior, the event of the nonevent.

We may not want to go so far as the Heidegger of *Being and Time* and define the singularity of human existence as being-toward-death (*Sein zum Tode*), that is, the anticipatory resoluteness of the end that compels one to confront the "nonrelational ownmost potentiality" (*eigenste, unbezügliche Möglichkeit*), which is labeled as "the possibility of the absolute impossibility of Dasein" (*die Möglichkeit der schlechthinnigen Daseinsunmöglichkeit*).[1] It would be difficult, however, to deny Blanchot's insight regarding dying as the "never-ending ending," in the Levinasian formulation,[2] the *impossibility of possibility*, which constantly informs the path of our being as "a presence

---

[1] Martin Heidegger, *Being and Time*, trans. Joan Stambaugh, revised and with a foreword by Dennis J. Schmidt (Albany: State University of New York Press, 2010), § 50, 241; *Sein und Zeit* (Tübingen: Max Niemeyer Verlag, 1993), 250. See Bernard N. Schumacher, *Death and Mortality in Contemporary Philosophy*, trans. Michael J. Miller (Cambridge: Cambridge University Press, 2011), 72–80.

[2] Emmanuel Levinas, *Proper Names*, trans. Michael B. Smith (Stanford: Stanford University Press, 1996), 132. See also text cited below at n. 10.

in the depth of absence," the possibility that secures our "greatest hope" of being human because it reminds us that "the future of a finished world is still there for us."[3] Contrary to what commonsense might dictate, the finality of death does not abrogate but rather engenders hope.[4] Alternatively expressed, instead of viewing the stasis of death as an "eternal present," the *nunc stans* that is without any future, as Merleau-Ponty opined,[5] an intrinsic nexus is forged between death and futurity. To cite Blanchot again: "Death works with us in the world; it is a power that humanizes nature, that raises existence to being, and it is within each one of us as our most human quality; it is death only in the world—man only knows death because he is man, and he is only man because he is death in the process of becoming... As long as I live, I am a mortal man, but when I die, by ceasing to be a man I also cease to be mortal, I am no longer capable of dying, and my impending death horrifies me because I see it as it is: no longer death, but the impossibility of dying."[6]

Death and the Surplus of Not Yet

What terrifies us about death is not that it is, as Heidegger surmised, the coming-to-an-end (*Zu-Ende-kommen*), the "mode of being in which each and every actual Dasein simply cannot be represented by someone else."[7] The angst surrounding death lies rather in the prospect of confronting

---

[3] Maurice Blanchot, *The Gaze of Orpheus and Other Literary Essays*, preface by Geoffrey Hartman, trans. Lydia Davis, ed. P. Adams Sitney (Barrytown, NY: Station Hill, 1981), 55.

[4] For a wide-ranging discussion of the more commonplace theme of death as the enemy of hope, see Bernard Schumacher, *A Philosophy of Hope: Josef Pieper and the Contemporary Debate on Hope*, trans. D. C. Schindler (New York: Fordham University Press, 2003), 153–202.

[5] Maurice Merleau-Ponty, *Phenomenology of Perception*, trans. Donald A. Landes (London: Routledge, 2012), 348: "A present without a future, or an eternal present, is precisely the definition of death, the living present is torn between a past that it takes up and a future that it projects."

[6] Blanchot, *The Gaze of Orpheus*, 55.

[7] Heidegger, *Being and Time*, § 48, 233; *Sein und Zeit*, 242. Compare Martin Heidegger, *The Concept of Time*, trans. Ingo Farin with Alex Skinner (London: Continuum, 2011), 38–39: "We would be ill-advised to base our investigation on the Dasein of others that has come to an end and is present as a finished whole. First of all, it is central to this Dasein that it too *is* no longer 'there' ['*da*'] as itself. But above all, the particular Dasein of others can never be substituted for the being of Dasein, as long as we wish to maintain that Dasein is in each case one's own [*jeweilig das meinige*]. I can never *be* the Dasein of others, although I may be together with them" (emphasis in original). This text, which was written in 1924 for the journal *Deutsche Vierteljahresschrift für Literaturwissenschaft und Geistesgeschichte* but only published posthumously in 2004 as volume 64 of the *Gesamtausgabe*, is considered the first draft of *Sein und Zeit*.

the fact that without contemplating the contingency of dying there is no more excess of lack but only the lack of excess, no more pondering the possibility of there being nothing more to ponder. Death does not signify the compulsory extinction that we must each endure in our existential-ontological aloneness—in Heidegger's memorable articulation, dying "is essentially and irreplaceably mine,"[8] or in the equally arresting expression of Reiner Schürmann, death is the *singular object of monstration*, which always arrives unexpectedly in the form of a "this" that cannot be subsumed under the general morphology of the species[9]—but rather the perpetual deferment of that obliteration, the postponement of a termination that can be present only by being absent. Not the certitude of death but the impossibility of dying, in Blanchot's provocative locution, is the source of our greatest consternation, since the hopefulness of being alive is inseparably entwined with the possibility of dying. Levinas alludes to this matter when he writes in his notebooks in 1942 that death is distinguished from all other aspects of human experience because it epitomizes the "extreme possibility" that is the "promise of transcendence."[10] The transcendence to which he refers is the relentless becoming of the future that signals the end that never ends in virtue of its being the consummate end.

Death, we might say, is not the deficiency of no more but the surplus of not yet.[11] Following this logic led Levinas in the third of the four lectures

---

[8] Heidegger, *Being and Time*, § 51, 243; *Sein und Zeit*, 253. See Schumacher, *Death and Mortality*, 71–72. For a critique of this Heideggerian assumption and a challenge to the very possibility that death is ever in our grasp as a phenomenological possibility, see Lilian Alweiss, "Heidegger and 'the Concept of Time,'" *History of the Human Sciences* 15 (2002): 117–32.

[9] Reiner Schürmann, *Broken Hegemonies*, trans. Reginald Lilly (Bloomington: Indiana University Press, 2003), 17–18.

[10] Emmanuel Levinas, *Oeuvres 1: Carnets de captivité suivi de Écrits sur la captivité et Notes philosophiques diverses*, ed. Rodolphe Calin, preface and explanatory notes by Rodolphe Calin and Catherine Chalier, general preface by Jean-Luc Marion (Paris: Éditions Grasset and Fasquelle, 2009), 61: "Toutefois la mort n'est pas un fait de l'existence comme un autre. Elle promet quelque chose d'exceptionnel. C'est tout de même une possibilité extrême, une promesse de transcendance." See, however, ibid., 68, where Levinas writes about the "impossibility of dying" (*l'impossibilité de mourir*), and 184, where he similarly uses the expression the "impossibility of death" (*l'impossibilité de la mort*).

[11] This sentiment is expressed movingly in a passage from *Zohar* 1:223b, the compilation of kabbalistic lore published in the sixteenth century after a long period of gestation that began in earnest with the circulation of manuscript fragments in the thirteenth and fourteenth centuries: "It has been taught: R. Eleazar said, 'Even if a person lives for a thousand years, on the day that he departs from the world it seems to him as if he has lived but one day.'" The anonymous kabbalist well captured the manner in which death attests

entitled "Time and the Other," delivered in 1946/47, to differentiate his view sharply from that of Heidegger:

> Death in Heidegger is an event of freedom, whereas for me the subject seems to reach the limit of the possible in suffering. It finds itself enchained, overwhelmed, and in some way passive... This is why death is never a present... The ancient adage designed to dissipate the fear of death—"If you are, it is not; if it is, you are not"—without doubt misunderstands the entire paradox of death, for it effaces our relationship with death, which is a unique relationship with the future.[12]

I would be remiss if I failed to note that Heidegger, too, wrote of the not-yet (*Noch-nicht*) as marking the constant "lack of wholeness" (*Unganzheit*) or the quality of being "outstanding" (*Ausstand*) that belongs essentially to Dasein. This sense of "being-ahead-of-itself-in-already-being-in" (*Sich-vorweg-sein-im-schon-sein-in*) is identified as the structure of care (*Sorge*), the anxiety about the future,[13] which is not the psychological sense of distress to which human beings seem routinely vulnerable on the level of ontic anthropology but rather the ontological structure that designates "the being of a possible being-in-the-world" (*des Seins eines möglichen In-der-Welt-seins*).[14] Ontologically, "being toward one's ownmost potentiality-for-being [*Sein zum eigensten Seinkönnen*] means that Dasein is always already *ahead* of itself in its being [*das Dasein ist ihm selbst in seinem Sein je schon* vorweg]. Dasein is always already 'beyond itself' [»*über sich hinaus*«], not as a way of behaving toward beings which it is *not*, but as being toward the potentiality-for-being which it itself is. This structure of being of the essential 'being concerned about' we formulate as the *being-ahead-of-itself* [Sich-vorweg-sein] of Dasein."[15]

From Heidegger's perspective, human existence is overshadowed by the gnawing sense that "what belongs together is not yet together" (*Nochnichtbeisammensein des Zusammengehörigen*),[16] that Dasein's being

---

not only to the fleetingness of our mortal lives but also to the hope we steadfastly bear that there shall be more time before the coming of the end that heralds the end of becoming.

[12] Emmanuel Levinas, *Time and the Other*, trans. Richard A. Cohen (Pittsburgh: Duquesne University Press, 1987), 70–71. Many have weighed in on the difference between the views of death promulgated by Heidegger and Levinas. For two representative studies, see Tina Chanter, *Time, Death, and the Feminine: Levinas with Heidegger* (Stanford: Stanford University Press, 2001), 154–62, and Eric Severson, *Levinas's Philosophy of Time: Gift, Responsibility, Diachrony, Hope* (Pittsburgh: Duquesne University Press, 2013), 93–99.

[13] Heidegger, *Being and Time*, § 41, 189; *Sein und Zeit*, 196.

[14] Heidegger, *Being and Time*, § 12, 57; *Sein und Zeit*, 57.

[15] Heidegger, *Being and Time*, § 41, 185; *Sein und Zeit*, 191–92.

[16] Heidegger, *Being and Time*, § 48, 233; *Sein und Zeit*, 242.

"remains forever *on its way to something (unterwegs zu)*."[17] The problem here is not the existentiell-ontical dilemma of not being able to apprehend "the not-yet of the character of Dasein," as we find, for example, in the case of perceiving the moon that is not yet full, but rather detecting the existential-ontological structure of "the possible *being* or *nonbeing* of this not-yet [*Noch-nicht*]. Dasein, as itself, has to *become*, that is, *be*, what it is not yet."[18] Heidegger insists, therefore, that "Dasein never becomes accessible at all as something objectively present [*Vorhandenes*], because being possible belongs in its own way to its kind of being."[19] This comportment, however, "finds its end in death,"[20] and hence the acceptance of one's mortality represents the "eminent possibility of Dasein" (*ausgezeichnete Möglichkeit*),[21] that is, the "most extreme not-yet" (*äußerste Noch-nicht*) to which Dasein relates itself as the end that is "imminent" rather than as "something not yet objectively present."[22] The "structural factor of care"—Dasein's being-ahead-of-itself (*Sich-vorweg*)—finds its "most primordial concretion" (*ursprünglichste Konkretion*) in "being-toward-death" (*Sein zum Tode*) that is divulged as "being-toward-the-end" (*Sein zum Ende*).[23] Ironically, humankind's "*ownmost* potentiality-of-being" (eigensten *Seinkönnen*)—its being-there (*Da-sein*)—is discerned from the "possibility of no-longer-being-able-to-be-there" (*die Möglichkeit des Nicht-mehr-dasein-könnens*).[24] The incompleteness of the not-yet terminates in the future that annuls the openness appropriate to a bona fide sense of futurity. "In death, Dasein is neither fulfilled nor does it simply disappear...Rather, just as Dasein constantly already *is* its not-yet as long as it is, it also always already *is* its end." The act of dying, consequently, "does not signify a being-at-an-end [*Zu-Ende-sein*] of Dasein, but rather a *being toward the end* [*Sein zum Ende*] of this being. Death is a way to be that Dasein takes over as soon as it is."[25] In that respect, the being-toward-the-end does not connote an ultimate ending but rather the end that is always also a beginning, the mortality that is the benchmark of our immortality, not in the promise of a postmortem life but in taking hold of the collapse of the difference between life and

---

17 Heidegger, *The Concept of Time*, trans. Ingo Farin with Alex Skinner, 38.
18 Heidegger, *Being and Time*, § 48, 234; *Sein und Zeit*, 243.
19 Heidegger, *Being and Time*, § 49, 239; *Sein und Zeit*, 248.
20 Heidegger, *Being and Time*, § 48, 233; *Sein und Zeit*, 242.
21 Heidegger, *Being and Time*, § 49, 239; *Sein und Zeit*, 248.
22 Heidegger, *Being and Time*, § 50, 240; *Sein und Zeit*, 250.
23 Heidegger, *Being and Time*, § 50, 241; *Sein und Zeit*, 251.
24 Heidegger, *Being and Time*, § 50, 241; *Sein und Zeit*, 250.
25 Heidegger, *Being and Time*, § 48, 236; *Sein und Zeit*, 245.

death in comprehending that the persistence of time consists in its passing, that time is insofar as it constantly is not.[26] Thus, commenting on the verse of Hölderlin, "Life is death, and death is also a life [*Leben ist Tod, und Tod is auch ein Leben*]," Heidegger writes, "Insofar as death comes, it vanishes. The mortals die the death in life. In death the mortals become *im*-mortal [un-*sterblich*]."[27]

In *Der Begriff der Zeit*, a lecture Heidegger delivered to the Marburg Theological Society in July 1924, he offered the following paradoxical account of temporal reversibility that buttresses the centrality accorded to the future in the phenomenological ontology of his earlier work:

> Dasein, as always specifically mine in each case, knows of its death and does so even when it wants to know nothing of it. What is it to *have one's own death in each case? It is Dasein's running ahead to its past, to an extreme possibility of itself that stands before it in certainty and utter indeterminacy.* Dasein as human life *is primarily being possible,* the Being of the possibility of its certain yet indeterminate past...This past, to which I can run ahead as mine, is not some 'what', but the 'how' of my Dasein pure and simple...*This running ahead* is nothing other than *the authentic and singular future of one's own Dasein.* In running ahead Dasein *is* its future, in such a way that in this being futural [*Zukünftigsein*] it comes back to its past and present. Dasein, conceived in its most extreme possibility of Being, is *time itself,* not *in* time...Being futural gives time, cultivates the present and allows the past to be repeated in how it is lived. With regard to time, this means that *the fundamental phenomenon of time is the future* (das Grundphänomen der Zeit ist die Zukunft).[28]

---

[26] Martin Heidegger, *What Is Called Thinking?* trans. Fred W. Wieck and J. Glenn Gray, with an introduction by J. Glenn Gray (New York: Harper and Row, 1968), 99: "And what is the temporal?...We are unmistakably reminded of what it is when we are told that someone's 'time was up.' The temporal is what must pass away. And time is the passing away of what must pass away...Time causes the passing away of what must pass away, and does so by passing away itself; yet it itself can pass away only if it persists throughout all the passing away. Time persists, consists in passing. It is, in that it constantly is not." Heidegger considered this "representational idea of time" as an essential supposition of the "metaphysics of the West." The metaphysical conception is determined by the notion of being as presence and hence what is thought to be in time is that which is present: "Only the 'now' is of the present time at each given moment. The future *is* the 'not yet now'; the past *is* the 'no longer now.' The future is what is still absent, the past is what is already absent" (p. 101, emphasis in original).

[27] Martin Heidegger, *Elucidation of Hölderlin's Poetry*, trans. Keith Hoeller (Amherst, NY: Humanity Books, 2000), 189–90; *Erläuterungen zu Hölderlins Dichtung* [GA 4] (Frankfurt am Main: Vittorio Klostermann, 1981), 165.

[28] Martin Heidegger, *The Concept of Time*, trans. William McNeill (Oxford: Blackwell, 1992), 11–14 (emphasis in original).

To know one's own death, which is not just to know that inevitably one must die but to know in such a way that one possesses one's death—seemingly a phenomenological impossibility—in the quality of mineness (*Jemeinigkeit*) or specificity (*Jeweiligkeit*) that is distinctive to Dasein's being, gives rise to the paradox of temporal reversibility: the running ahead (*Vorlaufen*) to one's past through which one confronts the extreme possibility (*äußersten Möglichkeit*) that stands before oneself in irrefutable certainty (*Gewißheit*) and utter indeterminacy (*Unbestimmtheit*). Obviously, we would have expected Heidegger to speak of running back to the past or running ahead to the future. What does he mean by running ahead to one's past and how is it the authentic and singular future of one's own Dasein (*die eigentliche und einzige Zukunft des eigenen Daseins*)?

We can respond to these queries if we listen carefully to what is hinted at in the statement "Being futural gives time [*Zukünftigsein gibt Zeit*], cultivates the present and allows the past to be repeated in how it is lived." Rather than thinking of the temporalization of time as the indeterminate future determined by the actuality of the past, Heidegger posits the indeterminate past determined by the possibility of the future. Hence, the past to which one runs ahead is not a fait accompli but an open occurrence subject to constant reformulation. Conceived from the vantage point of the "extreme possibility of Being" (*äußersten Seinsmöglichkeit*)—so extreme that the past itself is only past to the extent that it can be replicated as that which is yet to come—the primary mode of temporality for Dasein is the future, and inasmuch as the fundamental phenomenon of time is the future, Dasein is identified as time itself. As in *Being and Time*, so too in this lecture, Heidegger relates the future-orientation of Dasein to the quality of care: "Everything that is encountered in the world is encountered by Dasein as residing in the now; thus it encounters the time itself that Dasein in each case is, but is as present. Concern as absorption in the present is, as care [*Sorge*], nonetheless alongside a not-yet [*Noch-nicht*] that is first to be attended to in taking care of it. Even in the present of its concern, Dasein is the whole of time, in such a way that it does not get rid of the future. The future is now that to which care clings."[29]

The true import of identifying Dasein's ownmost possibility of being as being-toward-death is that Dasein comports the sense of futurity that is the elemental nature of time and thus we should not speak of "having time" or "being in time" but rather that "we are time." The hermeneutical foundation

---

29 Ibid., 16.

of the ontology of time is brought to light in the section of *Being and Time* where Heidegger describes temporality (*Zeitlichkeit*) as the *being of Dasein which understands being* (Sein des seinverstehenden Daseins); that is, time is *the horizon of the understanding of being* (Horizont des Seinverständnisses) whence "Dasein tacitly understands and interprets something like being at all."[30] Indeed, it is in virtue of this dimension of Dasein's being that we can utter the "fundamental assertion" (*Grundaussage*) that *time is temporal* (*die Zeit ist zeitlich*). At first glance, it would appear that this is nothing but a tautology. Heidegger insists, however, that this is not so; the statement imparts that time assumes meaning—becomes temporal—as a consequence of each individual human being running ahead to its past.[31] Time is thus the *principium individuationis*, and the paramount facet of that temporalizing principle of individuation (*Individuationsprinzip*) is the future of the past that we are destined to live in the present. "In being futural in running ahead, the Dasein that on average is becomes itself; in running ahead it becomes visible as this one singular uniqueness of its singular fate in the possibility of its singular past."[32]

In the time of everydayness (*Alltäglichkeit*)—what Heidegger also refers to as the "astronomical and calendrical *time-reckoning*" (*astronomische und kalendarische* Zeitrechnung)[33]—the now of the present is the metrics by which we chronoscopically measure past and future: the past is the irretrievable no-longer-present (*Nicht-mehr-Gegenwart*) and the future the indeterminate not-yet-present (*Noch-nicht-Gegenwart*).[34] The everyday standpoint presumes, therefore, both the irreversibility (*Nicht-Umkehrbarkeit*) of time and its assimilation into space expressed as the homogenization into now-points (*Homogenisierung auf Jetzpunkte*).[35] Authentic time, by contrast, is lived from the futural retrieval of the past in the present, an act that constitutes the nature of Dasein as historicity (*Geschichtlichkeit*), that is, the enigma of history that unravels in our being historical. For Heidegger, this is the first principle of all hermeneutics: "*The possibility of access to history* [Zugangsmöglichkeit zur Geschichte] *is grounded in the possibility according to which any specific present understands how to be futural* [zukünftig]."[36] In *Being and Time*, Heidegger argued that the "being of Dasein finds its

---

30 Heidegger, *Being and Time*, § 5, 17; *Sein und Zeit*, 17.
31 Heidegger, *The Concept of Time*, trans. William McNeill, 20–21.
32 Ibid., 21.
33 Heidegger, *Being and Time*, § 80, 392; *Sein und Zeit*, 411.
34 Heidegger, *The Concept of Time*, trans. William McNeill, 17.
35 Ibid., 18.
36 Ibid., 20.

meaning in temporality," which is defined more specifically as "the condition of the possibility of historicity [*Möglichkeit von Geschichtlichkeit*] as a temporal mode of being [*zeitlichen Seinsart*] of Dasein itself." As the determination of the constitution of the being of Dasein, historicity is prior to the world-historical occurrences (*weltgeschichtliches Geschehen*), which we call history. On the face of it, the historical propensity of the human being may be grounded in the fact that in its factical being (*faktischen Sein*) Dasein always is how and what it already was, that it possesses the past as a property that is still objectively present. However, the appropriation and narration of the past is possible only because Dasein is "its past in the manner of *its* being which, roughly expressed, on each occasion 'occurs' out of its future. In its manner of existing at any given time, and thus also with the understanding of being that belongs to it, Dasein grows into a customary interpretation of itself and grows up on that interpretation... Its own past... does not *follow after* Dasein but rather always already goes ahead of it."[37] The formulation here anticipates the anti-Hegelian emphasis in Heidegger's later thought on the historical destiny of the unthought of being as the "it gives" (*es gibt*), which comes into language in the words of essential thinkers:

> Therefore the thinking that thinks into the truth of being is, as thinking, historical [*geschichtlich*]. There is not a "systematic" thinking and next to it an illustrative history of past opinions... Thought in a more primordial way, there is the history of being [*Geschichte des Seins*] to which thinking belongs as recollection [*Andenken*] of this history, propriated [*ereignet*] by it. Such recollective thought differs essentially from the subsequent presentation of history in the sense of an evanescent past. History does not take place primarily as happening [*Geschehen*]. And its happening is not evanescence [*Vergehen*]. The happening of history occurs essentially as the destiny of the truth of being and from it [*Das Geschehen der Geschichte west als das Geschick der Wahrheit des Seins aus diesem*]... Being comes to its destiny in that It, being, gives itself. But thought in terms of such destiny this says: It gives itself and refuses itself simultaneously [*Es gibt sich und versagt sich zumal*].[38]

---

37 Heidegger, *Being and Time*, § 6, 19 (emphasis in original); *Sein und Zeit*, 19–20. See Jean Greisch, *Ontologie et Temporalité: Esquisse d'une interprétation intégrale de* Sein und Zeit (Paris: Presses Universitaires de France, 1994), 352–82; Françoise Dastur, *Heidegger and the Question of Time*, trans. François Raffoul and David Pettigrew (Atlantic Highlands: Humanities Press, 1998), 38–51.

38 Martin Heidegger, *Pathmarks*, ed. William McNeill (Cambridge: Cambridge University Press, 1998), 255; *Wegmarken* [GA 9] (Frankfurt am Main: Vittorio Klostermann, 2004), 335.

In light of this passage, and many others that could have been cited, I would take issue with the observation of Žižek that "the true *Kehre* from *Sein und Zeit* to the late Heidegger is the shift from ahistorical formal-transcendental analysis to radical historicity...Heideggerian historicity is the historicity of transcendental horizons themselves, of the different modes of the disclosure of being, with no agent regulating the process—historicity happens as an *es gibt* (*il y a*), the radically contingent abyss of a world-game."[39] I concur with the characterization of the *es gibt* as the world-game in which the real is disclosed—and here I would add the word "concealed," insofar as every disclosure is perforce a concealment, every bequeathing is a refusal to bequeath—as "a *given without givenness*," as that which is "just given, with no possibility of accounting for its being given by any agency of giving."[40] Indeed, this is the crux of my reading of Heidegger offered in *Giving Beyond the Gift*, a reading that invokes the ungifting of the gift, that is, the realization that there is naught but the giving that gives with no will to give and no desire to be given.[41] However, I would challenge Žižek's following the scholarly convention by temporalizing Heidegger's thinking. The notion of historicity elicited from Heidegger after the so-called turn is in evidence even in the early work.

Be that as it may, Adorno astutely criticized Heidegger on the grounds that his notion of Dasein's temporal transiency implies that it "is both absolutized and transfigured as eternal by the existential-ontological drafts. The concept of existence as the essentiality of transience, the temporality of temporal things, keeps existence away by naming it...This is the latest type of philosophical solace, the type of mythical euphemism—a falsely resurrected faith that one might break the spell of nature by soothingly copying it."[42] Similarly, from Levinas's perspective, the break with ontology turns on grasping death as the openness that foretells a future that can

---

[39] Slavoj Žižek, *Less Than Nothing: Hegel and the Shadow of Dialectical Materialism* (London: Verso, 2012), 890.

[40] Ibid., 890 n. 44.

[41] Elliot R. Wolfson, *Giving Beyond the Gift: Apophasis and Overcoming Theomania* (New York: Fordham University Press, 2014), 227–60, esp. 236–46.

[42] Theodor W. Adorno, *Negative Dialectics*, trans. E. B. Ashton (New York: Seabury Press, 1973), 131. Compare Theodor W. Adorno, *The Jargon of Authenticity*, trans. Knut Tarnowski and Frederic Will (Evanston, IL: Northwestern University Press, 1973), 88–89. For the contrast between Adorno and Heidegger on the matter of death, temporality, and the finitude of human existence, see Fred Dallmayr, *Life-world, Modernity and Critique: Paths between Heidegger and the Frankfurt School* (Cambridge: Polity Press, 1991), 51–52. See also Alexander García Düttmann, *The Memory of Thought: An Essay on Heidegger and Adorno*, trans. Nicholas Walker (London: Continuum, 2002), 52.

never be present except as what is yet to come, and thus the relativization of the temporal is not subject to the absolutization of being, even if the latter is conceived as the past that is eternally in the process of becoming, the reverberation of the same difference. When viewed this way we can appreciate the need to reverse the relationship between transience and temporality that emerges from Heidegger's ruminations on death as the authentic "having-come-to-an-end" (*Zuendegekommensein*).[43] Apparently, pushing back against Heidegger, Levinas writes, "What we have attempted to do is to think of time independently of the death to which the passive synthesis of aging leads us, to describe time independently of death or the nothingness of the end that death signifies. We have attempted to think death as a function of time, without seeing in death the very project of time."[44] It seems to

---

[43] Heidegger, *Being and Time*, § 47, 230; *Sein und Zeit*, 239.

[44] Emmanuel Levinas, *God, Death, and Time*, trans. Bettina Bergo (Stanford: Stanford University Press, 2000), 113. This is not the place to evaluate the accuracy and impartiality of Levinas's critique of Heidegger's position, but it does seem to me that Heidegger anticipates some of this criticism in his assessment of the theme of being-toward-death in Martin Heidegger, *Contributions to Philosophy (of the Event)*, trans. Richard Rojcewicz and Daniela Vallega-Neu Maly (Bloomington: Indiana University Press, 2012), § 161, 222–23; *Beiträge zur Philosophie (Vom Ereignis)* [GA 65] (Frankfurt am Main: Vittorio Klostermann, 1994), 283–84. After asserting that the consideration of being-toward-death in *Being and Time* was "thought only within 'fundamental ontology' and never conceived anthropologically or in terms of a 'worldview,'" Heidegger recasts the earlier discussion in light of his current thinking about *Ereignis* as the truth of beyng (*Seyn*): "The uniqueness [*Einzigkeit*] of death in human Da-sein belongs to the most original determination of Da-sein, namely, to be ap-propriated [*er-eignet*] by beyng itself in order to ground this latter in its truth (openness of self-concealing). In the unusualness and uniqueness of death, what opens up is the most unusual amid all beings, beyng itself, which essentially occurs as estrangement [*Befremdung*]. Yet in order to surmise anything at all of this most original nexus . . . what had to be made visible first . . . is the relation of Da-sein to death itself, i.e., the connection between resoluteness (openness) and death, i.e., the running-ahead [*Vor-laufen*]. Yet this running ahead toward death is not to be made visible for the sake of attaining mere 'nothingness' [*Nichts*], but just the opposite, so that openness for beyng might be disclosed—fully and out of what is most extreme . . . The essential context for the projection of death is the original *futurity* [*ursprünglichen* Zukünftigkeit] of Dasein within its very essence (as that essence is understood in fundamental ontology). In the framework of the task of *Being and Time*, this primarily means that death is connected to 'time,' which in turn is established as the domain for the projection of the truth of beyng itself. This already shows, clearly enough for anyone who wants to participate in the questioning, that there the question of death stands in an essential relation to the *truth of beyng* [Wahrheit des Seyns] and stands *only* in that relation. Accordingly, death is not taken there, and is never taken, as the denial of beyng [*Verneinung des Seyns*] or even, qua 'nothingness,' as the essence of beyng [*Wesen des Seyns*]. Instead, the exact opposite is the case: death is the highest and ultimate attestation of beyng [*der Tod das höchste und äußerste Zeugnis des Seyns*]." As this passage indicates, and the succeeding section makes even more clear, Heidegger was responding to critics who understood his analysis of being-toward-death as promoting a worldview (*Weltanschauung*) that led to nihilism. On the

me entirely apt to ascribe to death Levinas's description of the tragic as the "infinity of existence that is consumed in an instant, the fatality in which its freedom is congealed as in a winter landscape where frozen beings are captives of themselves. Time, far from constituting the tragic, shall perhaps be able to deliver us from it."[45] Reiterating the theme with a slightly different nuance in *Totality and Infinity*, Levinas writes:

> To be temporal is both to be for death and to still have time, to be against death...It is a relation with an instant whose exceptional character is due not to the fact that it is at the threshold of nothingness or of a rebirth, but to the fact that, in life, it is the impossibility of every possibility, the stroke of a total passivity alongside of which the passivity of the sensibility, which moves into activity, is but a distant imitation. Thus the fear for my being which is my relation with death is not the fear of nothingness, but the fear of violence—and thus it extends into fear of the Other, of the absolutely unforeseeable.[46]

In contrast to Heidegger's understanding of death as the existential-ontological structure of Dasein's *ownmost and nonrelational possibility*, Levinas depicts death as the relation with the instant whose exceptionality exhibits the impossibility of every possibility, the passivity of the subject overcome by the unpredictability of the other. Borrowing the jargon used by Benjamin to distinguish classical tragedy from the *Trauerspiel*, we can say that, for Levinas, death is not an "individual destiny" but the "form of a communal fate."[47]

I would propose, moreover, that to comprehend Levinas's reference to the instant of death, we must avail ourselves of his earlier conception of the instant as the hypostasis that constitutes the "pretemporal sensibility,"

---

contrary, the intent of the analysis of being-toward-death was to enact the "ultimate measuring out [*Ausmessung*] of *temporality* [Zeitlichkeit] and thereby the move into the *space* of the truth of beyng, *the indication of time-space* [die Anzeige des Zeit-Raumes]: thus *not* in order to deny 'beyng,' but rather in order to establish the ground of its complete and essential affirmability [*Bejahbarkeit*]." The "carrying out" (*Vollzug*) of being-toward-death is open to "every essential human being" (*wesentliche Mensch*), but it is incumbent "only on thinkers of the other beginning." With palpable irritation and a smidgen of sarcasm, Heidegger observes, "Being-toward-death would not be touched in its essentiality if it did not give scholars in philosophy an occasion for tasteless scoffing and journalists the right to know everything better" (*Contributions*, § 162, 223–24; *Beiträge*, 284–85).

[45] Emmanuel Levinas, *Existence and Existents*, trans. Alphonso Lingis, foreword by Robert Bernasconi (Pittsburgh: Duquesne University Press, 2001), 78.

[46] Emmanuel Levinas, *Totality and Infinity: An Essay on Exteriority*, trans. Alphonso Lingis (Dordrecht: Kluwer Academic Publishers, 1969), 235.

[47] Walter Benjamin, *The Origin of German Tragic Drama*, trans. John Osborne, with an introduction by George Steiner (London: Verso, 1998), 136. The passage is cited below in n. 176.

in the language of Tina Chanter, the "time that is not yet time."[48] Levinas insisted that one cannot understand the instant unless one is attuned to the problem of origin, a topic that escapes philosophical analysis because the law of contradiction does not apply to what is prior to the event of the beginning, the moment of which we must say that A is concurrently non-A. The "paradoxical duality" is rendered as follows:

> What begins to be does not exist before having begun, and yet it is what does not exist that must through its beginning give birth to itself, come to itself, without coming from anywhere. Such is the paradoxical character of beginning which is constitutive of an instant...A beginning does not start out of the instant that precedes the beginning; its point of departure is contained in its point of arrival, like a rebound movement. It is out of this withdrawal in the very heart of the present that the present is effected, and an instant taken up.[49]

The instant of death is the mirror image of the instant of the beginning and thus we can say of it that *its point of departure is contained in its point of arrival*, and much like the beginning, the end is a withdrawal in the very heart of the present. But unlike the beginning, which is the giving birth to oneself, death is letting go of oneself to give birth to another. Death incarnates the temporality that is expressive of the alterity that undergirds the infinite responsibility that one must assume in proximity to the other.[50] That is, just as the temporal invariably bears the inchoateness of the not yet, so the other ceaselessly eludes categorization, since it is always on the way to becoming what it is not and therefore cannot be apperceived as that which is the same. Expressed in the more technical terms adopted by Levinas, the diachrony of time signifies the "noncoincidence" and "inadequation" of the "absolutely other," the "In-visible" that cannot be "assimilated by experience," the something more that is the "*always* of the relationship, an aspiration and an awaiting."[51] As a matter of phenomenological exactitude, death cannot be treated under the taxon of temporal facticity; it is more suitably demarcated as that which transpires in time in relation to which time has expired.

---

48 Chanter, *Time, Death, and the Feminine*, 151. The author suggests that the idea of the instant may be viewed as "the germ of the notion that Levinas will later call the trace. As such, it also anticipates the structural tension and ambiguity that he will explore under the heading of the saying and the said."

49 Levinas, *Existence and Existents*, 75.

50 Levinas, *Time and the Other*, 104.

51 Ibid., 32 (emphasis in original).

Death falls outside the parameter of phenomenality—at least when construed from the vantage point of a genetic as opposed to a generative phenomenology. Applying the words that Blanchot relegates to the phenomenon of the disaster, we can say of death that it is not a fact or an event because there is no "I" to undergo the experience, and since this is so, we are led to the paradox that death can take place only after having taken place.[52] The time of death, accordingly, is the *future anterior*; that is, concerning death we can only say post factum that it will have been the event that it was to become.[53] There is, as Françoise Dastur wrote, an impasse shared by the phenomenology of eventuality and the phenomenology of mortality: "Death, as an event, is also that which always happens against all expectation, always too early, something impossible that nevertheless happens. It comes to us without coming from us. It takes place in the impersonal manner of this event that happens also to others and it is the most universal event for living beings. One could say that death is the event par excellence, except that it is never present, it never presently happens."[54]

Husserl already recognized the problem in wrestling with what he considered to be the inconceivability of imagining that everything that is presently immanent—that is, all beings constituted noetically in the enduring present of consciousness—would come to a halt such that there would then be nothing:

---

[52] Maurice Blanchot, *The Writing of Disaster*, trans. Ann Smock (Lincoln: University of Nebraska Press, 1986), 28.

[53] My thinking reflects the approach to the event more generally affirmed by Claude Romano, "Awaiting," in *Phenomenology and Eschatology: Not Yet in the Now*, ed. Neal DeRoo and John Panteleimon Manoussakis (Surrey: Ashgate, 2008), 46. See also Françoise Dastur, "Phenomenology of the Event: Waiting and Surprise," *Hypatia* 15 (2000): 178–89, esp. 182–83: "But what is an event, in fact? At first, we can only define it as what was not expected, what arrives unexpectedly and comes to us by surprise, what descends upon us, the accident... The event in the strong sense of the word is therefore always a surprise, something which takes possession of us in an unforeseen manner, without warning, and which brings us towards an unanticipated future. The *eventum*, which arises in the becoming, constitutes something which is irremediably excessive in comparison to the usual representation of time as flow. It appears as something that dislocates time and gives a new form to it, something that puts the flow of time out of joint and changes its direction... The event constitutes the critical moment of temporality—a critical moment which nevertheless allows the continuity of time... Against all expectation, even if it has been partially expected and anticipated, such is in fact the 'essence' of the event. Based on this we could say without paradox that it is an 'impossible possible.' The event, in its internal contradiction, is the impossible which happens, in spite of everything, in a terrifying or marvelous manner."

[54] Dastur, "Phenomenology," 183.

As soon as one conceives of the "then-not-being," one presupposes a "then-being," which conflicts with the non-being. One imputes the possible cessation of every conceivable particular being to a putative cessation of the stream of life. The cessation itself as the cessation of the object presupposes a non-cessation, namely, consciousness to which the cessation is given.[55]

Merleau-Ponty extends the point to birth as well: "Neither my birth nor my death can appear to me as my personal experiences, since if I conceive of them in this way, I must imagine myself as preexisting or as surviving myself in order to be able to experience them, and thus I could not genuinely conceive of my birth or my death. Thus, I can only grasp myself as 'already born' and as 'still living,'—I can only grasp my birth and my death as pre-personal horizons: I know that one is born and that one dies, but I cannot know my birth or my death."[56] Simply put, none of us can experience our own birth or our own death even as we know categorically that one is indisputable and the other inescapable. By this yardstick, death is quintessentially the nonevent of the terminus delimited as the limit always to be delimited, the limit beyond which there is no limit, and hence the limit of what cannot be delimited, the threshold that may be crossed only by not-crossing. Death signifies a radical experience of time as the erasure written from the abiding evanescence of the end that stops being an end once it is attained, the future that can never arrive because, as future, it is always still arriving.

Prima facie, the inability to reach the end, which temporalizes our existence in a distinctive manner, can be expressed as an apophasis of language. The point was well captured by Schürmann: "The singularizing withdrawal that death exerts on life would reduce language to zero if it were possible for us to see it in all its clarity. A radical *Aufklärung* on the subject of fantasms would deprive us of the common space where the give and take of speech proves to us that we are not dead."[57] This seems reasonable enough—all things being equal, the possibility of dialogue with another is a tell-tale sign that one is still walking amongst the living. The silence of not speaking may thus be correlated with death. Probing the matter from an

---

[55] Edmund Husserl, *Analyses Concerning Passive and Active Synthesis: Lectures on Transcendental Logic*, trans. Anthony J. Steinbock (Dordrecht: Kluwer Academic Publishers, 2001), 467. Husserl's position is discussed by Saulius Geniusas, "On Nietzsche's Genealogy and Husserl's Genetic Phenomenology: The Case of Suffering," in *Nietzsche and Phenomenology: Power, Life, Subjectivity*, ed. Élodie Boublil and Christine Daigle (Bloomington: Indiana University Press, 2013), 50.

[56] Merleau-Ponty, *Phenomenology of Perception*, 223.

[57] Schürmann, *Broken Hegemonies*, 18.

even more paradoxical perspective, however, we can say that human time-keeping is such that death is the signpost that illumines the way to the end that is still spoken, albeit spoken as unspoken. But how does one speak of what cannot be spoken? How does one discourse about death without traversing the coming of one's time—as in our saying "one's time has come"? Death—the unexpected, but yet altogether anticipated, end that comes unendingly as the end to come intermittently—opens consciousness to the moment that escapes objectification and thematization, a moment that may be rendered poetically as the confrontation with the face most visible when it can be seen no more. In this encounter—the effacement at the intersection wherein existence and nonexistence are indistinguishable, or, as Levinas put it, the "interval of discretion" that is the "third notion between being and nothingness"[58]—truth is disclosed in the concealment of its disclosure. The sign of the end, accordingly, would signify the end of the sign, but it is a sign nonetheless, indeed the ultimate sign inasmuch as it signifies that which cannot be signified, a semiosis of the end that is inherently endless.

Waiting for the End of Waiting

Beyond the complexities of delineating death as an abstract homogenization that would lead paradoxically to the positing of a singularity that does not allow for singularity, we must be cognizant of the fact that any thinking that attempts to grapple with the endtime more generally in an age inundated by severe fragmentation, heterogeneity, and disjointedness needs to engage the problem of the viability of system and the incommensurability of truth as the exception to exceptionality, the trace of transcendence that defies incorporation into totality. As Joanna Hodge summarized the situation in the twentieth century, which can easily be extended to the twenty-first century, "In place of completed systems or delimited position statements, philosophy has tended to be written under the sign of incompleteness, and thus has the open-ended form of a practice which requires the active participation of its inheritors."[59] Thinking in the

---

[58] Levinas, *Totality and Infinity*, 58.
[59] Joanna Hodge, "Poietic Epistemology: Reading Husserl Through Adorno and Heidegger," in *Adorno and Heidegger: Philosophical Questions*, ed. Iain Macdonald and Krzysztof Ziarek (Stanford: Stanford University Press, 2008), 66.

footsteps of Rosenzweig,[60] I would proffer that system does not denote an architectural structure, which is formed by assembling individual stones whose meaning is validated by the sense of the whole, but rather the striving on the part of individual entities for correlationality; the merit of a system is dependent, therefore, on postulating a unity incessantly in the making, a cohesiveness that displays an impulse for order that must be realized continually through negotiating the chaos. The idea of the open system is captured aptly by Hodge's expression "poietic epistemology," which she deploys to convey the idea that phenomenology is a practice of thinking that is always in the process of formation.[61] Rosenzweig elucidated his view by noting that, in the Hegelian system, each individual is anchored temporally in the whole and thus every present is an interval related exclusively to two others, the one that immediately precedes it as past and the one that immediately succeeds it as future, but in his notion of systematicity, the genuine novelty of each moment is not to be confirmed spatially by its occupying a median position sequentially between what came before and what comes after. To the extent that the moment is authentically novel—an event of presence that is always in excess of being present—it is experienced as the constant resumption of what is yet to be, the return of what has never been, the vertical intervention that opens the horizontal timeline to the spherical redundancy of eternity. In this manner, Deleuze famously cast Nietzsche's doctrine of eternal recurrence as the repetition that consists in conceiving the same on the basis of the different; that is, what is the same is the reiteration of difference,[62] and hence, as Heidegger pithily portrayed the paradox of temporal

---

[60] I am here restating the argument in Elliot R. Wolfson, *Language, Eros, Being: Kabbalistic Hermeneutics and Poetic Imagination* (New York: Fordham University Press, 2005), 88–89, and compare Elliot R. Wolfson, "Structure, Innovation, and Diremptive Temporality: The Use of Models to Study Continuity and Discontinuity in Kabbalistic Tradition," *Journal for the Study of Religions and Ideologies* 6 (2007): 156–57. Rosenzweig's notion of system has been explored by various scholars. See, for instance, Stéphane Moses, *System and Revelation: The Philosophy of Franz Rosenzweig*, foreword by Emmanuel Lévinas, trans. Catherine Tihanyi (Detroit: Wayne State University Press, 1992); Benjamin Pollock, *Franz Rosenzweig and the Systematic Task of Philosophy* (Cambridge: Cambridge University Press, 2009); and the essays in *Die Denkfigur des Systems im Ausgang von Franz Rosenzweig's »Stern der Erlösung«*, ed. Hartwig Wiedebach (Berlin: Duncker and Humblot, 2013).

[61] Hodge, "Poietic Epistemology," 65.

[62] Gilles Deleuze, *Difference and Repetition*, trans. Paul Patton (New York: Columbia University Press, 1994), 41; Gilles Deleuze, *Nietzsche and Philosophy*, trans. Hugh Tomlinson (London: Athlone Press, 1983), 48. For discussion of the Deleuzian perspective and the passage of Heidegger cited in the following note, see Wolfson, *Giving Beyond the Gift*, 243.

tensiveness, every "already" (*wieder*) is an "altogether otherwise" (*ganz anders*). Repetition, therefore, means "to *let* the *same*, the uniqueness of beyng, become plight *again* and *thereby out of a more original truth.*"[63]

For Rosenzweig, this paradox suggests that the renunciation of totality and the consequent turn to individuality are not an unmitigated toppling of system but a reorientation based on a notion of system according to which universality is revamped continuously in light of the entanglement of the general in the web of particularity. This notion of systematicity, as I have suggested elsewhere,[64] offers something of a corrective to the postmodern dismissal of essentialism, insofar as it entails a conception of integration and a mode of discursive coherence that provide the relatively stable framework through and in which the changing constellations evolve, dissolve, and revolve, without assuming that all tensions, inconsistencies, and contradictions are reconciled in a unified structure akin to a Hegelian ideal of sublation. What may be elicited from Rosenzweig is not conceptually far-off from Benjamin's idea that the expressionless points to the absolute, which is not a substance that can be reified ontotheologically but rather the infinitude (*Unendlichkeit*) of language that prevents the setting of definite limits and thus serves as the principle of falsification that shatters the whole into fragments—corresponding linguistically to the translatability of the *Ursprache* into the multiple languages of humankind[65]—"reducing it to the *smallest* totality of semblance, a totality that is a great fragment

---

[63] Heidegger, *Contributions*, § 33, 58 (emphasis in original); *Beiträge*, 73. It follows that, for Heidegger, the inceptuality of the beginning (*die Anfängnis des Anfangs*)—the event (*Ereignis*)—is a reiteration (*Wiederanfangen*) of what has already been that which is to come, the thinking of the first that is always a rethinking of the second, a point exploited by the anarchic drift of Derridean deconstruction. See Heidegger, *Contributions*, § 23, 46; *Beiträge*, 57; Martin Heidegger, *The Event*, translated by Richard Rojcewicz (Bloomington: Indiana University Press, 2013), §§ 252–53, 195–97; *Das Ereignis* [GA 71] (Frankfurt am Main: Vittorio Klostermann, 2009), 227–29: "The beginning is not inceptually in the inceptuality; the beginning commences in what has not begun, inasmuch as the beginning disentangles itself from that in order to emerge. The disentangling is what is concealed of the unconcealedness... The other beginning is *the* beginning *otherwise* than the first—the first is still otherwise than the other [*der erste ist anders noch als der andere*]... Beginning [*Anfang*] does not mean commencement [*Beginn*], and afortiori never means the commencement of beings... In order to think the beginning, we must already in advance be appropriated in the experience of being [*Erfahrung des Seins*], appropriated by being to this experience" (emphasis in original). See also Martin Heidegger, *Schwarze Hefte 1931–1938* [GA 94] (Frankfurt am Main: Vittorio Klostermann, 2014), II, § 237, 100, and IV, § 115, 243.
[64] Elliot R. Wolfson, "Revealing and Re/veiling: Menaḥem Mendel Schneerson's Messianic Secret," *Kabbalah: Journal for the Study of Jewish Mystical Texts* 26 (2012): 52.
[65] Andrew Benjamin, "The Absolute as Translatability: Working Through Walter Benjamin on Language," in *Walter Benjamin and Romanticism*, ed. Beatrice Hanssen and Andrew Benjamin (London: Continuum, 2002), 109–22.

taken from the true world, the fragment of a symbol."[66] Moving beyond the rhetoric of Rosenzweig and Benjamin, employing the strategies of more recent semiotic theory, enhanced by contemporary physics and mathematics, I would say that the complexity of any given system requires that each one of the interacting semantic signs is implicated in the production of the very system that produces it, a network of patterns that express the dynamical properties fashioned by an ever-changing interconnectivity; this ensemble of irreducible and yet mutually interdependent clusters, however, does not form a homogeneous and symmetrical whole devoid of ambiguity and incoherence.[67] Following Badiou, we may wish to adopt the notion of *universal singularity*—epitomized by Paul in his appeal to the "evental truth" that casts the universal messianically with reference to the singular and subjective occurrence of the resurrection, that is, the human becoming the ultimate subject by relinquishing integration into the totality (Greek wisdom) and abdicating the mastery of a literal tradition that triggers the deciphering of signs (Jewish ritualism and prophetism)[68]—in an effort to affirm the construction of imaginary identities that are shared but not subsumed under an axiomatic homogeny. In Lacanian terms, the world is "an interplay of the symbolic and the imaginary in response to the collapse of the real."[69] However, as Badiou himself acknowledges, this collapse

66 Walter Benjamin, *Selected Writings, Volume 1: 1913–1926*, ed. Marcus Bullock and Michael W. Jennings (Cambridge, MA: Harvard University Press, 1996), 225.

67 Paul Cilliers, *Complexity and Postmodernism: Understanding Complex Systems* (London: Routledge, 1988), 44–45, 94–95. See also David Bohm, *Thought as a System* (London: Routledge, 1994).

68 Alain Badiou, *Saint Paul: The Foundation of Universalism*, translated by Ray Brassier (Stanford: Stanford University Press, 2003), 14, 42. For a sustained critique of Badiou's approach to Paul, see Stephen Fowl, "A Very Particular Universalism: Badiou and Paul," in *Paul, Philosophy, and the Theopolitical Vision: Critical Engagements with Agamben, Badiou, Žižek, and Others*, ed. Douglas Harink (Eugene: Cascade Books, 2010), 119–34.

69 Alain Badiou, "St. Paul, Founder of the Universal Subject," in *St. Paul among the Philosophers*, ed. John D. Caputo and Linda Martin Alcoff (Bloomington: Indiana University Press, 2009), 28. Badiou's indebtedness to Lacan is well-documented in the conversations recorded in Alain Badiou and Élisabeth Roudinesco, *Jacques Lacan, Past and Present: A Dialogue*, trans. Jason E. Smith (New York: Columbia University Press, 2014). On the truth as universal singularity and Paul, see also Badiou, *Saint Paul*, 9–14, esp. 11: "For if it is true that every truth erupts as singular, its singularity is immediately universalizable. Universalizable singularity necessarily breaks with identitarian singularity." On the thesis that every universal is a singularity, see Alain Badiou, "Thinking the Event," in Alain Badiou and Slavoj Žižek, *Philosophy in the Present*, ed. Peter Engelmann, trans. Peter Thomas and Alberto Toscano (Cambridge: Polity Press, 2010), 29–31. See also Frederiek Depoortere, "Badiou's Paul: Founder of Universalism and Theoretician of the Militant," in *Paul in the Grip of the Philosophers: The Apostle and Contemporary Continental Philosophy*, ed. Peter Frick (Minneapolis: Fortress Press, 2013), 143–64.

"eliminates the event, and so fidelity to the event, which is the subjective essence of the truth. The world is then hostile to the process of truth insofar as it resists the universal of identity through homogeny or the adhesion to constructed identities."[70]

The relevance of this claim to the topic at hand should be obvious. The repudiation of homogeneity and symmetry calls into question the rigidity of positing a clearly marked beginning or end. For our purposes I will concentrate on the latter, although I readily admit that the correlativity of the two precludes their partition. In contemplating the end, we enter into the thicket of eschatology—literally, the discourse or thinking about the end—for there is no end that has commanded as much attention in Jewish theorizing about the end as the eschaton. Here, too, it is prudent to note the messianic paradigm embraced by Rosenzweig, which is to be contrasted with a conception of the climactic fulfillment of history as we find in some forms of Christian soteriology, Enlightenment utilitarianism, and Hegelian idealism. The teleological notion is upended by the possibility of the future diremptively breaking into the present at any moment, an incursion that disturbs the chronometric flow of time and undercuts the supposition that there is a progressive march towards an attainable goal. Messianic hope hinges on preparing for the onset of what takes place as the *purely present future*, that is, the future that is already present as the present that is always future, the *tomorrow that is now because it is now tomorrow*.[71] "Eternity is not a very long time," wrote Rosenzweig, "but a tomorrow that just as well could be today. Eternity is a future, which, without ceasing to be future, is nevertheless present."[72] It is specifically through adherence to Jewish law in the course of the annual liturgical cycle that one is "permitted to implore eternity into time."[73] The Jews are the eternal people because they ritually embody this sense of fulfilled time: "For it its temporality, this fact that the years recur, is considered only as a waiting, perhaps as a wandering, but not as a growing . . . For eternity is precisely this, that between the present

---

[70] Badiou, "St. Paul," 28.

[71] Elliot R. Wolfson, *Open Secret: Postmessianic Messianism and the Mystical Revision of Menaḥem Mendel Schneerson* (New York: Columbia University Press, 2009), 286; Elliot R. Wolfson, "Open Secret in the Rearview Mirror," *Association for Jewish Studies Review* 35 (2011): 417–18.

[72] Franz Rosenzweig, *The Star of Redemption*, trans. Barbara Galli (Madison: University of Wisconsin Press, 2005), 241.

[73] Ibid., 347.

moment and the completion time may no longer claim a place, but as early as in the today every future is graspable."[74]

Rather than viewing the nomadic quality of the Jew as a detriment, Rosenzweig interprets the stereotype of wandering as the spatial analogue to the temporal exploit of waiting for the end. The position taken by Rosenzweig is put into sharp relief when compared to Heidegger, who viewed both Jewish messianic faith and the nomadic status of the Jew prejudicially: the directive to wait for redemption as an incident in history that has not yet occurred is the temporal equivalent of spatial dislocation and the diasporic desire to return to the homeland.[75] Needless to

---

[74] Ibid., 348.

[75] Concerning Heidegger's view on Jewish messianism, see the passage from *The Phenomenology of Religious Life* cited and discussed in Wolfson, *Giving Beyond the Gift*, 232–33. On the disparaging depiction of the itinerant status of the Jewish exile, see especially the comment in Martin Heidegger, *Nature, History, State 1933–1934*, trans. and ed. Gregory Fried and Richard Polt (London: Bloomsbury, 2013), 55–56: "History teaches us that nomads have not only been made nomadic by the desolation of wastelands and steppes, but they have also often left wastelands behind them where they found fruitful and cultivated land—and that human beings who are rooted in the soil have known how to make a home for themselves even in the wilderness. Relatedness to space, that is, the mastering of space and becoming marked by space, belong together with essence and the kind of Being of a people ... From the specific knowledge of a people about the nature of its space, we first experience how nature is revealed in this people. For a Slavic people, the nature of our German space would definitely be revealed differently from the way it is revealed to us; to Semitic nomads, it will perhaps never be revealed at all." See the analysis of this text in Peter E. Gordon, "Heidegger in Purgatory," in Heidegger, *Nature, History, State*, 85–107, esp. 96–98. As Gordon rightly notes, Heidegger's deleterious comment has to be evaluated against his overall thinking regarding the themes of enrootedness, dwelling, homelessness, and homecoming, as they relate to the destiny of the human being in the world. On the political issues surrounding the topological-geographical elements of Heidegger's thinking in light of his affiliation with Nazism, see Jeff Malpas, *Heidegger's Topology: Being, Place, World* (Cambridge, MA: MIT Press, 2006), 17–27, 283–85; and Jeff Malpas, *Heidegger and the Thinking of Place: Explorations in the Topology of Being* (Cambridge, MA: MIT Press, 2012), 137–57. The matter is too complicated to deal with adequately in this note, but I would say briefly that Heidegger's sense of homecoming or enrootedness in place cannot be separated from his sensitivity to the matter of homelessness, and both are to be gauged from the vantage point of the proximity to or the distance from being, which is determinative of the fundamental character of human ek-istence (*Ek-sistenz*), that is, the ecstatic inherence as the "there" (*das »Da«*) that is the "clearing of being" (*Lichtung des Seins*). See the "Letter on 'Humanism'" (1946) in Heidegger, *Pathmarks*, 248; *Wegmarken*, 325. For Heidegger, these are not polar opposites, as the logic of noncontradiction and the principle of the excluded middle might prescribe, for what is nearby is concomitantly faraway, what is disclosed is concomitantly concealed. See Wolfson, *Giving Beyond the Gift*, 104 and references to other scholars cited on 366 n. 110, to which one could add Richard Capobianco, *Engaging Heidegger*, foreword by William J. Richardson (Toronto: University of Toronto Press, 2010), 52–69. Most importantly, after resigning from the rectorship in 1934, Heidegger seems to have shifted from a purely political sense of "the homeland" (*die Heimat*) and of "the German" (*das Deutsche*) to a theologico-poetic sense, in Lacoue-Labarthe's turn of

say, the distinction that Heidegger draws in the 1920–1921 lecture course, "Introduction to the Phenomenology of Religion," between the historical time of Jewish messianism and the kairetic time of Christian eschatology is too simplistic. One can discover in some versions of Jewish messianism the chiastic paradox that Heidegger associates with the structure of hope and the temporality of the enactment of life (*Vollzug des Lebens*) ritualized sacramentally by the Christian *parousia*: the future is already present as the present that is always future.[76] This form of hope is not expressed by waiting for something to take place in the ordinary procession of time but as an expectation of the unexpected, the renewal of what has already transpired.[77] Heidegger distinguishes Jesus's proclamation (*Verkündigung*)

---

phrase, which shares affinity with Benjamin's signature expression "theological-political." See Philippe Lacoue-Labarthe, "Poetry's Courage," in *Walter Benjamin and Romanticism*, 163–79. This is not to say that the geopolitical sense is completely obliterated in Heidegger, but only that it is somewhat attenuated. Consider, for instance, the following exposition of these lines from Hölderlin, "A sign is needed,/Nothing else, plain and simple" (*Ein Zeichen braucht es,/Nichts anderes, schlecht und recht*), in Martin Heidegger, *Hölderlin's Hymn "The Ister,"* trans. William McNeill and Julia Davis (Bloomington: Indiana University Press, 1996), 153 (*Hölderlins Hymne "Der Ister"* [GA 53] (Frankfurt am Main: Vittorio Klostermann, 1993), 191): "This alone is the singular need of journeying into the locality of what for the Germans is their ownmost [*der Wanderschaft in die Ortschaft des Eigensten der Deutschen*]: 'A sign' (a poet), 'Nothing else, plain and simple'—there is need of this unconditional founding of what remains." And see especially Heidegger's admonition, ad loc., n. 2: "There is no need for the affected extravagance, the loud gestures and bewildering din, or the immense monuments characteristic of the un-German monumental of the Romans and Americans. And such things are not needed if the sign remains plain, that is, oriented directly toward that which is to be said, and it has nothing to do with all those other things that are adverse and detrimental to one's own." That these words were written in 1942 is not insignificant. On the diasporic nature of Heidegger's "thinking poetics," see Alejandro A. Vallega, *Heidegger and the Issue of Space: Thinking on Exilic Grounds* (University Park, PA: Pennsylvania State University Press, 2003); Aubrey L. Glazer, *A New Physiognomy of Jewish Thinking: Critical Theory After Adorno as Applied to Jewish Thought* (London: Continuum, 2011), 31.

[76] Wolfson, *Open Secret*, 280–81; Elliot R. Wolfson, *A Dream Interpreted within a Dream: Oneiropoiesis and the Prism of Imagination* (New York: Zone Books, 2011), 254.

[77] Wolfson, *Giving Beyond the Gift*, 101–2, 231–32. I will not repeat here the other scholarly analyses of Heidegger's exegesis of Paul and Christian eschatology that I cited in that study, but I do want to take the opportunity to draw the reader's attention to some additional references: Thomas J. Sheehan, "Heidegger's 'Introduction to the Phenomenology of Religion,' 1920–21," *The Personalist* 55 (1979–1980): 312–4, reprinted in *A Companion to Heidegger's "Being and Time,"* ed. Joseph Kockelmans (Washington, D.C.: University Press of America, 1986), 40–62; Giorgio Agamben, *The Time That Remains: A Commentary on the Letter to the Romans* (Stanford: Stanford University Press, 2005), 33–34; Joachim L. Oberst, *Heidegger on Language and Death: The Intrinsic Connection in Human Existence* (London: Continuum, 2009), 17–47, esp. 28–36; Glazer, *A New Physiognomy*, 34–35; Sylvain Camilleri, *Phénoménologie de la religion et herméneutique théologique dans la pensée du jeune Heidegger: Commentaire analytique des Fondements philosophiques de la mystique médiévale (1916–1919)* (Dordrecht: Springer, 2008), 457–64; Justin D. Klassen, "Heidegger's Paul and Radical Orthodoxy on the Structure of Christian Hope," in *Paul, Philosophy, and*

of the coming of the kingdom of God in the synoptic gospels and Paul's notion of enactment, which in turn is based on the factical life experience (*Faktische Lebenserfahrung*) whose object is Jesus, the messiah that has already come. The factical life experience for the Christian "is historically determined by its emergence with the proclamation that hits people in a moment, and then is unceasingly also alive in the enactment of life."[78] The enactment of life, therefore, entails the ability for one to relive the historical moment—the Christ-event of the crucifixion—which from its inception bears the retroactive not yet.

In this regard, the messianic annunciation is not simply a "thankful memory" but rather the "having-become" (*Gewordensein*) that engenders the possibility of a "new becoming" that "always remains co-present."[79]

---

the Theopolitical Vision, 64–89; Simon Critchley, "You Are Not Your Own: On the Nature of Faith," in *Paul and the Philosophers*, ed. Ward Blanton and Hent de Vries (New York: Fordham University Press, 2013), 224–55; Judith Wolfe, *Heidegger's Eschatology: Theological Horizons in Martin Heidegger's Early Work* (Oxford: Oxford University Press, 2013), 61–65; Benjamin Crowe, "Heidegger and the Apostle Paul," in *Paul in the Grip of the Philosophers*, 39–56. Also relevant here is the discussion in Düttmann, *The Memory of Thought*, 258–63, of Heidegger's "Dionysian mysticism," which rests upon a "forgetting of the Messianism of Jewish mysticism." The catalyst for Düttmann's comments is the contrast between Heidegger and Derrida made by Jürgen Habermas, *The Philosophical Discourse of Modernity: Twelve Lectures*, trans. Frederick Lawrence (Cambridge, MA: MIT Press, 1987), 167: "Derrida passes beyond Heidegger's inverted foundationalism, but remains in its path. As a result, the temporalized *Ursprungsphilosophie* takes on clearer contours. The remembrance of the messianism of Jewish mysticism and of the abandoned but well-circumscribed place once assumed by the God of the Old Testament preserves Derrida, so to speak, from the political-moral insensitivity and the aesthetic tastelessness of a New Paganism spiced up with Hölderlin." It is beyond the confines of this note to evaluate Habermas's remark but Düttmann is correct to derive from it a portrait of a Heideggerian messianism devoid of any influence of Jewish eschatology.

[78] Martin Heidegger, *The Phenomenology of Religious Life*, trans. Matthias Fritsch and Jennifer Anna Gosetti-Ferencei (Bloomington: Indiana University Press, 2004), 83; *Phänomenologie des religiösen Lebens* [GA 60] (Frankfurt am Main: Vittorio Klostermann, 1995), 116–17. See Simon Critchley, *The Faith of the Faithless: Experiments in Political Theology* (London: Verso, 2012), 169–70.

[79] Heidegger, *The Phenomenology of Religious Life*, 84; *Phänomenologie des religiösen Lebens*, 117. Travis Kroeker, "Living 'As If Not': Messianic Becoming or the Practice of Nihilism?" in *Paul, Philosophy, and the Theopolitical Vision*, 40 n. 8, commented on the affinity between Heidegger's interpretation of Paul's notion of "having become" and Badiou's emphasis on becoming a subject. I would add that another similarity relates to the primacy accorded the now of the singularity of the event, or as Badiou, *Saint Paul*, 59, puts it, "every truth is marked by an indestructible *youthfulness*" (emphasis in original). I read Badiou's idea of the eventual truth as a further secularization of Heidegger's interpretation of Pauline eschatology and the hope engendered by waiting for the second coming. Consider the following summary given in an interview with Fabien Tarby in Alain Badiou, *Philosophy and the Event*, trans. Louise Burchill (Cambridge: Polity Press, 2014), 12: "In every situation, there are processes faithful to an event that has previously taken place. It's not a matter, then, of desperately awaiting a miraculous event but, rather of following

Commenting on Paul's observation that the appointed time has grown short or contracted itself, *ho kairos synestalmenos estin* (I Cor. 7:29), Heidegger writes in a conspicuously Kierkegaardian spirit[80] that the primordial Christian religiosity (*urchristlichen Religiosität*) demands that one live incessantly in the distress of the only-yet (*Nur-Noch*), a "compressed temporality" (*zusammengedrängte Zeitlichkeit*) instantiated in the moment of vision (*Augenblick*), in which there is no time for postponement.[81] The true believer ascertains that salvation partakes of the factical life experience that converts the temporal into the eternal. "The obstinate waiting," writes Heidegger, "does not wait for the significances of a future content, but for God. The meaning of temporality determines itself out of the fundamental relationship to God—however, in such a way that only those who live temporality in the manner of enactment understand eternity."[82]

Utilizing Ricoeur's discussion of Augustine's notion of time and eternity as it pertains to the psychological experience of *distentio animi*,[83] we can hypothesize that even at this early stage, Heidegger—in a manner that is consonant with Rosenzweig[84]—does not embrace a metaphysical

---

through to the very end, to the utmost degree, what you've been able to extract from the previous event and of being as prepared as possible, therefore, to take in subjectively what will inevitably come about. For me, truth is an undertaking; it is a process made possible by the event. The event is only there as a source of possibilities."

[80] Compare the analyses of Kierkegaard and Heidegger in Koral Ward, *Augenblick: The Concept of the 'Decisive Moment' in 19th- and 20th-Century Western Philosophy* (Burlington: Ashgate, 2008), 1–33, 97–124.

[81] Heidegger, *The Phenomenology of Religious Life*, 85; *Phänomenologie des religiösen Lebens*, 119.

[82] Heidegger, *The Phenomenology of Religious Life*, 83–84; *Phänomenologie des religiösen Lebens*, 117. For a critical assessment of Heidegger's view, see Theodore W. Jennings, Jr., *Outlaw Justice: The Messianic Politics of Paul* (Stanford: Stanford University Press, 2013), 82–83, 88, 134. Various scholars have explored the relation between time and eternity in Heidegger. Here I mention two studies worthy of attention: Gerd Haeffner, "Heidegger über Zeit und Ewigkeit," *Theologie und Philosophie* 64 (1989): 481–517; Jean Greisch, "The Eschatology of Being and the God of Time in Heidegger," *International Journal of Philosophical Studies* 4 (1996): 17–42.

[83] Paul Ricoeur, *Time and Narrative*, vol. 1, trans. Kathleen McLaughlin and David Pellauer (Chicago: University Press, 1984), 26. My discussion here is indebted to Greisch, "The Eschatology of Being," 20.

[84] Elliot R. Wolfson, *Alef, Mem, Tau: Kabbalistic Musings on Time, Truth, and Death* (Berkeley: University of California Press, 2006), 176–77: "The disavowal of time does not imply an abrogation or even a dialectical surpassing of temporality, but rather its radical deepening, an eradication of time by rooting oneself more deeply in the ground of time. Eternity, accordingly, is not the metaphysical overcoming of or existential escape from time but rather the merging of the three-dimensional structure of lived temporality through eternalization of the present in the continuous becoming of the being that has always been what is yet to come."

conception of eternity that is the ontological negation of time, but rather eternity is to be construed as the limiting idea that determines the horizon of and intensifies our experience of time. The intensification of the experience of time is the phenomenological content of the enactment of life identified by Heidegger as the primordial Christian religiosity. In *Der Begriff der Zeit*, a lecture delivered a few years later, Heidegger defines Christian faith (*Glaube*) as that which "is in itself supposed to stand in relation to something that happened in time—at a time, we are told, of which it is said: I was the time 'when time was fulfilled.'"[85] Heidegger distinguishes between the theologian's concern to understand time in relation to eternity (*Ewigkeit*), which is a matter of faith, and the philosopher's quest to understand time through time (*die Zeit aus der Zeit*) or in terms of that which exists perpetually (*aei*), which appears to be eternal but is actually a derivative of being temporal.[86] The dichotomy seems decisive: the theologian comprehends time from the standpoint of eternity and the philosopher, eternity from the standpoint of time. And yet, Heidegger is clear that faith dictates that the believer experiences eternity in relation to what has occurred at a given moment in time, an eternity that should be understood neither as *sempiternitas*, "the ongoing continuation of time" (*das fortgesetzte Weitergehen der Zeit*), nor as *aeternitas*, the "ever-enduring presence" (*immerwährende Gegenwart*) of the "standing now" (*nunc stans*), the two explanations of eternity offered by Heidegger in the lecture course on Hölderlin's hymn *Germanien* delivered in the winter semester 1934–1935 at the University of Freiburg.[87]

Heidegger's reading of Pauline eschatology and his interpretation of Christianity based thereon rest upon a third possibility that presumes the eternalization of the temporal without appeal to the two conceptions of eternity (*Ewigkeitsbegriffe*)—the incessant flow of time, a "never-ending sequence of 'nows,'" and the motionless and everlasting present, "an encompassing 'now' that remains standing ahead of time"—that spring from the experience of time as a *"pure sequential passing of 'nows'"* (reinen

---

85 Heidegger, *The Concept of Time*, trans. William McNeill, 1. The scriptural citation is from Galatians 4:4. It is of interest that Heidegger copied this introduction in the article with the same name "Der Begriff der Zeit," also written in 1924 (see above, n. 7). See Heidegger, *The Concept of Time*, trans. Ingo Farin with Alex Skinner, 37.

86 Heidegger, *The Concept of Time*, trans. William McNeill, 1–2.

87 Martin Heidegger, *Hölderlin's Hymns "Germania" and "The Rhine,"* trans. William McNeill and Julia Ireland (Bloomington: Indiana University Press, 2014), 52; *Hölderlins Hymnen "Germanien" und "Der Rhein"* [GA 39] (Frankfurt am Main: Vittorio Klostermann, 1999), 54–55.

Vergehens des Jetzt im Nacheinander). Insofar as this notion of time "does not grasp the essence of time"—the view already espoused in *Being and Time*—it follows that the concepts of eternity dependent upon it also will not "reach the essence of eternity."[88]

In addition to these perspectives, Heidegger proposes a third notion of eternity that is tagged as "the time that is essentially long" (*die wesen-haft lange Zeit*). Utilizing the following lines from the second version of Hölderlin's poem *Mnemosyne* as a springboard, "Long is/The time, yet what is true/Comes to pass" (*Lang ist/Die Zeit, es ereignet sich aber/Das Wahre*), Heidegger distinguishes the ascription of the quality of length to "everyday time" (*alltägliche Zeit*) and to "time of the peaks" (*die Zeit der Gipfel*), an expression derived from the poem *Patmos*. In the case of the former, the feeling that time is long is a sign of boredom, whereas in the case of the latter, it signifies that at the height of sublimity there "reigns a persistent waiting for and awaiting *the event* [*Ereignis*] ... There is no passing or even killing of time there, but a struggle for the duration and fullness of time that is preserved in awaiting."[89] In this context, Heidegger has unquestionably departed from the theistic mind-set operative in his exegesis of Paul. Nevertheless, there is a thread that ties together that discussion and his analysis of Hölderlin. Both instances demonstrate that Heidegger did not think of eternity as atemporal or supratemporal but rather as the elongation of time experienced in the adamant waiting for the event that is the "becoming manifest of beyng" (*das Offenbarwerden des Seyns*),[90] the repeatedly renewed conferral of the origin that remains permanently still to come.

Along similar lines, Agamben argued that Paul's technical term for the messianic event is *ho nyn kairos*, the time of the now, which is not the end of time that will happen in the future but the time of the end that is experienced as the interminable waiting in the present.[91] Messianic time is thus defined as "*the time that time takes to come to an end*, or, more precisely, the time we take to bring to an end, to achieve our representation of time. This is not the line of chronological time ... nor the instant of its end ... nor is it a segment cut from chronological time; rather, it is operational time pressing within the chronological time, working and transforming it from within; it is the time we need to make time end: *the time that is left us*."[92]

---

[88] Heidegger, *Hölderlin's Hymns*, 52; *Hölderlins Hymnen*, 55.
[89] Heidegger, *Hölderlin's Hymns*, 53; *Hölderlins Hymnen*, 55–56.
[90] Heidegger, *Hölderlin's Hymns*, 53; *Hölderlins Hymnen*, 56.
[91] Agamben, *The Time That Remains*, 61–62.
[92] Ibid., 67–68 (emphasis in original).

The seventh day emblematizes messianic time because the Sabbath "is not another day, homogenous to others; rather, it is that innermost disjointed-ness within time through which one may—by a hairsbreadth—grasp time and accomplish it."[93] The anticipation of the end, therefore, reveals a com-plex interplay between foresight and reminiscence, between the experience of absence and the nonexperience of presence, between the nongivenness of an event and the givenness of the nonevent, between the disappearance that has appeared and the appearance that will disappear.[94]

Rosenzweig himself attests to the fact that the messianic tenet of Judaism, in a manner congruent to, even though not identical with, Christian faith, betokens a tension between the absent presence of the past and the pres-ent absence of the future. That is to say, redemption is always of the future but a future that retrieves the past and ruptures the present, thereby bend-ing the timeline such that not-yet is already-there insofar as already-there is not-yet.[95] The eternal people live an eternal life in time, constantly antici-pating the end and thereby transposing it into the beginning. This rever-sal "denies time as resolutely as possible and places itself outside of it." To live in time means to live between beginning and end, but to live outside time—which is the necessary condition for one who lives eternally—must deny this between. From Rosenzweig's standpoint, the individual who adheres to Jewish ritual "experiences precisely the reversal of the between," and thus "disavows the omnipotence of the between and denies time."[96] Redemptive time, therefore, is concomitantly overflowing with and empty of quotidian time, a novel iteration that can disrupt the temporal flux at any and every moment. Instead of circumscribing the future as being-toward-death, Rosenzweig characterizes the future as the fecundity of the disten-sion that bears the paradox of the linear circularity of time, the restoration

93 Ibid., 72. See Eleanor Kaufman, "The Saturday of Messianic Time: Agamben and Badiou on the Apostle Paul," in *Paul and the Philosophers*, 297–309; Ryan L. Hansen, "Messianic or Apocalyptic? Engaging Agamben on Paul and Politics," in *Paul, Philosophy, and the Theopolitical Vision*, 198–223; Alain Gignac, "Agamben's Paul: Thinker of the Messianic," in *Paul in the Grip of the Philosophers*, 165–92.

94 My approach can be fruitfully compared to the discussion of the *parousia* in Jean-Yves Lacoste, "The Phenomenality of Anticipation," in *Phenomenology and Eschatology*, 15–33.

95 Stéphane Mosès, *The Angel of History: Rosenzweig, Benjamin, Scholem*, trans. Barbara Harshav (Stanford: Stanford University Press, 2009), 56–57. See Stéphane Mosès, "Walter Benjamin and Franz Rosenzweig," *The Philosophical Forum* 15 (1983–1984): 188–205, esp. 200–202. See also Pierre Bouretz, *Witness for the Future: Philosophy and Messianism*, trans. Michael Smith (Baltimore: Johns Hopkins University Press, 2010), 138–47.

96 Rosenzweig, *The Star of Redemption*, 443.

of what is to come.[97] This view resonates with Schwarzschild's observation that there is an "anticipation of the end-time within time, or, more properly perhaps, this vestige of the primaeval time within time."[98] Redemption is not the consequence of historical development, the effect of a causal chain that links the retention of the past and the protention of the future, but rather the corollary of an expectation that is realized as the expectation of what cannot be realized. "That which is future calls for being predicted. The future is experienced only in the waiting. Here the last must be the first in thought."[99]

The allure of the future, accordingly, is not to be assessed from the standpoint of an achievable goal but from the standpoint of the activity that the waiting for that goal incites. To utilize again the language of Schwarzschild: on the one hand, Judaism shows evidence of an "actionable Messianism," that is, the anticipation of the endtime affects behavior in the life of the present,[100] but, on the other hand, the duty conferred on the devout Jew is to believe in a savior who is always in the process of coming and not in one that has already come.[101] The expectation for the nonexpected

---

[97] See analysis in Beniamino Fortis, "Thinking the Future: Death and Redemption—Heidegger and Rosenzweig," *Daimon: Revista Internacional de Filosofía* 3 (2010): 249–56.

[98] Steven S. Schwarzschild, "An Introduction to the Thought of R. Isaac Hutner," *Modern Judaism* 5 (1985): 245. In that context, the author is discussing the eschatological thought of Levinas and Hutner. See below, n. 101.

[99] Rosenzweig, *The Star of Redemption*, 235.

[100] Steven S. Schwarzschild, *The Pursuit of the Ideal: Jewish Writings of Steven Schwarzschild*, ed. Menachem Kellner (Albany: State University of New York Press, 1990), 219, and see 363 n. 72, where the author notes this theme in thinkers as disparate as Martin Buber, Isaac Hutner, Ernst Bloch, and Walter Benjamin. For a more detailed discussion of Hutner's messianic view, especially in conversation with Cohen and Levinas, see Schwarzschild, "An Introduction," 238–56.

[101] Schwarzschild, *The Pursuit of the Ideal*, 209–11, cited in Wolfson, *Giving Beyond the Gift*, 116. The Cohenian influence of Schwarzschild has been noted by scholars. See Kenneth Seeskin, "The Rational Theology of Steven S. Schwarzschild," *Modern Judaism* 12 (1992): 284; Menachem Kellner, "Introduction," in Schwarzschild, *The Pursuit of the Ideal*, 10–11. A related but somewhat different issue is the question of a personal redeemer versus the ideal of redemption, a topic discussed by Schwarzschild in a 1956 essay, reprinted in *The Pursuit of the Ideal*, 15–28. In his later thought, Schwarzschild unequivocally renounced the belief in a personal messiah and sided with Cohen in affirming an asymptotic approach that conceives of the end as the ethical goal towards which we strive but which we can never attain. See also Schwarzschild, "An Introduction," 244. Commenting on Hutner's teaching concerning the ultimate actualization of the good and the disclosure of God's truth in the endtime, which is compared to Cohen's idea of noumenal knowledge as the rational formulation of the regulative ideal and to Rosenzweig's notion of messianic speech, Schwarzschild writes, "The eschatological future, in which evil has ceased, is, however, actually a restoration of Edenic existence, before sin entered the world in the first place. In short, it is not really future but outside of (historical) time, i.e., eternity."

transposes the temporal order by inverting the causal succession—what determines the present is not the past but the future. This transposition is communicated by Rosenzweig in language—"the last must be first in thought"—that calls to mind the dictum in the hymn *Lekha Dodi*, composed by the sixteenth-century kabbalist Solomon Alqabets, *sof ma'aseh be-maḥashavah teḥillah*, "the end of action is first in thought."[102]

Echoing Rosenzweig's view, Levinas noted that because Judaism does not identify salvation as the denouement of history, it remains possible at every moment.[103] This is the messianic mystery alluded to in the disquieting expression "awaiting without an awaited." To wait without an awaited implies that there can be no end to the waiting, the very condition that underscores the essential feature of time as the promise of a future.[104] Levinas thus explicitly identifies waiting for the Messiah as the "actual duration of time." The waiting attests to the procrastination that is germane to the relation with the Infinite, which can never enter fully into the present.[105] The continual deferral, the not-yet that is resolutely yet not at hand, is what eternalizes the temporal and temporalizes the eternal in a now that is persistently not now, the momentary present in which the future is made present as the withdrawal of being present. The tomorrow that is today is nevertheless still tomorrow. If the guarantee of there always being another tomorrow ignites a sense of hopefulness, it is a hopefulness that cannot be extricated from an insurmountable hopelessness. To paraphrase the comment of Kafka transmitted by Max Brod and recorded by Benjamin,[106] from the fact that there is plenty of hope, indeed an *infinite amount of hope*, we may infer that at any given moment the hope can never be spoken of in relation to us. One can be hopeful only in the recognition that the fulfillment of the hope one bears will never come to pass except

---

102 Regarding this dictum and its earlier philosophical sources, see Wolfson, *Open Secret*, 371 n. 160.

103 Emmanuel Levinas, *Difficult Freedom: Essays on Judaism*, trans. Seán Hand (Baltimore: Johns Hopkins University Press, 1990), 84. See Bettina Bergo, "Levinas's Weak Messianism in Time and Flesh, or the Insistence of Messiah Ben David," in *The Messianic Now: Philosophy, Religion, Culture*, ed. Arthur Bradley and Paul Fletcher (London: Routledge, 2011), 45–68, esp. 50–52; Wolfson, *Giving Beyond the Gift*, 117–18, and references on 380–81 n. 214 to a host of other scholars who have written on Levinas and messianism.

104 Levinas, *Time and the Other*, 32; Levinas, *God, Death, and Time*, 139.

105 Emmanuel Levinas, *Beyond the Verse: Talmudic Readings and Lectures*, trans. Gary D. Mole (London: Athlone Press, 1994), 143.

106 Walter Benjamin, *Selected Writings, Volume 2: 1927–1934*, trans. Rodney Livingstone and others, ed. Michael W. Jennings, Howard Eiland, and Gary Smith (Cambridge, MA: Harvard University Press, 1999), 798. The comments of Kafka were first reported in Max Brod, "Der Dichter Franz Kafka," *Die neue Rundschau* 11 (1921): 1213.

as the hope for fulfillment. As Schwarzschild correctly discerned, "The certainty of the expectation of the end-time contains a fundamental aporia."[107]

Analogously, although in slightly different terminology, Scholem noted that the messianic idea in Judaism is "anti-existenialist," since it has "compelled a *life lived in deferment,* in which nothing can be done definitively, nothing can be irrevocably accomplished." The presumably unending need to impede the coming of the end is both the "greatness" and the "constitutional weakness" of Jewish messianism.[108] Eliciting a similar conclusion from the messianic speculation attributed to the Hasidic master Naḥman of Bratslav, Marc-Alain Ouaknin observed:

> The messianic era is not the time when the Messiah is here. On the contrary: it is the time during which the Messiah is awaited ... the Messiah is made for not coming ... and yet, he is awaited. The Messiah allows time to be continually deferred, to generate time ... Messianic man (the one who is waiting) constantly projects himself into the "yet to come" (*à-venir*) of the future; he produces a difference, a suspense ... In this suspension of meaning, time is forever projected toward the yet-to-come by an act of anticipation. But this anticipation does not foresee anything; there is no fulfillment at the end of the road. It is the anticipation of an anti-anticipation.[109]

The Messiah is the one that comes by not-coming, the one that is present by being absent. Waiting for the end is the adjournment of time that occasions the fostering of time.

Messianic Time, Futural Remembering, and Historical Disjointedness

Writ large we can say that the delay of the end's historical concretization is what secures the potential of its constant implementation. In this respect, there is close affinity to Benjamin's notion of the present or the now-time (*Jetztzeit*) that is described in a passage from an earlier draft of

---

[107] Schwarzschild, "An Introduction," 243.

[108] Gershom Scholem, *The Messianic Idea and Other Essays on Jewish Spirituality* (New York: Schocken, 1971), 35 (emphasis in original). The bibliography on Scholem's messianism is immense, and here I mention one study that provides a good historical background to understand his ambivalence and reluctance to affirm a teleological understanding: Michael Löwy, "Messianism in the Early Work of Gershom Scholem," *New German Critique* 83 (2001): 177–91. Also pertinent to the theme of this essay is the analysis in Eric Jacobson, *Metaphysics of the Profane: The Political Theology of Walter Benjamin and Gershom Scholem* (New York: Columbia University Press, 2003), 52–81.

[109] Marc-Alain Ouaknin, *The Burnt Book: Reading the Talmud* (Princeton: Princeton University Press, 1995), 302.

"On the Concept of History"—a text composed in the early part of 1940, several months before Benjamin's suicide in September of that year[110]—as being "shot through with splinters of messianic time," the moment that is the "small gateway [*kleine Pforte*] in time through which the Messiah might enter."[111] The import of this statement is made clear from the opening of the fourteenth thesis: "History is the subject of a construction whose site is not homogeneous, empty time, but time filled full by now-time [*Jetztzeit*]."[112] The historian, in particular, is entrusted with the responsibility of bearing witness to the soteriological potential in the now-time that ensues from attending to the unrealized possibilities of the past. The narrative recapitulating affords one the opportunity to blast the past out of the continuum of history [*Kontinuum der Geschichte*] in the explosive and subversive manner[113] that Benjamin describes Robespierre's relationship to ancient Rome.[114] In the culminating sentence of the eighteenth and last thesis, Benjamin elaborates: "Now-time, which, as a model of messianic time, comprises the entire history of mankind in a tremendous abbreviation, coincides exactly with the figure which the history of

---

[110] For a comprehensive discussion and close reading of this text, see Michael Löwy, *Fire Alarm: Reading Walter Benjamin's 'On the Concept of History'*, trans. Chris Turner (London: Verso, 2005). The author uses the expression "talmudic analysis" to characterize his approach (p. 17).

[111] Walter Benjamin, *Selected Writings, Volume 4: 1938–1940*, trans. Edmund Jephcott and others, ed. Howard Eiland and Michael W. Jennings (Cambridge, MA: Harvard University Press, 2003), 397; Walter Benjamin, *Gesammelte Schriften*, vol. 1.2, ed. Rolf Tiedemann and Herman Schweppenhäuser (Frankfurt am Main: Suhrkamp, 1991), 704.

[112] Benjamin, *Selected Writings, Volume 4*, 395; Benjamin, *Gesammelte Schriften*, vol. 1.2, 701.

[113] Löwy, *Fire Alarm*, 88, calls our attention to a variant of thesis fourteen where "*Jetztzeit* is defined as an explosive [*Explosivstoff*] to which historical materialism adds the fuse. The aim is to explode the continuum of history with the aid of a conception of historical time that perceives it as 'full,' as charged with 'present,' explosive, subversive moments." For the original text, see Walter Benjamin, *Gesammelte Schriften*, vol. 1.3, ed. Rolf Tiedemann and Herman Schweppenhäuser (Frankfurt am Main: Suhrkamp, 1991), 1249.

[114] Benjamin, *Selected Writings, Volume 4*, 395; Benjamin, *Gesammelte Schriften*, vol. 1.2, 701. See text cited below at n. 150. Compare Richard Wolin, *Walter Benjamin: An Aesthetic of Redemption* (New York: Columbia University Press, 1982), 107–37; Werner Hamacher, " 'Now': Walter Benjamin on Historical Time," in *Walter Benjamin and History*, ed. Andrew Benjamin (London: Continuum, 2006), 38–68, esp. 40–41; Löwy, *Fire Alarm*, 87–89; Eli Friedlander, *Walter Benjamin: A Philosophical Portrait* (Cambridge, MA: Harvard University Press, 2012), 192–95. Agamben, *The Time That Remains*, 143–44, suggests that Benjamin's *Jetztzeit* parallels Paul's technical designation of messianic time as *ho nyn kairos* and that his view that the now-time is an abridgement of the totality of history corresponds to Paul's *anakephalaiōsasthai*, that is, the gathering together of all things in Christ in the fullness of time (Ephesians 1:10). See Löwy, *Fire Alarm*, 100, and the criticism of Agamben, 134 n. 161. Compare Roland Boer, "Agamben, Benjamin and the Puppet Player," in *Paul in the Grip of the Philosophers*, 57–68, esp. 63–65.

mankind describes in the universe."[115] The present, as Michael Löwy put it, is likened to a "messianic monad," for in every instant the entirety of history is reflected just as Leibniz had argued that each monad reflects the universe from its own perspective.[116] The redemptive power of the *Jetztzeit*, therefore, is a consequence of the historian's ability to alter the course of the future by eliciting from the moment the whole of the past that is abbreviated or condensed in the present.

This is the gist of Benjamin's remark in the second thesis that the "past carries with it a secret index by which it is referred to redemption." The "secret index" (*heimlichen Index*) relates to the human aptitude for the futural remembering that redeems the past.[117] Benjamin also alludes to this potential as the "secret agreement" (*geheime Verabredung*) between past generations and the present, an agreement that turns both on the redemptive potential of chronicling and narrating the past such that nothing is lost to history and also on the fact that since there can never be a total amelioration of past inequities, there is always unfinished business that will have to be addressed in some future time. Each generation, therefore, is "endowed with a *weak* messianic power [*eine* schwachen *messianische Kraft*], a power on which the past has a claim."[118] What has not been actualized in the past lingers as a "secretly insistent appeal" to us in the present.[119] In the fifth of the historical theses, Benjamin relates this idea to Gottfried Keller's statement "The truth will not run away from us." The image of history promoted by historicism—the image "pierced by historical materialism"—is "an irretrievable image of the past which threatens to disappear in any present that does not recognize itself as intended in that image."[120]

The historian must believe that the present is intended in the image of the past, and yet, as Benjamin argues in the sixth thesis, in language that

---

[115] Benjamin, *Selected Writings, Volume 4*, 396; Benjamin, *Gesammelte Schriften*, vol. 1.2, 703.

[116] Löwy, *Fire Alarm*, 99–100.

[117] With regard to this temporal reversal Benjamin's thinking can be compared profitably to the analysis of Bloch's reflections on memory and utopia examined in Vincent Geoghegan, "Remembering the Future," in *Not Yet: Reconsidering Ernst Bloch*, ed. Jamie Owen Daniel and Tom Moylan (London: Verso, 1997), 15–32, and the essay in the same volume by David Kaufmann, "Thanks for the Memory: Bloch, Benjamin, and the Philosophy of History," 33–52.

[118] Benjamin, *Selected Writings, Volume 4*, 390; Benjamin, *Gesammelte Schriften*, vol. 1.2, 693–94.

[119] Michael G. Levine, *A Weak Messianic Power: Figures of a Time to Come in Benjamin, Derrida, and Celan* (New York: Fordham University Press, 2014), 2–3.

[120] Benjamin, *Selected Writings, Volume 4*, 390–91.

parallels the Heideggerian idea of historicity mentioned above[121]—and this in spite of his explicit rejection of Heidegger's attempt "to rescue history for phenomenology abstractly through 'historicity' [*Geschichtlichkeit*]"[122]—to

[121] See text cited above at n. 37, and compare Andrew Benjamin, "Time and Task: Benjamin and Heidegger Showing the Present," in *Walter Benjamin's Philosophy: Destruction and Experience*, ed. Andrew Benjamin and Peter Osborne (Manchester: Clinamen Press, 2000), 212–45.

[122] Walter Benjamin, *The Arcades Project*, trans. Howard Eiland and Kevin McLaughlin, prepared on the basis of the German volume edited by Rolf Tiedmann (Cambridge, MA: Harvard University Press, 1999), 462; Walter Benjamin, *Gesammelte Schriften*, vol. 5.1, ed. Rolf Tiedemann (Frankfurt am Main: Suhrkamp, 1991), 577. See the translator's comment in *The Arcades Project*, 983, n. 4: "Benjamin, like Heidegger, plays on the archaic verb *wesen* ('to be') embedded in the *Gewesenen* ('what has been'); he cites the being in what has been." On the respective views of Benjamin and Heidegger on history, see David S. Ferris, "Introduction: Aura, Resistance, and the Event of History," in *Walter Benjamin: Theoretical Questions*, ed. David S. Ferris (Stanford: Stanford University Press, 1996), 1–26, esp. 3–10. See also Peter Fenves, *The Messianic Reduction: Walter Benjamin and the Shape of Time* (Stanford: Stanford University Press, 2011), 118–22. The author discusses Benjamin's criticism in a letter to Scholem from November 11, 1916 (*The Correspondence of Walter Benjamin 1910–1940*, ed. Gershom Scholem and Theodor W. Adorno, trans. Manfred R. Jacobson and Evelyn M. Jacobson [Chicago: University of Chicago Press, 1994], 82) of Heidegger's analysis of historical time and mechanical time of the physical sciences in the essay based on his inaugural lecture delivered on July 27, 1915, "Das Problem der historischen Zeit," even though he also acknowledges the shared lines of inquiry and terms of expression, which can be explained, in part, by the fact that Heidegger and Benjamin both participated in Heinrich Rickert's seminar on Bergson. For Benjamin's criticism of Heidegger's idea of historicity, see also Howard Eiland and Michael W. Jennings, *Walter Benjamin: A Critical Life* (Cambridge, MA: Harvard University Press, 2014), 91. See the comment of Benjamin in a letter to Scholem from January 20, 1930, in *The Correspondence of Walter Benjamin 1910–1940*, 359–60: "It now seems a certainty that, for this book [*Paris Arcades*] as well as for the *Trauerspiel* book, an introduction that discusses epistemology is necessary—especially for this book, a discussion of the theory of historical knowledge. This is where I will find Heidegger, and I expect sparks will fly from the shock of the confrontation between our two very different ways of looking at history." For Benjamin's disparaging assessment of Heidegger's book on Don Scotus, see the letter to Scholem from December 1, 1920, in *The Correspondence of Walter Benjamin*, 168, but see his somewhat more conciliatory assessment in the letter to Scholem from January 1921, op. cit., 172. Compare Benjamin's comment in the letter to Scholem from April 25, 1930, op. cit., 365, "We were planning to annihilate Heidegger in the summer in the context of a very close-knit critical circle of readers led by Brecht and me." On Benjamin's own reporting that he was considered a "follower of Heidegger," see his letter to Gretel Adorno from July 20, 1938, op. cit., 571. My own view is close to the assessment of Hannah Arendt, *Men in Dark Times* (San Diego: Harcourt Brace & Company, 1995), 201: "Without realizing it, Benjamin actually had more in common with Heidegger's remarkable sense for living eyes and living bones that had sea-changed into pearls and coral, and as such could be saved and lifted into the present only by doing violence to their context in interpreting them with 'the deadly impact' of new thoughts, than he did with the dialectical subtleties of his Marxist friends." For a criticism of Arendt, see Löwy, *Fire Alarm*, 3–4. The author refers to the passages noted in this text wherein Benjamin was unequivocally dismissive of Heidegger's thought and wherein he explicitly rejects the comparison of his thought to Heidegger. Löwy admits that there are affinities between the two thinkers concerning the theme of eschatology, the conception

portray the past historically does not mean to verify *the way it really was*, according to Leopold von Ranke's definition of the historian's task. To recount the past "means appropriating a memory as it flashes up in a moment of danger. Historical materialism wishes to hold fast that image of the past which unexpectedly appears to the historical subject in a moment of danger."[123] Benjamin's method, exemplified in *The Arcades Project*, was to liberate "the enormous energies of history that are bound up in the 'once upon a time' of classical historiography. The history that showed things 'as they really were' was the strongest narcotic of the century."[124] Parenthetically, this dynamic holds the key to understanding Benjamin's extolling the virtue of quotation as the bridge that links past and present in the dialectical fabrication of historical experience. Explicating Goethe's insight that "classical works do not really allow for their criticism," Benjamin proclaimed that "the exegesis, the ideas, the admiration and enthusiasm of past generations have become indissolubly part of the works themselves, have completely internalized them and turned them into the mirror-images [*Spiegel-galerien*] of later generations...And here, at this highest stage of investigation, it is vital to develop the theory of the quotation."[125] The resonance of Benjamin's perspective with traditional Jewish learning and the practice of citation should be obvious. Just as the rabbinic perspective on history, which is the basis for the textual reasoning that has spanned many centuries, rests on a contemporaneity of past, present, and future, so Benjamin's view, as opposed to the historicist notion of history, is one in which the past is a function of the present and the present a function of the future.[126]

Significantly, in *The Arcades Project*, the remark concerning the "dissolution of 'mythology' into the space of history...through the awakening of a not-yet-conscious knowledge of what has been [*eines noch nicht bewußten Wissens vom Gewesnen*]" is immediately followed by the aphorism,

of authentic temporality, and the openness to the past, but he insists nonetheless that it would be incorrect to call Benjamin a "follower" of Heidegger, especially since his critical conception of time took shape before the publication of *Sein und Zeit* in 1927. Löwy's objection is not persuasive inasmuch as Arendt spoke of affinities between Benjamin and Heidegger and did not refer to the former as a follower of the latter. See below, n. 153.

[123] Benjamin, *Selected Writings, Volume 4*, 391.

[124] Benjamin, *The Arcades Project*, 463; Benjamin, *Gesammelte Schriften*, vol. 5.1, 578.

[125] Benjamin, *Selected Writings, Volume 2*, 372; Benjamin, *Gesammelte Schriften*, vol. 6, ed. Rolf Tiedemann and Hermann Schweppenhäuser (Frankfurt am Main: Suhrkamp, 1991), 170.

[126] Bram Mertens, *Dark Images, Secret Hints: Benjamin, Scholem, Molitor and the Jewish Tradition* (Bern: Peter Lang, 2007), 42–51.

"This work has to develop to the highest degree the art of citing without quotation marks [*ohne Anführungszeichen zu zitieren*]. Its theory is intimately related to that of montage."[127] The threading together of different citations produces a "literary montage" (*literarische Montage*),[128] which is comparable to the intertwining of images in a photomontage. The ostensibly troublesome turn of phrase *citing without quotation marks* is not meant to justify plagiarism but rather to highlight the fact that the citation of the words of previous authors releases them from the discarded rubble of the past and resuscitates them into contemporary forms (*heutige Formen*). The "lost forms" (*verlorenen Formen*) of an epoch are retrieved in the guise of novel creations, and hence it is not necessary—indeed, it would be misleading—for the citations to be transmitted with quotation marks.[129] What was previously said has not yet been spoken.

Benjamin thus described his own undertaking: "I needn't *say* anything. Merely show" (*Ich habe nichts zu sagen. Nur zu zeigen*). Through the art of citation the thought-images (*Denkbilder*), excavated from the arcades of history, manifest themselves in narratological figurations of thought (*Denkfiguren*) that were never before written. "I shall purloin no valuables, appropriate no ingenious formulations. But the rags, the refuse—these I will not inventory but allow, in the only way possible, to come into their own: by making use of them."[130] Benjamin refers to this process as *Verfremdung*, the alienation that results by quoting out of context in order to devise a new context. The practice of quotation, therefore, preserves the continuity of tradition through its discontinuity.[131] The historian, in the words of Hugo

127 Benjamin, *The Arcades Project*, 458; Benjamin, *Gesammelte Schriften*, vol. 5.1, 571–72. My discussion has benefited from the analysis in Norbert Bolz and Willem van Reijen, *Walter Benjamin*, trans. Laimdota Mazzarins (Atlantic Highlands: Humanities Press, 1996), 53–54. On the notion of montage and *Das Passagen-Werk*, see Eiland and Jennings, *Walter Benjamin*, 288.

128 Benjamin, *The Arcades Project*, 460 and 860; Benjamin, *Gesammelte Schriften*, vol. 5.1, 574 and *Gesammelte Schriften*, vol. 5.2, ed. Rolf Tiedemann (Frankfurt am Main: Suhrkamp, 1991), 1030.

129 Benjamin, *The Arcades Project*, 458; Benjamin, *Gesammelte Schriften*, vol. 5.1, 472.

130 Benjamin, *The Arcades Project*, 460 and see the slightly altered version on 860; Benjamin, *Gesammelte Schriften*, vol. 5.1, 574 and vol. 5.2, 1030. On Benjamin's notion of the thought-image, see Sigrid Weigel, *Body- and Image-Space: Re-reading Walter Benjamin* (London: Routledge, 1996), 49–60.

131 Bolz and van Reijen, *Walter Benjamin*, 54: "In this way, quotation envisions the continued existence of tradition as discontinuity; it salvages the elements of tradition through seemingly brutal blows. Benjamin's hermeneutic practice of explication is actually a process of beating something out of its original context; for this reason, all interpretations have something violent about them." On citation and the dialectics of awakening, see also Eiland and Jennings, *Walter Benjamin*, 290–91.

von Hofmannsthal, the Austrian poet who published Benjamin's essay on Goethe's *Elective Affinities* in the *Neue Deutsche Beiträge* (1924–1925), is commended to "read what was never written,"[132] or in the language of Friedrich Schlegel paraphrased and interpreted by Benjamin, "the historian is a prophet facing backward."[133] The dialectical image, which "emerges suddenly, in a flash," is perceived through "the prophetic gaze [*Seherblick*] that catches fire from the summits of the past"[134] and thereby rescues what was in the "now of its recognizability" (*Jetzt der Erkennbarkeit*) "solely for the sake of what in the next moment is already irretrievably lost."[135] This method of temporal interruption, which coerces authorial voices "to appear before the tribunal of history,"[136] involves, in Bloch's expression mentioned by Benjamin, the "turn of remembrance" (*Wendung des Eingedenkens*), that is, a "dialectical reversal" of past and present that is compared to the experience (*Erfahrung*) of awakening from a dream: "Accordingly, we present the new, the dialectical method of doing history: with the intensity of a dream, to pass through what has been, in order to experience the present as the waking world to which the dream refers!"[137]

That the present is experienced as the dream to which the waking world refers does not mean, as Heidegger prosaically argued in his notes

---

[132] The remark is cited in Gerhard Richter, *Thought-Images: Frankfurt School Writers' Reflections from Damaged Life* (Stanford: Stanford University Press, 2007), 50.

[133] Benjamin, *Selected Writings*, *Volume 4*, 405. Benjamin offers two explanations of Schlegel's aphorism. The first one is the conventional sense that "the historian, transplanting himself into a remote past, prophesies what was regarded as the future at that time but meanwhile has become the past." The second, and more daring, explanation, and the one that conveys Benjamin's own thought, implies that "the historian turns his back on his own time, and his seer's gaze is kindled by the peaks of earlier generations as they sink further and further into the past. Indeed, the historian's own time is far more distinctly present to this visionary gaze than it is to the contemporaries who 'keep step with it.'... It is precisely this concept of the present which underlies the actuality of genuine historiography... Someone who pokes about in the past as if rummaging in a storeroom of examples and analogies still has no inkling of how much in a given moment depends on its being made present [*ihre Vergegenwärtigung*]." And see 407: "The seer's gaze is kindled by the rapidly receding past. That is to say, the prophet has turned away from the future: he perceives the contours of the future in the fading light of the past as it sinks before him into the night of times... To grasp the eternity of historical events is really to appreciate the eternity of their transience."

[134] Compare Benjamin, *Selected Writings*, *Volume 4*, 360, where Carl Gustav Jochmann is described as turning "his back on the future (which he speaks of in prophetic tomes), which his seer's gaze is kindled by the vanishing peaks of earlier heroic generations and their poetry, as they sink further and further into the past."

[135] Benjamin, *The Arcades Project*, 473; Benjamin, *Gesammelte Schriften*, vol. 5.1, 591–92.

[136] Benjamin, *The Arcades Project*, 363; Benjamin, *Gesammelte Schriften*, vol. 5.1, 459.

[137] Benjamin, *The Arcades Project*, 838; Benjamin, *Gesammelte Schriften*, vol. 5.2, 1006.

recording a conversation with Medard Boss on March 2, 1972,[138] that the dreamworld belongs to waking life as a manner of being-in-the-world, inasmuch as one speaks about dreams while awake but not about being awake

---

[138] Martin Heidegger, *Zollikon Seminars: Protocols—Conversations—Letters*, ed. Medard Boss, translated and with notes and afterwords by Franz Mayr and Richard Askay (Evanston, IL: Northwestern University Press, 2001), 230. Heidegger's implicit critique of the psychoanalytic approach to dreams appears in a letter to Boss from August 2, 1952, in Heidegger, *Zollikon Seminars*, 245: "Dreams are not symptoms and consequences of something lying hidden behind [them], but they themselves are in what they show and *only* this. Only with *this* does their emerging essence [*Wesen*] become worthy of questioning" (emphasis in original). See also Heidegger's criticism of Freud in the notes from the conversation with Boss on September 7, 1963, in Heidegger, *Zollikon Seminars*, 182–83: "Concealment is not the antithesis of consciousness but rather concealment belongs to the clearing. Freud simply did not see this clearing... In Freud's repression we are dealing with hiding [*Verstecken*] a representation [*Vorstellung*]. In withdrawal [*Entzug*] we are dealing with the phenomenon itself. The phenomenon withdraws itself from the domain of the clearing and is inaccessible—so inaccessible that this inaccessibility as such cannot be experienced anymore. What conceals itself remains what it is, otherwise I could no longer come back to it. Clearing is never mere clearing, but always the clearing of *concealment* [*Sich-Verbergen*]. In the proper sense the clearing of *concealment* [*Lichtung des Sich-Verbergens*] means that the inaccessible shows and manifests itself as such—as the inaccessible... What manifests itself as the inaccessible is the mystery [*Geheimnis*]" (emphasis in original). For the utilization of Heidegger's stance to provide an alternative to Freud's interpretation of the oneiric phenomenon, see Medard Boss, *"I Dreamt Last Night...*", trans. Stephen Conway, introduction by Paul J. Stern (New York: Gardner Press, 1977), 46, 182–83, 185–87. Boss draws on Heidegger's insights to articulate the view that dreaming and waking share in a concept of reality that is brought into openness (*Unverborgenheit*) from an originary hiddenness (*Verborgenheit*), two states that are "mutual determinants of each other" (p. 182). The common matrix of the two is the notion of *Dasein*, the human way of being-in-the-world, the standing-out (*ek-sistence*) or the ecstasy (*ekstasis*) disclosed in the opening-sheltering of the clearance (p. 185). On Heidegger's attitude to dreams, see as well the anecdotal comments of Medard Boss, "Martin Heidegger's Zollikon Seminars," *Review of Existential Psychology and Psychiatry* 16 (1978–79): 12–13. Heidegger's critique of Freudian psychoanalysis is assessed by Richard Askay, "Heidegger's Philosophy and Its Implications for Psychology, Freud, and Existential Psychoanalysis," in Heidegger, *Zollikon Seminars*, 308–12. See also Joseph J. Kockelmans, "Daseinanalysis and Freud's Unconscious," *Review of Existential Psychology and Psychiatry* 16 (1978–1979): 21–42; Richard Askay, "A Philosophical Dialogue between Heidegger and Freud," *Journal of Philosophical Research* 24 (1999): 415–43; Richard Askay and Jensen Farquhar, *Apprehending the Inaccessible: Freudian Psychoanalysis and Existential Phenomenology* (Evanston, IL: Northwestern University Press, 2006), 190–229; Richard Askay and Jensen Farquhar, *Of Philosophers and Madmen: A Disclosure of Martin Heidegger, Medard Boss, and Sigmund Freud* (Amsterdam: Rodopi, 2011), 113–18. On Heidegger and psychotherapy more generally, see the discussion in Dallmayr, *Life-world*, 210–37, and reference to other scholarly analyses cited on 234 n. 2. Noteworthy is the impact of Heidegger and Freud on Medard Boss's *Psychoanalysis and Daseinanalysis* (New York: Basic Books, 1963), but this is a matter than cannot be explored here. For an introduction to this topic, see F. Alec Jenner, "Medard Boss' Phenomenologically Based Psychopathology," in *Phenomenology and Psychological Science: Historical and Philosophical Perspectives*, ed. Peter D. Ashworth and Man Cheung Chung (New York: Springer, 2006), 147–68. See also Ludwig Binswanger, *Being-in-the-World: Selected Papers of Ludwig Binswanger*, ed. Joseph Needleman (New York: Basic Books, 1963), 206–21.

while dreaming; the intent, rather, is the far bolder claim that the present can be calibrated as the real world only vis-à-vis the past, which is like a dream. We awaken to the present that is the realization of the dream that is the past. Recollecting the past in the present is not merely the replication of the past; it is an act of consciousness that seeks a "teleological moment" by bestowing new reality on the past, the "moment of waiting" that is akin to the dream that "waits secretly for the awakening."[139] Benjamin identifies this inversion of past and present—the waking from the dream that one is waking from the dream—as the *Copernican revolution in historical perception* [*geschichtlichen Anschauung*], which he elaborates as follows:

> Formerly it was thought that a fixed point had been found in "what has been," and one saw the present engaged in tentatively concentrating the forces of knowledge on this ground. Now this relation is to be overturned, and what has been is to become the dialectical reversal [*dialektischen Umschlag*]—the flash of awakened consciousness [*Einfall des erwachten Bewußtseins*]. Politics attains primacy over history. The facts become something that just now first happened to us, first struck us; to establish them is the affair of memory. Indeed, awakening is the great exemplar of memory... There is a not-yet-conscious knowledge of what has been [*Noch-nicht-bewußtes-Wissen vom Gewesenen*]: its advancement has the structure of awakening... The new, dialectical method of doing history presents itself as the art of experiencing the present as waking world [*die Gegenwart als Wachwelt zu erfahren*], a world to which that dream we name the past refers in truth. To pass through and carry out *what has been* in remembering the dream [*Traumerinnerung*]!—Therefore: remembering [*Erinnerung*] and awaking [*Erwachen*] are most intimately related. Awakening is namely

---

139 Benjamin, *The Arcades Project*, 390; Benjamin, *Gesammelte Schriften*, vol. 5.1, 492. On the dream in Benjamin's thought, see Wolfson, *A Dream*, 326–27 n. 99, and reference to other scholarly analyses mentioned there. Many more sources could have been cited including Margaret Cohen, *Profane Illumination: Walter Benjamin and the Paris of Surrealist Revolution* (Berkeley: University of California Press, 1993), 46–51; Tyrus Miller, "From City-Dreams to the Dreaming Collective: Walter Benjamin's Political Dream Interpretation," *Philosophy and Social Criticism* 22 (1996): 87–111; Susan Buck-Morss, *The Dialectics of Seeing: Walter Benjamin and the Arcades Project* (Cambridge, MA: MIT Press, 1989), 253–86. See also Friedlander, *Walter Benjamin*, 90–111, esp. 94–95: "We should not understand waiting in terms of an objective, external determination of time... but rather in relation to the process of transformation internal to the dream's space of meaning, through which awakening can occur. However, this does not mean that all there is to waiting is patience, as though killing time until that transformation occurs. Waiting must be understood as holding to two distinct and opposed moments. On the one hand, waiting is the gathering of forces or of potential; on the other, waiting is the seeking of an opportunity to realize that potential... Waiting is the dialectical overcoming of the opposition between gathering energy and actively seeking 'experiences' that stimulate or awaken."

the dialectical, Copernican turn of remembrance [*die dialektischen, koperni-kanische Wendung des Eingedenkens*].[140]

Constructing a materialist historiography is facilitated by the act of remembrance that unsettles the monolithically irreversible causal sequence between past and future, the repetition of singularity and the singularity of repetition, and is thus comparable to the narrative space of the dreamtime (*Zeit-traum*) in which origin is the goal (*Ursprung ist das Ziel*), according to the phrase from Karl Kraus cited by Benjamin as the motto for the fourteenth thesis.[141] As in the remembering of the dream, so in the historian's retelling, we find neither the irreversibility nor the repeatability of events but rather the "contemporaneity of the noncontemporaneous," the prognosis of the future rooted in and hence already existent in—even though not yet having occurred—the past that is reshaped in the present.[142]

> In the dialectical image, what has been within a particular epoch is always, simultaneously, "what has been from time immemorial." As such, how- ever, it is manifest, on each occasion, only to a quite specific epoch— namely, the one in which humanity, rubbing its eyes, recognizes just this particular dream image as such. It is at this moment that the histo- rian takes up, with regard to that image, the task of dream interpretation

140 Benjamin, *The Arcades Project*, 388–89 (emphasis in original); Benjamin, *Gesammelte Schriften*, vol. 5.1, 490–91. On the dialectic of memory and forgetfulness in Benjamin, see Orietta Ombrosi, *The Twilight of Reason: Benjamin, Adorno, Horkheimer and Levinas Tested by the Catastrophe*, trans. Victoria Aris (Boston: Academic Studies Press, 2012), 81–92. See also Eiland and Jennings, *Walter Benjamin*, 289.

141 Benjamin, *Selected Writings, Volume 4*, 395; Benjamin, *Gesammelte Schriften*, vol. 1.2, 701. See Peter Szondi, *On Textual Understanding and Other Essays*, trans. Harvey Mendelsohn, foreword by Michael Hays (Minneapolis: University of Minnesota Press, 1986), 157–58. Szondi illumines Benjamin's dialectic of the messianic future and the historical past by citing the following passage about the origin (*Ursprung*) from Benjamin, *The Origin of German Tragic Drama*, 45–46: "The term origin is not intended to describe the process by which the existent came into being, but rather to describe that which emerges from the process of becoming and disappearance...That which is original is never revealed in the naked and manifest existence of the factual; its rhythm is apparent only to a dual insight. On the one hand it needs to be recognized as a process of restoration and re-establishment, but, on the other hand, and precisely because of this, as something imperfect and incomplete...Origin is not, therefore, discovered by the examination of actual findings, but it is related to their history and their subsequent development. The principles of philosophical contemplation are recorded in the dialectic which is inherent in origin. This dialectic shows singularity and repetition to be conditioned by one another in all essentials." For previous citation and analysis of this passage, see Wolfson, *Alef, Mem, Tau*, 120–21. See also Mosès, *The Angel of History*, 75–76.

142 Reinhart Koselleck, *Futures Past: On the Semantics of Historical Time*, trans. and with an introduction by Keith Tribe (New York: Columbia University Press, 2004), 95.

[*Traumdeutung*] ... The realization of dream elements in the course of waking up is the canon of dialectics. It is paradigmatic for the thinker and binding for the historian.[143]

The exigency of the dialectical motion—the "leap in the open air of history"[144]—enjoins the mission of brushing history against the grain,[145] the expectation of what was once upon a time and the commemoration of what is yet to come.[146] For Benjamin, the past does not cast its light on the present nor does the present cast its light on the past. The two modes of time converge in the image "wherein what has been comes together in a flash with the now to form a constellation. In other words, image is dialectics at a standstill [*Dialektik im Stillstand*]. For while the relation of the present to the past is a purely temporal, continuous one, the relation of what-has-been to the now is dialectical: it is not progression [*Verlauf*] but image [*Bild*], suddenly emergent [*sprunghaft*].—Only dialectical images are genuine images (that is, not archaic); and the place where one encounters them is language. Awakening."[147] The dialectic image, as opposed to a mimetic image, does not merely mirror the past; the present is thus marked by a "temporal rupture in which time and space are out of joint. This out-of-jointness is the *Sprunghaftigkeit*, possessing the qualities of leaps and cracks that characterize our relation to the past, the present, and the future, a relation that perpetually is at odds with itself."[148]

The writing of history proceeds from this out-of-jointness, the leap that bridges past and present and thereby brings together what remains at a distance, the constellated moment wherein time is, paradoxically, most fluid and most sedentary—*dialectics at a standstill.*[149] Accentuating the same point in the sixteenth of the theses on the concept of history, Benjamin

---

[143] Benjamin, *The Arcades Project*, 464; Benjamin, *Gesammelte Schriften*, vol. 5.1, 580.

[144] Benjamin, *Selected Writings, Volume 4*, 395.

[145] Ibid., 392.

[146] This dimension of Benjamin's thinking is attested in Scholem's poem "Paraphrase, aus der Prosa des ‚Tagebuchs'," written on May 12, 1918, and inspired by reading "The Metaphysics of Youth." See Gershom Scholem, *The Fullness of Time: Poems*, trans. Richard Sieburth, introduced and annotated by Steven M. Wasserstrom (Jerusalem: Ibis, 2003), 52–53: "Even as you die, Youth, you establish history ... The future was. The past shall be [*Die Zukunft war. Vergangenheit wird sein*]." The reversal of time that is affirmed here—the future already past and the past yet to come—is indicative of an anti-utopian spirit and a resignation to the fact that history is not redemptive.

[147] Benjamin, *The Arcades Project*, 462; Benjamin, *Gesammelte Schriften*, vol. 5.1, 576–77.

[148] Richter, *Thought-Images*, 62.

[149] Theodor Adorno, "Progress," *The Philosophical Forum* 15 (1983–1984): 69: "What Benjamin called dialectic at a standstill is certainly less a platonizing regression than an attempt to raise such a paradox to a philosophical consciousness. Dialectical images:

writes: "The historical materialist cannot do without the notion of a present which is not a transition, but in which time takes a stand [*einsteht*] and has come to a standstill. For this notion defines the very present in which he himself is writing history...He remains in control of his powers— man enough to blast open the continuum of history."[150] It follows that the "concept of historical time forms an antithesis to the idea of a temporal continuum. The eternal lamp is an image of genuine historical existence. It cites what has been—the flame that once was kindled—in perpetuum, giving it ever new sustenance."[151] The past, consequently, is not the irrevocable cause of the present; it is the trace that is reconfigured anew in each moment through the agency of anamnesis in the manner of the dream that is remembered upon waking. The remembering itself blurs the boundary between dream and wakefulness, since in recalling the dream, the dreamer is no longer certain if s/he is dreaming of being awake or evoking the dream once s/he has awoken. To be awakened, on this score, consists of waking to and not from the dream, that is, waking to the realization that what we call reality is a component of the dream from which we imagine that we awake,[152] a realization that sufficiently narrows, if not eviscerates, the distinction between interior and exterior—"the external world that the active man encounters can also in principle be reduced, to any desired degree, to his inner world, and his inner world similarly to his outer world, indeed regarded in principle as one and the same thing."[153]

Noteworthy is Benjamin's utilization of Bloch's expression "darkness of the lived moment" (*Dunkel des gelebten Augenblicks*) to illustrate the knowledge that is "secured on the level of the historical, and collectively."[154] Let me cite Bloch's words verbatim so that we get a better sense of the fuller context:

---

these are the historical-objective archetypes of that antagonistic unity of standstill and movement definitive for the most bourgeois concept of progress."

[150] Benjamin, *Selected Writings, Volume 4*, 396.

[151] Ibid., 407.

[152] Wolfson, *A Dream*, 101, 255–74.

[153] Benjamin, *Selected Writings, Volume 1*, 202. This passage from Benjamin's 1919 essay "Schicksal und Charakter" is discussed by Fenves, *The Messianic Reduction*, 70–71, in support of his contention that Benjamin, like Heidegger, rejected the Husserlian phenomenological reduction, which presumed the naturalness of the natural attitude, since for both thinkers, "the reduction of the 'natural' attitude has already taken place in everyday activity...Far from positing a world of things that affect consciousness and to which it reacts in return, there is only the 'working' situation, and the distinction between interior and exterior is purely functional, not substantial." The breakdown of the distinction between inside and outside corresponds to my claim regarding the inability to distinguish dream and reality.

[154] Benjamin, *The Arcades Project*, 389; Benjamin, *Gesammelte Schriften*, vol. 5.1, 491.

> Thus, once again, the unconstruable, the absolute question certainly also runs towards the moment, into its darkness. Not as a clearing, but as an unmistakable allusion to the immediate darkness of the Now, in so far as its central latency in terms of content nevertheless depicts itself in such astonished questioning, such questioning astonishment. If the content of what is driving in the Now, what is touched in the Here, were extracted positively... then conceived hope, hoped-for world would have reached their goal. *Once more: darkness of the lived moment; Carpe diem*... Even the feeling of internal and external stimuli, at the point where these plunge into the Now, participates in the latter's darkness... Together with its content, the lived moment itself remains essentially invisible, and in fact all the more securely, the more energetically attention is directed towards it: at this root, in the lived In-itself, in punctual immediacy, all world is still dark.[155]

With these penetrating and poignant words of Bloch in mind, we can circle back to Benjamin's description of the *Jetztzeit* as the present shot through with splinters of messianic time. The redemptive potential is connected to the present or, more specifically, to the recollection of the past in the present, the commemorative act that transforms the former by the latter and the latter by the former. And yet, the present in its punctual immediacy is essentially invisible, not in the manner of some past experience that is lost in the fog of oblivion, but as the memory that haunts the present like a ghostly figure that "constantly reappears" in the "opening in the passage of time," as Benjamin described the character of fate in his study on the origins of German tragic drama (*Trauerspiel*).[156] The past is a phantom that can be manifest only to the extent that it remains occluded, and like all manifestations of the imagination, according to Benjamin, the apparition is a "deformation [*Entstaltung*] of what has been formed. It is a characteristic of all imagination that it plays a game of dissolution with its forms."[157]

Remembering proceeds from the blind spot that is the darkness of the lived moment, the not-yet that is necessary for the possibility of there being something rather than nothing, the negation that impels the indeterminate emptiness that is the fullness of becoming.[158] To seize the moment—*Carpe*

---

[155] Ernst Bloch, *The Principle of Hope*, trans. Neville Plaice, Stephen Plaice, and Paul Knight (Cambridge, MA: MIT Press, 1986), 290–91 (emphasis in original). See the passage from *The Spirit of Utopia* cited below at n. 239.

[156] Benjamin, *The Origin of German Tragic Drama*, 135, and see analysis in Ilit Ferber, *Philosophy and Melancholy: Benjamin's Early Reflections on Theater and Language* (Stanford: Stanford University Press, 2013), 108–9.

[157] Benjamin, *Selected Writings, Volume 1*, 280.

[158] On Bloch's ontology of becoming and the demarcation of being in the mode of not-yet, see Schumacher, *Death and Mortality*, 81–82 n. 68.

diem—is to take hold of this darkness, for one can see the light only by gazing from within the darkness and not by dispelling it. Benjamin's assertion that each moment betrays the splintering of messianic time is indicative of the fact that he was incapable of ascribing to history as a whole the capacity for fulfillment. This crucial point is missed by many interpreters of Benjamin's utopianism. The more conventional approach is attested in the explication of Benjamin's idea of redemption and recollection offered by Stéphane Mosès:

> It is this break of historical temporality, this appearance of the unpredictable, that Benjamin called Redemption. But this is not located anywhere at the end of time; on the contrary, it happens (or it can happen) at any moment, precisely as each moment of time—grasped as absolutely unique—brings a new state of the world into being. The qualitative difference of each of the fragments of time always brings a new possibility of an unforeseen change, a brand-new arrangement of the order of things. In contrast to the Marxist idea of the "end of history," based on a quantitative and cumulative vision of historical time, what is drawn here is the idea, borrowed from Jewish messianism, of a *utopia appearing in the very heart of the present*, of a hope lived in the mode of today... It is thus that the Benjaminian notion of "recollection" (*Eingedenken*) continues the Jewish category of "re-remembering" (*Zekher*), which does not denote the preservation in memory of events of the past but their reactualization in the present experience... As for the messianic hope, it must not be conceived as aiming for a utopia destined to be realized at the end of time but as an extreme vigilance, a capacity to detect what at each moment shows the "revolutionary energy" of the new.[159]

There is much about this statement with which I am in agreement but it does obfuscate the fact that even after having espoused a leftist agenda with its professed belief in political insurgency as a harbinger of socio-economic reform, Benjamin was consigned to a deep-seated skepticism—one might even say Saturnine distrust[160]—about the redemptive potential

---

[159] Mosès, *The Angel of History*, 108–9 (emphasis in original). The expression "revolutionary energy" appears in a passage from Henri Focillon, *Vie des formes*, cited by Benjamin, *The Arcades Project*, 488 (*Gesammelte Schriften*, vol. 5.1, 611): "I have elsewhere pointed out the dangers of 'evolution': its deceptive orderliness, its single-minded directness, its use, in those problematic cases..., of the expedient of 'transitions,' its inability to make room for the revolutionary energy of inventors" (Henri Focillon, *The Life of Forms in Art*, trans. Charles Beecher Hogan and George Kubler [New York: Zone Books, 1989], 47). A proper attunement to Focillon's words confirms the interpretation of Benjamin that I have presented in this essay.

[160] Compare the important comment regarding the angelic form of Klee's *Angelus Novus* in the first version of the autobiographical fragment "Agesilaus Santander" (1933), in Benjamin, *Selected Writings, Volume 2*, 713: "By turning to his advantage that I was born under the sign of Saturn—the planet of slow revolution, the star of hesitation and

of history not only as the utopian future but also as it pertains to the potential of each present to serve as a stimulus for upheaval.[161] When Benjamin writes that the "concept of progress must be grounded in the idea of catastrophe," he does not only mean that the status quo has the "ever-present possibility" of being calamitous, but rather that the cataclysmic is "what in each case is given," and hence "hell is not something that awaits us, but this life here and now."[162] In a revealing comment in his essay on Kafka, published in December 1934 on the tenth anniversary of his death, Benjamin elaborates on Kafka's aphorism "Don't forget the best!", "But forgetting always involves the best, for it involves the possibility of redemption."[163] One would have reasonably expected Benjamin to affirm a connection between memory and redemption, and yet, he inverts Kafka's advice and substitutes forgetfulness for memory. The instruction was not to forget the best but Benjamin insists that through forgetfulness

---

delay—he sent his feminine aspect after the masculine one reproduced in the picture, and did so by the most circuitous, most fatal detour, even though the two had been such close neighbors." The text is cited as well in Gershom Scholem, *On Jews and Judaism in Crisis: Selected Essays*, ed. Werner J. Dannhauser (New York: Schocken, 1976), 207, and see his analysis, 219–20. Regarding this passage, see also Max Pensky, *Melancholy Dialectics: Walter Benjamin and the Play of Mourning* (Amherst, MA: University of Massachusetts Press, 1993), 13–14; Mosès, *The Angel of History*, 79–80; Moshe Idel, *Saturn's Jews: On the Witches' Sabbat and Sabbateanism* (London: Continuum, 2011), 91–94, 168 n. 26. On the theme of melancholia and Saturn, see Benjamin, *The Origin of German Tragic Drama*, 149–51, and analysis in Pensky, *Melancholy Dialectics*, 102–5. The classical study of this motif is Raymond Klibansky, Erwin Panofsky, and Fritz Saxl, *Saturn and Melancholy: Studies in the History of Natural Philosophy, Religion, and Art* (London: Nelson, 1964), 127–214. For other discussions of melancholia in Benjamin's oeuvre, see Scholem, *On Jews and Judaism*, 174 and 202; Pensky, *Melancholy Dialectics*; Ferber, *Philosophy and Melancholy*. For the larger intellectual and cultural milieu to assess Benjamin's depressive tendencies, see the discussion on "Melancholy Germans" in Jane O. Newman, *Benjamin's Library: Modernity, Nation, and the Baroque* (Ithaca: Cornell University Press, 2011), 138–84.

[161] Wolin, *Walter Benjamin*, 110. See, however, Löwy, *Fire Alarm*, 101–2. The author interprets Benjamin's image of the *Jetztzeit* being shot through with splinters of messianic time as a reference to "moments of revolt," and hence it conveys the "imminent or potential presence of the messianic era in history." Löwy reinforces his argument with a citation from Scholem's unpublished notebooks of 1917 where he reports that Benjamin once said, "The messianic kingdom is always there." Commenting on this passage, Löwy writes: "We are, here, in the rupture between messianic redemption and the ideology of progress, at the heart of the constellation formed by the conceptions of history of Benjamin, Scholem, and Franz Rosenzweig, who draw on the Jewish religious tradition to contest the model of thought that is common to Christian theodicy, the Enlightenment and the Hegelian philosophy of history. By abandoning the Western teleological model, we pass from a time of necessity to a time of possibilities, a random time, open at any moment to the unforeseeable irruption of the new." The influence of Rosenzweig's idea that the future can erupt at any moment is repeated, ibid., 104, and see 8, 122 n. 18. As Löwy explicitly acknowledges, 134 n. 165, his argument is indebted to Mosès.

[162] Benjamin, *The Arcades Project*, 473; Benjamin, *Gesammelte Schriften*, vol. 5.1, 593.

[163] Benjamin, *Selected Writings, Volume 2*, 813.

alone one can access the best, since forgetfulness involves the possibility of redemption.

At most, we should attribute to Benjamin the redolent title of one of Scholem's poems "Melancholy Redemption" (*Traurige Erlösung*), composed in 1926, three years after his arrival in Jerusalem, which already expresses disillusion with the possibility of the "untarnished ray" of the light of Zion attaining the "world's inmost core" (*Innere der Welt*).[164] In another poem composed in 1933, "With a Copy of Walter Benjamin's 'One-Way Street,'" Scholem reiterated the primacy accorded to melancholy in the religious outlook of Benjamin and in his own worldview: "In days of old all roads somehow led/to God and to his name./We are not devout. Our domain is the profane,/and where 'God' once stood, Melancholy takes his place [*und wo einst 'Gott' stand, steht Melancholie*]."[165] Scholem, like Benjamin, came to perceive reality as the "abyss of nothingness in which the world appears" (*der Abgrund des Nichts, in dem die Welt erscheint*).[166] At the conclusion of the *Theological-Political Fragment*, Benjamin asserts that the "task of world politics" (*Aufgabe der Weltpolitik*) is to strive for the "eternal and total passing away" (*ewigen und totalen Vergängnis*) that is characteristic of "the rhythm of messianic nature" (*der Rhythmus der messianischen Natur*) and hence the method befitting this "eternally transient worldly existence" is nihilism.[167] I thus assent to Gillian Rose's educing from this passage—which

---

[164] Scholem, *The Fullness of Time*, 68–69. The influence of Benjamin's preoccupation with mourning (*Trauer*) in Scholem's poem is duly noted by Wasserstrom, *The Fullness of Time*, 146. See also the emotive beginning of the poem "W.B." in the same volume, 62–63: "Mournful one, near to me yet always in hiding [*Trauernder, nah mir und doch stets verborgen*]."

[165] Scholem, *The Fullness of Time*, 98–99. Idel, *Saturn's Jews*, 91, perceptively notes that this "radical statement about melancholy as a form of hypostasis is, at the same time, a melancholic statement in itself."

[166] Scholem, *The Fullness of Time*, 96–97. One should here recall Scholem's expression "nothingness of revelation" (*Nichts der Offenbarung*) mentioned in the letter of Benjamin to Scholem from August 11, 1934, and in Scholem's response to Benjamin from September 20, 1934, in *The Correspondence of Walter Benjamin and Gershom Scholem 1932–1940*, ed. Gershom Scholem, trans. Gary Smith and Andre Lefevere, with an introduction by Anson Rabinbach (New York: Schocken, 1989), 135 and 142. See Elliot R. Wolfson, *Venturing Beyond: Law and Morality in Kabbalistic Mysticism* (Oxford: Oxford University Press, 2006), 233, and reference to other scholars cited in n. 166, to which one might add David Kaufmann, "Imageless Refuge for all Images: Scholem in the Wake of Philosophy," *Modern Judaism* 20 (2000): 154–55; Ilit Ferber, "A Language of the Border: On Scholem's Theory of Lament," *Journal of Jewish Thought and Philosophy* 21 (2013): 169–70.

[167] Walter Benjamin, *Selected Writings, Volume 3: 1935–1938*, trans. Edmund Jephcott and others, ed. Howard Eiland and Michael W. Jennings (Cambridge, MA: Harvard University Press, 2002), 306; Benjamin, *Gesammelte Schriften*, vol. 2.1, ed. Rolf Tiedemann and Herman Schweppenhäuser (Frankfurt am Main: Suhrkamp, 1991), 204. For an analysis of this text as the framework within which to evaluate Benjamin's early thinking on history

basically accords with the reading proffered by Taubes—that the political
agenda envisaged by Benjamin "presupposes the inner man in isolation,
able to bear a suffering that promises neither realization nor redemption.
E contrario, it implies misfortune which is unable to bear this suffering, a
thirst for the realization of entreated redemption, for the politics of the
world, and total perdition."[168]

The depth of Benjamin's dark luminosity—or what we may call his utopian pessimism[169]—is driven home in the ninth of his theses on the concept of history, which is offered as a midrashic exegesis of the fifth stanza
of the poem on Klee's *Angelus Novus*, "Gruß vom Angelus," which Scholem
composed in honor of Benjamin's twenty-ninth birthday, July, 25, 1921:
"My wing is ready for flight,/*I would like to turn back.*/If I stayed everliving
time,/I'd still have little luck."[170] The first thing to note is that in the use of

---

and redemption, see Jacobson, *Metaphysics of the Profane*, 19–51. See also the attempt
of Jacob Taubes, *The Political Theology of Paul*, ed. Aleida Assmann and Jan Assmann in
conjunction with Horst Folkers, Wolf-Daniel Hartwich, and Christoph Schulte, trans. Dana
Hollander (Stanford: Stanford University Press, 2004), 72–74, to read Benjamin's insistence
on world politics as nihilism in light of the use of the expression *hōs mē* ("as not") by
Paul in his description of the *kairós* in 1 Corinthians 7:29. On Heidegger's explication of
this locution, which he translates as *als ob nicht*, "as if not," see Agamben, *The Time That
Remains*, 33–34, whose reading has much affinity to my interpretation in *Giving Beyond the
Gift*, 231–32, of Heidegger's rendering of the expression *ouk edexanto*, "they received not,"
in 2 Thessalonians 2:10, as an "enactmental not" (*vollzugsmäßige Nicht*). For discussion of
Agamben and the structure of messianic time, and Paul's exhortation for the community
to love *hōs mē*, see Elizabeth A. Castelli, "The Philosophers' Paul in the Frame of the Global:
Some Reflections," in *Paul and the Philosophers*, 151–53. On *hōs mē* and Paul's meontology
according to Heidegger, see also Critchley, *The Faith of the Faithless*, 177–83; idem, "You
Are Not Your Own," 236–40. On Taubes's reading of Paul as a prism of his conflictual
relationship to Judaism and Christianity, see Larry L. Welborn, "Jacob Taubes—Paulinist,
Messianist," in *Paul in the Grip of the Philosophers*, 69–90.

[168] Gillian Rose, *Judaism and Modernity: Philosophical Essays* (Oxford: Blackwell, 1993),
189. Compare ibid., 181: "The object, style and mood of Benjamin's philosophy converge, not
in the Christian mournfulness or melancholy, discerned from the Baroque *Trauerspiel* to
Baudelaire, but in the Judaic state of desertion—in Hebrew, *agunah*—the stasis which his
agon with the law dictates.... Benjamin is the *taxonomist of sadness*, and he adds figures of
melancholy to the philosophical repertoire of modern experiences... stoicism, scepticism,
the unhappy consciousness, resignation and *ressentiment*" (emphasis in original). See also
Rebecca Comay, "Benjamin's Endgame," in *Walter Benjamin's Philosophy: Destruction and
Experience*, 246–85.

[169] The expression is derived from David McLellan, *Utopian Pessimist: The Life and
Thought of Simone Weil* (New York: Simon and Schuster, 1990).

[170] I am following the translation in Benjamin, *Selected Writings, Volume 4*, 392. The
German original appears in Benjamin, *Gesammelte Schriften*, vol. 1.2, 697. A different
translation of the entire poem appears in *The Correspondence of Walter Benjamin*, 184–85.
For a third translation of the poem and the original, see *The Correspondence of Walter
Benjamin and Gershom Scholem*, 79–81. Scholem included this poem together with some
others in a letter written to Benjamin on September 19, 1933. A fourth translation with

these words as the epigraph to his own text, Benjamin italicized the second line of this verse, *I would like to turn back*, a point of emphasis lacking in the original German "ich kehrte gern zurück." This may seem to be nothing more than a stylistic triviality but, in fact, it speaks very loudly as it underlines the redemptive potency of looking backward, the stance that is essential to historical writing. In Benjamin's own terms:

> This is how the angel of history must look. His face is turned toward the past. Where a chain of events appears before *us*, *he* sees one single catastrophe, which keeps piling wreckage upon wreckage and hurls it at his feet. The angel would like to stay, awaken the dead, and make whole what has been smashed. But a storm is blowing from Paradise and has got caught in his wings; it is so strong that the angel can no longer close them. This storm drives him irresistibly into the future, to which his back is turned, while the pile of debris before him grows toward the sky. What we call progress is *this* storm.[171]

From the vantage point of the angel of history—which we can assume is a symbolic configuration of the faculty of memory—what appears as a concatenation of discrete events is but one single catastrophe constituted by the conglomeration of wreckage piled upon wreckage. The angel desires to tarry in the past to revive the dead and to repair what has been shattered but the storm blowing in from Paradise drives him into the future as the mound of trash, which is the past, continues to expand heavenward. With searing cynicism, Benjamin notes that this storm is what we call progress. Adorno well understood what should be adduced from the labyrinth of Benjamin's messianic-utopian thought:

> The traces always come from the past, and our hopes come from their counterpart, from that which was or is doomed; such an interpretation may very well fit the last line of Benjamin's text on *Elective Affinities*: "For the sake of the hopeless only are we given hope."[172] And yet it is tempting to look for the

---

the German text appears in Scholem, *The Fullness of Time*, 64–67. Concerning this poem, see also Gershom Scholem, *Walter Benjamin: The Story of a Friendship*, trans. Harry Zohn (Philadelphia: Jewish Publication Society of America, 1981), 102; Robert Alter, *Necessary Angels: Tradition and Modernity in Kafka, Benjamin, and Scholem* (Cambridge, MA: Harvard University Press, 1991), 113–15; Weigel, *Body- and Image-Space*, 56–57.

171 Benjamin, *Selected Writings, Volume 4*, 392 (emphasis in original). See Rolf Tiedemann, "Historical Materialism or Political Messianism? An Interpretation of the Theses 'On the Concept of History,'" in *Benjamin: Philosophy, Aesthetics, History*, ed. Gary Smith (Chicago: University of Chicago Press, 1989), 175–209, esp. 177–81; Bouretz, *Witnesses for the Future*, 212–23; Eiland and Jennings, *Walter Benjamin*, 661.

172 The reference is to the concluding line in Benjamin's essay "Goethes Wahlverwandtschaften," written in 1919–1922 and published in *Neue Deutsche Beiträge*,

sense, not in life at large, but in the fulfilled moments—in the moments of present existence that make up for its refusal to tolerate anything outside it.[173]

Any hope we can muster to breathe is knotted with the suffocation of hopelessness. This is the intent of Benjamin's pronouncement that we have been given hope for the sake of the hopeless; that is, the hopelessness can never be eradicated by hope, for if hopelessness was truly eliminated, we would not be capable of exuding hopefulness. It is safe to assume that Benjamin's sense of the hopeless hope underlies Adorno's classification of his own thinking as "melancholy science," which he further identifies as the "true field of philosophy." To know the "truth about life in its imme-diacy," one "must scrutinize its estranged form, the objective powers that determine individual existence even in its most hidden recesses...Our perspective of life has passed into an ideology which conceals the fact that there is life no longer."[174]

Here it is relevant to recall as well the fragment entitled "Idea of a Mystery" that Benjamin attached to a letter to Scholem sent in November

---

1924–1925. An English translation, "Goethe's Elective Affinities," is found in Benjamin, *Selected Writings, Volume 1*, 297–360. The crucial line appears on 356: "Only for the sake of the hopeless ones have we been given hope."

[173] Adorno, *Negative Dialectics*, 378. Compare Adorno, "Progress," 56–57: "But the dependence of progress on totality is a thorn on its side. Consciousness of this dependence inspires Benjamin's polemic in his theses on the concept of history against the coupling of progress in the direction which one might crudely call politically progressive...The concentration of progress on the survival of the species is thereby confirmed: no progress should be supposed in such a way as to imply there already is such a thing as humanity which therefore simply could progress. Rather, progress would produce humanity itself, the perspective for which is opened in the face of extinction. It follows that the concept of universal history cannot be saved, as Benjamin further teaches; the concept is illuminating only as long as the illusion of an already existing humanity, harmonious and ascending to unity, remains credible. If humanity remains entrapped by its own self-made totality, then, as Kafka wrote, no progress has really yet occurred, while reference to totality alone allows it to be thought." But see ibid., 65: "The progress of domination of nature which, according to Benjamin's parable, proceeds in contradiction to that true progress with its *telos* in redemption, is still not without all hope. The two concepts of progress communicate with each other not just in fending off the final calamity, but much more in each actual form of the mitigation of persistent suffering."

[174] Theodor W. Adorno, *Minima Moralia: Reflections from Damaged Life*, trans. E. F. N. Jephcott (London: Verso, 1974), 15. The summation by Gillian Rose, *The Melancholy Science: An Introduction to the Thought of Theodor W. Adorno* (New York: Columbia University Press, 1978), 148, is worth citing: "The melancholy science is not resigned, quiescent or pessimistic. It reasons that theory, just like philosophy it was designed to replace, tends to overreach itself, with dubious political consequences. The social reality of the advanced capitalist society is more intractable than such theory is willing to concede, and Adorno had a fine dialectical sense for its paradoxes." The attentiveness to suffering and pain in Adorno's utopian speculations is appreciated as well by Ombrosi, *The Twilight of Reason*, 119–47.

1927. Benjamin wrote of representing "history as a trial in which man, as an advocate of dumb nature, brings charges against all Creation and cites the failure of the promised Messiah to appear. The court, however, decides to hear witnesses for the future. Then appear the poet, who senses the future; the artist, who sees it; the musician, who hears it; and the philosopher, who knows it. Hence, their evidence conflicts, even though they all testify that the future is coming."[175] In the continuation, Benjamin notes that the court could not "make up its mind" and thus it was necessary for "new grievances" to be introduced and for new witnesses to come forth, to the point that there was "torture and martyrdom," terms that seem inappropriate to the setting of a trial. Moreover, we are told that the jury did not trust the prosecutor or the witnesses, and by the end, fearing that they might be expelled from their places, the jurors fled and "only the prosecutor and witnesses remain."[176]

It is interesting to cogitate about what inferences may be drawn from the juxtaposition of the specific vocations listed on Benjamin's list of witnesses. A full exposition of this matter lies beyond the main concern of this essay, but I will offer two brief observations. First, the list obliges us to consider the intricate bond between poet and philosopher, since they are distinguished from the artist and musician, inasmuch as the medium for witnessing that they share is language. To be sure, Benjamin sets them apart by speaking of the poet who feels (*es fühlt*) as opposed to the philosopher who knows (*es weiß*), whence we can assume that the linguistic truths expressed by the former well forth from an experience of immediacy, whereas those of the latter are a matter of ratiocination.[177] Even so, Benjamin's celebrated notion of the linguistic nature of all being (*das sprachliche Wesen der Dinge*) and the depiction of the world as symbolic of a fallen state in relation to an

---

[175] Benjamin, *Selected Writings, Volume 2*, 68.

[176] Ibid. It is of interest to recall in this context the following passage from Benjamin, *The Origin of German Tragic Drama*, 136: "Death, as the form of tragic life, is an individual destiny; in the *Trauerspiel* it frequently takes the form of a communal fate, as if summoning all the participants before the highest court." And compare the distinction between the heavenly and earthly court in ibid., 234: "And while, in the earthly court, the uncertain subjectivity of judgment is firmly anchored in reality, with punishments, in the heavenly court the illusion of evil comes entirely into its own. Here the unconcealed subjectivity triumphs over every deceptive objectivity of justice, and is incorporated into divine omnipotence as a 'work of supreme wisdom and primal love', as hell."

[177] On the meaning of poetic existence in Benjamin, informed by Hölderlin, see Fenves, *The Messianic Reduction*, 18–43, esp. 35–38.

inexpressible *Ursprache*[178] insinuate a more proximate relation between poet and philosopher.[179]

Second, Benjamin speaks of history as a trial in which the human being serves as an advocate for "mute nature" (*stummen Natur*) by bringing a complaint against all creation in general and against the redeemer's non-appearance in particular. The prosecutor, the witnesses, and the members of the jury are all imagined to be present, but the defendant standing trial is the one persona on the scene that is absent. Indeed, the absence of the defendant is precisely what is being judged. I take this to mean that any investigation into messianic speculation must interrogate the deferment of the promise. Benjamin remarks that all of the witnesses testify to the Messiah's coming, but in truth, they accomplish this by testifying to his not having come. Scholem suggested that the aforecited arcanum "constitutes the first evidence of the influence on Benjamin of Kafka's novel *The Trial*...This was the beginning of his meditations on Kafka, which were intended as preliminary studies for an essay on *The Trial*."[180] I would add that Benjamin's comment regarding the absence of the promised Messiah (*das Ausbleiben des verheißnen Messias*) is reminiscent of Kafka's parabolic aphorism that the Messiah will come on the day after he has arrived, not the last day but on the very last day,[181] that is, the day after the last, a day that cannot come forth in the ebb and flow of time any more or less than the very first day, the first that would have to come before the first and therefore already be second.[182]

In a similar spirit, Benjamin upheld the notion of an end that can never be achieved insofar as it is the end, and thus he wryly noted that the drawing

---

[178] Irving Wohlfarth, "On Some Jewish Motifs in Benjamin," in *The Problems of Modernity: Adorno and Benjamin*, ed. Andrew Benjamin (London: Routledge, 1989), 157–215; Eiland and Jennings, *Walter Benjamin*, 88–90. The question of Benjamin's theory of language and the Jewish mystical tradition, particularly as it was interpreted through the lens of Scholem, has been discussed by a number of scholars. For an extensive analysis, see Jacobson, *Metaphysics of the Profane*, 85–153, and see the comments in Wolfson, *Language, Eros, Being*, 11–12, 405–6 n. 78.

[179] Noteworthy are the comments of Hannah Arendt in Walter Benjamin, *Illuminations*, ed. Hannah Arendt, trans. Harry Zohn (New York: Schocken, 1969), 14: "What is so hard to understand about Benjamin is that without being a poet he *thought poetically* and therefore was bound to regard the metaphor as the greatest gift of language. Linguistic 'transference' enables us to give material form to the invisible...and thus to render it capable of being experienced" (emphasis in original).

[180] Scholem, *Walter Benjamin: The Story of a Friendship*, 145. Scholem's surmise is elaborated in Wohlfarth, "On Some Jewish Motifs," 188–205.

[181] Franz Kafka, *Parables and Paradoxes* (New York: Schocken, 1971), 81.

[182] Blanchot, *The Writing of Disaster*, 143, cited in Wolfson, *A Dream*, 452 n. 157. The comment of Kafka (cited in previous note) and the explication of Blanchot were noted by Comay, "Benjamin's Endgame," 269.

near of surrealism to communism arouses the need for "pessimism all along the line."[183] The failure to arrive at the end has been appropriated by various postmodern thinkers—in no small measure due to the influence of Derrida's notion of messianicity and the emphasis he placed on the future (*l'avenir*) as the dawning of what is to come (*à-venir*) and consequently impervious to a thematics of time[184]—as an indicator of limitless hope. Typical of this stance is Derrida's insistence that the apocalyptic tone—the unveiling of the truth of the end that reveals itself as the advent of the end of truth—rests on the assumption that the end is beginning, that the end is imminent, a point corroborated by the fact that we are all going to die.[185] Nevertheless, the discourse of the end echoes the diction of John's apocalyptic prediction, "you will not know at what hour I shall come upon you" (Rev. 3:3), which is glossed by Derrida, "I shall come: the coming is always to come. The *Adôn* named as the aleph and the tav, the alpha and the omega, is the one who has been, who is, and who comes, not who shall be, but who comes, which is the present of to-come [*à-venir*]. *I am coming* means: I am going to come, I am to come in the imminence of an 'I am going to come,' 'I am in the process of coming,' 'I am on the point of going to come.'"[186]

Even though Derrida states clearly that the "apocalyptic desire" for elucidation or enlightenment consists of the critique that demystifies or deconstructs apocalyptic discourse itself and with it all speculation on vision of the end[187]—indeed the dismissal of a transcendental signifier leaves us with an horizon of temporality in which there is neither arche nor telos, neither foundational beginning nor eschatological ending—his emphasis on the inability of the future to come, its state of always coming, seemingly begets an unbounded optimism, since the future is, in Derrida's own terms, the "monstrous *arrivant*;" that is, inasmuch as the future is unpredictable, incalculable, and nonprogrammable, it is like a monster that is not recognized the first time it appears. Hence, we can welcome the future only as that for which we cannot prepare in the manner that we "accord hospitality

---

183 Benjamin, *Selected Writings, Volume 2*, 216.

184 Wolfson, *Giving Beyond the Gift*, 160–61, and references to other scholarly discussions cited on 406 n. 31. To the sources mentioned there, see now the analysis of Colby Dickinson, *Between the Canon and the Messiah: The Structure of Faith in Contemporary Continental Thought* (London: Bloomsbury, 2013), 43–114. On the privileging of the future in the Derridean conception of temporality, see Joanna Hodge, *Derrida on Time* (London: Routledge, 2007), 91–112.

185 Jacques Derrida, "On a Newly Arisen Apocalyptic Tone in Philosophy," in *Raising the Tone of Philosophy: Late Essays by Immanuel Kant, Transformative Critique by Jacques Derrida*, ed. Peter Fenves (Baltimore: Johns Hopkins University Press, 1993), 151–52.

186 Ibid., 153 (emphasis in original).

187 Ibid., 148.

to that which is absolutely foreign or strange."[188] This "waiting for the never enough of time," as one scholar artfully called it,[189] matches the "experience of the impossible" that Derrida assigns to the "deconstructive operation." Performatively, awaiting the future that can never arrive is "the experience of the other as the invention of the impossible, in other words, as the only possible invention... Deconstruction is inventive or it is nothing at all; it does not settle for methodical procedures, it opens up a passageway, it marches ahead and marks a trail... Its *process* [démarche] involves an affirmation, this latter being linked to the coming—the *venire*—in event, advent, invention. But it can only do so by deconstructing a conceptual and institutional structure of invention that neutralizes by putting the stamp of reason on some aspect of invention, of inventive power; as if it were necessary, over and beyond a certain traditional status of invention, to reinvent the future."[190]

Of course, for Derrida, the matter is more complex because the future is precisely what never comes except as what cannot be foreseen, and thus in some sense, it is always coming. Still, there is an indefatigable hopefulness implicit in the description of deconstruction as a means to reinvent the future. Benjamin and the thinkers of the Frankfurt school saw the matter differently, perceiving that the inability for closure also breeds pessimism and despair, a "mistrust in all reconciliation: between classes, between nations, between individuals."[191] We cannot reinvent the future; at best, we can rewrite the story of the past so that we can manage to survive in the present. In the conclusion of the sixth historical thesis, Benjamin observed, "The only historian capable of fanning the spark of hope in the past is the one who is firmly convinced that *even the dead* will not be safe from the enemy if he is victorious. And this enemy has never ceased to be victorious."[192] Utilizing the traditional language of Christian soteriology, Benjamin expresses this in the image of the messianic redeemer subjugating the Antichrist. For Benjamin, however, this is a conquest that will

---

[188] Jacques Derrida, *Points...: Interviews, 1974–1994*, ed. Elisabeth Weber, trans. Peggy Kamuf and others (Stanford: Stanford University Press, 1995), 386–87. See Marko Zlomislic, *Jacques Derrida's Aporetic Ethics* (Lanham, MD: Lexington Books, 2007), 237.

[189] Zlomislic, *Jacques Derrida's Aporetic Ethics*, 233–39.

[190] Jacques Derrida, *Psyche: Inventions of the Other*, vol. 1, ed. Peggy Kamuf and Elizabeth Rottenberg (Stanford: Stanford University Press, 2007), 15 and 23 (emphasis in original).

[191] Benjamin, *Selected Writings, Volume 2*, 217. See Paul Mendes-Flohr, " 'To Brush History against the Grain': The Eschatology of the Frankfurt School and Ernst Bloch," *Journal of the American Academy of Religion* 51 (1983): 631–50.

[192] Benjamin, *Selected Writings, Volume 4*, 391 (emphasis in original).

necessarily not reach its fruition—the enemy never has and never will cease to be victorious. If the efficacy of the Antichrist were to be subdued, this would beckon the extermination of Christ.

Perhaps even more pertinent is Benjamin's aside in the *Theological-Political Fragment*: "Only the Messiah himself completes all history, in the sense that he alone redeems, completes, creates its relation to the messianic. For this reason, nothing that is historical can relate itself, from its own ground, to anything messianic. Therefore, the Kingdom of God is not the telos of the historical dynamic; it cannot be established as a goal [*Ziel*]. From the standpoint of history, it is not the goal but the terminus [*Ende*]."[193] Departing from Cohen's asymptotic conception of progress towards an end that is endlessly approached but never finally achieved, and the consequent distinction he proposes between eschatology and messianism,[194] Benjamin maintained that history is not advancing towards some goal; the messianic is the terminus that cannot be realized either in the course of a future that is at an infinite distance from the present or even in the intervention of any particular moment at hand. The now is splintered with shards of light but the liberation of these shards can never dissipate the darkness. As Eli Friedlander succinctly summarized Benjamin's view, messianic temporality is "a scheme of actualization" that "does not involve the projection of a utopian end in a more or less distant future but rather the urgent revolution of the present by way of the recognition of its bond with the suffering of the past. The present transformed, what Benjamin calls the Now, rather than any dreams of the future, is the focal point of the messianic passion. This is why Benjamin opposes messianism as he understands it to all utopian or prophetic thinking."[195] Reaching a similar conclusion, Löwy offers the following somewhat sanguine assessment:

---

[193] Benjamin, *Selected Writings, Volume 3*, 305; Benjamin, *Gesammelte Schriften*, vol. 2, 203. For discussion of this text in light of the two strands of messianic speculation in Jewish sources—one that posits the Messiah as the sole agency of redemption and the other that assumes the Messiah is the consummation of a redemptive process set into motion by human initiative—see Jacobson, *Metaphysics of the Profane*, 24–31.

[194] Hermann Cohen, *Religion of Reason Out of the Sources of Judaism*, trans. with an introduction by Simon Kaplan, introductory essay by Leo Strauss, introductory essays for the second edition by Steven S. Schwarzschild and Kenneth Seeskin (Atlanta: Scholars Press, 1995), 49: "An important moment already comes to the fore, which lays down the bridge between the root of monotheism and its peak formed by Messianism: *the distinction between eschatology and Messianism*" (emphasis in original). See ibid., 290.

[195] Friedlander, *Walter Benjamin*, 193.

Walter Benjamin was far from being a "utopian" thinker. Unlike his friend Ernst Bloch, he was preoccupied less with the "principle of hope" and more with the urgent necessity of organizing pessimism; interested less in the "radiant future" and more in the imminent dangers looming over humanity. He is not far from a tragic world-view . . . the deep sense of an unbridgeable abyss between the authentic values one believes in and empirical reality. However . . . a fragile utopian dimension—because it is entirely shot through with romantic melancholy and the tragic sense of defeat—is present in his work. Against the dominant tendency in the historic Left, which has often reduced socialism to economic objectives of concern to the industrial working class—itself reduced to its male, white, "national," stably employed fraction—Benjamin's thinking enables us to conceive a revolutionary project with a general mission to emancipate.[196]

I would add that Benjamin does not guarantee that the revolution of the present will ever succeed to overpower societal inequality once and for all. Rebellion is not a remedy for the despondency endemic to being human. There is no way out of the abyss but through being ensconced in the abyss, no ascent but through descent, no memory of forgetfulness but through the forgetfulness of memory, no recuperation from alienation but through the alienation from alienation.[197]

Utopian Hope and Disenchantment of the Image

The implications of the dark utopianism were drawn overtly by Adorno, whose decidedly secular politics and aesthetics were rooted in what has been called the *Jewish passion for the impossible*,[198] a fidelity to the ideal of redemption that assumes the form of its refusal—in the traditional idiom, the Messiah can be present only in the absence of being present. In the first section of the introduction to *Negative Dialectics*, Adorno put his finger on the conceptual quandary and pragmatic ineptitude that envisaging a perpetually deferred future inescapably entails: "Theory cannot prolong the moment its critique depended on. A practice indefinitely delayed is no longer the forum for appeals against self-satisfied speculation; it is mostly the pretext used by executive authorities to choke, as vain, whatever critical thoughts the practical change would require."[199]

---

[196] Löwy, *Fire Alarm*, 112.
[197] Wohlfarth, "On Some Jewish Motifs," 165.
[198] Josh Cohen, *Interrupting Auschwitz: Art, Religion, Philosophy* (London: Continuum, 2005), 33.
[199] Adorno, *Negative Dialectics*, 3.

An analysis of Adorno's critical theory is clearly beyond the scope of this essay. However, I will focus briefly on one crucial aspect of his thinking, which likely bears the influence of Cohen's Neokantianism, the conjunction between the motif of messianic yearning and the apophatic injunction against images (*Bilderverbot*):[200] just as the latter translates philosophically into "an extreme ascesis toward any type of revealed faith,"[201] an atheistic contention dogmatically expressed as the "one who believes in God cannot believe in God"[202]—any positive representation of God, consequently, capitulates to conceptual idolatry, the absolutization of the finite as infinite and the invocation of truth as falsehood[203]—so the valid redemptive response involves turning away from redemption. Musing about the Augustinian ideas of progress, redemption, and the immanent course of history, Adorno makes the following observation that, in my judgment, can be applied more generally to any teleological conception of the historical justified by appeal to transcendence whether sacralized or secularized: "If progress is equated with redemption as simple transcendent intervention, it surrenders any comprehensive meaning with the dimension of time, and evaporates into ahistorical theology. But the mediation with history threatens to make it an idol, and with the absurdity, both in reflection on the concept and in reality, that—what inhibits progress—is what counts as progress. Auxiliary constructions of an immanent-transcendent concept of progress condemn themselves through their very nomenclature."[204]

The essence of the messianic ethos lies in the fact that the God of Judaism, in contradistinction to ancient mythological deities, confronts nature as nature's other and hence there is always the chance that the status quo of the world order might be perturbed. But this very scenario is

---

200 Elizabeth A. Pritchard, "*Bilderverbot* Meets Body in Theodor W. Adorno's Inverse Theology," *Harvard Theological Review* 95 (2002): 291–318. Pritchard, 291–92 n, 2, reviews previous scholars who discuss negative theology and the ban of images in Adorno. The negative redemption implied by the *Bilderverbot* is explored by Glazer, *A New Physiognomy*, 60–63. See also Düttmann, *The Memory of Thought*, 58–61, 70–87. On the critical theory of the Frankfurt school as a form of Jewish negative theology, see additional sources cited in Wolfson, *Giving Beyond the Gift*, 264 n. 29.

201 Theodor W. Adorno, *Critical Models: Interventions and Catchwords*, trans. and with a preface by Henry W. Pickford (New York: Columbia University Press, 1998), 142. See also Max Horkheimer and Theodor Adorno, *Dialectic of Enlightenment: Philosophical Fragments*, ed. Gunzelin Schmid Noerr, trans. Edmund Jephcott (Stanford: Stanford University Press, 2002), 17.

202 Adorno, *Negative Dialectics*, 401.

203 Düttmann, *The Memory of Thought*, 56–58, 96–97; Hent de Vries, *Minimal Theologies: Critiques of Secular Reason in Adorno and Levinas*, trans. Geoffrey Hale (Baltimore: Johns Hopkins University Press, 2005), 601–6, 629–30.

204 Adorno, "Progress," 58.

self-negating, since every undermining is subject to being undermined. Adorno insists that the *negation of negation* should not be equated with positivity—in simple arithmetic terms, minus times minus is a plus—a move he sees as the "quintessence of identification," which obscures the nonidentical that arises from the "negation of particularities," the negation of the negated that remains negative.[205] The function of the negative dialectic is to alter the direction of conceptuality by giving "it a turn toward nonidentity," which is to say, to ascertain the "constitutive character of the nonconceptual in the concept."[206]

In another passage in *Negative Dialectics*, Adorno identifies *cognitive utopia* as the use of "concepts to unseal the nonconceptual with concepts."[207] When placed in this utopian light, the endeavor of philosophy as self-critique is to include nonconceptuality within the purview of conceptual knowledge, to defy the dominating spirit of the identity principle of reason—the sine qua non of philosophical thought insofar as thinking cannot occur without it[208]—and its invariable apportioning of injustice to the nonidentical.[209] "Disenchantment of the concept" may be deemed the "antidote of philosophy,"[210] but there is no way to the nonconceptual except through the conceptual, no way to the nonidentity of the other but through the identity of the self. "Philosophical reflection makes sure of the nonconceptual in the concept... It must strive, by way of the concept, to transcend the concept."[211] Progress, therefore, is dialectical—not in a Hegelian sense—inasmuch as "one moment changes into its other only by literally reflecting itself, by reason turning reason upon itself and emancipating itself, in its self-limitation from the demon of identity."[212] The paradox at play here is expressed concisely by Adorno in an essay on the experiential content of Hegel's philosophy, "Only through reflection can reflective thought get beyond itself."[213] Hence, the "work of philosophical

---

[205] Adorno, *Negative Dialectics*, 158.
[206] Ibid., 12.
[207] Ibid., 10.
[208] Adorno, "Progress," 67.
[209] Ibid., 60.
[210] Adorno, *Negative Dialectics*, 13.
[211] Ibid., 13–15. See Axel Honneth, *Pathologies of Reason: On the Legacy of Critical Theory*, trans. James Ingram (New York: Columbia University Press, 2009), 26–27.
[212] Adorno, "Progress," 63.
[213] Theodor W. Adorno, *Hegel: Three Studies*, trans. Shierry Weber Nicholsen, with an introduction by Shierry Weber Nicholsen and Jeremy J. Shapiro (Cambridge, MA: MIT Press, 1993), 73.

self-reflection" consists, pace Wittgenstein,[214] in "uttering the unutterable,"[215] or literally, in the need "to say what will not let itself be said" (*was nicht sich sagen läßt*),[216] the nonlinguistic and nonsignifying moment of language, the imageless image,[217] the "mimetic consummation" of the "true language of art," exemplified in music, a language whose "expression is the antithesis of expressing something."[218] The sociopolitical context for Adorno's view is spelled out in the following comment in the lecture on metaphysics he delivered on July 20, 1965: "I believe that culture's squalid and guilty suppression of nature—a suppression which is itself a wrongly and blindly natural tendency of human beings—is the reason why people refuse to admit that dark sphere ... If what I have tried to explain—in extreme terms—about the concept of culture is true, and if it is the case that philosophy's only *raison d'être* today is to gain access to the unsayable, then it can be said that Auschwitz and the world of Auschwitz have made clear something which was not a surprise to those who were not positivists but had a deep, speculative turn of mind: that culture has failed to its very core."[219]

---

[214] For a comparative analysis of Adorno and Wittgenstein on the theme of saying the unsayable, see Roger Forster, *Adorno: The Recovery of Experience* (Albany: State University of New York Press, 2007), 31–56.

[215] Adorno, *Negative Dialectics*, 9.

[216] Theodor W. Adorno, *Negativ Dialektik* (Frankfurt am Main: Suhrkamp, 1966), 21, translation in Forster, *Adorno*, 32. In light of this need to say what will not let itself be said, it is of interest to consider the following exposition of Schoenberg's *Moses und Aron* in Theodor W. Adorno, *Quasi una Fantasia: Essays on Modern Music*, trans. Rodney Livingstone (London: Verso, 1998), 230: "Aaron, the man of images and mediation, has to sing in the opera, but makes use of language without images. Moses, on the other hand, who represents the principle of the ban on images, does not sing in Schoenberg, but just speaks. The only way in which he can dramatize the Old Testament taboo is by making him communicate in a manner which is not really possible according to the biblical story."

[217] Adorno, *Hegel: Three Studies*, 123: "Philosophy as a whole is allied with art in wanting to rescue, in the medium of the concept, the mimesis that the concept represses, and here Hegel ... disempowers individual concepts, uses them as though they were the imageless images of what they mean. Hence the Goethean 'residue of absurdity' in the philosophy of absolute spirit. What it wants to use to get beyond the concept always drives it back beneath the concept in the details." As Dallmayr, *Life-world*, 49–50, noted, following Hermann Mörchen, the aversion to representational thinking was shared by Adorno and Heidegger.

[218] Theodor W. Adorno, *Aesthetic Theory*, ed. Gretel Adorno and Rolf Tiedemann, trans. with introduction by Robert Hullot-Kentor (Minneapolis: University of Minnesota Press, 1997), 112. Compare the description of Bloch's understanding of music in Richter, *Thought-Images*, 77, as "the prime sphere in which we encounter the general other-directedness of signification, an other-directedness that music shares with other forms of signification but which it stages in music-specific ways, that is, beyond any obvious model of referentiality and prestabilized norms of meaning."

[219] Theodor W. Adorno, *Metaphysics: Concept and Problems*, ed. Rolf Tiedemann, trans. Edmund Jephcott (Stanford: Stanford University Press, 2000), 118.

In accord with this logic, we can say that the possibility of redemption is bound inescapably to the impossibility of its actualization. Adorno thus identified the prototype of the "utopian stance toward thought" with the "interpretative stance in philosophy" because the latter leads us to break through the surface of all phenomena by assuring the mind that "what exists is not the ultimate reality—or perhaps we should say: what exists is not just what it claims to be."[220] Translated politically, just as the negative deportment of the hermeneutical condition means becoming conscious of the shortcomings and fallibility of existence, so one must harbor a basic suspicion regarding the tenability of envisioning any social change that would bring about a final resolution. Expressed in a different terminological register, Adorno wrote:

> The concept of progress is philosophical in that it contradicts the movement of society while at the same time articulating it. Social in origin, the concept of progress requires critical confrontation with real society. The moment of redemption, however secularized, cannot be erased from it. The irreducibility of the concept to either facticity or the idea, suggests its own contradiction... Progress means: humanity emerges from its spellbound state no longer under the spell of progress as well, itself nature, by becoming aware of its own indigenousness to nature and by halting the mastery over nature through which nature continues its mastery. In this it could be said that *progress only comes about at the point when it comes to an end*... All the same, a theory of progress must absorb that which is sound in the invectives against faith in progress as an antidote against the mythology which is its malaise... It is a part of the dialect of progress that those historical setbacks instigated by the principle of progress... also provide the condition for humanity to find means to avoid them in the future. The delusion of progress supercedes itself.[221]

In the end, there is no way to speak of the end that would not conjure the end of speaking. Notably, in *Negative Dialectics*, Adorno characterizes hope as an act of transgression against the Jewish ban on images, a ban that was extended to pronouncing the ineffable name. To endorse the possibility of hope is on a par with erecting images and/or mentioning the name, antinomian gestures that counter the indifference of the temporal world "deeply embedded" in the "metaphysical truth" that "vainly denies history."[222] Particularly influenced by Scholem's approach to the mystical

---

[220] Theodor W. Adorno, *History and Freedom: Lectures 1964–1965*, ed. Rolf Tiedemann, trans. Rodney Livingston (Cambridge: Polity Press, 2006), 138.

[221] Adorno, "Progress," 59–65 (emphasis added).

[222] Adorno, *Negative Dialectics*, 402. Compare ibid., 297–98: "What would be different, the unperverted essence, is withheld from a language that bears the stigmata of

phenomenon as innately nihilistic,[223] Adorno presumed a heretical theology common to the kabbalah and to Christian mysticism—such as that of Angelus Silesius—that espoused a doctrine "of the infinite relevance of the intra-mundane, and thus the historical, to transcendence."[224]

Bracketing the accuracy of Adorno's claim, he looks to the allegedly heretical theological underpinnings of mysticism to find within tradition a challenge to the metaphysical supposition of a separation of the intra-mundane realm and the transcendental. But the very emphasis on turning back to the historical without recourse to metaphysical transcendence leaves the former without the possibility of ultimate perfectibility. Curiously, in its aniconism, Judaism plays a pivotal role in the disavowal of metaphysics. Thus, in the *Dialectics of Enlightenment*, Judaism is described as the religion in which the "idea of the patriarchy is heightened to the point of annihilating myth" and in which "the link between name and essence is still acknowledged in the prohibition of uttering the name of God." The eschatological quality of resisting the eschaton is related to the "disenchanted world" of Judaism that "brooks no word which might bring solace to the despair of all mortality... The pledge of salvation lies in the rejection of any faith which claims to depict it, knowledge in the denunciation of illusion."[225] The critical utopia[226] imagined by Adorno is one whose possibility is impossible and therefore possible. Progress is thus not a "conclusive category. It wants to disrupt the triumph of radical evil, not to triumph in itself... Then,

---

existence—there was a time when theologians would speak of the 'mystical name.'" For discussion of Jewish name mysticism in Adorno, see Steven M. Wasserstrom, "Adorno's Kabbalah: Some Preliminary Observations," in *Polemical Encounters: Esoteric Discourse and Its Others*, ed. Olav Hammer and Kocku von Stuckard (Leiden: Brill, 2007), 61–62; Glazer, *A New Physiognomy*, 52–55.

223 Wasserstrom, "Adorno's Kabbalah," 62–64. See also Wolfson, *Venturing Beyond*, 244–46. The influence of Scholem is also evident in Adorno, *Metaphysics*, 108, where he contests the commonplace assumption that mysticism places primary emphasis on the unmediated experience of the divine. The study of mystical texts indicates rather that the experiences are "very strongly mediated by education. For example, the intricate interrelationships between gnosticism, Neo-Platonism, the Cabbala and later Christian mysticism give rise to an area of historicity which is equal to anything in the history of dogma. And it is certainly no accident that the corpus in which the documents of Jewish mysticism are brought together more or less disconnectedly, the Cabbala, bears the title of tradition." Adorno proffers that the emphasis in mystical sources is on topoi of religious experiences, which are often mediated by sacred texts, and not on immediate vision or pure subjectivity. Much of my scholarly work on Jewish mysticism has sought to challenge the polarization of experience and interpretation that is so endemic to Scholem's approach.

224 Adorno, *Metaphysics*, 100.

225 Horkheimer and Adorno, *Dialectic of Enlightenment*, 17.

226 The expression was coined by Jürgen Habermas, *Philosophical-Political Profiles*, trans. Frederick G. Lawrence (Cambridge, MA: MIT Press, 1983), 42: "The German Idealism of the Jews produces the ferment of a critical utopia."

progress would become transformed into resistance against the ever-present danger of regression. Progress is precisely this resistance at all stages, not the capitulation to advancing through their course."[227] In the concluding aphorism of *Minima Moralia*, he writes:

> The only philosophy which can be responsibly practiced in face of despair is the attempt to contemplate all things as they would present themselves from the standpoint of redemption. Knowledge has no light but that shed on the world by redemption... It is the simplest of all things, because the situation calls imperatively for such knowledge, indeed because consummate negativity, once squarely faced, delineates the mirror-image of its opposite. But it is also the utterly impossible thing, because it presupposes a standpoint removed... from the scope of existence... Even its own impossibility it must at last comprehend for the sake of the possible. But beside the demand thus placed on thought, the question of the reality or unreality of redemption itself hardly matters.[228]

Adorno's utopianism encompasses a *noneschatological eschatology* or a *nonteleological teleology*—the "renunciation of redemption in exchange for the appearance of redemption," according to Agamben's gloss on Taubes's characterizing this passage as promoting an "aestheticization" of the messianic that assumes the form of an *as if* construction[229]—and hence he rejected any culmination in the geopolitical arena that might divert one from the ongoing critical enterprise, which brings to light the contradictions and fissures integral to conceptual thought. In the wake of the Holocaust, the only credible philosophical thinking is the mandate to contemplate reality from the standpoint of a redemption whose reality or unreality cannot be substantiated, to cultivate a knowledge that is both the simplest of things and utterly impossible, a knowledge marked by a negativity that yields the mirror image of its opposite, that is, a philosophy whose possibility is predicated on its very impossibility. The demand placed on thought is such that the impossibility must be contemplated for the sake of the possible but the possibility of the possible cannot be contemplated except from the standpoint of the impossible.

One can discern in this description of the impossible possibility of the end a phenomenological recasting of the rabbinic obligation to wait temporally for a redemption that cannot take place in time. The waiting provokes the longing for the advent of the nonevent, the present that Levinas identifies as the "mastery of the existent over existing," an occurrence that

---

[227] Adorno, "Progress," 69–70.
[228] Adorno, *Minima Moralia*, 247.
[229] Taubes, *The Political Theology of Paul*, 74–75; Agamben, *The Time That Remains*, 35.

"can no longer be qualified as experience," a phenomenon that is, technically speaking, "beyond phenomenology."[230] I have discussed the minutiae of Levinas's messianism elsewhere and do not intend to repeat my analysis here.[231] Suffice it to note my conjecture that the shift from Messiah as a distinct person to messianism as a personal vocation for all humanity is an outcome of the diachronic conception of temporal transcendence as a movement toward infinity expressed in the "ethical adventure of the relationship to the other person,"[232] a course set forth by a "pluralism that does not merge into unity."[233] For Levinas, there is no presumption of an abolition of human misery and affliction. As I noted above, that there can be no climax to the historical process portends that the possibility for salvation is always real. The hope of the "temporal transcendence of the present toward the mystery of the future"[234] depends on letting go of the conviction that an eschaton may be reached and a new era without hardship ushered in. Messianic awakening consists of being liberated from this expectation and realizing that the consummation of the end is in waiting for the end to be consummated, a truism that exposes the secret of the nature of time.[235] To wait for the Messiah, in other words, is not to wait for something or someone; it is to wait for the sake of waiting, and hence it induces the patience that is the *length of time*, "an awaiting without anything being awaited, without the intention of awaiting… Patience swallows its own intention; time is attested in being deferred [*se réfère en se déférant*]. Time is deferred, is transcended to the Infinite. And the awaiting without something awaited (time itself) is turned into responsibility for another."[236] Levinas's view is expressed aphoristically by Blanchot, "In waiting, there is always more to await than there are things awaited… Waiting is a wearing down that is not worn out."[237] As Levinas well understood, the Jewish messianic ambition is precisely this *wearing down that does not wear out*, a hope that grows stronger the more it is unfulfilled. The time of the Messiah, consequently,

230 Levinas, *Time and the Other*, 54.

231 Wolfson, *Giving Beyond the Gift*, 113–20. Some of that discussion is reworked here. For a list of other scholarly discussions of messianism in Levinas's thought, see ibid., 380–81 n. 214.

232 Levinas, *Time and the Other*, 33.

233 Ibid., 42.

234 Ibid., 94.

235 Emmanuel Levinas, *Beyond the Verse: Talmudic Readings and Lectures*, trans. Gary D. Mole (London: Athlone Press, 1994), 143.

236 Levinas, *God, Death, and Time*, 139.

237 Maurice Blanchot *Awaiting Oblivion*, trans. John Gregg (Lincoln: University of Nebraska Press, 1997), 59. On the inherent sense of waiting and Jewish messianism, see also text of Blanchot referred to above, n. 182. Compare Romano, "Awaiting," 47–51.

bespeaks the mystery of time more generally, the "*not yet* more remote than a future, a temporal *not yet*, evincing degrees in nothingness."[238]

In the final analysis, Levinas's diachrony is a phenomenological translation of the paradox that has impacted Jewish messianism through the centuries: the coming of the Messiah is the impossible possible, that which is possible because it is impossible—the Messiah who has come can never be the Messiah one believed is coming. Messianic time is the moment in time that is outside of time, the moment that cannot be gauged quantitatively, no matter how refined our tools of analytic computation, and hence there is no way to think of its occurrence but as the occurrence of what cannot occur save in the nonoccurrence of its occurrence. The nonoccurrence in no way affects the belief in the possibility of the eruption of the future; on the contrary, insofar as that eruption is contingent to the time that cannot materialize in time, the nonoccurrence is, strictly speaking, what guarantees its occurrence.

Not Yet Now and the Nothingness of the Future

Let me conclude by citing the following passage from Bloch's *The Spirit of Utopia*, written between 1915–1916, published in 1918 and then with revisions in 1923:

> Yet—*and this is of decisive importance*—the *future*, the *topos of the unknown within the future* . . . is itself nothing but *our expanded darkness, than our darkness in the issue of its own womb, in the expansion of its latency* . . . That means: the final, true, unknown, superdivine God, the disclosure of us all, already "lives" now, too, although he has not been "crowned" or "objectivated"; he "weeps," as certain rabbis said of the Messiah, at the question, what is he doing, since he cannot "appear" and redeem us; he "acts" in the deepest part of all of us as the "I am that I shall be," as "darkness: of the lived God," as darkness before his self-possession, before his face that will finally be uncovered, before the departure from the exile of true essence itself. So it seems, indeed it becomes certain, that this precisely is hope, where the darkness brightens. Hope is in the darkness itself, partakes of its imperceptibility, just as darkness and mystery are always related; it threatens to disappear if it looms up too nearly, too abruptly in this darkness.[239]

---

[238] Levinas, *Totality and Infinity*, 264 (emphasis in original).
[239] Bloch, *The Spirit of Utopia*, trans. Anthony A. Nassar (Stanford: Stanford University Press, 2000), 201.

The revolutionary politics proffered by Bloch is plagued by two conflict-
ing tendencies—the emphasis on the Western category of the telos,
the omega point at the end of history that pulls human emancipation
forward—expressed specifically as the triumph of Marxism—and the
subversive power of the utopian spirit to break into history disruptively,
the radical disjunction that is the essence of the not-yet of the future.[240]
Bloch's thought is both thoroughly messianic, inasmuch as his thinking
is typified by a defiant desire not to accept unjust suffering, and thoroughly gnostic, inasmuch as he accepts forlornness as the indigenous
state of the human condition. The petition to overcome moral injustice
is not bolstered by naïve buoyancy but is born from awareness of inexo-
rable torment. There is no recourse to a benevolent God, no pledge of a
transcendent light extinguishing darkness. The darkness is defeated by
political activism that accepts the perdurance of the darkness it seeks to
defeat. The hope of which we may speak is positioned in the place "where
the darkness brightens," that is, the *hope is in the darkness itself.* Bloch
does grant that the secret "quite precisely never stands in the dark, but
rather is called to dissolve it; *thus does the darkness of the lived moment
awaken in the resonance of the amazement that comes over us.*"[241] Hope
must lift itself out of the darkness of the now but the reciprocal connection between the two makes it impossible to imagine one without the
other. This, I suppose, is what Bloch meant when he used the term *revolutionary gnosis* in the 1963 Afterword to *The Spirit of Utopia* to characterize his thinking. "The world is untrue," he writes, "but it wants to
return home through man and through truth."[242] From that perspective,
what is not yet true is the actuality that looms in the potentiality of what
has already come to be untrue; the end restores us to the beginning, in
terms apposite to both the inceptual thinking of kabbalistic theosophy
and the Schellingian system of transcendental idealism, the pleromatic
void where absolute necessity is indistinguishable from pure possibility,
the dark ground of the present that is the propulsion of the nascent past
toward an inveterate future. As Habermas incisively put it, "Bloch's basic
experience is of the darkness, the open-endedness, the longing proper
to the lived moment, proper to the nothingness of the mystic that is

---

[240] See Tom Moylan, "Bloch against Bloch: The Theological Reception of Das Prinzip
Hoffnung and the Liberation of the Utopian Function," in *Not Yet: Reconsidering Ernst
Bloch*, 96–121, esp. 112.
[241] Bloch, *The Spirit of Utopia*, 202 (emphasis in original).
[242] Ibid., 279.

hungering for something...In this primordial hunger, the knot of the world presses toward resolution and, as long as it is unresolved, at each moment casts life back to its beginnings."[243]

With his denial of the world as God's creation and his avowed atheism, Bloch was at odds with the fundamental theological presuppositions of Judaism. Even so, due to his indebtedness to Jewish thinkers, perhaps prompted by the kabbalistic themes of exile and redemption mediated through Schelling,[244] but influenced especially by Cohen's idea of the messianic future as an "aspiration for infinity"[245] that degrades and destroys the "present political actuality,"[246] he developed his principle of hope and the epistemology of the not yet. To cite one evocative passage:

> The Authentic or essence is that *which is not yet, which in the core of things drives towards itself, which awaits its genesis in the tendency-latency of process*; it is itself only now founded, objective-real—hope...The tomorrow in today is alive, people are always asking about it. The faces which turned in the utopian direction have of course been different in every age, just like that which in each individual case they believed they saw. Whereas the *direction* here is always related, indeed in its still concealed goal it is the same; it appears as the only unchanging thing in history. Happiness, freedom, non-alienation, Golden Age, Land of Milk and Honey, the Eternally-Female, the trumpet signal in Fidelio and the Christ-likeness of the Day of Resurrection which follows it: these are so many witnesses and images of such differing value, but all are set up around that which speaks for itself by still remaining silent.[247]

Like the Marburg thinkers, Bloch accords a privileged position to the future as the truest dimension of time that transmutes history from an

---

[243] Habermas, *Philosophical-Political Profiles*, 68.

[244] Ibid., 38–40. Habermas speaks about Bloch's "Marxian appropriation of Jewish mysticism" as the culmination of a process that began with Benjamin, who sought to synthesize historical materialism and kabbalistic mysticism (38). Habermas suggests, moreover, that the Lurianic myth of the world arising from the divine contraction, exile, and restoration informed the fundamental axiom of Bloch's speculative materialism: matter is in need of redemption (39). Finally, it is proposed that Bloch was influenced by Schelling, who "had brought from the spirit of Romanticism the heritage of the Kabbalah into the Protestant philosophy of German Idealism," and hence "the most Jewish elements of Bloch's philosophy...are at the same time the authentically German ones" (40). See the expanded discussion of this theme in Habermas, *Philosophical-Political Profiles*, 67–69, and see below, n. 249.

[245] Cohen, *Religion of Reason*, 248.

[246] Ibid., 291.

[247] Bloch, *The Principle of Hope*, 1373–75.

empirical to an ideal construction.[248] The future inspires hopefulness in the present as the nothingness of what is not yet formed—indeed as future it can become actual only by never becoming actual, since the future, by definition, is what is still to be actualized—and therefore to speak for itself it must remain silent.

This is the intent of the aforementioned comment from *The Spirit of Utopia* that the Messiah cannot appear and thus he acts in the deepest part of us as the "I am that I shall be." Bloch has creatively interpreted the name of Yahweh revealed to Moses at the theophany of the burning bush, *ehyeh asher ehyeh* (Exod. 3:14), the most peculiar of names that does not name any being that is actually present but only the potential for future becoming. In *The Principle of Hope*, Bloch traces the consciousness of "utopia in religion" and of "religion in utopia" to this biblical narrative and the revelation of the name of the "original God of exodus," the "God of the goal," the Deus Spes (God of hope) as opposed to the Deus Creator (God of creation):

> For the Yahweh of Moses, right at the beginning, gives a definition of himself...which makes all statics futile: 'God said unto Moses, I will be who I will be' (Exodus 3,14)...Eh'je asher eh'je...places even at the threshold of the Yahweh phenomenon a god of the end of days, with futurum as an attribute of Being. This end- and omega-god would have been a folly in Delphi, as in every religion where the god is not one of exodus. However, God as time is in tension with God as beginning or origin, with which the Egyptian-Babylonian influenced teaching of the creation in the Bible begins...So Deus Spes is already laid out in Moses, although the image of a last leader out of Egypt, i.e. of the Messiah, does not appear until a thousand years later; messianism is older than this religion of the Messiah.[249]

---

[248] Cohen, *Religion of Reason*, 249: "The ideality of the Messiah, his significance as an idea, is shown in the overcoming of the person of the Messiah and in the dissolution of the personal image in the pure notion of time, in the concept of the *age*. Time becomes future and only future. Past and present submerge in this time of the future. This return to time is the purest idealization" (emphasis in original).

[249] Bloch, *The Principle of Hope*, 1235–37. In that context, Bloch, clearly influenced by Scholem, upholds the kabbalah, which he calls a "gnostic mysticism," as collapsing the difference between the Deus Creator and the Deus Spes, the God of the beginning and the God of the end, the alpha and the omega. The teaching of Isaac Luria, in particular, is mentioned by Bloch as an illustration of this collapse: "The world came into being as a contraction (tsimtsum) of God, is therefore a prison from its origin, is the captivity of Israel as of the spiritual sparks of all men and finally of Yahweh. Instead of the glory of the alpha or morning of creation, the wishful space of the end or day of deliverance presses forward; it allied itself to the beginning only as to a primal Egypt which must be set aside. Little though such ramifications of Mosaism accord with the solemn hymn of Genesis, they correspond precisely to the original God of exodus and the Eh'je asher eh'je, the God of the goal." See Bouretz, *Witnesses for the Future*, 468–71.

Commenting again on this name in *Atheism in Christianity*, Bloch is explicit about his indebtedness to Cohen's musing on hope and the openness of the messianic future:

> Hence, the singularly unsensual idea of God in the Bible, so foreign to the ancient concept of presence; hence too the difference between epiphany and apocalypse, and between the mere anamnesis of truth (re-membering, circular line) which stretches from Plato to Hegel, and the eschatology of truth as of something still open within itself, open with Not-yet-being. The basic sense and direction of this biblical thought appears again in Hermann Cohen's eschatology, which has its roots in and takes its power from *Messianism*; although he shares the attitude that will always so "reasonably" surrender the eschatological in its struggle versus antiquity, for the sake of Future-being. "This is the great cultural riddle of Messianism: all the nations put the golden age in the primordial past; the Jews alone hope for man's development, hope in the future" (*Religion der Vernunft*, 1959, p. 337).[250]

Bloch rightly goes on to note that the messianic ideal articulated by Cohen stems from the time of *ehyeh asher ehyeh*, that is, the time of the *ultimatum* that lies within the *Novum* and breaks through into the *Futurum*.[251]

Tellingly, Levinas discriminates Heidegger's privileging the ecstasy of the future in his notion of being-toward-death and the nothingness of the future in the Marxist utopianism of Bloch: "The nothingness of the utopia is not the nothingness of death, and hope is not anguish . . . But it is not death that, in Bloch, opens the authentic future, and it is relative to the future of utopia that death itself must be understood. The future of utopia is the hope of realizing that which is not yet."[252] In passing, I note that this is another striking example of Levinas offering a critical caricature of Heidegger based exclusively on his early work.[253] Lyotard already perceptively deduced that the "moment" in Heidegger's thought that is most contiguous with the thought of "the jews" relates to the fact that after the turn (*Kehre*) Heidegger would have readily admitted that the "only thought adequate to the disaster is that which remains available to the waiting for God." Specifically in the poems of Hölderlin, Heidegger finds evidence of the "interminably deferred." Through the "art of waiting" the poet becomes

---

[250] Ernst Bloch, *Atheism in Christianity: The Religion of the Exodus and the Kingdom*, with an introduction by Peter Thompson, trans. J. T. Swann (London: Verso, 2009), 44–45.

[251] Ibid., 46.

[252] Emmanuel Levinas, *Of God Who Comes to Mind*, trans. Bettina Bergo (Stanford: Stanford University Press, 1998), 37–38.

[253] In my chapter on Levinas in *Giving Beyond the Gift*, 90–153, I offer numerous other examples of this tendency. See above, n. 44.

the "guardian of the memory of forgetting. Here, as in Wiesel, the only narrative that remains to be told is that of the impossibility of narrative."[254] Surely, there is a bitter irony, and no small measure of audacity, to speak of Heidegger and Wiesel in one breath. But we should not throw out the baby with the bath water: Lyotard has a point in seeing in Heidegger a distinctively Jewish understanding of the moment as the time of waiting for what can be fulfilled only by not being fulfilled.

More importantly, Levinas neglects to emphasize that Bloch was keenly aware of the fact that the utopian hope renews itself sporadically as the hope postponed unremittingly. Gerhard Richter well expressed this overlooked point: "For Bloch, this thinking of the futurity of futurity is invested with the hope of the 'not-yet' (*das Noch-nicht*)—not a naïve or childish form of wishful thinking in an administered world of reified relations in which such thinking would be utopian in the worst sense, but with an abiding intuition that the non-self-identity of thoughts and actions, their internal self-differentiation, is more than a hermeneutic or administrative problem to be overcome in the name of implementing meanings and systems. The not-yet also signals a nameless otherness that, precisely by being at odds with itself and never coming fully into its own, promises an anticipatory glimpse, the Blochian *Vorschein*, of what still remains to be thought and experienced, of what has not yet been foreclosed."[255] We cannot avoid the predicament that is at the heart of this nonprogressive utopianism or nonteleological eschatology: if the end can only be imagined as the terminus that can never be terminated, the very source of hope is a source of despair. Not yet may not be enough to sustain confidence in the one who is coming or in a moment of reckoning and rectification. Neither pessimism nor optimism seems suitable to brand this bestowal of hope through its suspension. Maybe it is hopeless to imagine letting go of the inclination to hope, but then, we would do better to think of hope in Levinasian terms as an awaiting without an awaited, an awaiting with no anticipation, an awaiting wherein we can no longer sever present and future, since the future becomes present as the present that is the future that is both present and not present, present as not present, not present as present. Expectation as such can never be fulfilled but it is precisely because this is so that the expectation propels us to speak of an end that will not succumb to the end of speaking.

---

254 Jean-François Lyotard, *Heidegger and "the jews"*, trans. Andreas Michel and Mark Roberts, introduced by David Carroll (Minneapolis: University of Minnesota Press, 1990), 79.
255 Richter, *Thought-Images*, 76.

INTERVIEW WITH ELLIOT R. WOLFSON
JULY 25, 2012

Hava Tirosh-Samuelson and Aaron W. Hughes

Professor Wolfson, you're a scholar of Jewish mysticism, historian of religions, historian of ideas, and a Jewish philosopher. Please tell us about your life, your intellectual training, and intellectual trajectory. How did you become the scholar that you are?

Let me start by telling you about my upbringing. I was raised in a traditional Orthodox Jewish home. In fact, my father was an Orthodox rabbi. So, from a very early age, I was surrounded by Jewish textuality and did quite a bit of study at home which supplemented my study in traditional yeshivot. In addition to the kind of standard text that one studies in an Orthodox Jewish home, I also was exposed when I was a teenager to the Hasidic works of Nachman of Bratslav and Chabad. And both of those sects were quite present physically in my environment, so it wasn't just book study, but I interacted with Hasidim from both of those groups. And that was really my initial entry into kabbalah, or Jewish mysticism.

When I went to college, I began to pursue the study of philosophy, focusing primarily on ancient Greek philosophy and then modern philosophy, and then what used to be called continental philosophy, mostly, hermeneutics and phenomenology. And it was through that study, particularly through Heidegger and William James, that I became more and more interested in the phenomenon of mysticism, more generally, and that started to lead me to branch out of Judaism to study other religious traditions.

When I went to graduate school, I initially went to study philosophy, but wasn't totally pleased since the program was lopsidedly analytic. And then I had a decision to make. I was either going to go study Eastern religions or pursue Jewish philosophy and for a variety of reasons, personal and intellectual, I chose the latter. I went to Brandeis University and started to study both medieval Jewish philosophy and modern Jewish philosophy. But within a year or so, it became clear to me that what I really wanted to pursue was the study of Jewish mysticism, since it seemed to me that mastery of this domain would require a combination of intellect and imagination, mathematics and poetry, a combination that was, and remains, very appealing to me. The study of Jewish mysticism was not to the exclusion of Jewish philosophy, but I decided that the sources of Jewish mysticism would become my primary focus for philosophical inquiry. So, that sort of gives you some sense of the steps that led me on my path as a scholar.

Since you grew up in an Orthodox environment, why did you decide to study at a secular university? Was the move from the yeshiva world to the secular university difficult? What did it signify religiously? Did you experience a crisis of faith? If so, how did you overcome it?

To be precise, I grew up in a modern Orthodox environment that embraced both Torah learning and secular knowledge. The home I grew up in was filled with Jewish and non-Jewish books, and the yeshivot I attended all shared the ideological presumption that a life of piety must be based on both adherence to tradition and attentiveness to the contemporary environment, epitomized in the rabbinic expression *yafeh torah im derekh eretz*. In this spirit, it was not only permissible but mandatory to learn science, mathematics, philosophy, and literature. The pursuit of these cultural forms did not compromise the autonomy and preeminence of tradition. Hence, there never was a question about my attending a university. In fact, when I toyed with the idea of staying in a yeshiva in Jerusalem after finishing high school, my parents were insistent that I return to the States to enter college. It is true that the preference was for me to enroll in Yeshiva University, so that I could have the best of the two worlds, reflected in the motto *torah u-madda*.

I spent three semesters at Yeshiva University and then transferred to CUNY Graduate Center/Queens College because my interest in philosophy was growing and I wanted a more robust program. I did not experience a crisis of faith because of the university per se but I did eventually experience something of a breaking point in graduate school when I began to think of the biblical and Talmudic canons in a more critical and historically determined way. I had to reassess all the beliefs that structured my life experience. I have never been able to return to the simplicity of my childhood faith. And yet, the love of texts, which was so crucial to the path of Orthodoxy, has continued to shape my sensibility in the world. This love has always encompassed all forms of wisdom without prejudice. Indeed, in my work, I have been critical of xenophobic statements in rabbinic and kabbalistic sources—this is not to say that I do not recognize that there are other perspectives to be culled from this material—out of my conviction that the deeper one digs into one path, the greater the chance one will find the way to other paths. I embrace a universalism rooted in the singularity of each tradition.

Who were the major philosophers, thinkers, or even artists, who have shaped your intellectual identity, contributed to or helped you formulate your own intellectual voice?

Well, there have been many. The thinkers that had the most profound influence on me and still do were the German and French philosophers of hermeneutics and phenomenology. Nietzsche, Husserl, Merleau-Ponty, Heidegger, Sartre, Bergson were very important. Overtime, Levinas has become crucial, as has Derrida. That is pretty much the philosophical discourse with which I'm most comfortable. But there have been many other voices as well. At some point I became very interested in feminist theory; Irigaray was probably the most important feminist theorist that shaped my thought, but Kristeva too has been important. Of other French intellectuals, I owe a debt to Paul Ricoeur and Gilles Deluze. Within the Anglo-American tradition, because of my work on William James, I became very interested in process philosophy and spent a lot of time with Whitehead. Wittgenstein also happens to be an extremely important thinker for me. I often go back to read Wittgenstein for philosophical clarity and inspiration. The study of all of these thinkers has fertilized my thought.

Did you study them systematically or on your own?

Well, I started already as an undergraduate. As I already stated, I began at Yeshiva University and then I transferred to a program at the CUNY Graduate Center in conjunction with Queens College. And that was an excellent program because it allowed me to take graduate seminars in philosophy. And at the time, the philosophy department at Queens was truly exceptional. I studied Heidegger with Henry Wolz. He published several works, including a monograph on Plato and Heidegger, but, most importantly, he studied with Heidegger in Germany before emigrating to the United States. (He eventually earned his doctorate at Fordham University.) So that was an excellent opportunity. I also studied with Edith Wyschogrod, whom I still consider to be one of my most important teachers. Wyschogrod's primary focus was in the area of continental philosophy (some of her main interlocutors included Kierkegaard, Hegel, Nietzsche, Husserl, Heidegger, Merleau-Ponty, Sartre, Levinas, Gadamer,

Ricoeur, Deleuze, Derrida, and Badiou), but her work also demonstrates competence in ancient and medieval philosophy (with special interest in the Neoplatonic writings of Plotinus and Iamblichus) as well as in the analytic tradition (Frege, Quine, and Wittgenstein). Beyond her mastery over these philosophical sources, Wyschogrod's work is characterized by a far wider range of influence and inspiration, including interest in Judaism, Christianity, and Buddhism. My interest in comparative religions is in no small measure indebted to her. It was in the course of both my undergraduate and then subsequent graduate work that I did study these thinkers pretty systematically.

When you encountered philosophy at Queens College for the first time, what was your emotional response? What did you think philosophy was trying to do? Did philosophy present a fascination or a spiritual challenge/threat, or both?

I started reading philosophy long before Queens College. Already in high school, I was studying some philosophical works on my own, especially the classics of medieval Jewish thought, Saadya, Halevi, and Maimonides. I also had begun studying kabbalistic and Hasidic texts, which I tended to interpret philosophically, including the *Tanya* of Shneur Zalman of Liadi, *Liqquṭei Moharan* of Nahman of Bratslav, and *Orot ha-Qodesh* of Rav Kook. I recall as well reading several essays by Joseph B. Soloveitchik, and more importantly, attending some of his public lectures, which were masterful in their philosophical exegesis of Jewish texts. Indeed, I would have to say that it was from Soloveitchik that I drew inspiration for the possibility of rendering traditional sources in a philosophical key. At Yeshiva University I took several courses in philosophy, but I eventually transferred to the B.A./M.A. program sponsored by Queens College and the Graduate Center at the City University of New York. From the moment I immersed myself in philosophy, it felt like a homecoming. I had the feeling of finally finding kindred spirits, who were asking the questions that occupied my mind from a relatively young age. To this day I accept the Platonic notion that philosophy begins and ends in wonder, rooted, as it is, in an openness to the mystery of being—the ultimate metaphysical question, why is there something rather than nothing—and the quest to understand the complex interface between mind and matter. Philosophy is the mode of thinking that displays the inherent quality of lacking an inherent quality, and thus one who is philosophically attuned is overcome by the feeling of the uncanny, in German *unheimlich*, literally, unhomely, which is experienced most profoundly only when one is at home. Derrida articulated the paradox by noting the double bind that philosophy's way of being at home with itself consists in not being at home with itself. In this regard, philosophy converged with my upbringing by reinforcing the sense I have borne my whole life that the Jewish way of being in the world consists of belonging by not-belonging. The Judaism of my childhood was one that would cast suspicion on the Jew who felt totally at home in his or her environment.

Did your religious upbringing train you to read philosophical texts or did it pose a hurdle? In what way was your religious upbringing conductive or detrimental to your philosophical interest?

While it is the case that the study of philosophy led me to question some of the beliefs with which I was indoctrinated, I never felt that my religious upbringing was detrimental to my philosophical interest. On the contrary, the emphasis that traditional Judaism places on textual reasoning provided a useful methodological basis to pursue the study of philosophy. Moreover, the mandate to question, which is an integral part of the Jewish hermeneutic, has served me well in the pursuit of philosophical understanding. I would go so far as to say that the movement of thought proper to both rabbinic textuality and philosophical speculation is not grasping an idea definitively but being able to question it from multiple perspectives. The celebrated stereotype of the Jewish penchant for questioning dovetails with the Heideggerian notion that questioning is essential to the path of thinking—to be underway on that path one must constantly interrogate what one assumes to be true, for only the question, properly speaking, is thought provoking, the gift of the unthought that continuously gives food for thought.

When you say that various thinkers, Jewish and non-Jewish, are very important to you, are they part of your intellectual landscape or intellectual makeup? If so, how? When you write, do you just hear their voices in the background or do you actively converse with them as you sort out your ideas? Do you debate with these thinkers?

At the beginning of my work, these voices were more in the background or were relegated to the footnotes. But over time, they have surfaced much more and now I'm engaging them much more directly. But I've always felt that my interest in Jewish mysticism was such that this body of material could be studied through the prism of those philosophical disciplines. I remember once at a job interview, someone asked me if I considered myself to be a disciple of Scholem or Idel, and I said that I am a disciple of neither of them.

For me, the goal (and hence this interview) was not getting into Jewish mysticism as an academic field; it was never about being a scholar of Jewish mysticism. It was about finding a repository of texts that were rich and that could be investigated or interrogated from the standpoint of these philosophical disciplines.

Why did you choose to go to Brandeis University for graduate work? In retrospect, how do you assess the graduate training you received?

I began my doctoral work in philosophy at Johns Hopkins but decided to switch after one year. I was considering two options at the time—to pursue Asian religions or Jewish studies, with an emphasis on Jewish philosophy and mysticism. At that time, there were not too many graduate programs in Jewish studies in North America and Brandeis emerged as the most suitable choice. I was fortunate to study with good scholars at Brandeis and others who were visiting annually at Harvard. My philological-textual training was excellent and I was given the space to pursue my own theoretical interests. I am especially grateful that I had the opportunity to work with Professor Altmann. Although he was long retired by the time I started the program, at a certain point Professor Fox introduced me to him and he immediately became interested in my progress. He participated in one of my comprehensive examinations and also served on my dissertation committee. The choice of my dissertation topic—a critical edition of Moses de León's *Sefer ha-Rimmon*—was Altmann's suggestion. Overall I was satisfied with my training. It has served me well through the years. All of my speculative excursions and flights of fancy commence and terminate with the text, and that is the way I have trained my own graduate students for the last three decades.

Your training at Brandeis and your scholarship make many people want to pigeon-hole you as a scholar of Jewish mysticism. But your work bridges many disciplines and thinkers. How would you define yourself?

I would define myself as a phenomenologist and an archaeologist of texts. That's how I would define myself. But you are quite right, that has been a frustration of mine, because even when I write on topics that have nothing to do with Jewish mysticism, that's how I'm pigeon-holed. And that is a source of personal frustration, but I also think it opens up a much larger question about the positioning of Jewish thought: how people look upon a thinker who is not only Jewish by an ethnic demarcation, but who has chosen to somehow participate in the long history of Jewish textual interpretation.

Which of the following labels are you most comfortable with: "secular Jew," "nonobservant Jew," "textual Jew," "scholar of Judaism," and "comparative religionist"? If no label fits you, please explain why?

Although I prefer to avoid definitions, not only of myself but also of others, I will try to respond to your question. It is not easy to find the right label. Clearly, I am no longer an observant Jew, but this does not make me a secular Jew. I resist this dichotomy, a binary that I find too simplistic to address the complex construction of identity that has shaped my path these many years. I am undoubtedly a scholar of Judaism but this is not sufficient to capture my lifelong involvement with the tradition. There is something more than scholarship at the heart of my scholarship. It is precisely because I cannot name that surplus that it continues to be the wellspring of my creativity. As mystics in many different traditions and in many different historical periods have recognized, the yearning to communicate stems from the incommunicable. I happily accept the tag of "comparative religionist" inasmuch as my study of Jewish sources has been informed by Christian, Islamic, Hindu, Taoist, and Buddhist texts. But none of these classifications is sufficient. If pushed to the wall, I would say that I have aspired to be the consummate outlaw, the one who is inside by being outside. Through my scholarly prose, poetry, and painting, I have sought to transform the Judaism of my youth. But I have done so without any pretensions regarding disciples or followers. I have never aspired to be a leader or a spokesperson. Indeed, I subscribe to the wisdom of Leonard Cohen's lyric, "Follow me the wise man said, but he walked behind."

What is the purpose of your scholarship? When you say "archaeology of the texts," archaeology of knowledge, do you give it a Foucaldian or a Nietzschean meaning? The phrase can be interpreted in a variety of ways. So what is the telos of your scholarship?

Well, it's multi-faceted. I do want to be part of this long chain of interpreters of Jewish texts that I embrace. I'm not embarrassed by that self-definition, and I think I have tried to contribute to that by expanding the canvas, so to speak, of how one approaches these sources. What voices does one have in one's head when one looks at these sources? All the voices are potentially present in my mind, but the ones that emerge at any given point in time are determined by the texts I am studying. I also hope that the work is a contribution to the humanities, more generally. And that, as I put it in one of my works and I often tell it to students, by digging deep into one tradition, one finds the paths to other traditions. I think of my work as a kind of comparative philosophy where the comparison doesn't turn on a model of a universal truth that I'm looking for in each of the particular traditions. But rather some space of discourse between the different traditions where both sameness and difference may appear.

And, if you don't mind us pushing this point further, why is it so important to you? Why has the mining of the tradition or traditions become your life's work?

Well, there's a beauty to thinking. As far as my memory stretches back, truly, I have somehow been pondering thoughts. As I already stated, William James had a formative influence on me as well as process thought. Therefore, I don't think of the self atomistically; the self is part of a very complex fabric. I think of the self relationally. So, of course, my work with the tradition is stamped with my own particularity, but it is part of something much larger. And I do think that there's an aesthetic dimension to thinking within tradition. There's a beauty of thinking along with others who have belonged to a community of mind or spirit. There's also an ethical dimension to it. Thinking is in the service of critique of traditions.

Why do you say "critique" and not "affirmation"?

Well, critique and affirmation are not binary opposites. I mean in order to critique a tradition, you also have to, in some sense need to, appropriate and affirm it. I just think that that's one of the tasks of philosophy. Not just Jewish philosophy, but philosophy in general; all philosophy is about critique.

How do you understand philosophy and Jewish philosophy, and how does Jewish philosophy relate to Jewish theology? Is there a difference between them? How do you answer these questions as a philosopher

and as a historian of ideas? Since you also look at texts in terms of the social institutions that produced them, can you also reflect on these categories as an intellectual historian?

Each of those is a very large and complex category that requires explication. Yes, I agree that all these categories inform my work, but I'm not sure I can really articulate the way that the different instruments in the orchestra in my mind, so to speak, come together. Somehow they do in each of the projects I set out to do. My training in Jewish studies is partly responsible for what you call intellectual history. I do try to be mindful of and am careful about historical context; ideas don't just emerge in vacuums. At the same time, I was trained in philosophy and my true love really is philosophy, rather than history. As I see it, there is some way in which philosophy doesn't negate the historical context but helps shed light on defining and reconfiguring historical context. Philosophy and history work together for me as I seek to reconstruct the meaning of texts. I try to be responsible to the historical context, but I also try to illumine the nature of the text from a standpoint of a different conception of temporality, one that isn't necessarily limited by a diachronic view of history.

Earlier you said that philosophy is about critique. Is it about critique or is it about clarification? Do you seek to determine the precise meaning of what the text says or rather figure out what is problematic in the statement? What exactly is philosophy for you?

For me, philosophy, to put it most simply, is reflective thinking or thinking about thinking. It's the constantly calling into question the presuppositions of what we think about any number of topics. That, to me, is what philosophy is all about. So, in that way, it really goes back to Plato's portrayal of Socrates. He was the prototypical philosopher.

You already elicited a musical analogy when you said that somehow the various voices join to create the symphony in your mind. Using this analogy, if you always ask the questions about the supposition, it sounds to me that philosophy for you is more like music theory, than music performance.

No, I would respectively disagree with that statement. One of the unique things about philosophy as a discipline is you can't really teach philosophy without engaging in being a philosopher, even if you're doing the work of an intellectual historian. For example, when you present the views of Judah Halevi to students, you have to enter into the space of his thinking. In so doing, you have to perform as a philosopher and enter a philosophical conversation. So, the philosophical text, for me, is like a musical score, actually, in the sense that you have to perform it. Now, part of that performativity is the clarification or the critique.

Does this performance and critique have an ethical dimension? Since Socrates is the paradigmatic philosopher, he clearly taught that philosophy has an ethical mission. So where is the ethical mission in your way of doing philosophy?

Yes I embrace the ethical mission of philosophy, although I don't have an overall definition of the ethical. I don't have a conception of what constitutes the basis for our moral decisions. But I have some sense of it in the studying of traditions, the responsibility of the scholar is to lay bare, to clarify, what certain assumptions have been in the past. And that I see as part of the ethical mandate of all forms of scholarship.

This sensitivity to the ethical, I would say, accounts for my interest in feminist theory; it was driven by ethical concerns. As we know, not everybody has been pleased with what I've had to say. And I think there's no greater critic of my work than myself, because I'm constantly rethinking it. And if I found a reason to change my opinion, I say it openly, as I have done most recently in my book on Menachem Mendel Schneerson, where I did find a shift away from the phallocentrism. My availing myself of feminist theory was part of a critique of the tradition as is my work on the negative attitudes towards the non-Jews that I've found in these sources.

Let's focus again on Jewish philosophy. What, in your opinion, is Jewish philosophy? Can there be Jewish philosophy? Is it theology? Do you define yourself as a "Jewish philosopher"?

That's also a very complex question. Before we get to how I see myself, let me address the question, "what is a Jewish philosophy?" From one standpoint, it seems that the phrase "Jewish philosophy" is an oxymoron, or that it cannot exist, because we wouldn't think, for instance, of a Jewish algebra. We might think of a Jew who does algebra, but we wouldn't necessarily consider what that person was doing to be a Jewish algebra. So how is philosophy particularized in this way, be it Jewish, Muslim,

Christian, or Buddhist? If by "Jewish philosophy" we refer to the philosophical investigation of the fundamental beliefs relative to this cultural system, then there is no problem at all. That's what Jewish philosophy is, and the history of Jewish philosophy has been precisely that. Namely, the investigation of what the fundamental beliefs are and those, of course, shift and change over time. This is what Maimonides said in the twelfth century and what Mendelssohn did in the eighteenth century. These thinkers shared a common goal or ambition, if by "Jewish philosophy" we refer to exposition of beliefs. But I'm not sure that yields an adequate definition of Jewish philosophy, or of a Jewish philosopher. What exactly would be the contours of a Jewish philosophy that wasn't the way that we just defined? Clearly, we would not say that every single philosopher who was ethnically Jewish is doing Jewish philosophy. Hence, I do not consider Henri Bergson a Jewish philosopher. Conversely, we need to ask: can a non-Jew produce a Jewish philosophy? I am not talking about a non-Jew who writes as an intellectual historian and who studies the Jewish philosophical past. Can a non-Jew *construct* Jewish philosophy? That's a big question.

It is possible for a non-Jew to think constructively about difference, about otherness, or about bridging between Jews and non-Jews. In that way a non-Jew could do constructive Jewish philosophy.

Yes, there are a few non-Jews who write in such a way, but I still wonder if that kind of work has a lot to contribute to the conversation. In this case, is the non-Jewish philosopher really doing constructive work, or simply studying Jewish thinkers? It's very tricky.

Would the constructive aspect make the difference between "Jewish philosophy" and "Jewish theology"? Whenever we engage in the interpretation of texts, there's always a constructive dimension.

That's true.

The texts at your disposal constitute the data for philosophical work. So the philosopher must always relate to this textual data, right?

I would agree with that. Therefore, philology and textuality are the anchors of what a Jewish philosophy would be.

If so, the Jewish philosopher is always engaged in an ongoing conversation with certain voices, with certain thinkers, with certain texts, and with certain questions.

Right, but the philosopher has to be mindful that each of them in their moment had a very complicated negotiation of what's inside and outside, and that's always changing. The textual tradition is not a static thing that we can identify as "Jewish." That category itself is ever-changing, because its boundaries are porous.

Several Jewish thinkers included in the Library of Contemporary Jewish Philosophers don't identify themselves as philosophers and specifically state that they are not even interested in philosophy. Contrary to you, they see Judaism as an eternal essence that never undergoes any sort of change. How would you respond to this viewpoint?

My view is diametrically opposed to that statement. What makes the juxtaposition of "philosophy" and "Jewish" viable for me is that both lack in essence! The essence of both Judaism and philosophy is not to have an essence.

Derrida said that the philosopher belongs by not belonging, which he linked to his own sense of being a Jew in the world. So my view is a total opposite of essentialism: there is no essence and there is no singular thing that is Judaism. There are Judaisms. But I do agree with the earlier point about the multivocality of the Jewish tradition: it is still framed within some sense of coherence over time and that goes back to the texts.

Your analogy from music is useful here once again: the voices you hear as you compose the score of the orchestra are not infinite, because you hear these voices rather than others. In other words, the textual tradition itself determines which voices you will hear and utilize in the composition of the score. The tradition may be very broad, but it is also sufficiently defined, and that's what makes it Jewish. In terms of music, we can easily identify a given piece of music as either Bach's or Mozart's, and even if we think about atonal music of Schoenberg or Alban Berg, their atonality also stands within the tradition they tried to disrupt.

Right. This interview is being held in my home, and as you can see its walls are lined with books. There are a lot of books in this room, in this apartment, but relative to the scope of Jewish textuality, the number of books here is itself very limited. Because of my interest in the voices of the past, I'm reading these texts, thinking about them, writing about them, teaching them, and interpreting them, but I also keep in mind many other voices that come to bear on my work as a Jewish philosopher.

As for the phrase "Jewish philosopher" if we understand it in the way that we just described, that is, in terms of being a link in this chain of Jewish and textual interpretation, then I would embrace it. But I'm a little bit troubled by the categorization. I'll give you an example that explains why I am weary of categorization. Some scholar quoted a comment of mine from *Language, Eros, Being*, on the problem of unsaying and saying, and how they work together in the context of mystical phenomena. And yet, when I was quoted, the author found it necessary to say, "As the Jewish scholar, Elliot Wolfson, writes. . . ." Throughout the entire essay, the only marking or identification in that way was me. Why wasn't Derrida marked as the Jew? So, why was I marked in that way? Why is it relevant that I am a Jewish scholar? Or, in what way is being Jewish relevant to my analysis of mysticism? To some extent, the need to qualify me as a Jew reflects on the author of the essay (for which I did not harbor any ill will), but beyond it, I think this indicates a much larger issue that we have to deal with.

If the particular Jewish person has dedicated his or her life to the study of Jewish texts, then it makes sense to mark the scholar in this way. In this regard, Derrida should clearly be referred to as a Jewish scholar, since he actually has written a lot about his Jewish identity.

It is true that Derrida was compelled to reflect about his Jewish identity because a lot of people tried to link his deconstruction to Judaism in a way that he was uncomfortable with. And yet Derrida is not marked that way; he is not marked as a "Jewish philosopher."

Even Levinas is not marked as a "Jewish philosopher," and a lot of people who write or talk about Levinas don't know that Levinas was actually Jewish. As for Derrida, how many people know that he's an Algerian Jew, even though this biographical fact is most relevant to the project of Deconstruction.

Right, but wouldn't you agree that it would be unfortunate if Derrida were marked in that way? Let's take another contemporary Jewish philosopher, Judith Butler, who is now writing about her Jewish identity and the question of Zionism. She is not going to be marked as "Judith Butler, the Jew," or "the Jewish philosopher, Judith Butler."

Judith Butler admits that her Jewish identity has evolved over time: she is not today where she was two decades ago or where she will be ten years from now. She is a secular Jew who for a long time marginalized or suppressed her own Jewish identity. In recent years, perhaps because of her contact with Daniel Boyarin at Berkeley, she finally came to term with her Jewishness and she is now positioning herself in certain ways that she couldn't do twenty-five years ago.

Right, but you see my point: Butler's legacy will not ever turn on the term "Jewish." Similarly, my philosophical, intellectual, and scholarly work should not be reduced to being Jewish; the label, "Jewish," should not be used as a marker. I am troubled by the fact that I am so commonly labeled as a "Jewish scholar," no matter what I write about. In my recent book, *A Dream Interpreted within a Dream*, the first chapter is a detailed discussion of neuroscience and phenomenology in which I engage many non-Jewish scientists and philosophers. Those communities will either never be interested in what I have to say or those who are interested in what I have to say will continue to frame it within this much more narrow scope of "Jewish" scholarship.

Whether a scholar regards the category "Jewish" as unfortunate or fortunate depends on the kind of value you put on it; it is up to each person to decide how they want to be known.

Well, I feel such labeling is unfortunate for the positioning of Judaism in the culture at large, because it perpetuates the marginalization of Jews and of Judaism.

That brings up the question of audience. Who is your intended audience? To whom do you write either ideally or practically, if there is a difference?

I don't have a single answer, because there are different audiences. Obviously I'm writing in part for the academic fields of Jewish mysticism, Jewish philosophy, and Jewish studies. But then I'm also writing, hopefully, for a broader audience, people who are interested in cultural studies, people who are interested in the history of religion and in theology. You asked me earlier about theology, or about being a Jewish theologian, and I am uncomfortable with the classification.

Is it not a primary identity for you?

No, I'm interested in theological questions and in theology as an intellectual discourse because of people like John Caputo or Catherine Keller, who have tried to revive theology by the use of either phenomenology or Derrida's deconstruction. I read the work of contemporary theologians and I stay informed. But no, I don't think of myself as being a major contributor to a Jewish theology. If anything, what I'm writing is an a-theology.

Do you refer to the deconstruction of Jewish theology?

Yes. I can't affirm a transcendent God along the lines of classical Jewish monotheism. And I don't think I have much to affirm along those lines.

Would you say that your discomfort with classical Jewish monotheism reflects your postmodern or postmodernist identity or self-understanding? If so, what does post-modernism mean to you?

Well, postmodernism means that there is no more grand narrative. There is no story that's being told which each of the details fits in. There's no overriding system. And there is no ultimate truth other than perhaps the truth that there is no ultimate truth.

What happens when you apply that statement to Judaism? If there is no grand narrative, can we still talk about a sacred myth, or sacred story, by virtue of which Jews are Jewish? What happens to Judaism once we endorse the postmodernist position?

I'm not certain what happens next. You used the term "sacred myth" to talk about Judaism. I suppose that category allows you to work in a variety of ways which resist the postmodernist critique. But it seems to me the more difficult problem is that the self-consciousness regarding that narrative is that it hasn't been a myth. For Jewish believers, the grand narrative, or sacred myth, engenders truth about the nature of the human being and the nature of the world at large, or the relationship between the Jewish people and other ethnicities.

Indeed. Myth is not mere fiction. In the Platonic sense of the term, myth is a narrative that tells us truth that cannot be stated propositionally. So in that sense, you could say Judaism has a narrative that expresses deep truths. The question is how does a postmodern or postmodernist Jew relate to the sacred that has shaped the identity and history of this particular group?

Well, I think, that the voice of Derrida has not been unimportant, although Derrida wouldn't have necessarily considered himself an advocate of postmodernism. But those who articulate a kind of Jewish postmodernism would agree with Derrida's emphasis on an all-encompassing textuality. Derrida taught us that there's nothing outside of the text. Consequently, the notion of multivocality merges deconstruction and postmodernism with classical Jewish textuality. Several scholars (e.g., Susan Handelman and Daniel Boyarin) have made the point quite convincingly. One can be committed to postmodernism and affirm Jewishness at the same time.

Does postmodernism somewhat help Jews to be Jewish today? Do multivocality, ambiguity, and ambivalence characterize contemporary Jewish existence?

I don't think so. I was just trying to answer hypothetically what one could do. But I don't really think it helps that much. There are so many elements of that myth or narrative that seem no longer to be tenable or viable. Nonetheless, Judaism survives in the world, it persists in the world, it keeps going and maybe that's part of its strength and its own genius: the ability to constantly adapt and change. Even so, there are fundamental facets of the story which are no longer viable and do not sit well with the postmodern sensibility.

Can you be more specific?

Well, the notion of "chosenness" isn't viable today, the narrative of creation, and even the messianic belief, whose most recent version is Chabad, are not intellectually credible. Let's discuss the messianic belief. There are lots of people who have used the work of Levinas, Derrida, and Benjamin to describe messianism without a messiah; an open-endedness of the future. I understand this interpretation and why it is attractive in its own way. But when you think about it in terms of a specific community who has held the belief in the one who is coming, namely, the messiah, and when that turns out to be false, then the consequences of that messianism are most significant.

Sociologically speaking, Chabad ideology has generated a number of figures who were and are extreme in their messianic beliefs; they think that the Rebbe is going to rise from the grave, literally speaking. Then there are a number of people who have left out of disillusionment and in the middle there are those who stay as members of Chabad but for whom the messianic rhetoric has shriveled. It's been denuded, or neutralized.

Is it appropriate to say that in Judaism certain beliefs are necessarily foundational because without those beliefs the entire structure falls apart. By contrast, postmodernism and deconstruction are anti-foundational because they critique the logical possibility of any foundation?

Right, but some thinkers have tried to say that the foundation of Judaism is anti-foundational. That is its foundation, or what I said before, that its essence is not having one. If one wants to persist in using the language of essence, then I would say the operative metaphor is that of the open center, the middle that is the potentiality to become. There are texts and rituals that have shaped Jewish practice for centuries but what remains distinctive is that openness, that sense of nothing at the core, the matrix through and by which there is constant change and regeneration. Temporally speaking, I have referred to this paradox in my work as the coming to be of what has always been that which is yet to come. Repetition, on this score, is not the mechanical return of the same, but the creative reclamation of difference, the constant verbalization of a truth spoken as what is yet to be spoken. Torah study is a form of disciplined spontaneity that ideally instigates an innovative replication, the saying again of what has never been said, a reiteration that always occurs in the moment.

What makes your position unique is the fact that you see your exposition of Jewish text to be philosophical. Unlike other scholars who either refuse to call themselves philosophers, or say that they do constructive theology, or even call into question the whole idea of Jewish philosophy, you see textual interpretation as philosophy for the sake of doing philosophy.

Right. As I noted above, for me philosophy is a way of being in the world, which is inherently critical.

How do you understand the existential position of the philosopher? As a critic, is the philosopher always on the fence, so to speak, or on the margins? If Socrates is the paradigmatic philosopher, we should remind ourselves that the citizens of Athens put him on trial, found him guilty, and executed him.

The philosopher is necessarily on the margins of society, he or she is not "on the fence" since this expression implies equivocation and lack of commitment.

The philosopher may be said to be "on the fence," in the sense of the poem of Hayyim Nahman Bialik that tries to capture the relationship of the modern Hebrew poet to the Jewish tradition. The poet both belongs to the tradition while rebelling against it; his relationship to the past is inherently ambivalent and ambiguous. Likewise, the Jewish philosopher, no matter how critical, belongs to some tradition; he or she is never a total outsider. The philosopher is an insider, but from a distance, observing and looking at it from the outside in.

Well, Spinoza is a kind of paradigm here, right? Spinoza was unique in his time, because he didn't choose to become a Christian.

That's right. But even in Spinoza there is some rootedness. He reads certain texts, he refers to certain thinkers, he definitely talks about the Bible and he addresses people who read the Bible.

Yet, if we didn't have his *Theological-Political Treatise*, we would not be able to associate Spinoza with a particular tradition. If we only had Spinoza's *Ethics* and some of the other works, we would not be able to identify his cultural identity. Spinoza is an example of the pure philosopher.

Can we say that Spinoza is an example of a philosopher who belongs and doesn't belong at the same time?

That's true.

Earlier you suggested that philosophy is an ethical pursuit. It means that philosophy impacts the way we live and act. But if the philosopher is going to be effective socially, he or she must be active in the social sphere and through social institutions, even if the philosopher wishes to transform the society. So a philosopher can never be a total outsider.

Perhaps, the place of the philosopher is better explained by Kafka's famous parable of the man before the door of the law. He wrote this scene separately and later inserted it into *The Trial*.

In the parable the man learns just before he perishes that this door was made only for him. But he can't go through the door to get to the law. As I read that story, Kafka's telling us that this person, who symbolizes either the Jew or humanity more generally, is on the inside by being outside. I resonate with this parable; this I find to be very sympathetic to my own life. I am on the outside, but that's my way of being inside. That way of being is being at the margins in the center. This position allows one to keep negotiating the inside/outside binary and challenge it. To know what is in the center and what is on the margins one has to take a somewhat longer view of history. One never knows the implications of one's work. You just don't know.

It may not happen in one's own time. It may not happen at all, but one can be in the margin in one generation and move to the center later, or vice versa. One can be very "famous" in one generation and totally forgotten by history in later generations.

Within the large Jewish tradition, there's a particular body of knowledge that you engage more specifically and that's kabbalah, or more broadly, the Jewish mystical tradition. So, what is the relationship between your understanding of philosophy and the fact that a lot of your scholarship pertains to the exposition of kabbalistic texts? Does your philosophy frame your interpretation of kabbalistic texts, or is the other way around, that kabbalah shapes your philosophy?

Certainly, kabbalah and philosophy affect one another. I would hope that the interplay of philosophy and kabbalah will be seen as one of my contributions to the field, precisely because I challenged the field in that regard. The study of kabbalistic texts should not be seen as something distinct from the study of philosophical thinking in the Middle Ages. Now this statement is both a historical and a conceptual justification of my work. Historically, the kabbalists were well-versed in philosophical literature.

There's no question about that, even though they didn't have access to all the sources that some other individuals whom we identify as "philosophers" did; the kabbalists knew a fair amount of philosophical texts, and there is no reason to distinguish them from the so-called philosophers. In fact, it's hard to imagine the emergence of kabbalah as a historical literary phenomenon without philosophy. Secondly, beyond the historical facts and conceptually speaking, it seems to me that the kabbalists are engaged in living philosophically. Notwithstanding the famous statement of Moses of Burgos that the kabbalists stand on the shoulders of the philosophers, meaning that kabbalah goes beyond where the philosophers can go, the philosophers and the kabbalists live the same kind of life, the contemplative life.

To bring it back to you: can your own philosophical thinking be characterized as kabbalistic? Is there something kabbalistic about the way you do philosophy? After all, the kabbalist has a particular way of formulating questions and addressing them.

That's true, yes. That's what I meant by saying that the kabbalists lived philosophically.

The key issue for the kabbalists is the meaning of nothing or nothingness (*ayin*).

I would say that the key issue for kabbalists is secrecy (*sod; raz*), but that turns on the problem of nothing.

If so, does the kabbalistic focus on nothingness affect the way one philosophizes? There's something in kabbalah that shifts the way you think about philosophy. Right?

Right, but only on the assumption that kabbalah is part of philosophy, not as a foreign element; kabbalah itself is part of philosophy. Well, now, we're in agreement about the relationship of kabbalah and philosophy, but keep in mind that there were scholars of previous generations who thought that kabbalah and philosophy are diametrically opposed. They would not agree. In fact, some of my own teachers, obviously, would not have agreed with my understanding of the relationship between philosophy and kabbalah; they would still see these two intellectual traditions to be in conflict with each other.

Given your understanding of the relationship between philosophy and kabbalah, what should be the ideal training of scholars of kabbalah? Should the scholar of kabbalah today be trained in philosophy and vice versa, should the philosopher be trained in kabbalah?

I think so. Ideally, I think it should be both. But minimally, I would say that you cannot train in kabbalah without training in philosophy. I think that you could do it the other way around. Although I don't think it's ideal, in part echoing what you just said. Just by studying these texts, it shifts your orientation. And also I do believe kabbalah is part of the history of Jewish philosophical thinking. So I can't say with great confidence right now that there's perfect symmetry. But at least those for whom I'm responsible in training do a significant amount of study of philosophy, both medieval and contemporary.

If kabbalah is philosophy, how do you understand the unique literary features, or more broadly, artistic dimension of kabbalah? Kabbalah is an art and some might say that it is *the* art of the Jewish tradition. If that's true, (a) how do you understand the artistic dimension of kabbalah philosophically, and (b) how does kabbalah as art relate to Jewish philosophy?

What do you mean exactly by "artistic"?

The word "artistic" refers to creativity. Philosophy is not about creativity per se, but about clarification, precision, and accurate use of terms. The goal of philosophy is to clarify the language we use and get rid of problems, or offer better answers to apparent problems.

Don't you think philosophy is creative activity? What about the philosophical dialogues in the Middle Ages analyzed by Aaron Hughes? Those are artistic works that make philosophical claims. Aren't they?

Fair enough. The artistic or creative dimension of kabbalah refers to its narrativity and its use of imagery. Philosophy is not about a story, and it does not use imagery as much. It is true that the narrative style appears in some philosophical schools, especially in continental philosophy, but on the whole in Western and in Jewish philosophy, the focus is on arguments not on narratives.

Okay.

So, if for you kabbalah is philosophy, how does it relate to art and to literature? How does the philosophic dimension of kabbalah relate to the poetic? What's the role of the imagination in philosophy and in kabbalah?

The relationship of the imagination and philosophy is a tricky one. Historically, philosophy spoke derogatorily about the imagination. But since Kant, we have gained a different understanding of the imagination: without the imagination, we wouldn't have any knowledge. Now, that actually goes back to Aristotle, who argued that knowledge derives from reason abstracting from the sense data that derives from our experience of the world. Kant was just reformulating an Aristotelian principle and hence forth, at least in the so-called continental tradition, imagination has been given pride of place.

What about the connection between imagination and error, which goes back to Plato?

Well, that's why the imagination was typically seen as philosophy's other, because the imagination is subject to a greater possibility of false claims. Hence, in relationship to reason, the imagination is problematic. But again, already in Aristotle there is a sense that without the imagination, you couldn't have any kind of knowledge because the imagination is feeding the sense data that reason needs in order to abstract knowledge, and Kant sort of returns to that view. I don't see any tension between the deceptiveness of imagination and the certitude of reason. I admit that this is exactly the way that my mind works. I take from Nietzsche, Heidegger, and incidentally I find it in Rosenzweig as well, that just as there can't be revelation without some mode of concealment, so there can't be truth without some degree of untruth.

Thus, for me, the imagination is the perfectly apt mechanism by which we try to access a truth that will only be able to reveal itself through some concealment, through some garb of untruth. And I think this is one of the more profound elements of kabbalah: the Ein Sof is the ultimate reality but it can never be revealed without being concealed, which means that we can never really have access to a naked truth, a truth that is fully laid bare. Truth itself is a matter of dissimulation, or a garment, or as the Sufis like to think of it, a veil.

In the book, _Rending the Veil,_ you seem to suggest that the act of interpretation offers a way to remove the veils that conceal the truth.

Right, but the paradox is that interpretation not only reveals the truth it also re-veils, or re-conceals the truth! That, to me, is the paradox at the heart of everything, be it religion, philosophy, art, or life. To see truth without a veil is to see that there is no seeing of truth but through the veil of truth. In many of my works I have articulated this insight. In the absence of imagination there is no form, not even the form of the formless, and without form there is no vision and hence no knowledge. Alternatively expressed, there is only the semblance of truth unveiled in the veil of untruth. If the secret is imagined to be a truth that is completely disrobed—that is, a truth divested of all appearance—then the secret is nothing to see. By contrast, the truth that is truly apparent is disclosed in and through the garment of its concealment.

As you know, the analytic philosopher understands the task of philosophy as the clarification of ordinary language. Language is important in analytic philosophy as it is in continental philosophy or in kabbalah, yet these intellectual traditions understand the function of language very differently. If I understand you correctly, for you language functions dialectically: it conceals truth in order to protect it, while at the same time revealing or unveiling the truth.

This is indeed how I understand the role of language, but I do not impose it on the sources; the paradoxes of language or the dialectical operation of language can be elicited from the kabbalistic sources. The analytic tradition may have a different approach to language, but continental philosophy, and certainly Heidegger and Derrida, deeply resonate with the kabbalistic approach.

Can you explain the dialectics of veiling and unveiling? What is the significance of the process, philosophically, aesthetically, ethically, spiritually, or epistemically? If I get it right, the process of interpretation must involve intentional obfuscation: every saying is necessarily an unsaying; every uncovering of the truth is but another covering.

Think about Levinas and the distinction he makes between the saying and the said. The purpose of language is to bring to the fore the unsaid of the saying at the core of every utterance that is said. The saying, which is never coincidental with the said, gestures toward the being that is otherwise than being. We are caught here in an unassailable paradox: language always exceeds the limits of what can be expressed, inasmuch as it is a bridge to the other, and hence it can let things be understood only without making them understandable. Meaning consists of implication or allusion rather than the conventional forms of signification determined by the criteria of systematic simultaneity and logical conceptualization. The model is the poetic word—also referred to as "the prophetic said" (*le dit prophétique*)—which, like the Tetragrammaton, is endlessly spoken because inherently unspeakable, infinitely interpreted because innately inscrutable.

I will not go as far as saying that the process of interpretation is intentional obfuscation. But for me, admittedly, it embraces a profound paradox. And that in itself is the contribution of kabbalah to our understanding of the inherent paradoxical nature of truth and knowledge. Epistemically, this approach is also an act of ultimate humility. That is, if one can come to see that the quest is to unveil, or to get to the bottom of things, to get to the truth, then to be truly enlightened means to comprehend that there is no seeing without a veil; all seeing, or understanding of truth, requires a veil through which to see.

Let me give you an example from Chabad literature, which I think crystallizes the point. Chabad masters use the scriptural idiom *mashal qadmoni* (the "primordial parable") to describe the nature of the Torah. The word *mashal* ("parable") for them is identical with the word *levush* (or garment). So what they mean by that primordial parable is that the Torah in its ultimate metaphysical sense embodies the light of the essence of the Infinite. But to embody the light of the Infinite, it has to give it some kind of cloak; it has to give it some kind of shape, or form, which will both reveal it and conceal it at the same time.

Philosophically, this notion is not different from the Aristotelian dynamics between matter and form. Perhaps we need to clarify the different ways we use the word "truth." Is truth to be capitalized to signify some preexistent or eternal reality, or is truth to be written in lower case "t" or even put in quotation marks. Do you believe in the existence of truth? What does the word "truth" mean to you?

Do I believe in truth? Well, I believe in the truth in the way that I've just articulated it. I don't believe in truth without a measure of untruth. I don't think human beings, in principle, have the capacity to know the "naked truth," so to speak. To me, this has implications even into the scientific domain: to discover truth we must always proceed by this dialectical process of veiling and unveiling.

Is this process necessarily linguistical? Must the uncovering of truth always take place through language?

Well, yes! It is for me primarily through language, but my understanding of language is more expansive, since it is not limited to just linguistic gesticulation. I think that all that we do as human beings is an expression of language, and I don't agree with those in the scientific community who maintain that language is present in other species, such as whales or primates, even though there is some symbolic communication among them, In my judgment, when we call that communication "language," we simply anthropomorphize the behavior of other animals. That is to say, whales communicate with one another as do chimps or elephants, but the communicative function is just one element of human language. Human language does much more than communication.

Could you elaborate on the other elements besides communication that characterize human language?

All of our experience, it seems to me, all of our sensual experience is enframed in some primordiality of language. Not necessarily in the Aristotelian understanding of the human as a rational animal. Although human beings are indeed rational animals, and as such they are privileged because of their use of language, language is not only the mark of rationality. Aristotle's notion is still too limited. There's a way that our being in the world is still very much linked to language, and language isn't something that exceeds who we are. Language can't simply be reduced to the different dialects that people speak. More fundamentally, language is the opening through which being—always beyond language—reveals and conceals itself.

Human beings use many forms to communicate or express meaning. I have in mind music, painting, sculpture, dance—in short, the arts, which are nonverbal languages.

Well, to me, all of those would be linguistic expressions, and they are characteristically human activities. There are experiments in which chimps were given iPads and they started to poke around and then used it to create something. But it doesn't prove anything. There never will be a time, I'm pretty confident, that the chimp will create a sentence or move computer technology to another level. Humans will always be one step ahead of the chimp. And this is the dimension of transcendence that I am still willing to affirm. By using this term I do not mean to suggest that I affirm some supernatural phenomenon in order to flee the cognitive implications of the naturalistic approach to the human predicament. Indeed, transcendence, as I regard it, precludes that possibility. There is nothing beyond nature that is not already part of nature. In the Deleuzian sense, beholden in no small measure to Spinoza, we are prepared to affirm that the transcendental field is to be located on the pure plane of immanence.

Today the challenge to the uniqueness of human beings comes not from animals who can presumably do what humans do, but from superintelligent machines that will eventually (so the prediction goes) supersede human intelligence. We have to worry about robots who will become decision-making machines more than about chimps.

Well, that's interesting too. But do those machines have language?

Yes! Computers do have a language, and the prediction is that at some point in the not so distant future, these machines will compute by themselves and make human beings obsolete. That's the cutting edge in artificial intelligence and robotics.

That's an intriguing phenomenon and I will have to think more about the computer language. To what extent is it similar and different from human language? I know that some have argued that we are moving to a point that we may be able to create an artificial intelligence that will be superior to our own intelligence. I am not so confident that this will be the case, but even as a possibility, it is frightening and demands careful philosophical scrutiny.

In the background of this discussion about language and about technology lies an important philosopher who has been a sort of taboo in Jewish studies: Heidegger. What is your view of Heidegger? Given Heidegger's influence on many Jewish philosophers, would you say that Heidegger is a source of Jewish philosophy?

Well, yes. The obvious thing to start with is there are those who would say because of his connection to Nazism that discredits him as a credible source for Jewish philosophy.

Some people would say that his whole theory is grounded in his Nazism.

I don't agree with that claim. There's no question of Heidegger's human failings, I refer not so much to the fact that he joined the Nazi party and whatever he did in those few years when he was a Rector of Freiburg University, because, you know, he did step down from the rectorship within a year, but mostly his inability to ever acknowledge his mistakes in judgment and his embracing explicit anti-Semitic stereotypes.

But he managed to fire a few Jewish professors before he did that.

Yes, Heidegger dismissed Jewish professors and contributed to Jewish suffering, but that is not the worst failure as a human being. The big problem is that he never owned up to it after the war. That is really his ultimate human shortcoming. However, with respect to Heidegger's intellectual work, there is no question that there's a curious disregard for Judaism, for Hebrew scriptures, even in the early theological writings when he readily discussed the New Testament and interpreted many passages from it. But rarely do you have Heidegger gesturing towards Hebrew scripture. So that has to be said and acknowledged when we seek to understand Heidegger's relationship to Jews, Judaism, or Jewish philosophy.

Nonetheless, to my mind, especially in studying the kabbalistic material, I have come to the conclusion that Heidegger is one of the best prisms through which to look at this material and to translate it into another philosophical idiom. Especially the so-called "later Heidegger" is relevant to kabbalah, that is, the writings from the 1930s on when he talks about the event of Being as the self-withholding projection, or the disclosive nature of truth as the concealment of concealment. Heidegger's discussion of concealment as disclosure is very fruitful and I think in many ways appropriate to the kabbalistic literature. The connection between Heidegger and kabbalah can be made historically if we consider that the German philosopher Schelling exerted deep influence on Heidegger, and Schelling most likely had familiarity with Christian kabbalah. So the affinity between Heidegger and kabbalah is not just pie in the sky, or a figment of my imagination; it is well grounded and rooted in the texts themselves.

The question is whether you need Heidegger's philosophy to make sense of kabbalistic texts. After all, Heidegger's language is very peculiar and has its own idiosyncratic markers that do not help us interpret the kabbalistic text.

That is right. You don't need Heidegger to read kabbalah. One could say about my work that it's idiosyncratic. In response I would say that Heidegger's philosophy helped me illumine the nature of esotericism, insofar as I've used Heiddegerian tropes to shed light on the complexities of esotericism. In this respect, my exposition goes beyond the dialectic of concealment and disclosure, which was noted already by Scholem. I could take the explanation further because I understand how Schelling feeds right into Heidegger and why there is no dialectical resolution of concealment and disclosure; every moment of concealment is itself a disclosure of the concealment. But, to return to your point, one does not need Heidegger. In this regard, Heidegger is not unique. No one tool is necessary or sufficient. Nevertheless, this is part of the task of the thinker, to read the texts of the past through new interpretive prisms. I do disagree with your statement that Heidegger does not help us interpret the kabbalistic texts. That is a frontal challenge to my work and while I concede that one does not necessarily need Heidegger, I do not acquiesce to the further claim that using his thought is of no avail.

Isn't that dynamic evident in daily life? For example, in a therapeutic encounter, you have similar dynamics of concealment and disclosure: you conceal by revealing and reveal by concealing.

Granted that this is the case in classic psychoanalysis whose goal is to get to disclosure of concealed (or repressed) material. But what I'm saying is different from the psychoanalytic method, according to which the disclosure of truth is salvific in some way. For me, there is no moment in which there can be a disclosure that is not in itself a concealment. I don't think that's a therapeutic model.

In other words, there's no resolution, there's no closure, and there is no end to the process. This is an ongoing, infinite process, of disclosure and concealment.

Right. Heidegger is the philosopher who has provided an apparatus to really articulate this process which is the core of the kabbalistic worldview. Of course, other people may disagree with my reading of the kabbalistic texts. But my scholarship for the past few decades has brought to bear a lot of evidence for this reading.

The affinity between Heidegger and Jewish sources might account for the fact that in the 1920s Heidegger had many Jewish students and Jews were influenced by him.

Right.

Do you feel close to any of Heidegger's Jewish students?

The two who contributed most to my thinking are Hans Jonas and Hannah Arendt. And both of them in quite different ways saw themselves as making a contribution to Judaism.

Can you explain how your thinking relates to Jonas and Arendt?

Well, I admire both of them, I read both of them, and I think from within their conceptual framework, even though I'm less interested in the political than Arendt. Over the years, I have found Arendt to be one of the more subtle thinkers of the twentieth century; she deserves much more attention than she gets. She is an incredibly sophisticated reader of Heidegger, but she's rarely mentioned in the Heideggarian literature which I find very odd.

What about the large body of scholarship about Arendt, especially among feminists or among political theorists of the Left?

Indeed there is interest in Arendt in these circles, but I still think that at least in terms of the history of Heideggarian interpretation, she deserves more attention. By the way, she excused him to the end, and she was absolutely wrong to do so.

That is Arendt's major failure, as Hans Jonas, her closest friend, noted.

Arendt wrote an essay, "Heidegger at 80," where she says that a philosopher's thought has nothing to do with historical context, and I think she is wrong about that generalization. As for Jonas, I have been influenced by his early work on Gnosticism and I admire his attempt to incorporate science in his more mature philosophical thinking.

As you well know, Jonas was also a major critic of Heidegger. Does Jonas's criticism matter to you?

There is no question that Jonas was a critic of Heidegger, but in his first book on Gnosticism, he's much closer to the Heideggarian tropes, most likely because that work was done as a doctoral dissertation under Heidegger's supervision.

Jonas understood the connection between Heidegger and the horrors of World War II, and after the war he moved away from Heidegger. In fact, Jonas's philosophy of biology, his study of metabolism, and his attempt to restore moral value to nature all emerged as a response to what Jonas considered the Gnostic tendencies of Heidegger.

There is no question about that and I am sympathetic to Jonas's disappointment and disapproval of Heidegger's politics, even as I am not certain all of his thought is tainted by overtly immoral actions. But I still find Jonas's early work on Gnosticism to be not unimportant for the study of kabbalah and there Heidegger is very present.

Another important German-Jewish philosopher in the 1920s was Franz Rosenzweig. What is your relationship to Rosenzweig? Did Rosenzweig serve as a source for your understanding of reality as an infinite unfolding of disclosure and concealment?

Rosenzweig is not unimportant to me. That's true and particularly with respect to the dialectic of disclosure and concealment rather than the structure of his theopoetics. In a way, although I didn't understand it at the time but only much later, my book *Through a Speculum That Shines* could be read as a commentary on Rosenzweig's *Star of Redemption*, which ends with an affirmation of a vision of redemption that exceeds the dialogical language of revelation.

My book contains material that Rosenzweig didn't have access to, but because he was such a genius, he picked up on things about kabbalah here and there, so that his own work had kabbalistic elements in it, even though he didn't really immerse himself in the study of kabbalah. Actually, how much he immersed himself in any Jewish text is still a question.

How do you deal with the concept of chosenness in Rosenzweig? His discussion of the holy land, the holy people, the holy law seems to be in conflict with your own views.

The holy land for him is not geographical or topological in nature. So in that regard there is no problem with Rosenzweig's views. But certainly his commitment to the singularity of the Jews as the eternal people is not part of the story that I've been most comfortable with or interested in. Obviously, the events of the twentieth century showed the limits of his thinking. Rosenzweig's religious philosophy is quintessentially diasporic, and it's hard to look at it now and celebrate it in the same way. The horrors of the Holocaust also proved that his notion of the Jew as the meta-historical presence in history is insufficient, or even untenable. History has shown that such a perspective is not adequate or beneficial.

Given the shortcomings of Rosenzweig, how do you explain the kind of renaissance of Rosenzweig among Jewish scholars of Jewish philosophy? It seems like practically everybody is writing on Rosenzweig nowadays, not only Jewish scholars, but non-Jews too.

It's an interesting phenomenon and I'm not sure I know how to explain it. I could explain my own interest in Rosenzweig because there's a profundity to his thinking which I find intellectually attractive. I also think he has great affinity with kabbalah, on the one side, and Schelling and Heidegger, on the other side, that make it possible for me to resonate with him. Hegel was Rosenzweig's most important conversation partner, but Schelling too is extremely important: Schelling's whole notion of myth philosophy is critical to our understanding of what Rosenzweig was up to in his thought. So, for me personally, Rosenzweig is a very deep thinker who in his own way has tried to translate his experience of Judaism into an idiom that musically vibrates.

As to the larger interest in him, that's a very, very interesting question, because it is not just limited to Jews writing in the diaspora. Obviously not. I don't think we can pigeon-hole it in that way. I don't know. I'm not exactly sure what accounts for it. Maybe it has something to do with his personality, which people have found so compelling, and his tragic disability, which evokes a lot of sympathy.

The popularity of Rosenzweig might have something to do with his artistry. Like other artists, he expresses nonspatial ideas in space and through space and that is why people find him so attractive. Rosenzweig's philosophy is a picture and he thinks very much like a painter.

Is the spatial more important than the temporal for Rosenzweig? I actually think that Rosenzweig privileges the temporal over spatial. The temporal is a vital part of his thinking.

If his philosophy is about temporality, why bother with the shape of the Star of David?

Let me clarify my point: Rosenzweig's thought is not just about temporality, but even when he conveys his ideas spatially, he constructs an interesting kind of space, a temporal space, a space of temporality. The Star of David is a constellation made up of both spatial and temporal coordinates. Rosenzweig is not interested in concrete physical entities, for instance, concreteness of land. I see him not so much as a painter, but as a poet who privileges language.

Since you mentioned poetry, it might be a good way to reflect on your own artistic work, as a poet and a painter. You rarely talk about your art because it is beyond language. Is your art private?

Oh, no it is not private, but it's just a different language, a language beyond language. It is true, however, that I have not been aggressive in displaying my artwork, even though I have done so in a limited way. I am torn between the lack of interest in dealing with the art world and knowing that the work of a painting is for it to be seen. Right now, for the most part, the art is concealed from others, although I still would resist referring to it as private.

How about your poetry? Could you talk about how your poetry intersects with your work on kabbalah? Can you say something about your life as a poet?

Well, the emergence of poetry is itself a very mysterious process; it always has been that way to me. In a very particular way, the poet is the vessel through which the event of poesis is happening; at its best, there's a sense in which the poet is not at all in control of the process, which remains very enigmatic. Obviously, my poetry is very informed by all that I've studied, but curiously, if you look at the poems, and there are hundreds of them by now, you will find that rarely do I use the word "God" and rarely, rarely do I use a technical term from kabbalistic symbolism. So there's a real translation going on in the poems: whatever is coming from all of these sources is being alchemically transformed into something else. The major affinity to the kabbalah is my understanding of the poetic language as a form of speech that unsays what it says in the act of saying the unsaid. Here I follow Celan who spoke of the poem as coming into being through intercourse with that language that remains invisible.

The big themes of my scholarly work all show up in the poems: imagination, language, concealment and disclosure, the erotic, and gender. A lot of people have criticized my work on gender, but if they read the poems, they would see an entirely different side of me. In the poems there is a shifting of gender identity, indeed, a bending of gender insofar as the female voice can morph into the male and the male into the female.

Do you mean that you write as a female, or that you use both male and female voices?

You never know; you never know the gender identity of the voices in the poems. So what I try to accomplish in the poems is exactly what I don't find in the kabalistic sources for the most part.

Earlier in the interview you said that there is a primordial linguistical reality that channels itself through your writing.

Right. This is what Heidegger meant when he said that language is the house of being.

This is precisely the creative aspect of language, which is very different from what most philosophers, at least those in the analytic tradition, are doing. Of course, continental philosophy sees the task of philosophy differently and affirms the role of creative language in philosophy. Would you say that the continental philosopher is closer to poetry and to being a poet?

Some, perhaps.

If so, does it mean that philosophy has nothing to do with logical reasoning or with reason?

Well, Husserl demonstrates that continental philosophy is about logical thinking.

Yes but what you just said is very different from both Husserl and Heidegger. So we go back to the question: what is philosophy?

Now, let me remind you that Heidegger eventually does create a philosophical *poesis*. He's writing philosophy in a poetic idiom, which I think Nietzsche already anticipated. Nietzsche was already moving in that direction. Heidegger eventually does enunciate a philosophical rhetoric that is an act of *poesis* and is itself poetic. It is not accurate to say this has nothing to do with logical reasoning. The logos, both as reason and discourse, assumes a different character and serves a different function. The belonging-together of logos and being has to be thought differently from the poetic standpoint.

Is you poetry philosophy poeticized? Is your poetry an attempt to give shape to pure linguisticality?

Yes, it's something like that. That's how Celan understood the craft of writing poetry. That's how he describes it: poetry is language taking shape.

You referred to the way gender ambiguity is present in your poetry as a way to state openly what remained unstated or ambiguous in kabbalah. You have written extensively on gender in kabbalah, especially in regard to the Shekhinah symbolism, which had become most popular in recent years. How do you explain the popularity of kabbalah in contemporary culture? Is it just a fad, or is there something really deep here? What's your take on it?

There are a variety of different ways in which kabbalah has entered into a more public consciousness, and there is a bit of a difference between the place of kabbalah among Jews in Israel and in the diaspora, although, there are, obviously, shared elements as well. For some, kabbalah in the popular imagination is pretty much about magic and it pertains to amulets or verbal formula, i.e., blessings, that you can hang on your car, your house, or your body, so you're protected against evil. Some people also go to consult with a kabbalist when they are ill and want a prayer for healing, or if a woman is sterile and she wants to be blessed with a child, or for other types of maladies. In this regard, kabbalah belongs to folk religion.

And then there are those who are interested in kabbalah because they're seeking some kind of richer spirituality. And they know enough about kabbalah to know that it offers a place where they can go to be "juiced up," as it were, because kabbalistic texts have a certain kind of spiritual energy that can revitalize their own spirituality. I don't think that engagement is very deep, but I would certainly not stand in criticism of people who seek out that kind of spiritual energy. That seems to me a very genuine hunger on the part of a lot of people.

Why don't these people turn to Jewish philosophy to find spiritual energy?

Right, that's an interesting question. I think we can be certain that many people who seek to be energized by kabbalah don't understand the kabbalistic texts themselves, for the most part. There's the exotic element to kabbalah because it is sufficiently foreign that makes it fascinating and attractive to spiritual seekers.

What about the symbolic dimension or, more broadly, the artistic dimension? The theurgic aspect of kabbalah, namely, the notion that humans can impact God, could also be appealing to people. Right?

All of those things would have to be translated down. It is true that people with artistic bend resonate with kabbalah. For example, at NYU, where I have been teaching for twenty-five years, most of my undergraduates in the last five years come from fields like film studies or other kinds of artistic-driven programs. The artistic, visual, and poetic aspects of kabbalah are clearly attractive and people find them spiritually meaningful.

Would that explain why people (Jews and non-Jews) are attracted to kabbalah rather than to philosophy? Might this account for the fact that kabbalah is thriving and philosophy does not seem to be thriving today?

That is correct, but let me also note the paucity of the kabbalah which is presented today as art, divested from its philosophical dimensions. This is not a message that enthusiasts of kabbalah like to hear or are willing to accept.

Another factor that accounts for the popularity of kabbalah is gender and sexuality, and you have written on that more than others.

Yes.

What message do you want the general, nonscholarly reader to grasp about the role of gender in kabbalistic literature?

It was important for me, using the tools of feminist theory, to clarify to myself first, and then articulate for others, how gender works in kabbalah.

The so-called celebration of the feminine in kabbalistic literature is more problematic than many have presented. Although other scholars before me also explicated the role of gender categories in kabbalah, in my mind they weren't investigating the symbolism adequately. I never thought and still don't think, that the work of the scholar would impede changes in the social reality of the Jewish communities. Those changes, and I refer to the role of women in society and culture, have been underfoot and they're quite dramatic.

Feminism has brought about many important changes that I celebrate and think of proudly. I am proud that Judaism was able to make changes in regard to the role of women in Jewish religious life so as to create a more equal space for women within the community. Equality of women clearly varies within Jewish denominations, so that modern Orthodoxy will be doing it less than Reconstructionist Judaism, but even modern Orthodoxy has made dramatic changes in regard to women, and Jewish religious life will continue to change. Who knows what it's going to look like in a few decades. I never thought that my work in any way would impede that process or clash with that process. But I still thought that as a scholar, it was necessary for me to make clear what seemed to me to be the case about gender categories in kabbalah. It was important for me to say that kabbalah was a far more androcentric (that is, male-centered) and phallomorphic (namely, that gender identity is determined from the standpoint of the phallus) literature than other scholars were presenting.

Now, why was that important to me? Because, and now I go back to the beginning of our conversation, there's a certain intrinsicality of thinking that has its own integrity and its own value to me. I am committed to the truth of the text, that is, a relative truth, not an absolute truth. I want the reader to understand kabbalistic texts for what they actually say. I do not want to misconstrue or misinterpret the text, even if I wished the texts said something different. That is my commitment to the integrity of the text.

That approach suggests the need to respect the text; one cannot read into the text, or impute meanings to the texts, if the meaning is not there.

Right, right.

So, was it the quest for truth that drove your interest in gender categories in kabbalah, or is there another factor?

The interest in gender is part of a larger interest in the question of embodiment, which, in turn, comes out of my study of phenomenology. The philosophy of Merleau-Ponty is probably the most important voice in this regard. I could not have written about kabbalah or gender in kabbalah without his insights. All of us who have studied kabbalah are immediately struck by the use of gender images. So gendered imagery has to be investigated; you can't avoid it if you wish to understand a kabbalistic text.

I remember that after the *Speculum* was published, somebody said to me: "I hope that the publication of the book burns out the interest in gender from you." He probably meant to say, "You exhausted what you had to say on gender and you won't write any more." I looked at him and I said, "Well, that's very unlikely for two reasons. First, because I'm probably just beginning to try to understand what's going on here. And secondly, I can't stop writing about gender unless I stop reading kabbalistic material." Because it's not that I impose gender analysis on the texts; kabbalistic texts are suffused with gendered imagery and symbolism that calls for gender analysis.

The popularity of kabbalah today is curious because we are in a very unique moment in terms of human embodiment. We live in cyberspace and are becoming more and more virtual people. We create identities in cyberspace (in video games and chat rooms, for example) and the Internet moves us away from embodied relations. There are millions of people in cyber-communities who never meet face to face. What is the meaning of embodiment (which is so central to kabbalah and to Judaism) in contemporary virtual life? In Europe right now, there is an infatuation with being a virtual Jew, namely, taking on a constructed Jewish identity often for the sake of critiquing society and culture. What is the meaning of embodiment in an environment which becomes more and more digital and virtual?

My grandmother would say, "This is not good for the Jews." Judaism and kabbalah in particular are all about embodiment: rituals are performed in the body; the body of the Jewish male is circumcised, and Jewish social life requires the presence of embodied Jews as virtual and not virtual Jews as embodied.

Here's a point of interesting intersection with what you just said. I like to use Henri Corbin's term "imaginal body" in order to understand or to articulate what the kabbalists had in mind, when they were envisioning this divine body (Shiur Qomah in Hebrew). The kabbalists spoke of the embodiment of God even though they were deeply familiar with Maimonides who made it very clear that we cannot think about God as a corporeal body, subject to generation and decay. The kabbalists also affirmed verbally that God is not a body, but they did so quite differently from Maimonides; they weren't willing to simply say that anthropomorphic language is only a metaphorical way to talk about God, a language that describes that which is beyond description, or in principle cannot be described. So, for them, there's some kind of ontic reality to which the description of the divine body refers. That reality is embodied, but in a non-corporeal manner. The best way to make sense of it is to use Corbin's term, "imaginal body," which he used to describe Islamic mystical sources.

I find that term to be a very fecund locution. It denotes a kind of virtual reality, where virtuality is the reality! And when you add the linguistic dimension, this notion becomes even more interesting in light of the computer. The operating language of a computer, what makes the hardware do its work, can be analogous to the "imaginal body." The kabbalists, of course, did not speak in the mathematical language of computers, but for them too the virtual or imaginal body is made of letters of the Hebrew alphabet. So the body of God is non-corporeal as the operating language of the computer is non-corporeal.

Can we say that the imaginal body is made of information?

Well, yes, you could translate the kabbalistic ideas into the idiom of information.

It's no coincidence that people who are interested in artificial intelligence are also fascinated with kabbalah and that certain film makers, for example, Darren Aronofsky who created the film *Pi* understood something very deep about kabbalah and about information technology. Kabbalists may have the right intuition about virtual reality but they did not have the technology to execute it. Today, computer technology enables us to realize some of the insights or intuitions of kabbalah.

Right, and historically, it's very peculiar what the kabbalists were up to in their visualizations of the imaginal. Even the Muslim mystics that Corbin studied are not quite the same as the kabbalists. There's a way that the kabbalists articulated in much greater detail these virtual realities.

The kabbalistic imagination was very rich and detailed, but instead of visualizing it in space, as Christians did in stained-glass windows, the kabbalists expressed their artistic and pictorial imagination in words. Their pictorial imagination was in their heads, so it remained noncorporeal and nonspatial, in order to abide by the Jewish prohibition on iconism.

Right, right. The sefirotic diagrams that the kabbalists did draw are very primitive, although their imagination was very rich. We should keep in mind that for the kabbalists, the domain of the imagination was the heart. The heart is the space or the locus of the imagination.

Within the academy, the study of kabbalah is carried out mostly in the context of the discipline of Jewish studies. For most of your academic career you have worked in one academic institution: New York University. Unlike other institutions where Jewish studies is a Program, at NYU Jewish Studies is a full-fledged Department. What are the benefits or detriments of having a Jewish Studies Department (as opposed to teaching Judaism as part of a discipline such as history, religious studies, etc.)?

The program at NYU was modeled very much on the basis of the Department of Near Eastern and Judaic Studies at Brandeis University. There are benefits and detriments. The most obvious benefit is that one does not have to struggle to establish coherence for the program. It is imposed structurally by the existence of a department. It is also advantageous for students in mysticism and philosophy to take courses in other subdisciplines in Jewish studies. The biggest detriment is that Jewish studies is an eclectic phenomenon and it is not always clear what the different fields have in common methodologically. Hence, there is a danger of balkanization, not to mention ghettoization. When we started the department at NYU we had hopes that students would become familiar with the various fields contained within the rubric of Jewish studies. Typically, in my first decade of teaching, my seminars in Jewish mysticism and philosophy were attended by students specializing in history, rabbinics, and even on occasion, the Bible. In the course of time that changed as the emphasis was placed on a more narrow focus. I understand why this is the case but I still lament that it is so. I have always found the seminar room benefits from diversity of interests on the part of students. The other major challenge of a program like the one at NYU is to encourage students to broaden the scope of their training by taking courses in cognate fields. I have always strongly suggested to my students that their minor comprehensive should be in a field other than Jewish philosophy or mysticism, for example, in gender theory, hermeneutics, phenomenology of religion, or comparative mysticism.

How do you assess the place of Jewish studies in the discipline of religious studies? Has there been a change over the past three decades since you entered the field?

In the last three decades, Jewish studies has grown appreciably and there have been more programs within the context of religious studies and this has generated more positions. The growing interest in topics such as gender, the status of the body, hermeneutics, and textuality in religious studies has had a positive and transformative impact on Jewish studies. Judaism is well represented in most departments of religion. This does represent a substantial change from the time I entered the field in 1987. Nevertheless, in some critical way, the dominant approach to Jewish studies is still the historical-philological one rather than the methodologies that are more endemic to scholars of religion. I do not mean to suggest that religious studies should be ahistorical or that a competent scholar of religion should avoid historical context. What I mean is that the study of religion has the potential to offer a diverse way to construe the historical that does not succumb to historical positivism. The preponderance of Jewish studies scholars have not really adopted the hermeneutical assumptions about the nature of time that is crucial to the discipline of religious studies. This is curious insofar as traditional Jewish learning could provide a model of time that is more conducive to what I am identifying as pervasive in scholars of religion. The rabbinic perspective on history rests on an assumption regarding the contemporaneity of past, present, and future. This stands in opposition to the historicist notion in which the present is a function of the past and the future a function of the present. Historical continuity from the traditional perspective means that both past and future can be experienced as real through the memory that is enacted in the present. The coalescence of the three temporal modes in the present alters the commonplace notion of causality based on the criteria of irreversibility and synchronicity. Through that act of commemoration the past is as much determined by the future as the future is by the past.

Twice your books received awards of the American Academy of Religion. What do these awards signify to you? What would you like the scholar of religious studies to take from them?

I am honored to have these awards although each of my books is precious to me like a child, even the ones that have not received any award. *Through a Speculum That Shines: Vision and Imagination in Medieval Jewish Mysticism* won the AAR Award in 1995 in the category of Historical Studies, and *A Dream Interpreted within a Dream: Oneiropoiesis and the Prism of Imagination* won the AAR Award in 2012 in the category of Constructive and Reflective Studies. Both awards are surely meaningful but I was especially humbled by the second one because this is not a category that is usually awarded to books that deal with Judaism. I have always felt that my work is not meant exclusively for Jewish studies and it is has been my desire for many years that my books and essays be read particularly by philosophers and scholars of religion. In the preface to *Open Secret: Postmessianic Messianism and the Mystical Revision of Menaḥem Mendel Schneerson* (2009), I wrote, "It is my hope, though by now not my expectation, that the readership of this book will not be limited to Jewish scholars or even to scholars of Judaica. In line with Rosenzweig's assessment of *The Star of Redemption*, I am willing to describe this work as a 'Jewish book,' if it is understood that this locution does not imply that it deals exclusively with 'Jewish things,' but rather that it enfolds and exceeds the principle that the particular, in all of its unpredictability, sheds light on a universal that must repeatedly articulate its universality from the vantage point of the particular. And, as Rosenzweig expressed his own aspiration, if others will be responsive to the 'Jewish words,' they have the potential of renewing the world." Sadly, the book was marketed for a "Jewish" audience and thus far I have little evidence that my hope has been fulfilled. I believe the issue I am raising is not unique to my situation. Scholars of Judaica have a particular challenge. The default position is that this is a narrow or even parochial area of studies. We must always resist this ghettoization and continue to make the case that the universal is to be calibrated from the perspective of the particular.

How do you understand the place of philosophy and kabbalah in Jewish studies?

There's a way in which the place of Jewish philosophy and kabbalah now is quite secure. Those battles have been won, because there are courses in universities and colleges around the world where one can study Jewish philosophy and/or kabbalah. I think there are fewer people doing Jewish philosophy than there were two decades ago, but Jewish philosophy is still an accepted part of the canon of Jewish studies.

The question is will Jewish studies be able to keep going on without significantly evolving by engaging different disciplines and different models of thinking. This seems to me to be the challenge. The possibility of creating a significant conversation between Judaism and science, or the attempt to think about kabbalah in terms of computer technology, are areas of potential growth for the discipline of Jewish studies.

In general, religious studies seems to be able to grow because the field has engaged the relationship of religion and science. The same should happen in the areas of Jewish philosophy and Jewish mysticism. So the task for Jewish studies is to create training programs that are able to ground students in the historical and philological skills necessary for working with Jewish texts, and at the same time allow them to think more expansively and creatively about these texts in light of contemporary science and technology.

That's the challenge which will not be easily addressed. It's not easy because especially at the graduate level it requires a lot, both in terms of skills and in terms of time. And sometimes we find graduate students who are more sophisticated with theoretical and methodological speculation but are weaker in terms of philological skills, and conversely we have students who are strong in the philological skills but who lack the capacity for theoretical sophistication. If the field of Jewish studies is to grow we need to train students who will have both sets of skills.

Beyond the walls of the academy, to whom does Jewish studies matter? Does it matter to Jews at all? Should Jews care about Jewish studies?

Well, I hope that Jewish studies matters not only to Jews but to everybody, inside the academy and in the society at large. Jewish studies would be a failure if it matters only to Jews. In this regard I like to recall Levinas's term "universalist singularity." Even if I may not agree with him totally, the rudiment of his idea seemed to me correct: if the Jews are going to somehow maintain something of their singularity, it has to be in the service of some universality. Levinas turned the trope of the Jews' otherness on its head; the Other is turned from a negative into a positive notion. The Jew represents the irreducible other, and thus as Jews we share an irreducible singularity, which makes us not only different from non-Jews,

but also different from one another. To apply this insight to Jewish studies, we could say that Jewish studies should gain its significance only if it
extends beyond the particularity of the Jewish people, understanding its
singularity as universal.

As for the connection between Jewish studies and the community,
or the culture of the Jewish people, that's also a bit of a problem. And
I think that we're living in a very precarious moment where there have
been certain institutions that have infiltrated into the academy with their
money, and they seem to be controlling to some extent the conversation
and the discourse, particularly in the area of Jewish philosophy and Jewish
thought. In my mind it is a problem when scholarship on Jewish thought
(or Jewish studies more generally) becomes controlled by nonacademic
interests, whether they are to the right or to the left, politically speaking.
The political orientation of private funding doesn't matter to me, what
matters to me is that the academy is now controlled by or answerable
to nonacademic interests. There is something profoundly anti-intellectual
about that development which I see as detrimental to the future of Jewish
philosophy and Jewish studies more generally.

Another challenge lies in the fact that Jewish studies has become
increasingly a conversation for Jews, by Jews, and about Jews, driven by
questions of Jewish identity. Today whatever props up, what supports
Jewish existence, and what celebrates being a Jew in the world, dominates
the discourse of Jewish studies. In this manner Jewish studies becomes
increasingly particularized and its universal significance is diminished or
becomes unrecognized. That to me is the greatest challenge for Jewish
studies and for Jewish existence because they become increasingly con-
strained by ideological and ethnic concerns and more in the service of
wealthy funders and private foundations.

**In other words, you are saying that the discipline of Jewish studies suf-
fers and will suffer even more from a growing insularity that has crept
up in the past two decades.**

I think so. But, let us be honest and remind ourselves that many of these
academic positions for which we owe our livelihood came to be because
of Jewish patronage. You know, the universities were happy to take Jewish money for their own financial reasons. And that enabled programs of
Jewish studies to grow all over the U.S. This is fine to get it going, but it's
not enough to sustain it as a real, genuine intellectual contribution.

To say that makes you a social critic. So, is the role of the philosopher to be a social critic?

Well, I think so. As a social critic, the philosopher is on the margins, as I have noted earlier in the interview. This position, I find, is itself empowering.

To whom?

Well, to society at large, because the philosopher can pay attention to various social problems; and to the philosopher, because the philosopher sees the center better and understands the problem of the society better from the vantage point of the margins That should be the role of the philosopher, and of the Jewish philosopher. But I fear that with the infiltration of private funding and institutional agendas, the social role of the Jewish philosopher is being compromised.

What future, either near-term or long-term, do you envision for Jewish philosophy?

I have a hope more than a vision. I hope that eventually there will be a restored balance between academic scholarship and ideological interests. And I hope that enough people will continue to do serious thinking without being indebted to these money changers, as I call them.

And that will be enough for me. If there remain a handful of people who continue to do genuine scholarship, I will be pleased. As a matter of fact, I'm not as bleak on the whole situation, as I may sound. I think there's still a lot of talent out there and there are individuals who are continuing to do their work. And that will, I think, keep a certain healthy balance.

Do you see a role for non-Jews in the future of Jewish studies?

Absolutely. Jewish studies is not just for Jews; it is for non-Jews as participants, contributors, interpreters, and so forth. The future of Jewish studies will have to also come from the wider community. There has to be a change in consciousness here. And we're not there yet.

Here is a personal example from my book that Columbia University Press published on the Chabad leader, Menachem Mendel Schneerson.

The press insisted on having on the cover a picture of Schneerson, against my protest. I didn't want it, but the decision was driven by the marketing people because they decided that the primary target audience for the book was going to be the Jewish community and even more specifically the Chabad community, so putting his picture on the cover was meant to help sell the book. That was deeply insulting to me personally, but it underscores the dilemma of Jewish studies more generally. On the one hand, Columbia Press has agreed to publish my book on a very Jewish subject, which is a major accomplishment in terms of scholarly recognition, but on the other hand, they marketed the book in a certain way which is against the grain of the book. In the preface of the book I mentioned Rosenzweig's assessment of the *Star* as a Jewish book and, as I noted earlier, I wrote that "I am willing to describe this work as a 'Jewish book,' if it is understood that this locution does not imply that it deals exclusively with 'Jewish things,' but rather that it enfolds and exceeds the principle that the particular in all of its unpredictability sheds light on a universal that must repeatedly articulate its universality from the vantage point of the particular." And I concluded the reference to Rosenzweig by saying, "And, as Rosenzweig expressed his own aspiration, if others will be responsive to the 'Jewish words,' they have the potential of renewing the world." So that to me encapsulates all of my efforts.

You seem to imply something redemptive in your scholarly work. Is that correct?

It's a hope. There's no certainty of this but there's a hope.

This statement may lack certainty but it suggests a utopian, future oriented, and creative impulse. You want something to change in the world as a result of this writing.

Right. But in its moment, my scholarship changes nothing, or at least so far it has changed nothing. I have to tell you that thus far the book has not really garnered much attention. The book has all kinds of conversations about the nature of apophatic embodiment, the question of particularity and universality, language and materiality, concealment and disclosure, and even a discussion of the posthuman overcoming of theism and egoism, although I do not use that precise term. All of these issues emerge from the Chabad sources themselves that I show seek to go beyond theism, thereby undoing their own messianism from within. I don't think Chabad practitioners are anywhere close to being able to enact this dimension of the messianic teaching, but what I say could be of interest to contemporary philosophers such as Jean-Luc Marion and John Caputo, who are writing about a-theology. But it requires on their part a willingness to enter the complexity of Jewish texts. There's something more profound here. It will require on their part a willingness to tolerate a certain style of Jewish textual interpretation towards the service of something greater than its own particularity.

So what you're saying is that the academy is not interested in Jewish studies or even has a vested interest in keeping Jewish studies distinctly particularistic because in this matter they continue to marginalize Jews.

I think this is evident in the cases of both Derrida and Levinas. The particularity is emphasized at the expense of the universal message. And in a way, there's a certain celebration of the particular or the singular, right? That's a quality of postmodernism.

So why not embrace the singularity of a very rich textual tradition? Because doing so requires one to learn to be able to read texts differently, and that is what people resist.

The problem exists for Jews as well: the inability to read the Christian texts, be they historical (e.g., the New Testament) or contemporary (constructive theology). The problem is less acute in regard to Islamic texts, but we do not see Jewish scholars engaged in interpreting Christian texts. Amy-Jill Levine or Daniel Boyarin are exceptional cases that prove the rule. So, we, Jews, have our own blind spots and our own blinders that prevent us from entering the symbolic world of another tradition, another culture, another civilization and work with its richness.

Right. I would agree that it is very difficult to do, but I have tried in my own way.

As scholars we try to engage cross-cultural interpretation, but in the end we all remain "children of our own tradition," as Gadamer called it. We read texts as Jews, trained as we are by the rules of our own intertextuality, which differ from Christian theology.

It would be lamentable if this continues. I would have thought by now we actually would have been at a different place, a hermenutical place in which it is possible to read texts in a particular way without promoting boundaries in simple binarian terms. I think it is vitally important to read the texts of a tradition in their own language—this is my ongoing commitment to philology—but I do not think that this necessarily means we simply remain children of our own tradition. The contours of any given tradition are constantly being formed and deformed, the relationship between inside and outside constantly being renegotiated.

What do you consider to be the most challenging issues for contemporary Jewish existence? Why and how do these issues challenge Jewish existence?

The challenges for contemporary Jewish existence are immense even though in some ways the threat of anti-Semitism has diminished in certain parts of the civilized world. The animosity toward Israel has been growing the last few decades but one must be careful of identifying specific critiques of Israel with a more general hatred of the Jews. The real challenges, as I see them, are much more internal. The level of Jewish literacy is at an all-time low, and while there have been adult educational programs, they have not really succeeded in overcoming this chasm. For the vast majority of Jews there is little, if any, desire to affiliate with Jewish tradition, however it is conceived. Like other religious faiths, it is not always clear to me that many of the traditional beliefs are sustainable and the cosmology underlying those beliefs is no longer tenable. Thinking of God as up in heaven is an inappropriate metaphor in the universe as it is presently conceived by physicists. Religious practices and beliefs need to be enriched by current cosmological assumptions.

How can scholars (especially scholars of Jewish studies) help address these challenges?

Not all the challenges belong to the prerogative of the scholar. What we can do, at best, is to continue to educate people. I think it is laudable for scholars to be involved in adult education, but I still would maintain that it is not the scholar's primary purpose to address the existential problems of the Jewish community. Some space must be preserved if scholarship is to fulfill its unique mission.

In the diaspora leaders are most concerned about the future of Jewish survival given the high percentage of intermarriage and the poor quality of education. Do you share these concerns? If not, why not?

I have already noted that I do share the concern with the poor quality of education. While I am sympathetic to those who would see intermarriage as a major concern, I personally do not think this is a threat to Jewish survival, and I certainly do not think it is the business of a scholar to weigh in on such an issue. Far more central and pertinent is the matter of knowledge. In this domain, the scholar can make a useful contribution.

How do you see the challenges to the State of Israel? Are you concerned about the ability of the State of Israel to survive? Does politics matter to you? If not, why not?

I am not concerned about the ability of the State of Israel to survive, not because I do not care about the State of Israel but because I believe its survival is not endangered. To be sure, Israel has many enemies—and the threat of extremists to wage a holy war against Israel or to establish a caliphate dedicated to the extermination of the Jews is troubling—but it also is very powerful militarily and it has the resolute support of the United States in the international community. It is time for Israeli politicians to let go of this rhetoric about survival. I am not saying that I think Israel can or should ignore defending its citizens. My point is that the constant appeal to security has and will continue to legitimate subjugation of the other. The endless cycle of violence needs to stop. Yes, politics matter to me—we are, as Aristotle put it, political animals. Not to be concerned with politics would be an abdication of our human responsibility. But I think the academic has a distinctive political role to play, a role that is determined by questioning, by problematizing rather than by finding definitive solutions.

Earlier you said that you are not as political as Arendt was. Can the Jewish philosopher ignore politics if the philosopher, as you also say, has a social mission?

I meant to say that I was not interested in writing political philosophy like Arendt. I do not think the philosopher can ignore politics. But I also do not think it is necessary for the political to overwhelm one's philosophical engagement. My critiques of phallomorphism and xenophobia in kabbalistic sources are political gestures. I have sought through criticism to reform these texts. This is part of the social mission to which I alluded.

Should Jewish philosophy be apolitical? Should the same be true about Jewish studies more generally?

I do not think Jewish philosophy, or Jewish studies more generally, should be apolitical. At the same time, I am wary of identity politics dominating the field. Jewish philosophy must be open to critical thinking and this thinking should not be constricted or dominated by the needs of the community. For me, the ultimate freedom consists of the ability to question and to doubt. This is the genuine political act that a philosopher can assume. Too often in Jewish philosophy this freedom to be skeptical is constricted by the need to affirm some position that serves a communal purpose rather than the genuine search for truth.

Thank you, Professor Wolfson, for taking the time to do the interview and for participating in the Library of Contemporary Jewish Philosophers. Your penetrating thought about Jewish philosophy, kabbalah, Hasidism, postmodernism, linguisticality, textuality, art, and the social role of the philosopher invite us to think anew about Judaism and to find new ways to frame our future tasks.

Thank you for inviting me to participate in the project.

SELECT BIBLIOGRAPHY

Books

1. *The Book of the Pomegranate: Moses de León's Sefer ha-Rimmon.* Brown Judaic Series 144. Atlanta: Scholars Press, 1988.
2. *Through a Speculum That Shines: Vision and Imagination in Medieval Jewish Mysticism.* Princeton, NJ: Princeton University Press, 1994.
3. *Along the Path: Studies in Kabbalistic Myth, Symbolism, and Hermeneutics.* Albany: State University of New York Press, 1995.
4. *Circle in the Square: Studies in the Use of Gender in Kabbalistic Symbolism.* Albany: State University of New York Press, 1995.
5. *Abraham Abulafia—Kabbalist and Prophet: Hermeneutics, Theosophy, and Theurgy.* Los Angeles: Cherub Press, 2000.
6. *Pathwings: Poetic-Philosophic Reflections on the Hermeneutics of Time and Language.* Barrytown, NY: Station Hill/Barrytown Press, 2004.
7. *Language, Eros, Being: Kabbalistic Hermeneutics and Poetic Imagination.* New York: Fordham University Press, 2005.
8. *Alef, Mem, Tau: Kabbalistic Musings on Time, Truth, and Death.* Berkeley: University of California Press, 2006.
9. *Venturing Beyond—Law and Morality in Kabbalistic Mysticism.* Oxford: Oxford University Press, 2006.
10. *Footdreams and Treetales: 92 Poems.* New York: Fordham University Press, 2007.
11. *Luminal Darkness: Imaginal Gleanings from Zoharic Literature.* London: Oneworld Publications, 2007.
12. *Open Secret: Postmessianic Messianism and the Mystical Revision of Menaḥem Mendel Schneerson.* New York: Columbia University Press, 2009.
13. *A Dream Interpreted within a Dream: Oneiropoiesis and the Prism of Imagination.* New York: Zone Books, 2011.
14. *Giving Beyond the Gift: Apophasis and Overcoming Theomania.* New York: Fordham University Press, 2014.

Edited Volumes

15. (With A. Ivry and A. Arkush) *Perspectives on Jewish Thought and Mysticism.* Australia: Harwood Academic Publishers, 1998.
16. *Rending the Veil: Concealment and Secrecy in the History of Religions.* New York: Seven Bridges Press, 1999.
17. (With R. Gibbs) *Suffering Religion.* New York: Routledge, 2002.
18. (With A. W. Hughes) *New Directions in Jewish Philosophy.* Bloomington: Indiana University Press, 2010.
19. (With D. Engel and L. H. Schiffman) *Studies in Medieval Jewish Intellectual and Social History: Festschrift in Honor of Robert Chazan.* Leiden: Brill, 2012.

Book Chapters

20. "Female Imaging of the Torah: From Literary Metaphor to Religious Symbol." In *From Ancient Israel to Modern Judaism: Intellect in Quest of Understanding: Essays in Honor of Marvin Fox,* edited by J. Neusner, E. Frerichs, and N. Sarna, 2:271–307. Atlanta: Scholars Press, 1989.
21. "Letter Symbolism and Merkavah Imagery in the Zohar." In *Alei Shefer: Studies in the Literature of Jewish Thought Presented to Rabbi Dr. Alexandre Safran,* edited by M. Hallamish, 195–236 (English section). Ramat-Gan: Bar-Ilan Press, 1990.
22. "Images of God's Feet: Some Observations on the Divine Body in Judaism." In *People of the Body: Jews and Judaism from an Embodied Perspective,* edited by H. Eilberg-Schwartz, 143–81. Albany: State University of New York Press, 1992.
23. "Beautiful Maiden without Eyes: Peshat and Sod in Zoharic Hermeneutics." In *The Midrashic Imagination: Jewish Exegesis, Thought, and History,* edited by M. Fishbane, 155–203. Albany: State University of New York Press, 1993.
24. "Forms of Visionary Ascent as Ecstatic Experience in the Zoharic Literature." In *Gershom Scholem's Major Trends in Jewish Mysticism 50 Years After,* edited by J. Dan and P. Schäfer, 209–35. Tübingen: J. C. B. Mohr, 1993.
25. "Yeridah la-Merkavah: Typology of Ecstasy and Enthronement in Early Jewish Mysticism." In *Mystics of the Book: Themes, Topics, and Typologies,* edited by R. Herrera, 13–44. New York: Peter Lang, 1993.
26. "The Image of Jacob Engraved upon the Throne: Further Speculation on the Esoteric Doctrine of German Pietism." In *Massu'ot:*

Studies in Kabbalistic Literature and Jewish Philosophy in Memory of Prof. Ephraim Gottlieb, edited by M. Oron and A. Goldreich, 131–85. Jerusalem: Mosad Bialik, 1994 (Hebrew).

27. "Woman—The Feminine as Other in Theosophic Kabbalah: Some Philosophical Observations on the Divine Androgyne." In *The Other in Jewish Thought and History: Constructions of Jewish Culture and Identity*, edited by L. Silberstein and R. Cohn, 166–204. New York: New York University Press, 1994.

28. "From Sealed Book to Open Text: Time, Memory, and Narrativity in Kabbalistic Hermeneutics." In *Interpreting Judaism in a Postmodern Age*, edited by S. Kepnes, 145–78. New York: New York University Press, 1995.

29. "Metatron and Shiʿur Qomah in the Writings of Haside Ashkenaz." In *Mysticism, Magic, and Kabbalah in Ashkenazi Judaism*, edited by K. Grözinger and J. Dan, 60–92. Tübingen: J. C. B. Mohr, 1995.

30. "On Becoming Female: Crossing Gender Boundaries in Kabbalistic Ritual and Myth." In *Gender and Judaism*, edited by T. M. Rudavsky, 209–28. New York: New York University Press, 1995.

31. "Weeping, Death, and Spiritual Ascent in Sixteenth-Century Jewish Mysticism." In *Death, Ecstasy, and Other Worldly Journeys*, edited by J. Collins and M. Fishbane, 207–47. Albany: State University of New York Press, 1995.

32. "Walking as a Sacred Duty: Theological Transformation of Social Reality in Early Hasidism." In *Hasidism Reconsidered*, edited by A. Rapoport-Albert, 180–207. Oxford: Litman Library of Jewish Civilization, 1996.

33. "Effacer l'effacement: sexe et écriture du corps divin dans le symbolisme kabbalistique." In *Transmission et passages en monde juif*, edited by E. Benbassa, 65–97. Paris: PUBLISUD, 1997.

34. "Eunuchs Who Keep the Sabbath: Becoming Male and the Ascetic Ideal in Thirteenth-Century Jewish Mysticism." In *Becoming Male in the Middle Ages*, edited by J. J. Cohen and B. Wheeler, 151–85. New York: Garland, 1997.

35. "The Face of Jacob in the Moon: Mystical Transformations of an Aggadic Myth." In *The Seduction of Myth in Judaism: Challenge and Response*, edited by S. Daniel Breslauer, 235–70. Albany: State University of New York Press, 1997.

36. "The Engenderment of Messianic Politics: Symbolic Significance of Sabbatai Ṣevi's Coronation." In *Toward the Millennium: Messianic Expectations from the Bible to Waco*, edited by P. Schäfer and M. Cohen, 203–58. Leiden: E. J. Brill, 1998.

37. "Mystical Rationalization of the Commandments in the Prophetic Kabbalah of Abraham Abulafia." In *Perspectives on Jewish Thought and Mysticism*, edited by A. Ivry, A. Arkush, and E. R. Wolfson, 311–60. Australia: Harwood Academic Publishers, 1998.

38. "Re/membering the Covenant: Memory, Forgetfulness, and History in the *Zohar*." In *Jewish History and Jewish Memory: Essays in Honor of Yosef Hayim Yerushalmi*, edited by E. Carlebach, D. S. Myers, and J. Efron, 214–46. Hanover and London: Brandeis University Press, 1998.

39. "Occultation of the Feminine and the Body of Secrecy in Medieval Kabbalah." In *Rending the Veil: Concealment and Revelation of Secrets in the History of Religions*, edited by E. R. Wolfson, 113–54. New York: Seven Bridges Press, 1999.

40. "Sacred Space and Mental Iconography: *Imago Templi* and Contemplation in Rhineland Jewish Pietism." In *Ki Baruch Hu: Ancient Near Eastern, Biblical, and Judaic Studies in Honor of Baruch A. Levine*, edited by R. Chazan, W. Hallo, and L. H. Schiffman, 593–634. Winona Lake: Eisenbrauns, 1999.

41. "Beyond the Spoken Word: Oral Tradition and Written Transmission in Medieval Jewish Mysticism." In *Transmitting Jewish Traditions: Orality, Textuality and Cultural Diffusion*, edited by Y. Elman and I. Gershoni, 166–224. New Haven and London: Yale University Press, 2000.

42. "Gazing Beneath the Veil: Apocalyptic Envisioning the End." In *Reinterpreting Revelation and Tradition: Jews and Christians in Conversation*, edited by J. T. Pawlikowski and H. G. Perelmuter, 77–103. Franklin: Sheed and Ward, 2000.

43. "Judaism and Incarnation: The Imaginal Body of God." In *Christianity in Jewish Terms*, edited by T. Frymer-Kensky, D. Novak, P. Ochs, and M. Signer, 239–54. Boulder: Westview Press, 2000.

44. "Martyrdom, Eroticism, and Asceticism in Twelfth-Century Ashkenazi Piety." In *Jews and Christians in Twelfth-Century Europe*, edited by J. Van Engen and M. Signer, 171–220. Notre Dame: University of Notre Dame Press, 2001.

45. "Messianism in the Christian Kabbalah of Johann Kemper." In *Millenarianism and Messianism in the Early Modern European Culture: Jewish Messianism in the Early Modern World*, edited by M. D. Goldish and R. H. Popkin, 139–87. The Netherlands: Kluwer Academic Publishers, 2001.

46. "Before Alef/Where Beginnings End." In *Beginning/Again: Towards a Hermeneutics of Jewish Texts*, edited by A. Cohen and S. Magid, 135–61. New York: Seven Bridges Press, 2002.

47. "Beyond Good and Evil: Hypernomianism, Transmorality, and Kabbalistic Ethics." In *Crossing Boundaries: Ethics, Antinomianism and the History of Mysticism*, edited by J. J. Kripal and W. Barnard, 103–56. New York: Seven Bridges Press, 2002.

48. "The Cut That Binds: Time, Memory, and the Ascetic Impulse." In *God's Voice from the Void: Old and New Studies in Bratslav Hasidism*, edited by S. Magid, 103–54. Albany: State University of New York Press, 2002.

49. "Divine Suffering and the Hermeneutics of Reading: Philosophical Reflections on Lurianic Mythology." In *Suffering Religion*, edited by R. Gibbs and E. R. Wolfson, 101–62. New York and London: Routledge, 2002.

50. "Asceticism and Eroticism in Medieval Jewish Philosophical and Mystical Exegesis of the Song of Songs." In *With Reverence for the Word: Medieval Scriptural Exegesis in Judaism, Christianity, and Islam*, edited by J. D. McAuliffe, B. D. Walfish, and J. W. Goering, 92–118. Oxford and New York: Oxford University Press, 2003.

51. "Circumcision, Secrecy, and the Veiling of the Veil: Phallomorphic Exposure and Kabbalistic Esotericism." In *The Covenant of Circumcision: New Perspectives on an Ancient Jewish Rite*, edited by E. W. Mark, 58–70. Hanover and London: Brandeis University Press, 2003.

52. "Seven Mysteries of Knowledge: Qumran E/sotericism Reconsidered." In *The Idea of Biblical Interpretation: Essays in Honor of James L. Kugel*, edited by H. Najman, 173–213. Leiden: Brill, 2003.

53. "Beneath the Wings of the Great Eagle: Maimonides and Thirteenth-Century Kabbalah." In *Moses Maimonides (1138–1204)—His Religious, Scientific, and Philosophical Wirkungsgeschichte in Different Cultural Contexts*, edited by G. K. Hasselhoff and Otfried Fraisse, 209–37. Würzburg: Ergon Verlag, 2004.

54. "Suffering Eros and Textual Incarnation: A Kristevan Reading of Kabbalistic Poetics." In *Toward a Theology of Eros: Transfiguring Passion at the Limits of Discipline*, edited by V. Burrus and C. Keller, 341–65. New York: Fordham University Press, 2006.

55. "Angelic Embodiment and the Feminine Representation of Jesus: Reconstructing Carnality in the Christian Kabbalah of Johann Kemper." In *The "Jewish Body" in the Early Modern Period*, edited by M. Diemling and G. Veltri, 395–426. Leiden: Brill, 2008.

56. "Murmuring Secrets: Eroticism and Esotericism in Medieval Kabbalah." In *Hidden Intercourse: Eros and Sexuality in the History of Western Esotericism*, edited by J. Kripal and W. Hanegraff, 65–109. Leiden: Brill, 2008.

57. "Revisioning the Body Apophatically: Incarnation and the Acosmic Naturalism of Habad Hasidism." In *Apophatic Bodies: Infinity, Ethics, and Incarnation*, edited by C. Boesel and C. Keller, 147–99. New York: Fordham University Press, 2009.

58. " 'Sage Is Preferable to Prophet': Revisioning Midrashic Imagination." In *Scriptural Exegesis: The Shapes of Culture and the Religious Imagination: A Festschrift in Honor of Michael Fishbane*, edited by D. A. Green and L. S. Lieber, 186–210. Oxford: Oxford University Press, 2009.

59. "Light Does Not Talk But Shines: Apophasis and Vision in Rosenzweig's Theopoetic Temporality." In *New Directions in Jewish Philosophy*, edited by A. W. Hughes and E. R. Wolfson, 87–148. Bloomington: Indiana University Press, 2010.

60. "The Status of the (Non)Jewish Other in the Apocalyptic Messianism of Menahem Mendel Schneerson." In *Kabbalah and Modernity: Interpretations, Transformations, Adaptations*, edited by B. Huss, M. Pasi, and K. von Stuckard, 221–57. Leiden: Brill, 2010.

61. "Immanuel Frommann's Commentary on Luke and the Christianizing of Kabbalah: Some Sabbatian and Ḥasidic Affinities." In *Holy Dissent: Jewish and Christian Mystics in Eastern Europe*, edited by G. Dynner, 171–222. Detroit: Wayne State University Press, 2011.

62. "Echo of the Otherwise: Ethics of Transcendence and the Lure of Theolatry." In *Encountering the Medieval in Modern Jewish Thought*, edited by A. W. Hughes and J. A. Diamond, 261–324. Leiden: Brill, 2012.

63. "Imagination and the Theolatrous Impulse: Configuring God in Modern Jewish Thought." In *The Cambridge History of Jewish Philosophy: The Modern Era*, edited by Z. Braiterman, M. Kavka, and D. Novak, 663–703. Cambridge: Cambridge University Press, 2012.

64. "Textual Flesh, Incarnation, and the Imaginal Body: Abraham Abulafia's Polemic with Christianity." In *Studies in Medieval Jewish Intellectual and Social History: Festschrift in Honor of Robert Chazan*, edited by D. Engel, L. H. Schiffman, and E. R. Wolfson, 189–226. Leiden: Brill, 2012.

65. "Becoming Invisible: Rending the Veil and the Hermeneutic of Secrecy in the Gospel of Philip." In *Practicing Gnosis: Ritual, Magic, Theurgy and Liturgy in Nag Hammadi, Manichaean, and Other Ancient Literature: Essays in Honor of Birger A. Pearson*, edited by A. D. DeConick, G. Shaw, and J. D. Turner, 113–35. Leiden: Brill, 2013.

66. "Configuring of Untruth in the Mirror of God's Truth: Rethinking Rosenzweig in Light of Heidegger's Alētheia." In *Die Denkfigur des Systems im Ausgang von Franz Rosenzweigs 'Stern der Erlösung'*, edited by H. Wiedebach, 141–62. Berlin: Duncker and Humblot, 2013.

67. "Le corps de la letter: l'herméneutique soufie et kabbalistique." In *Histoire des relations entre juifs et musulmans du Coran à nos jours*, edited by Abdelwahab Meddeb and Benjamin Stora, 817–32. Paris: Albin Michel, 2013.

68. "Patriarchy and the Motherhood of God in Zoharic Kabbalah and Meister Eckhart." In *Envisioning Judaism: Studies in Honor of Peter Schäfer on the Occasion of his Seventieth Birthday*, vol. 2, edited by R. Boustan, K. Hermann, R. Leicht, A. Yoshiko Reed, and G. Veltri, with A. Ramos, 1049–88. Tübingen: Mohr Siebeck, 2013.

69. "Zoharic Literature and Midrashic Temporality." In *Midrash Unbound: Transformations and Innovations*, edited by M. Fishbane and J. Weinberg, 311–33. Oxford: Littman Library, 2013.

70. "Bifurcating the Androgyne and Engendering Sin: A Zoharic Reading of Genesis 1–3." In *Hidden Truths from Eden: Esoteric Readings of Genesis 1–3* (Semeia Studies), edited by S. Scholz and C. Vander Stichele, 83–115. Atlanta: SBL Publications, 2014.

71. "Skepticism and the Philosopher's Keeping Faith." In *Jewish Philosophy for the Twenty-First Century: Personal Reflections*, edited by H. Tirosh-Samuelson and A. W. Hughes, 481–515. Leiden: Brill, 2014.

Journal Articles

72. "Left Contained in the Right: A Study in Zoharic Hermeneutics." *Association for Jewish Studies Review* 11 (1986): 27–52.

73. "Circumcision and the Divine Name: A Study in the Transmission of Esoteric Doctrine." *Jewish Quarterly Review* 78 (1987): 77–112.

74. "Circumcision, Vision of God, and Textual Interpretation: From Midrashic Trope to Mystical Symbol." *History of Religions* 27 (1987): 189–215.

75. "The Hermeneutics of Visionary Experience: Revelation and Interpretation in the Zohar." *Religion* 18 (1988): 311–45.

76. "Light through Darkness: The Ideal of Human Perfection in the Zohar." *Harvard Theological Review* 81 (1988): 73–95.

77. "Mystical Rationalization of the Commandments in *Sefer ha-Rimmon*." *Hebrew Union College Annual* 59 (1988): 217–51.

78. "Anthropomorphic Imagery and Letter Symbolism in the Zohar." *Jerusalem Studies in Jewish Thought* 8 (1989): 147–81 (Hebrew).

79. "By Way of Truth: Aspects of Naḥmanides' Kabbalistic Hermeneutic." *Association for Jewish Studies Review* 14 (1989): 103–78.

80. "The Problem of Unity in the Thought of Martin Buber." *Journal of the History of Philosophy* 27 (1989): 419–39.
81. "God, the Intellect, and the Demiurge: On the Usage of the Word *Kol* in Abraham ibn Ezra." *Revue des études juives* 149 (1990): 77–111.
82. "The Secret of the Garment in Naḥmanides." *Da'at* 24 (1990): 25–49 (English section).
83. "Merkavah Traditions in Philosophical Garb: Judah Halevi Reconsidered." *Proceedings of the American Academy for Jewish Research* 57 (1990–1991): 179–242.
84. "Hai Gaon's Letter and Commentary on Aleynu: Further Evidence of R. Moses de León's Pseudepigraphic Activity." *Jewish Quarterly Review* 81 (1991): 365–410.
85. "The Influence of the Ari on the Shelah." *Jerusalem Studies in Jewish Thought* 10 (1992): 423–48 (Hebrew).
86. "The Theosophy of Shabbetai Donnolo, with Special Emphasis on the Doctrine of Sefirot in Sefer Ḥakhmoni." *Jewish History* 6 (1992): 281–316.
87. "The Mystical Significance of Torah Study in German Pietism." *Jewish Quarterly Review* 84 (1993): 43–78.
88. "The Tree That Is All: Jewish-Christian Roots of a Kabbalistic Symbol in *Sefer ha-Bahir*." *Journal of Jewish Thought and Philosophy* 3 (1993): 31–76.
89. "Mysticism and the Poetic-Liturgical Compositions from Qumran." *Jewish Quarterly Review* 85 (1994): 187–204.
90. "Negative Theology and Positive Assertion in the Early Kabbalah." *Da'at* 32–33 (1994): 5–22.
91. "The Doctrine of Sefirot in the Prophetic Kabbalah of Abraham Abulafia." *Jewish Studies Quarterly* 2 (1995): 336–71 and 3 (1996): 47–84.
92. "Iconic Visualization and the Imaginal Body of God: The Role of Intention in the Rabbinic Conception of Prayer." *Modern Theology* 12 (1996): 137–62.
93. "Coronation of the Sabbath Bride: Kabbalistic Myth and the Ritual of Androgynisation." *Journal of Jewish Thought and Philosophy* 6 (1997): 301–44.
94. "Facing the Effaced: Mystical Eschatology and the Idealistic Orientation in the Thought of Franz Rosenzweig." *Zeitschrift für Neuere Theologiegeschichte* 4 (1997): 39–81.
95. "*Tiqqun ha-Shekhinah*: Redemption and the Overcoming of Gender Dimorphism in the Messianic Kabbalah of Moses Ḥayyim Luzzatto." *History of Religions* 36 (1997): 289–332.

96. "Constructions of the Feminine in the Sabbatian Theology of Abraham Cardoso, with a Critical Edition of *Derush ha-Shekhinah*." *Kabbalah: A Journal for the Study of Jewish Mystical Texts* 3 (1998): 11–143.

97. "Fore/giveness On the Way: Nesting in the Womb of Response." *Graven Images: Studies in Culture, Law, and the Sacred* 4 (1998): 153–69.

98. "Hebraic and Hellenistic Conceptions of Wisdom in *Sefer ha-Bahir*." *Poetics Today* 19 (1998): 147–76.

99. "*Megillat Emet we-Emunah*: Contemplative Visualization and Mystical Unknowing." *Kabbalah: A Journal for the Study of Jewish Mystical Texts* 5 (2000): 55–110.

100. "Ontology, Alterity, and Ethics in Kabbalistic Anthropology." *Exemplaria* 12 (2000): 129–55.

101. "Phantasmagoria: The Image of the Image in Jewish Magic from Late Antiquity and the Early Middle Ages." *The Review of Rabbinic Judaism: Ancient, Medieval, Modern* 4 (2001): 78–120.

102. "Assaulting the Border: Kabbalistic Traces in the Margins of Derrida." *Journal of the American Academy of Religion* 70 (2002): 475–514.

103. "Gender and Heresy in Kabbalah Scholarship." *Kabbalah: A Journal for the Study of Jewish Mystical Texts* 6 (2002): 231–62 (Hebrew).

104. "Iconicity of the Text: Reification of the Torah and the Idolatrous Impulse of Zoharic Kabbalah." *Jewish Studies Quarterly* 11 (2004): 215–42.

105. "Language, Secrecy, and the Mysteries of Law: Theurgy and the Christian Kabbalah of Johannes Reuchlin." *Kabbalah: A Journal for the Study of Jewish Mystical Texts* 13 (2005): 7–41.

106. "New Jerusalem Glowing: Songs and Poems of Leonard Cohen in a Kabbalistic Key." *Kabbalah: A Journal for the Study of Jewish Mystical Texts* 15 (2006): 103–52.

107. "Secrecy, Modesty, and the Feminine: Kabbalistic Traces in the Thought of Levinas." *Journal of Jewish Thought and Philosophy* 14 (2006): 195–224. Reprinted in *The Exorbitant: Emmanuel Levinas Between Jews and Christians*, edited by K. Hart and M. Signer, 52–73. New York: Fordham University Press, 2010.

108. "Imago Templi and the Meeting of the Two Seas: Liturgical Time-Space and the Feminine Imaginary in Zoharic Kabbalah." *RES* 51 (2007): 121–35.

109. "Inscribed in the Book of the Living: *Gospel of Truth* and Jewish Christology." *Journal for the Study of Judaism* 38 (2007): 234–71.

110. "Oneiric Imagination and Mystical Annihilation in Habad Hasidism." *ARC, The Journal of the Faculty of Religious Studies, McGill University* 35 (2007): 131–57.

111. "Structure, Innovation, and Diremptive Temporality: The Use of Models to Study Continuity and Discontinuity in Kabbalistic Tradition." *Journal for the Study of Religions and Ideologies* 18 (2007): 143–67.

112. "Kenotic Overflow and Temporal Transcendence: Angelic Embodiment and the Alterity of Time in Abraham Abulafia." *Kabbalah: Journal for the Study of Jewish Mystical Texts* 18 (2008): 133–90. Revised version in *Saintly Influence: Edith Wyschogrod and the Possibilities of Philosophy of Religion*, edited by E. Boynton and M. Kavka, 113–49. New York: Fordham University Press, 2009.

113. "*Via Negativa* in Maimonides and Its Impact on Thirteenth-Century Kabbalah." *Maimonidean Studies* 5 (2008): 393–442.

114. "The Anonymous Chapters of the Elderly Master of Secrets: New Evidence for the Early Activity of the Zoharic Circle." *Kabbalah: Journal for the Study of Jewish Mystical Texts* 18 (2009): 143–278.

115. "Undoing Time and the Syntax of the Dream Interlude: A Phenomenological Reading of *Zohar* 1:199a–200a." *Kabbalah: Journal for the Study of Jewish Mystical Texts* 22 (2010): 33–57.

116. "Apophasis and the Trace of Transcendence: Wyschogrod's Contribution to a Postmodern Jewish Immanent A/Theology." *Philosophy Today* 55 (2011): 328–47.

117. "Nihilating Nonground and the Temporal Sway of Becoming: Kabbalistically Envisioning Nothing Beyond Nothing." *Angelaki* 17 (2012): 31–45.

118. "Paul Philip Levertoff and the Popularization of Kabbalah as a Missionizing Tactic." *Kabbalah: Journal for the Study of Jewish Mystical Texts* 27 (2012): 269–320.

119. "Revealing and Re/veiling Menaḥem Mendel Schneerson's Messianic Secret." *Kabbalah: Journal for the Study of Jewish Mystical Texts* 26 (2012): 25–96.

120. "Nequddat ha-Reshimu—The Trace of Transcendence and the Transcendence of the Trace: The Paradox of Ṣimṣum in the RaShaB's *Hemshekh Ayin Beit*." *Kabbalah: Journal for the Study of Jewish Mystical Texts* 29 (2013): 75–120.

Printed by Printforce, the Netherlands